APPRECIATIVE INQUIRY
Handbook

PREMIUM EDITION
SECOND EDITION

David L. Cooperrider, Ph.D.
Case Western Reserve University
Weatherhead School of Management

Diana Whitney, Ph.D.
Corporation for Positive Change
and Saybrook Graduate School and Research Center

Jacqueline M. Stavros, EDM
Lawrence Technological University
College of Management

Foreword by Ronald Fry

Crown Custom Publishing, Inc.
Brunswick, OH

Crown Custom Publishing, Inc.
1656 Pearl Road
Brunswick, Ohio 44212
(330) 273-4900
(877) 225-8820
www.crowncustompublishing.com

Ordering Information

Individual sales: This book can be ordered direct from Crown Custom Publishing, Inc. at the address above.

Quantity sales: Special discounts are available on quantity purchases by corporations, associations, and others. For details, contact Crown Custom Publishing, Inc. at the address above.

Orders for college textbook/course adoption use: Please contact Crown Custom Publishing, Inc. at (877) 225-8820.

Orders by U.S. wholesalers: Please contact Crown Custom Publishing:
Tel: (877) 225-8820; Fax (330) 225-9932;
E-mail: carl@crowncustompublishing.com or visit
www.crowncustompublishing.com

ISBN 978-1-933403-199
Printed in the United States of America

Library of Congress Cataloging-in-Publication Data
First Edition   10 9 8 7 6 5 4 3 2

Publisher: Carl Wirick
Production Editor: Roger Williams
Copyediting: Marianne Miller
Design: Tia Andrako

Contents

Detailed Contents

PART 2   Application of the 4-D Cycle of Appreciative Inquiry

Chapter 4: Discovery: *What Gives Life?*

Chapter 5: Dream: *What Might Be?*

Chapter 6: Design: *How Can It Be?*

PART 3   Learning Applications and Resources

List of Tables, Figures, and Exhibits

Foreword

"Be the change you want to see in the world."
—Gandhi

This second edition of the *Appreciative Inquiry Handbook* signals a period of tremendous growth in the application and dissemination of AI throughout the world. No fewer than 20 new books on AI have appeared during the four short years since the Handbook first appeared—books ranging in focus from organizational capacity building to building of dynamic relationships, from peace making to knowledge management, from leadership to coaching and program evaluation, and from socially responsible enterprises to multistakeholder strategy creation. A steadily growing number of workshops, certificate programs, and master's degree programs emphasizing AI and related strength-based change methods are being conducted in most continents and in multiple languages. There is no doubt that AI has established itself as a maturing community of practice that carries on the legacy of Kurt Lewin's memorable notion that nothing is so good as a practical theory.

As the praxis of AI matures, so does our understanding of the theoretical underpinnings that remain valid and that provide confidence for the practitioner, as well as our recognition of new frontiers for thought and action. This *Appreciative Inquiry Handbook* instructs and guides us in both areas. I would like to offer a few observations on the healthy "state of the discipline" as we receive the second edition of the Handbook:

- **The fundamentals are sound.** I believe the core principles (Chapter 1) and their theoretical roots (mini-lectures) remain the bedrock of this practice. Fundamentally, AI is still about changing attitudes, behaviors, and practices through appreciative conversations and relationships—interactions designed to bring out the best in people so that they can imagine a preferred future together that is more hopeful, boundless, and inherently good. It is still about socially constructing a shared future and enacting human systems through the questions asked. And it is still about anticipatory learning—finding those positive, anticipatory images of the future that compel action toward them. Even the academic critics (another sign of a maturing science!) of AI avoid any serious debate of the basic principles; these basic assumptions still signal a verifiable way (not *the* way) to understand and activate positive change in human systems.

- **The scale is limitless.** From pairs to populations, from a team to a global network of thousands of stakeholders, the scope of AI in practice is ever-expanding. The advent of the AI Summit methodology and other adaptations of large-group interventions using AI combined with today's information technology enable global systems to connect in ways never imagined. World Vision can engage nearly 5,000 of its members and stakeholders to create strategic goals in four days, working 24 hours a day in three languages. The BBC can engage all 22,000 employees worldwide in the design and creation of a culture for innovation. In ten summits, the U.S. Navy can engage thousands across seven different commands to foster a culture of engaged and empowered leaders at every level. A cadre of more than 1,000 appreciative leaders throughout Nepal can mobilize to shape a peaceful and prosperous future for their country (including the voices of more than 150,000 village women!). Those are just a few examples. Every day AI practitioners are discovering more effective way to engage all stakeholders—the whole system at once—in the center of strategy formation, planning, and implementation.

- **A greater scope is calling.** One of the great scholars of leadership and management over the past century, Peter Drucker, has said that all of the world's greatest challenges are business opportunities. Since AI has become an established means for designing, transforming, and growing effective organizations, it is well suited to help address the more difficult issues and/or questions of our time. This is an important frontier for AI—to increasingly tackle the difficult questions that will require engaging stakeholders and parties with wildly opposing world views, mental models, learned values, and the like. The methods, tools, and insights in this Handbook enable the reader/learner to find the strengths (positive core) of organizations (particularly businesses) and to apply those strengths toward shaping business to be an agent for world benefit, toward eco-innovations, toward business as an agent of peace, toward business models to eradicate poverty, and so on. They have helped the United Nations Global Compact and the Academy of Management create a new, enduring partnership to merge research of consequence to assist the aims of businesses in fulfilling the Millennium Development Goals. For Green Mountain Coffee Roasters, AI has been instrumental in its record setting economic growth and its continuing recognition as one of the world's most socially responsible organizations.

- **The focus is on generativity.** As with any maturing phenomena, there is a danger of superficial understanding or application that manipulates for an outcome rather than that opens for inquiry and searches for new understanding. I believe the field of AI is at that stage, particularly with respect to the tendency for many to be drawn to the "positive-ness" of AI as an end or outcome. There is little doubt that one of the attractions to AI is that it honors or privileges the experience of positive effect—and that our need for this, or attraction to it, is a commentary on the state of today's social systems that tend to provoke the opposite (vicious) effect much of the time. However, the place of positive effect in AI is more a means than an end. The burgeoning fields of Positive Psychology and Positive Organization Scholarship are revealing that human systems are not entropic; rather, they are capable of virtuous acts resulting from members finding more energy to cooperate with each other—that the desire to put more effort, more time, and more attention toward an activity of mutual benefit is the consequence of certain kinds of inquiry and conversation. Negative, critical, radical, or fringe voices are not excluded from this formula. AI choreographs dialogic inquiry to increase the likelihood of generating new cooperative acts. This is the meaning of the use of positive in labeling a type of scholarship, a field of psychology, or a type of change.

- **The inquiry is what really counts.** Similar to the "trap" of seeking just to be positive is the tendency for those using AI to seek only to be acting or engaging in appreciative ways. So often I hear of AI "exercises" being used to begin key meetings, strategic planning workshops, and so on, as warm-ups to get all of the voices in the room to reconnect with some high-points and to begin on an "appreciative note." It would be a tragedy for this Handbook to serve merely for that purpose. Rather, let it be your guide to *inquiry*, to a particular type of search and exploration for shared meaning that can lead to powerful images of the future that then call for action to realize that preferred future. In other words, AI is more about learning and understanding something (the affirmative topic, Chapter 2)—and thereby *valuing* it—than it is about expressions of appreciation.

This Handbook remains the best and most complete and practical set of materials for anyone wanting to read about AI and to begin to practice the AI 4-D methodology. It remains the basic primer for "what to do," "how to do it," and "why to do it" and for using AI theory and methods. This second edition contains more examples of applications and measured impacts, more evidence of positive change from longitudinal interventions, and more tools and new insights about the *Design* phase of the AI process (4 Ds) in Chapter 6. The resources brought forth are a rich companion to anyone engaged or wanting to engage in AI. I expect no matter your prior experience with AI ideas and processes, you will want to reference this book again and again. Once again the authors have amassed in one place all of the foundation concepts and latest concepts, cases, and resources necessary to learn and apply AI at any level.

However, there is one shortcoming of this great foundation book about AI in that it cannot really convey what the authors model in their practice: the "be-ing" of AI. David, Diana, and Jackie are great practitioners and teachers, not just because of what they know, but because of how they "be AI" in their everyday lives. When, in their company, you experience the gift of their ability to be what they write about, as I have, you suddenly realize the essence of this wonderful idea of appreciative inquiry—that we can actually be in the moment we are in, working toward the change we want to realize, and that this be-ing with each other is the change happening, as we engage. We do not have to plan for it, measure it, wait for a date to have it, or announce that it is here; positive change is what life—living—can be all about. It is not a Cartesian concept to be objectified or even measured as much as it is a quality of experience—of being connected to others in shared hopes, activities, and exchanges that help each of us to flourish in the moment.

Ronald Fry
Weatherhead School of Management
Case Western Reserve University
Cleveland, Ohio
Fall 2007

Preface

"The ageless essence of leadership is to create an alignment of strengths in ways that make a system's weaknesses irrelevant."
—Peter Drucker

Better ways of leading change are spreading throughout the world. Could it be, as Drucker's provocative manifesto so clearly implies, that the leadership of change is *entirely* about the discovery and elevation of strengths? Certainly we know that *strengths perform*. But what about the idea that strengths do far more than perform—*that strengths transform*? As many are now experiencing, an exciting nondeficit model of positive change is rapidly spreading that puts something powerful and full of life deep inside the heart of every type of business and organizational change.

Some call it the "strengths revolution"— a movement that has profound implications for everyone interested in leading with hope and optimism and winning the future through the highest engagement of human strengths. Fascinating questions on this topic are many. Why, for example, would discovering and moving from strength to strength in human systems activate, energize, and elevate change? What would it mean to ignite an entire change paradigm around new combinations, configurations, and chemistries of strengths? What good are positive emotions, words, images, inquiries, and constructions as we seek to understand the positive psychology and expansive economy of human strengths—especially in turbulent, difficult, and complex times? And what if we took the strengths logic to the hilt: where are all of the new tools, and where would we—as managers, change leaders, parents, and friends—start? Equally important, what becomes of all of the "deficiencies," "threats," "breakdowns," "gaps," and "problems" if we truly explore what's involved in Drucker's ever-curious phrase in *ways that make a system's weaknesses irrelevant?*

This book is that invitation to an imaginative and fresh perception of organizations and the process through which they change. Its "metacognitive" stance is choicefully affirmative. Its central thesis—as an extension of the Lewinian premise that human action depends on the world as constructed rather than the world as it is—is pragmatic and hopeful. This book teaches how to build and sustain an organization from its strengths—positive core. This book offers a fresh approach to using the contributions of any and all stakeholders to design and redesign the systems within organizations for a more effective and sustainable future.

In its most practical construction, Appreciative Inquiry (also referred to as AI) is a form of transformational inquiry that selectively seeks to locate, highlight, and illuminate the life-giving forces of an organization's existence. It is based on the belief that human systems are made and imagined by those who live and work within them. AI leads these systems to move toward the creative images that reside in the positive core of an organization. This approach is based on solid, proven principles for enabling creativity, knowledge, and spirit in the workplace. These principles call people to work toward a common vision and a higher purpose.

AI seeks out the best of "what is" to help ignite the collective imagination of "what might be." The aim is to generate new knowledge that expands the "realm of the possible" and helps members of an organization envision a collectively desired future. Furthermore, it helps to implement vision in ways that successfully translate images of possibilities into reality and belief into practice. The methodology results in a win-win situation.

This book provides a comprehensive presentation, the theory and the practical application of AI methods. Theories and activities in this book have been developed from the work of small and large corporations, government organizations, and international organizations working on issues of sustainability. Research on AI has been conducted in organizations in more than 100 countries around the world.

Material in this book is designed to facilitate theoretical understanding and the effective use of AI by organization leaders, managers, members, and consultants. This book is the expanded second edition that provides new developments of AI, updated case information, new worksheets, additional resources, and new case applications. It contains everything needed to plan, design, and lead an AI initiative. We invite readers to adapt it to their needs, in accordance with the copyright guidelines.

As Goethe reminds us, "Whatever you can do or dream you can, begin it. Boldness has genius, power and magic in it." When you are prepared to believe in people, trust them, and acknowledge that they know best about what needs to be done—at work and in their lives—Appreciative Inquiry is for you.

David L. Cooperrider, Diana Whitney and Jacqueline M. Stavros

Acknowledgments

Creating a second edition for a book takes a great deal of time, effort, and depth of conversations with and contributions from many people. We wish to acknowledge these efforts that took place over the past year.

We would like to thank the following people who contributed to the creation and content of the first *Appreciative Inquiry Handbook*: Frank Barrett, Steve Cato, David Chandler, Joep de Jong, Marsha George, Mette Jacobsgaard, Ralph Kelly, Jackie Kelm, Jim Lord, Jim Ludema, Ada Jo Mann, Adrian McLean, Bernard Mohr, Ravi Pradhan, Anne Radford, Diane Robbins, Judy Rodgers, Marge Schiller, Barbara Sloan, and Jane Watkins.

Other colleagues and friends who contributed resources to this Handbook include Stan Baran, Gervase Bush, Diane Ruiz Cairns, John Carter, Dawn Cooperrider Dole, Ronald Fry, Pamela Johnson, Ed and Martha Kimball, Jason Kirk, Claudia Leibler, Anne Kohnke Meda, Mary Grace Neville, Karla Phlypo, Charleysee Pratt, Thomas Price, Maryanne Rainey, Leslie Sekerka, Tony Silbert, Suresh Srivastva, Paul Stavros, Amanda Trosten-Bloom, Rita Williams, and Susan Wood.

Another group of contributors that joined us in the second edition to provide case applications, reviews, and updates include Gervase Bushe, Patty Castelli, Joep de Jong, Harry Dorman, Kathy Driver, Ken Elstein, David Gilmour, Donna Havens, Todd Hillhouse, Alex Jaccaci, Lynn Gurski Leighton, Carolyn Miller, Rick Pellett, Anne Radford, Nila Rinehart, Diana Sadighi, Pamela Skyrme, Patti Smith, Joseph Sprangel, Karen Stefaniak, Cheri Torres, Amanda Trosten-Bloom, Michele Waite, Carolyn Weisenberger, Rosemary Williams, and Susan Wood. We are immensely grateful for the time and effort they spent on their case applications in order to share their work with us.

We also would like to thank Michael Feinson, Jen Hetzel-Silbert, Sally Lee, Bernard Mohr, Ada Jo Mann, and Heidi Ramsbottom for helping to update the AI Initiative Table with the great work they are doing across the world.

Our clients and first edition readers have contributed to this book in ways both visible and subtle. Our readers shared with us what they liked about the first edition and what content to keep and what to add more of. At each of these organizations, hundreds, if not thousands, of people deserve credit. We are grateful to many people from the following organizations who provided insights, examples, and tools:

- Alice Peck Day Health Systems
- Avon Mexico
- Boulder County Aging Service Division
- BP Castrol Marine
- British Airways
- British Technologies Global Services
- Canadian Tire
- Cleveland Clinic
- DTE Energy Services
- EPA's Office of Research and Development
- Fairmount North America
- FCI Automotive
- GTE Telecommunications
- Head Start Agency
- Health Resources and Services Administration (six Pennsylvania Community Hospitals)
- Human Value (Japan)
- Hunter Douglas Window Fashions Division
- Imagine Chicago
- Imagine Nagaland (India)
- Lawrence Technological University
- Lovelace Health Systems
- McDonald's
- Merck (Latin America)
- Metropolitan School District
- Myrada
- NASA
- Nielsen Media Research
- North American Steel, Inc.
- Nutrimental (Brazil)
- Potawatomi Casino
- Princeton Group Health
- Roadway Express
- Save the Children (Zimbabwe, Africa)
- Scandinavian School System
- Syntegra
- Tendercare, Inc.
- United Nations Global Compact
- United Religions Initiative
- Unity
- University of Kentucky Hospital/UK Children's Hospital
- U.S. Agency for International Development
- U.S. Navy
- World Vision Relief and Development

We want to once again thank Ron Fry, our dear colleague and friend, who made many contributions to the field of AI since it emerged. He took the time to write the foreword for this second edition, capturing the growth and impact of AI across the globe in a variety of ways and industries.

We thankfully acknowledge the direction, commitment, and support of the editorial, design, and production team from Crown Custom Publishing and Berrett-Koehler for taking this book to its second edition. These behind-the-scenes people are the ones who bring the book to you!

And once again, we thank our families and friends for their support and patience during this adventurous journey.

With loving appreciation,
David, Diana, and Jackie

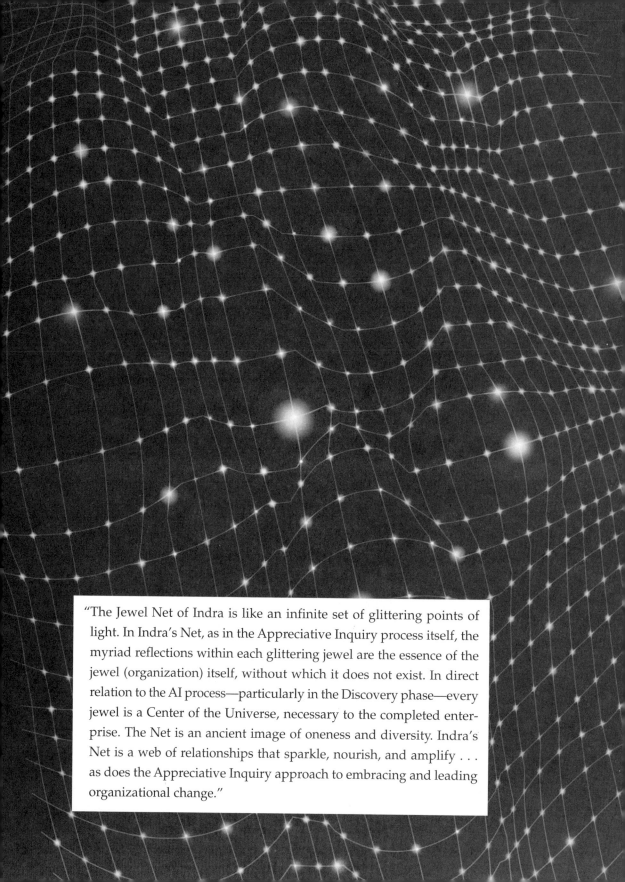

"The Jewel Net of Indra is like an infinite set of glittering points of light. In Indra's Net, as in the Appreciative Inquiry process itself, the myriad reflections within each glittering jewel are the essence of the jewel (organization) itself, without which it does not exist. In direct relation to the AI process—particularly in the Discovery phase—every jewel is a Center of the Universe, necessary to the completed enterprise. The Net is an ancient image of oneness and diversity. Indra's Net is a web of relationships that sparkle, nourish, and amplify . . . as does the Appreciative Inquiry approach to embracing and leading organizational change."

Introduction

Welcome to the second edition of *Appreciative Inquiry Handbook*, the comprehensive resource for learning and creating an Appreciative Inquiry (AI) initiative. This material is usable as is or may be customized to meet specific needs. This section of the book will:

- Provide background information about AI.
- List what is new in the second edition.
- Describe the contents of this book.
- Set the stage for launching an AI initiative.

The Focus of Appreciative Inquiry

AI is a philosophy that incorporates an approach, a process (4-D Cycle of *Discovery, Dream, Design, and Destiny*) for engaging people at any or all levels to produce effective, positive change. Currently, AI is used throughout the world in both small- and large-scale change initiatives. It has been used as an adaptable change method in combination with other organizational processes such as strategic planning, coaching, leadership and management development, redesign of structures and systems, mergers and acquisitions, cultural transformation, team building, valuing diversity, and social and sustainable development issues.

AI is an exciting way to embrace organizational change. Its assumption is simple:

Every organization has something that works right—things that give it life when it is most alive, effective, successful, and connected in healthy ways to its stakeholders and communities. AI begins by identifying what is positive and connecting to it in ways that heighten energy, vision, and action for change.

AI begins an adventure. Its call to adventure has been experienced by many people and organizations, and it will take many more to fully explore this emergent paradigm. Current practitioners and organizations sense an exciting direction in AI's language and theories of change; they sense an invitation to "a positive revolution."

The words *positive revolution* were first used by GTE (now Verizon) to describe the impact of years of work to create an organization in full voice, a center stage for a positive revolution. Based on significant and measurable changes in stock prices, morale survey measures, quality/customer relations, union-management relations, and so on, GTE's whole system change initiative was given professional recognition by the American Society for Training & Development (ASTD). GTE won the National ASTD award for best organization change program in the country. AI was cited as the backbone of that change.

AI has exhibited staying power and longevity within organizations such as Hunter Douglas, Tendercare, British Airways, and Roadway/Yellow Trucking—all of which are highlighted in this section and discussed in more detail in other chapters. Long-term applications of AI are iterated in Table I.1. Recently, the AI process has undergone change, particularly in the *Design* phase, where the concept of altering an organization's "social architecture" has been somewhat refined and broadened, consistent with the broader notions of design as a discipline.

Approach of the Handbook

This book provides an approach to launching an AI initiative. It is written to help people and their organizations take a long-term view of current activities and to achieve positive results by involving stakeholders. AI has proven to be a positive experience of a new way of living and organizing at work. Through the 4-D Cycle, people can transform the present state of their organization into a future state by building on a "positive core" of strengths to create its destiny. AI is an engaging participative process that, once begun, moves quickly to remarkable results.

Audience

This book is for trainers, executives, consultants, and students who want to be catalysts for organizational and social change. AI has been used by senior executives, line and staff managers, specialists in human resources and organizational development, leaders of nongovernmental organizations, and union management teams. The book is designed for those familiar with AI and its potential, as well as for those just beginning to explore the possibilities of AI.

The first edition of this book has been a valuable resource in many MBA and doctorate programs in business, organizational development, organizational behavior, and human resource development. This second edition also serves the needs of students who will be leading strategic change efforts, as well as practitioners.

Because the AI focus is innovation and creativity, its effectiveness is not limited to organizations of a particular type, size, demographic, or industry. Both for-profit and nonprofit organizations have found AI to be effective, and it works equally well at all levels of an organization. AI is ideal for anyone who wants to be part of a positive revolution in change.

What's in This Book?

This book contains the following:
- 11 chapters of text material and resources
- Exciting examples of AI topic choices, interview guides, reports, and cases
- An AI reference and bibliography list
- "Appreciative Insights" by AI users
- Contact information
- Sample participant worksheet handouts
- Course outlines and agendas
- Detailed description of the 4-D Cycle: Discovery, Dream, Design, and Destiny
- Customizable training workshops
- A series of the original classic published articles on AI
- A glossary of terms
- An invitation to be a member of Appreciative Inquiry Consulting, LLC

This book contains everything needed to understand the principles of AI and the way they apply. It includes a complete set of tools to design and deliver AI initiatives as well as detailed instructions and agendas for setting up multiple types of AI sessions:
- One-Hour AI Introduction
- Two-Hour Executive Overview
- Four-Hour Introductory Meeting
- Two-Day AI Program and Detailed Project Plan
- Detailed Project Plan

Each session can be used by itself or in combination with a planned initiative. Although this book covers a great deal of material, it is not exhaustive. The reader is encouraged to develop an appreciative learning library (refer to the bibliography).

What's New in the Second Edition

- Table updates are provided on new and existing uses by organizations, demonstrating the sustainability of AI.
- An expanded resource section provides new worksheets and an updated bibliography with 125 additional sources and more than 45 doctorate dissertations and master theses completed on AI.
- Chapter 1 includes the mini-lecture "Why AI Works."
- Chapter 9, made up of case applications, is new and consists of nine

case studies on for-profit, nonprofit, and government applications using AI.

- To exemplify sustainability in the AI process (in the sense of longevity of the initiative), all Case Clippings in Chapters 4–7 have been updated.
- *The Fairmount Minerals Sustainable Development Appreciative Inquiry Summit Workbook* is offered in Chapter 8.
- Throughout this book, the larger meaning of sustainable enterprise has been referred to in terms of the "triple bottom line," rephrased in AI terms as "people, prosperity, and planet."
- Chapter 3 provides a detailed employee development and healthcare project plan, an agenda, and an interview guide.
- Chapter 3 offers an expanded list of questions (up to 71) to consider when getting started.
- Chapter 6 provides two new powerful ways in which the Design phase can unfold to allow for creativity and innovation.
- Chapter 10 provides a complete illustration of all worksheets by the EPA ORD Summit on "Igniting Leadership at all Levels."
- Chapter 11 includes a soon-to-be classic article, "Strategic Inquiry with Appreciative Intent: Inspiration to SOAR!" This is a seminal article on AI and strategic planning.

How to Use This Book

This book contains everything needed to launch an AI initiative—background information on the topic, sample project plans, designs, agendas and interview guides, overheads, participant worksheets, and resources.

Before starting an AI initiative, the reader should review the structure and content of the entire book in order to understand the complete process. Chapter 3, Introducing, Defining, and Planning an Appreciative Inquiry Initiative, provides several illustrations and agendas that can help in designing a project plan. Part 2: Application of the 4-D Cycle of Appreciative Inquiry, evolves chapter by chapter to fully explain each phase: Discovery, Dream, Design, and Destiny. The bibliography presents new and updated information that has appeared in books, newsletters, and articles and on Web sites—an ongoing process.

AI is a robust intervention that can be molded to fit any organization's situation. While the reader or organization is going through the process, comparing Part 2 and Part 3 (Learning Applications and Resources) can help show how various organizations have used AI. However, the examples in the book are just that—examples. Creativity and innovation in developing or modifying the existing materials are encouraged and are a natural offshoot of an evolving process.

This book is designed for the novice as well as the experienced AI practitioner. For those just starting out, developing the first AI intervention will likely prove to be a time-consuming task. Sufficient time must be allowed to prepare and modify the plan. New practitioners should be patient and flexible and experience fun in embracing change. Experienced users will find this book a useful reference for further developing their AI initiatives.

This book details the transformational process needed to design, lead, and implement an AI initiative anywhere in an organization. The process starts with four simple, powerful questions being asked in an appreciative interview:

The Appreciative Interview
1. What would you describe as being a high-point experience in your organization, a time when you were most alive and engaged?
2. Without being modest, what is it that you most value about yourself, your work, and your organization?
3. What are the core factors that give life to your organization, without which the organization would cease to exist?
4. Assume you go into a deep sleep tonight, one that lasts ten years. But while you are asleep, powerful and positive changes take place, real miracles happen, and your organization becomes what you want it to be. Now you awaken and go into the organization. It is 2018, and you are very proud of what you see. As you take in this vision and look at the whole, what do you see happening that is new, changed, better, or effective and successful?

Those questions start a dialogue to discover and dream a new, more compelling image of the organization and its future. From anecdotal images, the future of the human systems within the organization is designed and the organization begins to move toward its destiny.

An AI initiative is more than just a training program. It is an opportunity to create an exciting and *dynamic* organization. To explain, the following definition is offered:

> *Dynamic: characterized by continuous change, activity, or progress; characterized by vigor and energy.*[1]

AI recognizes that every organization is an open system that depends on its human capital to bring its vision and purpose to life. AI focuses on what gives life to an organization's system when it is operating at its best. An organ-

---

1 Stavros, J., & Torres, C. (2005). *Dynamic relationships: Unleashing the power of appreciative inquiry in daily living.* Chagrin Falls, OH: Taos Institute Publishing.

ization will cease to exist without a human system to lead and support it. AI identifies and leverages the positive core of an organization to ensure its ongoing success.

The outcome of an AI initiative is a long-term positive change in the organization. AI has helped many organizations increase employee satisfaction; enhance productivity; increase levels of communications among stakeholders; decrease turnover; stimulate creativity; and align the whole organization around its vision, mission, objectives, and strategies. AI is applicable to any profit, nonprofit, or governmental organization.

To be effective, business leaders need to move away from the traditional problem-solving approach to organizational change and move toward viewing organizations as a mystery to be embraced. AI provides a fresh approach to organizational change that motivates all stakeholders to contribute to the organization. When an organization uses AI to solve problems, embrace challenges, create opportunities, make decisions, and initiate action, the whole system works toward a shared vision.

AI is a powerful approach to positive change. The process is simple, and it can engage everyone in the organization. Through collaborative inquiry and a connection to their positive core, many organizations have cocreated **whole systems processes** to:

- Create a common-ground vision and strategy for the future.
- Accelerate organizational learning—speeding the spread of innovation and amplifying the power of even the smallest victories.
- Unite labor and management in new, jointly envisioned partnerships.
- Create dialogue to foster shared meanings.
- Improve communications.
- Strengthen implementations of major information technology changes.
- Work toward sustainability.
- Demonstrate positive intent and trust with stakeholders.
- Build dynamic relationships and high-performance teams to facilitate change.

AI can revitalize virtually every process or program that may have been deficit-based, such as quality programs, focus groups, surveys, and reengineering efforts. AI is important because it works to bring the whole organization together to build on its positive core, one that allows for engagement in both transactional (action planning) and/or transformational change (values-vision-mission identification and alignment). AI encourages people to work together to promote a more complete understanding of the human system, the heartbeat of the organization.

AI Insight

Appreciative Inquiry can get you much better results than seeking out and solving problems. That's an interesting concept for me—and I imagine for most of you—because telephone companies are among the best problem solvers in the world. We troubleshoot everything. We concentrate enormous resources on correcting problems that have relatively minor impact on our overall service performance . . . . When used continually and over a long period of time, this approach can lead to a negative culture. If you combine a negative culture with all the challenges we face today, it could be easy to convince ourselves that we have too many problems to overcome—to slip into a paralyzing sense of hopelessness.

And yet if we flip the coin, we have so much to be excited about. We are in the most dynamic and most influential business of our times. We ought to be excited, motivated, and energized. We can be if we just turn ourselves around and start looking at our jobs (and ourselves) differently—if we kill negative self-talk and celebrate our successes. If we dissect what we do right and apply the lessons to what we do wrong, we can solve our problems and re-energize the organization at the same time . . . . In the long run, what is likely to be more useful: Demoralizing a successful workforce by concentrating on their failures or helping them over their last few hurdles by building a bridge with their successes?

Don't get me wrong. I'm not advocating mindless happy talk. Appreciative Inquiry is a complex science designed to make things better. We can't ignore problems. We just need to approach them from the other side.

Thomas H. White
President, GTE Telephone Operations
Vital Speeches of the Day, 1996

Hundreds of organizations are embracing this positive revolution through AI. Table A.1 highlights some of these organizations and their initiatives.

Table A.1 Appreciative Inquiry Initiatives

Organization	AI Initiative/Award

Academy for Educational Development, Addis Ababa, Ethiopia
More than 100 educators, government ministers, donors, and NGOs reflected on their many accomplishments and envisioned the future of education in Ethiopia for the next ten years.

ANZ Bank, Melbourne, Australia
ANZ Bank launched an inquiry into its purpose, involving more than 1,000 people—the largest engagement activity ever at the bank. Within a month, the bank crafted its purpose and had it adopted by the board of directors.

Avon Mexico
Avon Mexico addressed the issue of gender equity and a pilot project for Avon globally. It won the 1997 Catalyst Award as the best place in the country for women to work.

BAE Systems
BAE Systems created a five-year strategic plan for its Armament Systems Division with internal stakeholders and customers using the SOAR framework.

Boulder County Aging Services Division
This organization was awarded the 2007 Local Government Award "Planning with Vision" by the Denver Regional Council of Governments.

British Airways North America
British Airways created and sustained delivery of "Excellence in Customer Service."

City of Longmont, Colorado
Longmont completed the AI Core Project of the Year by the International Association for Public Participation and was awarded "All America City" by the National Civic League (2006).

Cleveland Clinic
The Cleveland Clinic discovered what made the clinic function successfully (first AI initiative).

DTE Energy Services
Its employees created a culture of choice.

EcoLogic Development Fund

This firm guided a participative strategic planning process that made it a world leader in collaborative, community-led conservation of biological and cultural diversity.

Fairmont Minerals

This firm launched a Sustainable Development Summit that created a vision and plan for 3 Ps: people, profits, and planet. It included a sustainable development design of the organization's purpose and principles in day-to-day operations, products, and services in addition to employees' personal lives.

FCI Automotive

It improved supply chain management and inventory quality.

Green Mountain Coffee Roasters

The firm increased its *Positive World Benefit through Phenomenal Sustainable Growth* while making a profit. AI is being used at all levels by providing employees with a process that fits with the strategy and culture.

Group Health Cooperative

This healthcare organization improved performance of its healthcare delivery system in the areas of cost, quality, and service.

GTE Telecommunications

GTE received the Best Organization Change Project Award from the American Society of Training & Development, 1997.

Guyana Democratic Consolidation and Conflict Resolution (GDCCR) Project—Guyana, South America

This agency inspired peace building and community development initiatives through increased citizen participation in policy reform and decision making, specifically targeting youth education, inter-religious collaboration, and participative governance.

Hunter Douglas Window Fashions Division

The company created shared vision and reinstilled the "positive core" factors (creativity, flexibility, intimacy, and sense of community) that had contributed to the division's original success, while building a sustainable leadership within the organization. It was ranked in the "Top Ten Places to Work" in Denver, Colorado (2004) and in Colorado (2006).

Imagine Chicago

This organization was the first to use AI intergenerational interviews, where young people interviewed elders to discover civic engagement and to nurture hope. Imagine Chicago has received many awards and today is helping to spawn "Imagine" projects on six continents focused on long-term sustainable development in large cities.

Imagine Nagaland (India)

This organization brought various ministries together with young people to discover the future they wanted to create. UNICEF helped guide the project, and a major film producer created a movie documentary showing the movement from hopelessness and conflict to new vision and collaboration.

Jefferson Wells

Jefferson Wells created a strategic operational plan that resulted in accelerated growth and performance, moving the selected office from rankings of sixth in the firm in revenues and eighth in profits to first in both revenues and profits with a turnover rate of 30% moving to under 10%. The office won the 2006 Global Office of the Year Award given by Manpower.

John Deere Harvester

To break through years' worth of apathy and distrust, John Deere initiated a five-day summit, the last two days focused exclusively on "tactical implementation." Participants selected ten projects they believed were most critical to organizational effectiveness and long-term performance.

Lancaster County, Pennsylvania Historical Society

The Society created a strategic plan to guide the institution for the next five years. The initiatives focused on twentieth-century history, affirmed Lancaster County's diversity, and championed the growth of technological capabilities to increase presence in the community.

Lawrence Technological University

The school completed an environmental scan and identified the core values of the university in support of the strategic plan.

Lovelace Health Systems

It improved nursing quality and retention.

Managua, Nicaragua

Nicaraguan citizens from a variety of political persuasions sponsored a two-day, 500-person AI event on civil society to create a society around shared interests, purposes, values, and vision. One of the projects resulted in a 100,000-person peaceful march (with all political parties represented) through the streets of Managua to draw attention to citizen responsibility in the electoral process.

McDonald's

McDonald's applied the Appreciative Inquiry approach in the Human Resources area and became among the best employers in each community around the world by putting "People First."

Milton Hershey School
This school designed a pioneer program that enables seniors nearing graduation to experience an advanced level of independence in life outside the residential school setting. AI is also used in the evaluation of this program.

Myrada
This organization built capacity within a network of Southern India NGOs.

NASA
NASA created a strategic plan for its OHR division to align with the larger NASA vision. This resulted in a more inclusive, participative culture.

Newark Beth Israel Medical Center
The hospital increased patient safety by redesigning the process of handing off patients from one nurse to another in a 670+ bed hospital. The staff built on their most effective handoff experiences, resulting in a 23.3% increase in patient satisfaction.

North American Steel, Inc.
This company celebrated its 40th year and tapped into the positive core of its history. The information was used for strategic planning, as 250 factory workers and managers were interviewed relative to positive experiences.

Nutrimental
The company created an innovative whole-system approach to strategic planning and decision making to achieve qualitative and quantitative outcomes; for example, a 600% increase in profits as well as a 75% reduction in absenteeism rates. The company has used the AI Summit method to do strategic planning for the past six years.

PA Community Hospitals
This group enhanced patient care delivery by improving the retention of nurses—Program: Building Capacity for Better Work and Better Care.

Princeton Group Health
Five hundred medical people—doctors, nurses, administrators, union leaders, patients, and many others—participated in whole-system planning by using AI and Future Search.

Roadway Express
This company engaged its unionized workforce to strategize about its future and increased throughput and productivity to move it from being a good organization to a great organization. The initial initiative was to reduce costs and rapidly increase business. Unionized workers, management, and staff worked together on this plan.

Save the Children
The organization changed how it could be re-created and achieved and sustained its mission.

Scandinavian School System
It received the Award for Educational Achievement, 1998.

Star Island Corporation
This firm obtained widespread, substantial involvement in the strategic planning system by including the Star Community in the process.

Syntegra – 109
The firm built a new leadership team and strategy to better approach and service its market.

Tendercare, Inc.
The company identified the positive care core needed to increase census while placing the residents in the center of the circle of quality care.

United Nations
The UN supported the Global Compact through a Leaders Summit that included more than 1,400 organizational members from business, civil society, and government to constructively engage in cocreating action plans in support of its principles.

United Religions Initiative
This group created a global interfaith organization dedicated to peace and cooperation among people of different religions, faiths, and spiritual traditions.

United States Agency for International Development (USAID)
This organization offered innovative management and leadership training to Private Voluntary Organizations (PVOs) to understand how NGOs built their capacities.

United States Navy
The focus of the initiative was to create enlightened leadership at every level of the Navy. The Navy brought together admirals and sailors at all levels for an AI Summit that included more than 250 people, and 30 projects were created to support the vision. A film was created of the event. Currently, AI Summits have occurred throughout the Navy, including the entire Pacific Fleet, to build leadership at every level.

Unity
Unity created a high-performance organizational culture congruent with its spiritual "new thought" philosophy.

Utah Education System
The teacher's union (UEA) has been using AI for more than three years. A statewide summit with legislators, media, people from the community, the board of education, teachers, administrators, university faculty, parents, and students joined together for a "Leap of Learning" facilitated by members of the Positive Change Core. In 2007, the school district committed to infusing the AI philosophy in classrooms.

World Vision Relief and Development
The organization built collaborative alliances to bring help and developmental assistance to thousands of children in hundreds of orphanages across Romania. More than 300 organizations were connected in a partnership, building on a strength- based analysis of each. Many papers were written about the effort, making possible the new "knowledge alliance" and resulting in millions of dollars in medical support.

Structure of the Book

AI Insight

AI was first used in 1980, when David Cooperrider, a doctoral student at Case Western Reserve University, was helping Al Jensen undertake his dissertation on physician leadership at one of the top tertiary care medical centers in the world, the Cleveland Clinic. They asked physician leaders to tell stories of their biggest successes as well as their biggest failures. But when Cooperrider looked at the data, he was drawn only to the success stories. Listening to their narratives of strength and strong leadership, he was amazed by the level of positive cooperation, innovation, and egalitarian governance at the clinic—by consensus, this was when organizational members were most effective. With the intellectual collaboration and prodding of his adviser, Suresh Srivastva, and the permission of the clinic's chair, David decided to look at the data exclusively in search of the positives—everything that served to give life to the system and to people when they were most alive, effective, committed, and empowered. Everything else was considered irrelevant.

The method of analysis was to systematically and deliberately "appreciate" everything of value, then use the positive analysis to speculate on the potentials and possibilities for the future. A theory of future possibility was created, and momentous stories were used to vivify the potentials. History was used as a source of positive possibility. In a report to the board of governors, Cooperrider and Srivastva called their method Appreciative Inquiry (AI). Thus, this was the first organizational analysis using AI. The results of the study created such a powerful positive stir that the board requested that this AI method be used at all levels of the 8,000-person organization to facilitate change. Cooperrider wrote his dissertation on the holistic process and created a scholarly logic for this, a new form of action research. This experience set the stage for the AI learning community!

To facilitate conceptual understanding and effective practical use of AI, the material in the book is presented in three parts. *Part 1: Essential Elements of Appreciative Inquiry* provides a powerful learning approach to (1) gaining an understanding of basic AI principles, (2) selecting an affirmative topic on which to build from the positive core, and (3) starting an AI initiative. The material presented in this section is a call to working with people, groups, and organizations in a more positive, collaborative, and constructive approach than perhaps they have utilized in the past. It provides all of the essential ingredients to design and lead strengths-based positive change in one's organization or community.

The 4-D appreciative learning model is the focus of *Part 2: Application of the 4-D Cycle of Appreciative Inquiry.* The process is dynamic and interactive. It builds on imagination and flexibility for its success. It starts with Discovery. At this stage, the "best of what is" in a system is identified as the positive core. The second stage is Dream. This stage teaches a visioning process to suggest "what might be." The third stage is Design. The Design chapter outlines the steps to create the ideal system for an organization. It builds on the positive core and the envisioned results of the first two stages. It allows for coconstructing the ideal design, "how it can be." The final stage is termed Destiny. The Destiny chapter covers the implementation and model for sustaining an appreciative learning environment, "what will be." Thus, Part 2 moves through the phases of discovery, dream, design, and destiny—the "4 Ds."

The tools needed for an AI initiative or training program are included in *Part 3: Learning Applications and Resources,* along with several case applications. A glossary, index, and a list of additional resources are also included. Today more than 500 scholarly papers pertaining to AI have been published worldwide; in addition, a dozen books and many Web sites are devoted to the practice of AI.

How Can AI Make a Difference?

This book is not a recipe; it is an adventure. AI is an effective way to get members of an organization involved in unleashing a positive revolution in today's dynamic global environment. The objectives of the book are to teach the founding principles and theories of AI, present a wide range of applications of the theory and the AI 4-D Cycle, and facilitate the training of trainers who will introduce and use AI. Therefore, the final section of this book includes resources to facilitate group teaching, learning, and application.

An organization's guiding force is its people. This book offers those people a framework for an appreciative learning journey that has proven to be successful in cocreating organizational systems that feature each organization operating at its best.

Where Can AI Make a Difference?

AI can make a difference with a single person or with any collective human system. To illustrate, AI has been successfully used in the following ways:

- Innovations leading toward the ideal organization
- Strategic planning
- Leadership and management development
- Work process redesign
- Team development
- Organizational culture change
- Employee development
- HR practices: staffing, orientation, and performance management
- Coaching
- Communications
- Collaborative alliances and joint ventures
- Community relations and customer relations
- Diversity initiatives
- Focus groups
- Generative benchmarking
- Surveys
- Meetings
- Global change initiatives
- Evaluation to valuation of performance systems
- New product development

AI is a proven paradigm for accelerating organizational learning and transformation. It can be used in any situation where the leaders and organizational members are committed to building positive, life-centered organizations.

You are ready to begin the journey.

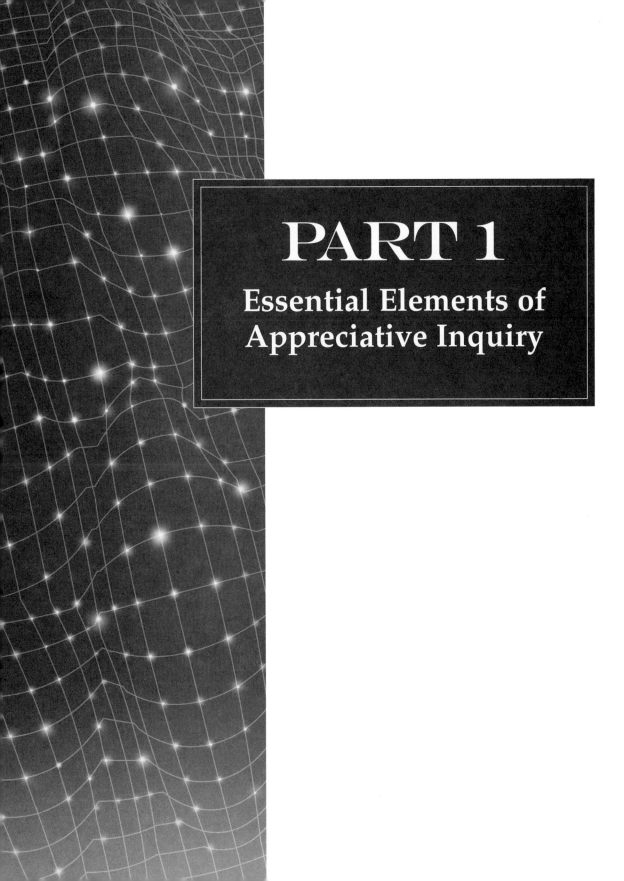

PART 1

Essential Elements of Appreciative Inquiry

Part I: Essential Elements of Appreciative Inquiry (AI)

Since the publication of the first edition in 2003, much has happened in the practice of Appreciative Inquiry (AI) and in the creation of new and connecting theories, as is apparent from the additional 125 resources and 40 studies/dissertations that were completed. (You can find these in the updated Bibliography.) The field of AI has "come of age" and has taken its place as a prominent change process within the field and textbooks of organizational development, behavior, and change.

Part 1 seeks to impart a powerful learning approach to gaining a better understanding of basic AI principles, theories, and applications. Chapter 1 touches briefly on the evolutionary changes in AI over the past several years. In addition, as in the first edition, this book gives a brief but *precise* review of the theory of AI with nine mini-lectures that includes one new piece on why AI works and sustains itself. These mini-lectures have been found to be useful in introducing AI to an organization.

AI as a strength-based approach and a process (4-D Cycle) has recently exhibited resonance with broader definitions of *sustainable development* and *sustainable enterprise*. Sustainable development is defined by the World Business Council for Sustainable Development (WBCSD) as "forms of progress that meet the needs of the present without compromising the ability of future generations to meet their needs" (http://www.wbcsd.org). The sustainable enterprise is a firm or an organization that maintains and re-creates itself over time while simultaneously attending to the triple bottom line of social, environmental, and economic benefits being distributed to the entire world. These concepts are connected to AI in Chapter 2 and in the case study of Fairmount Minerals, more fully developed in Chapter 8.

Chapter 3 presents the basics of starting an AI initiative that includes 60 new questions to consider in the planning phases, together with sample agendas ranging from a one-hour brief introduction to a two-day AI workshop. A new case application in healthcare, The University of Kentucky Hospital/UK Children's Hospital, is included with a project overview, agendas, the interview guide, and summit materials.

1

The Theoretical Basis of Appreciative Inquiry

Ap-pre'ci-ate, *v.*, 1. to value; recognize the best in people or the world around us; affirm past and present strengths, successes, and potentials; to perceive those things that give life (health, vitality, excellence) to living systems. 2. to increase in value, e.g., the economy has appreciated in value. Synonyms: value, prize, esteem, and honor.

In-quire', *v.*, 1. to explore and discover. 2. to ask questions; to be open to seeing new potentials and possibilities. Synonyms: discover, search, systematically explore, and study.

This chapter begins by introducing the theory and creation of AI. **Appreciative Inquiry** is an organization development (OD) process and approach to change management that grows out of social constructionist thought and its applications to management and organizational transformation. Through its deliberately positive assumptions about people, organizations, and relationships, AI leaves behind deficit-oriented approaches to management and vitally transforms the ways to approach questions of organizational improvement and effectiveness. Such questions include culture change, survey analysis, strategic planning, organizational learning, customer focus groups, leadership development, team building, quality management, measurement systems, joint ventures and alliances, diversity training, performance appraisal, communications programs, internal online networks, corporate history writing and others.

Presented here is a thesis, a proposition regarding the future of OD and change management. The thesis is a significant shift from "traditional" problem-solving methodologies. AI exhibits embedded wisdom that is reminiscent of early pioneers such as Kurt Lewin, Mary Parker Follett, Herb Shepard, and others. The thesis might be summarized this way:

> We may have reached the end of traditional problem solving. AI is a powerful approach to transformation as a mode of inquiry capable of inspiring, mobilizing, and sustaining human system change. The future of OD belongs, instead, to methods that affirm, compel, and accelerate anticipatory learning involving larger and larger levels of collectivity.

The new methods are distinguished by the art and science of asking powerful and unconditional positive questions. (Someday there will be an "encyclopedia of questions" that brings together classic formulations such as Maslow's interview protocols on peak human experience and Peters and Waterman's studies of organizational excellence or Vereena Kast's exceptional studies of joy, inspiration, and hope.) The new methods view realities as socially constructed. Therefore, they will become more radically relational, widening the circles of dialogue to groups of hundreds, thousands, and perhaps (due to cyberspace) millions. The arduous task of intervention will give way to the speed of imagination and innovation. Instead of negation, criticism, and spiraling diagnoses, there will be discovery, dream, design, and destiny.

AI: A Brief Introduction

AI has been described in many ways. Here is a practitioner-oriented definition:

> *Appreciative Inquiry is the cooperative co-evolutionary search for the best in people, their organizations, and the world around them. It involves the discovery of what gives "life" to a living system when it is most effective, alive, and constructively capable in economic, ecological, and human terms. AI involves the art and practice of asking questions that strengthen a system's capacity to apprehend, anticipate, and heighten positive potential. The inquiry is mobilized through the crafting of the "unconditional positive question," often involving hundreds or thousands of people. AI interventions focus on the speed of imagination and innovation instead of the negative, critical, and spiraling diagnoses commonly used in organizations. The discovery, dream, design, and destiny model links the energy of the positive core to changes never thought possible.*

AI is based on the simple assumption that every organization has something that works well, and those strengths can be the starting point for creating positive change. Inviting people to participate in dialogues and share stories about their past and present achievements, assets, unexplored potentials, innovations, strengths, elevated thoughts, opportunities, benchmarks, high-point moments, lived values, traditions, core and **distinctive competencies**, expressions of wisdom, insights into the deeper corporate spirit and soul, and visions of valued and possible futures can identify a "positive core." From this, AI links the energy of the positive core directly to any change agenda. This link creates energy and excitement and a desire to move toward a shared dream.

AI, an approach to organizational analysis and learning, is also intended for discovering, understanding, and fostering innovations in social organizational arrangements and processes. In this context, AI refers to:

- A search for knowledge.
- A theory of collective action designed to evolve the vision and will of a group, an organization, or a society as a whole.

AI is deliberate in its life-centric search. Carefully constructed inquiries allow the practitioner to affirm the symbolic capacities of imagination and mind as well as the social capacity for conscious choice and cultural evolution. The art of "appreciation" is the art of discovering and valuing those factors that give life to a group or an organization. The process involves interviewing and storytelling to draw out the best of the past, to understand what one wants more of, and to set the stage for effective visualization of the future.

The following propositions underlie the practice of AI:

1. **Inquiry into "the art of the possible" in organizational life should begin with appreciation.** Every system works to some degree. Therefore, a primary task of management and organizational analysis is to discover, describe, and explain those "exceptional moments" that give life to the system and activate members' competencies and energies. The appreciative approach takes its inspiration from "what is." This is the first step of the process in the 4-D Cycle: *Discovery.* Valuing, learning, and inspired understanding are the aims of the appreciative spirit.

2. **Inquiry into what is possible should yield information that is applicable.** Organizational study should lead to the generation of knowledge that can be used, applied, and validated in action.

3. **Inquiry into what is possible should be provocative.** An organization is an open-ended, indeterminate system capable of becoming more than it is at any given moment and learning how to actively take part in guiding its own evolution. Appreciative knowledge of "what is" becomes provocative to the extent that the learning stirs members to action. In this way, AI allows use of **systematic management** analysis to help an organization's members shape an effective future according to their imaginative and moral purposes.

4. **Inquiry into the human potential of organizational life should be collaborative.** This principle assumes an immutable relationship between the process of inquiry and its content. A unilateral approach to the study of social innovation is a direct negation of the phenomenon itself.

In its most practical construction, AI is a form of organizational study that selectively seeks to locate, highlight, and illuminate what are referred to as the life-giving forces of the organization's existence, its positive core.

In this sense, two basic questions are behind any AI initiative:

1. What, in this particular setting and context, gives life to this system—when it is most alive, healthy, and symbiotically related to its various communities?

2. What are the possibilities—expressed and latent—to provide opportunities for more effective (value-congruent) forms of organizing?

AI seeks out the exceptional best of "what is" (*Discovery*) to help ignite the collective imagination of "what might be" (*Dream*). The aim is to generate new knowledge of a collectively desired future. It carries forth the vision in ways that successfully translate images into possibilities, intentions into reality, and beliefs into practice.

As a method of organizational analysis, AI differs from conventional managerial problem solving. The basic assumption of problem solving is that "organizing is a problem to be solved." The task of improvement traditionally involves removing deficits by (1) identifying the key problems or deficiencies, (2) analyzing the causes, (3) analyzing solutions, and (4) developing an action plan.

In contrast, the underlying assumption of AI is that an organization is a "solution to be embraced" rather than a "problem to be solved." The phases are shown in Figure 1.1, Appreciative Inquiry 4-D Cycle. It starts with selecting a topic: affirmative topic choice. What follows are *Discovery* (appreciating and valuing), *Dream* (envisioning), *Design* (coconstructing the future), and *Destiny* (learning, empowering, and improvising to sustain the future). These are the essence of dialogue woven through each step of the process.

Figure 1.1: Appreciative Inquiry "4-D" Cycle

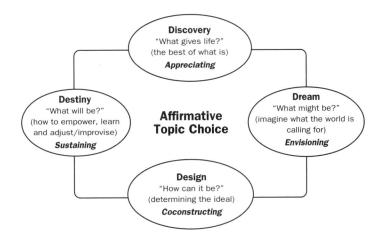

The first step in this process is to discover and value those factors that give life to the organization. For example, the organization might discover and value its commitment and identify when that commitment was at its highest (affirmative topic choice: highest commitment). Regardless of how few or infrequent the moments of highest commitment were, the organization's task is to focus on them and discuss the factors and forces that served as fertile ground for that exceptional level of commitment.

The First D is *Discovery*

The list of positive or affirmative topics for *Discovery* is endless: high quality, integrity, empowerment, innovation, customer responsiveness, technological innovation, team spirit, best in class, and so on. In each case, the task is to discover the positive exceptions, successes, and most vital or alive moments. Discovery involves valuing those things that are worth valuing. It can be done within and across organizations (in a benchmarking sense) and across time (organizational history as positive possibility).

As part of the *Discovery* process, individuals engage in **dialogue** and meaning-making. This is simply the open sharing of discoveries and possibilities. Through dialogue, a consensus begins to emerge whereby individuals in the organization say, "Yes, this is an ideal or a vision that we value and should aspire to." Through conversation and dialogue, individual appreciation becomes collective appreciation, individual will evolves into group will, and individual vision becomes a cooperative or shared vision for the organization.

AI helps create a deliberately supportive context for dialogue. It is through the sharing of ideals that social bonding occurs. What makes AI different from other OD methodologies at this phase is that every question is positive.

From *Discovery* to *Dream*

Second, participants *Dream*, or envision what might be. It occurs when the best of "what is" has been identified; the mind naturally begins to search further and to envision new possibilities. Valuing the best of "what is" leads to envisioning what might be. Envisioning involves passionate thinking, creating a positive image of a desired and preferred future. The *Dream* step uses the interview stories from the *Discovery* step to elicit the key themes that underlie the times when the organization was most alive and at its best.

Articulated *Dream(s)* to *Design*

Third, participants **coconstruct** the future by the *Design* of an **organizational architecture** in which the exceptional becomes everyday and ordinary. This design is more than a vision. It is a provocative and inspiring statement of intention that is grounded in the realities of what has worked in the past combined with what new ideas are envisioned for the future. It enhances the organization by leveraging its own past successes and successes that have been experienced elsewhere with a "strategic intent." Strategic intent signals what the organizations wants more of and recognizes that the future is built around what can be and what is.[1]

Design to *Destiny*

Fourth, the *Design* delivers the organization to its *Destiny* through innovation and action. AI establishes a momentum of its own. Once guided by a shared image of what might be, members of the organization find innovative ways to help move the organization closer to the ideal. Again, because the ideals are grounded in realities, the organization is empowered to make things happen. This is important because it is precisely through the juxtaposition of visionary content with grounded examples of the extraordinary that AI opens the status quo to transformations via collective action. By seeking an imaginative and fresh perception of organizations (as if seen for the very first time), the appreciative eye takes nothing for granted, seeking to apprehend the basis of organizational life and working to articulate the possibilities for a better existence.

Part 2 of the book covers the 4-D Cycle of AI in detail.

The principles that underlie AI are deeply grounded in scientific research (refer to "Positive Image, Positive Action: The Affirmative Basis of Organizing" in Chapter 11) and are highlighted in the remainder of this section in Mini-lectures I–IX. While the practitioner need not have a thorough understanding of these principles, it is often helpful when introducing AI to an organization to provide some of the supporting theory and research. The following presentation ideas are organized into nine brief mini-lectures. Each one refers to the theoretical constructs on which AI is based. Practitioners can successfully introduce AI by introducing and adapting these key concepts to the language and culture of the organization.

---

1 deKluyver, C., & Pearce, J. A. (2006). *Strategy: A view from the top.* Upper Saddle River, NJ: Prentice Hall.

Mini-lecture I: Five Principles of AI

The following five principles inspired and moved the foundation of AI from theory to practice:

1. The Constructionist Principle
2. The Principle of Simultaneity
3. The Poetic Principle
4. The Anticipatory Principle
5. The Positive Principle

Launching an AI initiative requires an understanding of these principles to fully grasp AI theory and to internalize the basis of the 4-D Cycle.

The full conceptual article on these principles, "Appreciative Inquiry into Organizational Life," is located in Chapter 11.

1. **Constructionist Principle:** Social knowledge and organizational destiny are interwoven. A constructionist would argue that the seeds of organizational change are implicit in the first questions asked. The questions asked become the material out of which the future is conceived and constructed. Thus, the way of knowing is fateful.[2] To be effective as executives, leaders, **change agents**, and so on, one must be adept in the art of reading, understanding, and analyzing organizations as living, human constructions. Knowing organizations is at the core of virtually every OD task. Because styles of thinking rarely match the increasingly complex world, there must be a commitment to the ongoing pursuit of multiple and more fruitful ways of knowing.

   The most important resource for generating constructive organizational change is cooperation between the imagination and the reasoning function of the mind (the capacity to unleash the imagination and mind of groups). AI is a way of reclaiming imaginative competence. Unfortunately, people's habitual styles of thought include preconscious background assumptions, root metaphors, and rules of analysis that come to define organizations in a particular way. These styles have often constrained the managerial imagination and mind.

---

2 For more information, refer to Gergen, K. *Realities and relationships.* (1994). Cambridge, MA: Harvard University Press and *Social construction: Entering the dialogue.* (2004). Chagrin Falls, OH: Taos Institute Publishing.

2. **Principle of Simultaneity:** This principle recognizes that inquiry and change are not truly separate moments; they can and should be simultaneous. Inquiry is intervention. The seeds of change are the things people think and talk about, the things people discover and learn, and the things that inform dialogue and inspire images of the future. They are implicit in the very first questions asked. One of the most impactful things a change agent or OD practitioner does is to articulate questions. The questions set the stage for what is "found" and what is "discovered" (the data). These data become the stories out of which the future is conceived, discussed, and constructed.

3. **Poetic Principle:** A useful **metaphor** in understanding this principle is that human organizations are an "open book." An organization's story is constantly being coauthored. Moreover, pasts, presents, and futures are endless sources of learning, inspiration, or interpretation (as in the endless interpretive possibilities in a good work of poetry or a biblical text). The important implication is that one can study virtually any topic related to human experience in any human system or organization. The choice of inquiry can focus on the nature of alienation or joy in any human organization or community. One can study moments of creativity and innovation or moments of debilitating bureaucratic stress. One has a choice.

4. **Anticipatory Principle:** The most important resource for generating constructive organizational change or improvement is collective imagination and discourse about the future. One of the basic theorems of the anticipatory view of organizational life is that the image of the future guides what might be called the current behavior of any organism or organization. Much like a movie projected on a screen, human systems are forever projecting ahead of themselves a horizon of expectation that brings the future powerfully into the present as a mobilizing agent. In the final analysis, organizations exist because people who govern and maintain them share some sort of discourse or projection about what the organization is, how it will function, what it will achieve, and what it will likely become.

5. **Positive Principle:** This last principle is more concrete. It grows out of years of experience with AI. Put most simply, momentum for change requires large amounts of positive affect and social

bonding, attitudes such as hope, inspiration, and the sheer joy of creating with one another. Organizations, as human constructions, are largely affirmative systems and thus are responsive to positive thought and positive knowledge. The more positive the questions used to guide a group building an OD initiative, the more long-lasting and effective is the change.[3] In important respects, people and organizations move in the direction of their inquiries. Thousands of interviews into "empowerment" or "being the easiest business in the industry to work with" will have a completely different long-term impact in terms of sustaining positive action than a study of "low morale" or "process breakdowns."

These five principles are central to AI's theoretical basis for organizing for a positive revolution in change. These principles clarify that it is the positive image that results in the positive action. The organization must make the affirmative decision to focus on the positive to lead the inquiry.

For more detailed information and application of the AI principles, refer to *Dynamic Relationships: Unleashing the Power of Appreciative Inquiry in Daily Living* by Jackie Stavros and Cheri Torres (Chagrin Falls, OH: Taos Institute Publishing, 2005).

Mini-lecture II:
Positive Image — Positive Action

The power of positive imagery, as illustrated in the fifth principle, is a key factor in the AI dialogue. There are six main areas of research to support this premise: research into the placebo effect, Pygmalion effect, positive effect, internal dialogue, positive imagery, and metacognitive competence. This section briefly elaborates on each area. The original article "Positive Image, Positive Action: The Affirmative Basis of Organizing" appears in Chapter 11.

1. **Powerful Placebo:** The **placebo effect** is a fascinating process in which projected images, as reflected in positive belief, ignite a healing response that can be as powerful as conventional therapy or any other intervention. In the twentieth century, the placebo effect

---

3 See Bushe, G., & Coetzer, G. (March 1994). Appreciative inquiry as a team-development intervention: A controlled experiment. *Journal of Applied Behavioral Science*, 31, 13.

is accepted by most medical professions as genuine. Between one-third and two-thirds of all patients show marked physiological and emotional improvement in symptoms simply by believing they were given an effective treatment, even when that treatment was a sugar pill or some other inert substance. While the complex mind-body pathways are far from being completely understood, there is one area of clear agreement: positive changes in anticipatory reality through suggestion and belief play a central role in all placebo responses.

2. **Pygmalion Effect:** In the classic Pygmalion study,[4] on the basis of "credible" information, teachers are led to believe that some of their students possess exceptionally high potential while others do not. Thus, the teachers are led, on the basis of some expert opinion, to hold a positive image (PI) or expectancy of some students, and a negative image (NI) or expectancy of others. Unknown to the teachers, however, is the fact that the so-called high-potential students were selected at random. In objective terms, all student groups were equivalent in potential and were merely dubbed as high, regular, or low in learning potential. As the experiment unfolds, differences quickly emerge— not on the basis of any innate intelligence factor or some other predisposition, but solely on the basis of the manipulated expectancy of the teacher. Over time, subtle changes among students evolve into clear differences, as the high-PI students began to significantly overshadow all others in actual achievement.

   The key lesson is that cognitive capacities are cued and shaped by the images projected through another's expectations. For example, what is seen is believed. As a result, actions and behaviors take on a whole new tone based on the perceived image. In turn, the resulting differential behavioral treatment makes the people receiving this treatment begin to respond to the positive images that others have of them. The greatest value of the Pygmalion research is that it provides empirical understanding of the relational pathways of the positive image—positive action dynamic.

3. **Positive Effect and Learned Helpfulness:** While still in the formative stages, early results on this issue suggest that positive imagery evokes positive emotions and positive emotions move people

---

4 Rosenthal, R. (1969). *Pygmalion in the classroom.* New York: Holt, Rinehart and Winston.

toward a choice for positive actions. Positive emotions are intimately connected with social helpfulness. This line of research is an expansion on an earlier, empirically validated theory of learned helplessness articulated by Martin Seligman and others in the growing field of positive psychology. Somehow, positive emotions draw people out of themselves, pull them away from self-oriented preoccupations, enlarge their focus on the potential good in the world, increase feelings of solidarity with others, and propel people to act in more altruistic and positive ways.[5] For more than a dozen years, Dr. Barbara Fredrickson has been studying the effect of positive emotions in the workplace. Her work has demonstrated the improvement in individual and collective functioning, psychological well-being, and physical health due to positive imagery.[6]

4. **Inner Dialogue (2:1):** It is argued that all human systems exhibit a continuing "cinematographic show of visual imagery" or ongoing "inner newsreel" that is best understood through the notion of inner dialogue. For example, a study of a stressful medical procedure indicated that people may have thoughts that impede the aim of the clinical intervention (this procedure may kill me, a negative image) or that facilitate the goals of the care (this will save my life, a positive image). Hence, the inner dialogue functions as an inner dialectic between positive and negative adaptive statements. One's guiding imagery is presumably an outcome of such an inner dialectic. In addition, studies show that there is a definite imbalance in the internal dialogue in the direction of positive imagery for those groups of individuals identified as more psychologically or socially functional. Functional groups are characterized by a 2:1 ratio of positive images to negative images, whereas mildly dysfunctional groups demonstrate equal frequencies—a balanced 1:1 internal dialogue.

The AI dialogue creates guiding images of the future from the collective whole of the group. It exists in an observable, energizing, and tangible way in the living dialogue that flows through every living system, expressing itself anew at every moment, thereby enhancing the chances of the 2:1 imagery to prevail in a group setting.

---

5 Seligman, M. (1992). *Helplessness: On development, depression, and death*. New York: W. H. Freeman.

6 For more information on the broaden-and-build theory, refer to Fredrickson, B. (2003). The value of positive emotions. *American Scientist*, 91, 330–335.

5. **Positive Imagery as a Dynamic Force:** Various scholars have noted that the underlying images that a civilization or a culture holds have an enormous influence on its fate. In his study of Western civilization, the Dutch sociologist Fred Polak argued this point concerning the tendency of the positive image. For him, the positive image of the future is the single most important dynamic and explanatory variable for understanding cultural evolution. Therefore, as long as an organization's or society's image is positive and flourishing, the dynamic culture is growing toward the positive images of the future. When there is a vision or a bright image of the future, the people flourish.

6. **Metacognition and Conscious Evolution of Positive Images:** Metacognition is awareness of one's own cognitive systems and knowledge and insight into its workings. It is the awareness that prompts a person to write reminders to himself or herself to avoid forgetting something.[7] The **heliotropic** hypothesis states that human systems have an observable tendency to evolve and move in the direction of those positive images that are the brightest and boldest, most illuminating, and promising. To the extent that the heliotropic hypothesis has some validity, questions of volition and free agency come to the fore.

   • Is it possible to develop metacognitive capacity and thereby choose positive ways of construing the world? If so, with what result?
   • Is the quest for affirmative competence, the capacity to project and affirm an ideal image as if it is already so, a realistic aim or merely a romantic distraction?
   • Is it possible to develop the affirmative competence of large collectives, that is, of groups, organizations, or whole societies affirming a positive future together?[8]

With the exception of the last question (where not enough research has been completed), most of the available evidence suggests quite clearly that affirmative competence can be learned, developed, and honed through experience and disciplined, formal training. One example is that imagery techniques are becoming important to the successful training of athletes. Experimental evidence indicates that the best athletes may be successful because of a high-

---

7 Ashcraft, M. (1997). *Fundamentals of cognition.* Englewood Cliffs, NJ: Prentice Hall.
8 Ibid.

ly developed **metacognitive** capacity of differential self-monitoring. In brief, this capacity involves being able to systematically observe and analyze successful performances (positive self-monitoring) or unsuccessful performances (negative self-monitoring) and to be able to choose between the two cognitive processes when desired. The professional athlete wills himself or herself to succeed by envisioning (imagining) a positive outcome to his or her next action or series of actions.

These examples demonstrate the power of positive imagery leading to positive actions and demonstrate that such imagery on a collective basis may be the strongest approach to cocreating a positive future. It is time to concentrate as never before on the power of positive images in leading to positive actions. Through such studies, new knowledge and images of possibility have been created. To learn more about the relationships between positive imagery and positive action, refer to the article in Chapter 11, "Positive Image, Positive Action: The Affirmative Basis of Organizing."

Mini-lecture III:
Social Constructionism

A central premise of AI is that the appreciative process of knowing is socially constructed. In other words, knowing takes place through interaction with and within a social system. That is why AI views organizations as centers of human relatedness. Thus, by getting people to unite on a central theme or idea, AI allows people who share a related objective to project or construct their future—in this case, the future of an organization.

The idea that a social system creates or determines its own reality is known as **social constructionism**. AI takes this theoretical framework and places it in a positive context. This positive spin on social constructionism is central to AI. Many of its principles flow from the idea that people control their destiny by envisioning what they want to occur and developing actions to move toward this end result. There is considerable overlap between the AI model and social constructionism theory. Some areas of overlap include the following:

1. The social order at any given point is viewed as the product of broad social agreement.

2. Patterns of social/organizational action are not fixed by nature in any direct biological or physical way; the vast share of social conduct is virtually stimulus-free, capable of infinite conceptual variation.

3. From an observational point of view, all social action is open to multiple interpretations, not one of which is superior in any objective sense. The interpretations favored in one historical setting may be replaced in the next.

4. Historical narratives and theories govern what is taken to be true or valid. To a large extent, such narratives determine what scientists and laypersons are able to see. An observation, therefore, is filtered through conventional stories, belief systems, and theoretical lenses.

5. To the extent that action is predicated on the stories, ideas, beliefs, meanings, and theories embedded in language, people are free to seek transformations in conventional conduct by changing patterns of narration.

6. The most powerful vehicle communities have for changing the social order is through the act of dialogue made possible by language. Therefore, alterations in linguistic practices hold profound implications for changes in social practice.

7. Social theory can be viewed as a highly refined narrative account with a specialized grammar all its own. As a powerful linguistic tool (created by trained linguistic experts), theory may enter the conceptual meaning system of a culture and, in this way, alter patterns of social action.

8. Whether intended or not, all theoretical accounts are normative and have the potential to influence the social order. Therefore, all narrative accounts (including social theory) are morally relevant. They have the potential to affect the way people interact with one another. This point is a critical one because it implies that there is no such thing as a detached, technical, scientific mode for judging the ultimate worth of value claims.

9. Value knowledge or social theory is, therefore, a narrative creation, not an aspect of the physical world. Social knowledge is not "out there" in nature to be discovered through detached, value-free, observational methods (**logical empiricism**); nor can it be relegated to the subjective minds of isolated individuals (**cognitivism**). Viewed from this perspective, social knowledge resides in the stories of the collectivity; it is created, maintained, and put to use by the human group. Dialogue, free from constraint of distortion, is necessary to determine the "nature of things" (social constructionism).

More information on the social constructionist viewpoint can be found in Kenneth and Mary Gergen's work listed in the References and Bibliography at the end of the book. Visit http://www.taosinstitute.net for a detailed listing of their publications.

Mini-lecture IV:
Beyond Problem Solving to AI

Since the 1930s, organizations have used a **deficit-based approach to problem solving**. It begins with seeking out the problem, the weak link in the system. Typically, there is a diagnosis; then alternative solutions are recommended. AI challenges this traditional paradigm with an "affirmative" approach, embracing an organization's challenges in a positive light. AI offers an alternative—to look for what is good in the organization, its success stories.

In Figure 1.2, Paradigm 1's basic assumption is that an organization is a problem that needs to be solved. Paradigm 2's basic assumption is that an organization is a mystery that should be embraced as a human center of infinite imagination, infinite capacity, and potential. The word mystery signifies, literally, a future that is unknowable and cannot be predicted. And this is true of organizations because nobody knows when or where the next creative insight will emerge that can shift everything or how a fresh combination of strengths will open to horizons never seen before. Paradigm 1 depicts organizations as broken-down machines in need of fixing; they are problems to be solved. Therefore, every analysis begins with some variation of the same question: What is wrong? What are the problems? What are the causes?

Figure 1.2 Two Paradigms for Organizational Change

Paradigm 1: Problem Solving	Paradigm 2: Appreciative Inquiry
"Felt Need" Identification of Problem	Appreciating "Valuing the Best of What Is"
⇓	⇓
Analysis of Causes	Envisioning "What Might Be"
⇓	⇓
Analysis of Possible Solutions	Dialoguing "What Should Be"
⇓	⇓
Action Planning (Treatment)	Innovating "What Will Be"
Organizing is a problem to be solved.	*Organizing is a mystery (infinite capacity) to be embraced.*

Paradigm 2 says something quite different. Organizations are not problematic. Indeed, no organization was created as a "problem." Organizations, if anything, are meant as solutions. But even more than that, organizations are not even singular solutions. They are creative centers of human relatedness, alive with emergent and unlimited capacity. Paradigm 2 is "life-centric." It searches for everything that gives life to a human system when it is most alive. It is creative and in a healthy relationship with its extended communities. AI is an approach to organizational change that is unique and refreshing. Detached observers of AI say that it is one of the most powerful, yet largely unrecognized models available to the OD and change management fields.

Mini-lecture V:
Vocabularies of Human Deficit

AI Insight

While AI was still evolving, Frank Barrett and David Cooperrider teamed up to work with a hotel that was experiencing low occupancy, with the staff and management locked in a setting of distrust and backbiting. Both sides were extremely negative toward each other, and neither was able to move past this to see a more positive option. In order to turn this hotel around, the AI team knew the first step was to shift the focus from a negative mind-set to one of openness. The AI team took the group to experience a four-star hotel. The staff and management did an inquiry to focus on what made this property an award-winning hotel. They focused on what worked well. From this inquiry, they learned they could work in similar ways to transform their hotel to a four-star hotel. Negative conversations turned into discussions of how they could be more than what they were. The transformation began, and the hotel became a top-rated four-star hotel. Frank Barrett and David Cooperrider coauthored a major paper on the breakthrough called "Generative Metaphor Intervention," and it received Best Paper of the Year Award at the Academy of Management's OD Division in 1988.[9]

---

9 See Barrett, F., & Cooperrider, D. (1991). Generative metaphor intervention: A new approach to intergroup conflict. *Journal of Applied Behavioral Science*, 26.

A fundamental assumption underlying AI is that the language one uses creates one's reality. Therefore, the emotional meaning of words such as dysfunctional, codependent, and stressed out affect one's thinking and acting, as illustrated earlier in the Pygmalion effect. This deficit-based vocabulary can inhibit the vision for a better and brighter future and limit growth.

Examples of deficit-based vocabularies are prolific in everyday conversation. Organizations, too, have adopted this mentality and spend considerable resources to train managers to remain vigilant at uncovering problems and identifying issues. As a result, many believe that a manager's job is to solve problems. This mentality constantly seeks to reinforce the idea that only by focusing on the problems can a better organization be created.

These tremendous expansions in vocabularies of human and organizational deficit can best be illustrated in Table 1.1, Vocabularies of Human Deficit,[10] and Table 1.2, Vocabularies of Organizational Deficit.

Table 1.1: Vocabularies of Human Deficit

Depressed	Midlife Crisis	Extremely Controlled
Bulimic	Kleptomaniac	Obsessive-Compulsive
Antisocial Personality	Neurotic	Low Self-Esteem
Paranoid	Anorexic	Identity Crisis
Posttraumatic Stress	Psychopathic Co-dependent	
Sadomasochistic	Dysfunctional Family	
Brief Psychotherapy		

Table 1.2 Vocabularies of Organizational Deficit

Organizational Stress	Theory X	Job Dissatisfaction
Work Alienation	Turfism	Neurotic Organization
Authoritarian Management	Low Morale	Executive Burnout
Role Conflict	Groupthink	Intergroup Conflict
Defensive Routines	Peter Principle Inflexibility	Structural
Bureaucratic Red Tape	Labor-Management Mistrust	Dilbert Bureaucracy
Interpersonal Incompetence	Organizational Diagnosis	Organization Learning Disabilities

---

10 All of these terms have come into common usage only within the past century (several only in the last two decades). See Gergen, K. (1991). *The saturated self.* New York: Basic Books.

To break through this negative vocabulary framework, AI proposes an affirmative vocabulary of organizing for the future. Why? As noted earlier, human systems and organizations move in the direction of what they study. The sooner the unconditional positive question is asked, the sooner the right answers can be obtained. This principle leads to the affirmative theory of organizing.

Mini-lecture VI: Toward a Theory of Affirmative Organization

The AI adventure truly begins with the appreciative mind-set, eye, thoughts, and vocabulary based upon the following concepts:

1. Organizations are made and imagined.

2. No matter what the durability to date, virtually any pattern of action is open to alteration and reconfiguration.

3. Organizations are "heliotropic" in character in the sense that organizational actions have an observable and largely "automatic" tendency to move in the direction of images of the future.

4. The more an organization experiments with the conscious evolution of positive imagery, the better it will become. There is an observable self-reinforcing, educating effect of affirmation. Affirmative competence is the key to the self-organizing system.

5. Paradoxically, the following is also true: the greatest obstacle in the way of group and organizational well-being is also the positive image, the affirmative projection that guides the group or organization.

6. Organizations do not need to be fixed. They need constant reaffirmation.

7. Leadership = Affirmation.

8. The challenge for organizational learning and development is creating the condition for organization-wide appreciation. This is the single most important act that can be taken to ensure the conscious evolution of a valued and positive future.

Once these simple, yet powerful concepts are internalized, the conditions that are essential to becoming an affirmative organization of change fall into place.

Mini-lecture VII: Assessing Organizational Inner Dialogue

Too often there is a tendency for OD interventions and even business meetings and organizational task forces to become gripe sessions or exercises in problem solving. Transforming the human system and its organization toward an affirmative learning and working environment requires a conscious effort to maintain a positive focus on the dialogue. In so doing, positive affirmations or comments should be encouraged, while negative dialogues should be minimized or avoided altogether. Listening for key phrases and/or activities can facilitate this process.

By way of example, the following positive discourse categories are offered:[11]

I.   Positive Categories

1. Positive Valuing: Any mention of positive values, past or present.

2. Hope toward future: Any mention of hope, optimism, or positive anticipation toward the future.

3. Skill or Competency: Any mention of skill, competency, action, or positive quality about self or others.

4. Openness, Receptivity, Learning: Any mention of receptivity in self or others accompanied by a positive outcome; also, any noticing of one's or others' learning or interests.

5. Active Connection, Effort to Include, Cooperation, or Combination: Any noticing of efforts to include, cooperate, connect, and relate that may be accompanied by at least an inferred positive outcome.

6. Mention of Surprise, Curiosity, or Excitement: Any mention of curiosity, surprise, openness to fresh insights, or excitement in self or others.

7. Notice of Facilitating Action or Movement toward a Positive Outcome: Any mention of a facilitating action or movement toward a real or imagined positive outcome or any mention of a facilitating object or circumstance. Also, noticing of any event that enhances another event, an effective state, or a person; noticing facilitative or positive cause and effect.

---

11 From Barrett, F., Cooperrider, D., Tenkasi, R., & Joseph, T. Unpublished manuscript, Case Western Reserve University, Cleveland, OH.

8. Effort to Reframe in Positive Terms: Any mention of a negative emotion or action accompanied by the possibility of a positive desired outcome; also, any mention of a change in mood from negative to positive, including any mention of an obstacle that is temporary or getting over a negative static state, or reframing a negative situation into more positive terms.

9. Envisioned Ideal: Any mention of a vision/value end-state articulation of a positive outcome envisioned for a future that is **utopian** or **pragmatic**.

Then for the organization to process, there must be a commitment to let go of the negative discourse categories that drain the organization's resources. These include the following:

II. Negative Discourse Categories

1. Negative Valuing: Any mention of negative valuing; for example, fatalism, apathy, or dislike. Any description of person, a group, a circumstance, or an event as a problem or an obstacle.

2. Concern, Worry, Preoccupation, Doubt: Any mention of concern, worry, or preoccupation without mention of a possible model to alleviate concern or to enhance understanding; any mention of doubt, suspicion, or lack of confidence in future outcomes.

3. Unfulfilled Expectation: Any mention of any event, action, state, or person that does not match intention, wish, desire, goal, or other unfulfilled expectation.

4. Lack of Receptivity, Absence of Connection: Any mention of a lack of receptivity in self or others, including a lack of collaboration, a lack of understanding, a failure to listen or failure to agree, or any explicit mention of an absence of connection.

5. Deficiency in Self or Others: Any mention of a sense that something is missing; for example, a deficiency in self or others or a lack of motivation, appropriate effort, skill, or competence or an absence of resources (such as time or money).

6. Negative Effect: Any mention of feelings of dissatisfaction, selfishness, sadness, defensiveness, irritation, or anger without mentioning a possible antidote or relief or effort to understand.

7. Withdrawal or Suppression: Any mention of avoidance, ignoring, withdrawal of energy or surrender, or suppressing of self or others.

8. Control or Domination: Any notice of effort or action to disrupt, dominate, wield control, or halt a mood or an action in self or other.

9. Wasted Effort: Any mention of excessive investment of time, resources, or energy without mention of reward or positive outcome.

10. Prediction, Image of a Negative Future: Any mention of prediction, vision, image, or expectation of a negative future.

11. Attribution of Control by Others in Combination with Self-Deprecation: Any notice of effort or action in others to disrupt, dominate, or wield control in combination with attribution of helplessness to self or self-pity.

12. Negative Cause-and-Effect Relation: Any explicit notice of a cause-and-effect relationship leading to a negative outcome.

13. Reframing a Situation in Negative Terms: Any mention of a positive emotion with the possibility of a negative outcome; mention of experiencing a change in mood from positive to negative or getting into a negative state, focusing on possible obstacles, or reframing a positive situation into more negative terms.

The responsibility of the AI moderator—whether a consultant, a manager, or an appointed team leader—is to facilitate positive discourse and minimize negative discourse to foster constructive change dialogue.

Mini-lecture VIII: History as Positive Possibility

Three factors that give life to healthy organizations are continuity, novelty, and transition. Research[12] has established that visionary organizations and their leadership have the capacity to learn and apply lessons from the best of the past (**continuity**), to surface and develop ideas for creative acts (**novelty**), and to enact actual changes in systems and behaviors to progress toward a desired state (**transition**). The importance and effectiveness of AI stems in part from its natural focus on all three of these generative factors.

---

12 See Collins, J., & Porras, J. (1994). *Built to last: Successful habits of visionary companies.* New York: Harper Business and Jonas, H., Fry, R., & Srivastva, S. (1989). The office of the CEO: Understanding the executive experience. *Academy of Management Executive*, 3(4).

Continuity

AI begins with a focus on organizational continuity, the understanding and appreciation of the system's connective threads of identity, purpose, pride, wisdom, and tradition that perpetuate and connect day-to-day life in the organization. It is paramount to recognize that continuity is a necessary part of change or transformation. As Jim Collins, coauthor of Built to Last: Successful Habits of Visionary Companies, puts it, ". . . change is good, but first know what should never change."[13]

Steven Covey also emphasizes the importance of valuing continuity in human development:[14]

> *People cannot live with change if there's not a changeless core inside them. The key to the ability to change is a changeless sense of who you are, what you are about, and what you value.*

In attending to continuity, the dialogue is built around the system's founding stories, turning points, proudest achievements, best practices, empowering traditions, intergenerational wisdom, legacies, and amazing moments. It is a discovery of the organization's history-as-positive-possibility. This inquiry reveals the bases on which healthy management of continuity can be sustained by:

- Knowing what people do best.
- Ensuring human and technical resources to support basic core tasks.
- Orienting to maintain the most valued aspects of the culture.

The function of continuity is between the individual and the organization.

Table 1.3 Functions of Continuity

For the Individual	For the Organization
Social Connectedness	Strengthened Commitment
Moral Guidance	Better Sense-Making and Decision Making
Confidence to Act	Consistent Values and Mission
Personal Welfare	Decentralized Control
Pride, Hope, and Joy	Basis for Organizational Learning
Freedom	Long-Term Thinking
	Customized Change

---

13 Ibid.
14 See Covey, S. (1990). *The 7 habits of highly effective people.* New York: Simon & Schuster.

Novelty

In attending to novelty, the AI dialogue and process provides the opportunity for unexpected newness to be offered up. A space for true valuing of novel thinking and acting is created. Hierarchy is suspended; harmony is postponed in favor of curious questioning. Symphonies of logical rationales are replaced with cacophonies of wild, half-baked notions; and typical incentives to conform are supplanted with celebration of those who constructively challenge the status quo. Such flowerings in an organization—what Dee Hock terms "creative chaos"[15] — enable the healthy management of novelty through:

- Intentional processes for learning from collective experience.
- Practices that actively search for new ideas: internally and externally.
- Investments in individual growth and development as a stimulus for new paradigm thinking.

This is where the affirmative topic choices come into the AI process.

Transition

In attending to transition, the dialogue uncovers ways in which new ideals (novelty) are transformed into visible changes that are experienced by everyone as positive movement toward a change target with minimal disruption (threat to continuity). The system is enlivened through a shared sense of enacting a "common script," whereby everyone recognizes the positive reason to change, the desired state to be achieved, and the next few steps to be taken. This allows for healthy management of transition through:

- A common vision, from which priorities are determined.
- Helpful feedback/measurement mechanisms on key success factors.
- Support for purposeful experimentation.
- Involvement strategies to promote a common script.

AI: The Foundational Questions

For visionary organizations, continuity, novelty, and transition are necessary capacities that exist in healthy tension. Too much attention on continuity may create myopic, rule- bound systems that constrain. Too much attention to nov-

---

15 Hock, D. *Birth of the chaordic age* (1999). San Francisco: Berrett-Koehler.

elty can result in ivory-tower leadership that loses credibility with those doing the core work. Too much emphasis on transition can create a sense of directionless change-for-the-sake-of-change. As a process, AI is instrumental in finding and sustaining a healthy balance among these life-giving capacities. The following foundational questions provide an opportunity to address the three necessary elements of continuity, novelty, and transition. The first three AI generic questions focus on continuity:

- What would you describe as being a high-point experience in your organization, a time when you were most alive and engaged?
- Without being modest, what do you value most about yourself, your work, and your organization?
- What are the core factors that give life to your organization, without which the organization would cease to exist?

The next step for the organization is to open itself to novelty, the unexpected newness or the new possibilities in its human systems. It is a time to dream. What is it that the organization can become?

- Imagine you have awakened from a long, deep sleep. You get up to realize that everything is as you always dreamed it would be. Your ideal state has become the reality. What do you see? What is going on? How have things changed?

Finally, there is the transition, the intentional change of the human systems in the organization. How will the organization achieve the dream that was discovered? It is in the Design phase that transition begins, continuing through the Destiny phase. The final AI foundational question addresses the future :

- What three wishes do you have to enhance the health and vitality of your organization?

All organizations have something to value about their past. This element must be appreciated so that change becomes a positive experience without unnecessary resistance from a sense of disruption. The AI process helps in honoring the past (continuity) and searching for newness (novelty) in order to embrace movement toward the new future (transition), as illustrated in Figure 1.3. Simultaneously, AI brings all three areas into balance and harmony.

Figure 1.3 Managing Change: Continuity, Novelty, and Transition[16]

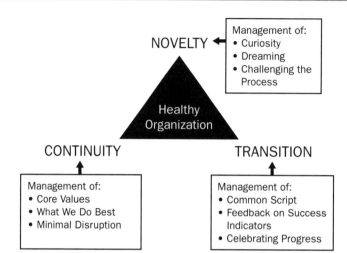

Mini-lecture IX: Why AI Works: The Liberation of Power

Adapted with permission from Whitney, D., & Trosten-Bloom, A. (2003). The power of appreciative inquiry. San Francisco: Berrett-Koehler.

For over two decades, organizations and communities around the globe have experienced extraordinary transformations through the use AI for organizational and social change. Those working with AI began asking the following questions:

- Why do people get so excited and want to participate in AI efforts?
- Why does participation so readily lead to positive results such as innovation, productivity, employee satisfaction, and profitability?
- What creates the space for people to be their best at work and for personal transformation?
- What are the conditions that foster cooperation throughout a whole system of highly diverse groups of people?

16 From Srivastva, S., & Fry, R. (1992). *Executive continuity.* San Francisco: Jossey-Bass.

In keeping with the spirit of AI, an inquiry into *why Appreciative Inquiry works* was conducted by Diana Whitney and Amanda Trosten-Bloom. They created a set of questions, held focus groups, and conducted formal and informal interviews in several organizations—most notably Hunter Douglas Window Fashions Division. (The Hunter Douglas Case Clipping is at the end of Chapter 7.) Their key finding is that AI works by generating six essential conditions within an organization. These conditions through which AI liberates power and unleashes human potential are called the Six Freedoms. Following is a brief description of each "freedom," along with quotes from stakeholders involved in the process.

1. **AI creates a context in which people are "Free to Be Known in Relationship."** Human identity forms and evolves within relationships; yet all too often in work settings, people are related in their roles rather than as unique individuals. AI interrupts the cycle of depersonalization that masks people's sense of being and belonging. It offers people the chance to truly know one another—both as unique individuals and as a part of the web of relationships. AI doesn't just build relationships. It also levels the playing field and builds bridges across boundaries of power and authority.

   > *For instance, at Hunter-Douglas, a machinist exclaimed, "Appreciative Inquiry blew the communication gap wide open." Similarly, a printer commented on the ways in which AI in general—and the interviews in particular—helped to make other people and their ideas more accessible: "Appreciative Inquiry gave us opportunities to be known across the boundaries. As our inquiry got fully under way, other people became excited, just like me. I didn't feel alone. For the first time, it was 'me with the world.'"*

2. **AI makes a space in which people are "Free to Be Heard."** Someone can listen without truly hearing or getting to know the other person. On the other hand, "being heard" is relational. To be heard requires that someone listen actively with sincere curiosity, empathy, and compassion. It requires an openness to know and to understand another person's story.

   Through one-on-one **appreciative interviews**, people who might otherwise feel as though they are ignored and do not have a voice are invited to come forward with information, ideas, and innovations that are subsequently put into action throughout the organization.

   To illustrate, a supervisor of a technical maintenance group initiated an inquiry among his team's internal customers: engineers, technical support staff, etc. He and his staff conducted interviews and collected stories of exceptional service. They invited people to dream about the service they had always wanted and to describe it in detail. In the process, the group built relationships across functions—in particular, between engineering and technical support.

3.   **AI opens the opportunity for people to be "Free to Dream in Community."** In today's complex world, visionary leadership means unleashing the dreams of people at all levels of organizations. It means creating organizations as safe places where large, diverse groups of people dream and share their dreams in dialogue with one another.

   For example, in a nonprofit organization, interviews with more than 1,200 stakeholders worldwide yielded a vision of an entirely new model of service: from sending people out to do good to linking people and organizations of similar intent around the globe. This vision was so compelling—and its momentum so great—that by the first anniversary of the summit, close to 30 new initiatives were launched using this "sister organization" model as a template. Then in the two years that followed, close to 200 new initiatives—dreams—unfolded.

4.   **AI establishes an environment where people are "Free to Choose to Contribute."** Work can separate people from what matters most to them, or it can provide a forum for enacting and realizing their deepest calling. Freedom of choice liberates power, but it also leads to commitment and a hunger for learning. When people choose to do a project and commit to others to do it, they become very creative and determined. They do whatever is necessary and learn whatever is needed to get the job done.

   For example, a frontline employee who had volunteered to lead an innovation team went to her personnel department to ask for coaching. She stated that for her team to succeed, she needed to learn how to facilitate meetings and how to help her team make decisions. Her determination paid off for the team, the organization, and herself. The team's project was finished in record time and led to significant process improvements in the company. She was promoted to a supervisory position, and her new team is thriving with her leadership.

5.   **AI provides the context for people to be "Free to Act with Support."** To act with support is the quintessential act of positive interdependence. When people know that large numbers of people recognize and care about their work and are anxious to cooperate, they feel safe to

experiment, innovate, and learn. In other words, whole-system support stimulates people to take on challenges and draws people into acts of cooperation that bring forth their best self and work.

To break through several years' worth of apathy and distrust, John Deere Harvester Works initiated a five-day summit—the last two days focusing exclusively on what it called "tactical implementation." Participants selected ten projects they believed were most critically important. Then to their surprise, they began working with one another there in the summit to plan, line up resources, and initiate the projects.

When people are truly free to act with support, their contributions are profound and their lessons sometimes surprising. Another employee at Hunter Douglas shows that this freedom liberates individual and organizational power—even when the intended actions fail to reach fruition:

> *My coworkers and I worked hard to make the case for and create a cross-training program. It was ready for implementation, and then . . . nobody signed up!!! I was deeply disappointed—but ultimately OK. In the end, the only thing I really accomplished was getting an answer: people simply weren't that interested. But an answer was a big thing. It meant that I had the power to get an answer.*

6. **AI opens the way for people to be "Free to Be Positive."** In organizations today, it is not the norm to have fun, to be happy, or to be positive. Time and again people allow themselves to be swept away in collective currents of negativity, despite the pain it causes. A long-term employee of an organization mired in deficit discourse shared the following with dismay:

> *"I have ulcers because of this negative thinking and talking. Every day I come to work and hear nothing but complaints and criticism and blaming. I hate coming to work."*

Over and over again, people say that AI works, in part because it gives people permission to feel positive and to be proud of their working experiences.

The effect of AI is so strong and powerful that it can even transform deficit discourse and negative thinking. In the words of one employee,

> *"I am a very positive thinker, so this suits me very well. But I believe*

this process is powerful enough to influence all of the staff—not just those of us who are already this way."

AI works because it unleashes all of the Six Freedoms over the course of a 4-D Cycle. It creates a surge of power and energy that, once liberated, won't be recontained. A supervisor at Hunter Douglas said, "As people tried and got results, they gained confidence. That led to five times as much input and the desire to get more involved." In short, through the liberation of power, AI creates a self-perpetuating momentum for positive change.

Summary

The nine mini-lectures provide the theoretical foundations and research citations that move human and organizational systems toward a positive, generative future. In addition, it is manifest that human systems within organizations move in the direction of what they study and that the study begins with an inquiry. The best way to understand AI is to discover how it works. That will be the focus of the next chapter: to show how these theoretical foundations move people into action—a way forward.

2

The Appreciative Inquiry Process: How It Works

Overview

AI is premised on the idea that organizations move toward what they study. For example, when groups study human problems and conflicts, they often find that the number and severity of complex and problematic issues grow. In the same manner, when groups study lofty human ideals and achievements (such as teamwork, quality, or peak experiences), these phenomena tend to flourish. People in organizations construct and enact worlds that, in turn, affect their behavior. What they study is what they become knowledgeable about and skilled in carrying out. Problem-focused study builds organizational knowledge, wisdom, and capacity about those problems. On the other hand, the study of organizations operating at their best builds knowledge, wisdom, and replicable capacity about how to bring out the best in the organizations. In this sense, the AI approach accepts the notion that knowledge and organizational destiny are interwoven: *the way we seek to know people, groups, and organizations is fateful*. To understand AI at a fundamental level, one simply must understand these two points. First, organizations move in the direction of what they study. Second, AI makes a conscious choice to study the best of an organization, its **positive core**.

Chapter 1 laid out the theoretical foundation for AI: the principles upon which it is founded, *what* AI is and *why* it works. From this point forward, the focus will be on *how* AI works. This chapter begins with an overview of the positive core. The central theme of the positive core is fundamental to AI. It is the dominant principle and established basis for the 4-D Cycle and how it facilitates the AI intervention. The chapter concludes with an overview of the 4-D process.

The **4-D Cycle** is a method that allows the user to follow a well-coordinated series of steps (or phases) to help an organization identify its positive core and initiate the concrete operational steps needed to achieve its vision and desired goals. *Discovery, Dream, Design*, and *Destiny* were discussed briefly in the previous chapter. The concept of the affirmative topic choice, however, is new to this discussion. Yet that is where the AI process begins.

The first step in the AI process involves choosing the life-affirming factors as the focus of inquiry. What is it that you want more of? This step is important because what is studied becomes reality. Therefore, the right topics need to be created or chosen. These topics ultimately guide the formulation of questions and, through inquiry, create the learning agenda for an organization. This approach, known as the affirmative topic choice, lies at the center of the 4-D Cycle, illustrated in **Figure 2.1**.

Figure 2.1 Appreciative Inquiry 4-D Cycle

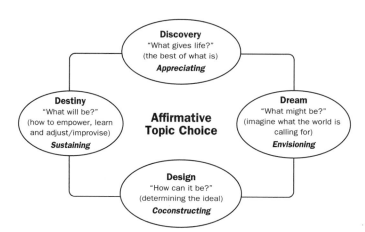

The Positive Core

The *positive core* of organizational life is one of the greatest, yet least recognized resources in the change management field today. AI has demonstrated that human systems grow in the direction of their persistent inquiries, and this propensity is strongest and most sustainable when the means and ends of inquiry are positively correlated. In the AI process, the future is consciously constructed on the positive core strengths of the organization. Linking the energy of this core directly to any change agenda suddenly and democratically creates and mobilizes topics never before thought possible.

The concept of the positive core is separate from yet central to the 4-D Cycle. As has been stated several times, AI is more than the 4-D Cycle. It is a strength-based philosophy (based on its core principles in Mini-lecture I: Five Principles of AI) created as "a way of being" in organizational life. The 4-D Cycle is the approach or process that allows the practitioner to access and mobilize the positive core. The positive core lies at the heart of the AI process. In this respect, the organization's positive core is the beginning and the end of the inquiry. This is where the whole organization has an opportunity to value its history and embrace novelty in transitioning into positive possibilities.

This positive core is woven throughout the 4-D Cycle. It is identified in the *Discovery* phase, mobilizing a whole-system inquiry into the positive core— *that which gives meaning to the organization*. It is amplified throughout the *Dream* phase, creating a clear results-oriented vision in relation to the discovered potential and in relation to questions of higher purpose. It is woven into the organizational architecture through the *Design* phase, creating provocative propositions of the ideal organization—an organizational design that people believe is capable of magnifying the positive core. Finally, it is implemented throughout the *Destiny* phase, strengthening the affirmative capability of the whole system. Thus, AI begins and ends with valuing that which gives life to an organization. In this sense, the organization's positive core can be expressed in any one of a number of ways, all of which can be identified through the inquiry. Following are some of the ways in which the positive core is expressed:

- Achievements and awards
- Best business practices
- Core and distinctive competencies
- Elevated thoughts
- Embedded knowledge
- Financial assets
- Innovations
- Leadership and management capabilities
- Market and/or strategic opportunities
- Organizational achievements
- Organizational wisdom
- Positive emotions
- Positive macro trends
- Product, service, and/or operational strengths
- Relational resources
- Social capital
- Technical assets
- Values and value chain
- Visions of possibility
- Vital traditions
- Strengths of partners and organizational stakeholders
- Capacities worldwide

Affirmative Topic Choice: A Fateful Act

Once the basic concept of the positive core is understood, the 4-D Cycle can be better explained. The first step in an AI application is selecting the **affirmative topic choice**.

This is, in short, the selection of topic(s) that will become the focus of the intervention.

Selecting the affirmative topic choice begins with the constructive discovery and narration of the organization's "life-giving" story. The topics, in the initial stages, are bold hunches about what gives life to the organization. Most importantly, the topics (usually three to five for an inquiry) represent what people really want to discover or learn more about. The topics will likely evoke conversations about the desired future.

The seeds of change are implicit in the first questions asked. The following two broad questions form a basis by which groups and organizations can create their own customized topics.

- *What factors give life to this organization when it is and has been most alive, successful, and effective?* This question seeks to discover what the organization has done well in the past and is doing well in the present.

- *What possibilities, expressed and latent, provide opportunities for more vital, successful, and effective (vision-and-values congruent) forms of organization?* This question asks the participants to dream about and design their most preferred future.

Since human systems typically grow in the directions about which people inquire, affirmative topic choices encourage people to select topics they want to see grow and flourish in their organizations. The choice sets the stage for AI through the application of the 4-D Cycle.

Careful, thoughtful, and informed choice of topics defines the scope of the inquiry, providing the framework for subsequent interviews and data collection. When AI was first being used, the design was an open topic choice, the "homegrown topic." The power of this type of discovery and dream led to the affirmative topic(s) that the organization would study, beginning with the AI foundational questions, as follows:

- What would you describe as being a high-point experience in your organization, a time when you were most alive and engaged?
- Without being modest, what is it that you value most about yourself, your work, and your organization?
- What are the core factors that give life to your organization— when it is at its best, without which the organization would cease to exist?
- What three wishes do you have now to enhance the health and vitality of your organization?

Since the first edition of the *Appreciative Inquiry Handbook*, many practitioners have replaced the *three wish question* with a more imaginative series of questions:

Imagine your organization five . . . years from now, when everything is just as you always imagined it would be. What has happened? What is different? How have you contributed to this future?

Pre-selected Topic Choices

Some organizations have succeeded with preselected topic choices. For example, a midsized long-term care company located in the Midwest had been struggling with census development (attracting patients) in its nursing homes and assisted living centers. The company's centers provided a high quality of care, as evidenced by both regional and statewide awards (such as the Governor's Award for Quality of Care). But many centers were experiencing a declining census base due to increased competition. The company decided to employ an AI initiative to focus on census development.

The objective of the initiative (called the Plus 1 campaign) was to jumpstart the census development effort by designing an inquiry that would include the center's stakeholders in working toward this common goal within a six-week budget period.

In an effort to focus the census campaign, the four key topics shown in **Table 2.1** were preselected in a subgroup planning discussion based on the four original topics.

Table 2.1 Appreciative Inquiry Key Topic Choices:
"Plus 1 Campaign" Example

Original Topics	Preselected Appreciative Inquiry Topics
Center of Choice	Provider of Choice
Customer Loyalty	Resident Loyalty
Treatment of Staff and Residents	Genuine Appreciation
Teamwork	The Exceptional Team

The company embraced the idea that larger gains would be made and sustained by expanding its initial goal of census development to include these preselected AI topic choices in order to understand best how to collectively achieve its census goal.

Another example is referenced in **Table 2.2**. A large global automotive firm had a rough idea of what it would take to build the positive core of a certain division.[1] However, the company wanted to make its topics more boldly affirmative. Therefore, the AI consultant worked with the group and suggested the following preselected AI topics:

---

1 A helpful resource to assist in determining preselected topic choices is the *Encyclopedia of positive questions: Volume One.* (2002). Garfield Heights, OH: Crown Custom Publishing (http://www.crowncustompublishing.com).

Table 2.2 Appreciative Inquiry Key Topic Choices: Automotive Example

Original Topics	Preselected AI Topics
Communications	Compelling Communications
Learning and Development	Continuous Learning
Management Behaviors	Integrity in Action
	Inspirational/Irresistible Leadership
Commitment and Enthusiasm	Culture As a Strategic Advantage
	Fun at Work
	Let's Do It

Who to Involve?

Selecting an affirmative topic choice can be a rich and satisfying experience, especially when it engages large numbers of people. At a minimum, a topic selection team should consist of people who have an important stake in the organization and its future. The team comprises any level of organizational participants from line staff to board of directors in order to create a "representative" steering committee.

Ideally, the topic selection team involves a microcosm of the organization. More people is better in terms of the organization's commitment to the process. Finally, the team must contain a variety of "voices," for in diversity comes a greater richness of relationship, dialogue, and possibility. **Table 2.3** details a list of potential stakeholders to consider for the topic team.

Table 2.3 Potential Representatives for Topic Team Selection

Potential Team Members

- Senior management
- Board of directors
- Middle management
- Staff or employee groups
- Union
- Customers
- Suppliers (vendors)
- Strategic partners
- Trade and professional associations

An important criterion in selecting participants is their ability to bring viewpoints and experiences from many different levels of the organization and from many different perspectives about the organization. Therefore, the list of potential participants is not necessarily limited to employees. The broad-based participant list is also the reasoning behind the statement "more is better." The more the intervention allows the participants to capture the true spirit of development, the better. In short, greater input will yield a stronger base of dialogue.

Once participants have been identified, a qualifier about team dynamics becomes important. Every participant in the topic selection team should have an active and equal role. The organization's leaders, executives, and/or managers must not control the dialogue. The participants must use a watchful eye to prevent this from happening on either a conscious or subconscious level. All who participate must be encouraged to speak their minds and say what is in their hearts.

The ABCs of Topic Choice: How to Do It

The topic selection team meets for a one- to two-day period. (The material in **Chapter 3** provides examples that can help lead to the affirmative topic choice.) Whether a two-hour executive overview or a one-day introduction, the process begins with a brief introduction to the initiative and goes directly into "mini-interviews," given the broad categories of topics initially selected. For these interviews, team members should be assigned to partners who are different from themselves with respect to functions, management levels, gender, age, tenure, and ethnicity. The goal is to get diverse opinions and to create dialogue. The mini-interview is an opportunity to create a genuine one-to-one relationship with the partner, and that opportunity should not be wasted. A simple rule is to have someone interview someone else that he or she has not spoken to before or barely knows.

The four AI starting questions are generally used for the mini-interviews. These questions have been used in many variations. Thus, you should tailor the basic questions to suit the needs of the inquiry and the organization. The four questions are given in **Table 2.4.**

Table 2.4 The Four Appreciative Inquiry Foundational Questions

1. What was a peak experience or "high point"?
2. What are the things valued most about...
    • Yourself?
    • The nature of your work?
    • Your organization?
3. What are the core factors that "give life" to organizing?
4. What are three wishes to heighten vitality and health?

A worksheet for preparing for topic selection using the four foundational AI questions is available in **Chapter 10**.

Following the mini-interviews, topic selection team members should organize into groups of six to eight members, staying with their original partners. In this smaller group, each member should introduce his or her partner, share stories and highlights, and begin to find common threads within the group. The groups must allow adequate time and space for dialogue and relationship building. They also must do whatever is necessary to prevent people from identifying themes before team members have really talked. The team must take time to dialogue, listen, and reflect. They must listen and take good notes. Next, within these groups, team members must identify key patterns and/or themes that have emerged.

When the time is right, these groups reassemble into the full group. The full group shares highlights and feedback from the small groups and discusses emerging themes and patterns. Are any of the themes related? Do any of the themes speak more loudly than another? less than another? Will any of the themes have a greater or lesser impact on the organization? Subgroups continue talking and working, if necessary, moving in and out of the large group.

The facilitator of this session also may be a participant in the process. This is acceptable because the facilitator is a member of the group. The facilitator must not monopolize; however, the facilitator can add value by sharing insights and ideas that have emerged.

On a final note, throughout this process, considerable dialogue and deliberation over particular words or phrases are not "just semantics"; they are essential. In an AI intervention, a fundamental assumption is that "words create worlds"; so the words chosen will have enormous impact on what is shared, what is learned, and where the group is headed with the inquiry. This is especially true at this stage of the inquiry. The selection of the affirmative action topic(s) drives the process from this point forward. A difference of one or several words may lead to different conclusions later in the process. Therefore, the moderator must allow for ample time and discussion over points that may seem irrelevant to some. For example, in the discussion that ensued from the topics provided in **Table 2.1**, a theme that emerged constantly was the treatment that staff and residents extended to each other and received from other stakeholders. A large group dialogue ensued, discovering that what the organizational members wanted was to better understand what "appreciation" meant and how "appreciation" was to be given and received as part of the culture and not as a specific event or award. This is how the topic choice of study moved from *treatment of staff and residents* to *genuine appreciation*.

Characteristics of Good Topics

Topics can be anything related to organizational effectiveness. Two such examples are provided in **Table 2.5**. Topics can include technical processes, human dynamics, customer relations, cultural themes, values, external trends, and market forces. Topics must be positive affirmations of the organization's strengths and the potential it seeks to discover, learn about, and become. In the end, somewhere between three and five compelling topics should be identified, all of which meet the following criteria:

- Topics are affirmative or stated in the positive.
- Topics are desirable. They identify the objectives people want.
- The group is genuinely curious about them and wants to learn more.
- The topics move in the direction the group wants to go.

The following principles apply as the group proceeds through the process:

- Organizations move in the direction of their images of the future.
- Their images of the future are informed by the conversations they hold and the stories they tell.
- The stories they tell are informed by the questions asked, so . . .
- The questions asked are **fateful** (i.e., they affect the answers given).

Table 2.5 Affirmative Topic Choice Samples

British Airways	Other Organizational Examples
1. Happiness at Work	1. Revolutionary Partnerships
2. Harmony and Sharing among All Employees	2. Customer Intimacy
3. Continuous People Development	3. Optimal Margins
4. Exceptional Arrival Experience	4. Lightning-Fast Consensus
	5. Transformational Cooperation
	6. Leadership at Every Level

These topics are used in sample interview guides available in **Chapter 8**. These two examples help illustrate that topics can be anything an organization considers strategically and humanly important, such as technical processes, market opportunity identification, sustainability, or social responsibility.

Table 2.6 summarizes useful guidelines to help create affirmative topic choices.

In the case of topic choice, the stated premise is still true: *human systems grow in the direction of their deepest and most frequent inquiries*. The AI process truly begins when a conscious choice is made to focus on the affirmative.

Table 2.6 Affirmative-Topic Choice Guidelines

Main Points

Topic choice is a fateful act.
Organizations move in direction of inquiry.
Vocabulary is not "just semantics"; words create worlds.
People commit to topics they have helped develop.
  • Everyone is an active participant.
  • Diversity is essential.

Critical Choice

Build a representative steering committee, or
Start with senior executive-level team, or
Involve the whole system to whatever extent is possible.

Rules of Thumb

No more than five topics are ultimately selected.
Topics are phrased in affirmative terms.
Topic is driven by curiosity—spirit of discovery.
Topic is genuinely desired. People want to see it "grow."
Topic is consistent with the overall business direction and intentions of the organization.
Topic choice involves those that have an important stake in the future.
Topic choice should take up to two days.

The *Discovery* Phase

Identify what gives life.
Appreciate the best of what is.

The primary task in the *Discovery* phase is to identify and appreciate the best of "what is." This task is accomplished by focusing on "peak times" or high-point experiences of organizational excellence—when people have experienced the organization as most alive and effective. Seeking to understand the unique factors (e.g., leadership, relationships, technologies, core processes, structures, values, learning processes, external relationships, and planning methods) that made the high points possible, people deliberately let go of analyses of deficits and systematically seek to isolate and learn from even the smallest wins. Recognizing that organizations are not always at their best, during discovery, people seek to uncover and learn from times and situations when the organization was at its best.

In the *Discovery* phase, people share stories of exceptional accomplishments, discuss the core life-giving factors of their organizations, and deliberate on the aspects of their organization's history that they most value and want to bring forward to their work in the future. In this phase, members come to know their organization's history *as positive possibility* rather than a static, eulogized, romanticized, or forgotten set of events. Empowering and hopeful conceptions of organizations frequently, if not always, emerge from stories that are grounded in the realities of the organization operating at its best. Appreciation is alive, and stakeholders throughout an organization or a community are connected in a dialogue of discovery. Hope grows and organizational capacity is enriched. *Capacity* is the ability or potential to mobilize resources and achieve objectives. It is everything necessary to construct the relationships required to achieve an organization's vision, mission, and goals.[2]

This is where the storytelling begins. The distinguishing factor of AI in this phase is that every carefully crafted question of the topic choice is unconditionally positive and seeks to inquire deeply into where the affirmative topic choice can help move the organization in the direction it wants to go.

---

2 See Stavros, J. (1998). *Capacity building using an appreciative approach: A relational process of building your organization's future.* Unpublished dissertation, Case Western Reserve University, Cleveland, OH.

The *Dream* Phase

Identify what might be.
Envision results the world is calling for.

The *Dream* phase amplifies the positive core and challenges the status quo by envisioning more valued and vital futures than those that are currently envisioned by organization members and stakeholders. The *Dream* phase asks the people whose future it is to engage with one another to create more vital and life-giving images for their own future. The primary purpose of the *Dream* phase is to expand or extend people's sense of what is possible.

Especially important today is the envisioning of potential results—the organization's contributions to the **triple bottom line** (i.e., profit, people, and planet).[3] Organizations today, be they business or social-profit, realize that financial well-being is one of three important criteria for success. The other two criteria are environmental sustainability and social well-being.

AI is uniquely suited to enhance an organization's contribution to the triple bottom line because it engages all stakeholders in envisioning their future together. When people who previously thought of themselves as adversaries, such as management and unions or corporations and environmentalists, meet and engage in dialogue through AI, they are able to create images of a future that works for all.

The *Dream* phase is practical in that it is grounded in the organization's history. It is also generative in that it seeks to expand the organization's potential, keeping in mind the voices and hopes of its stakeholders.

One aspect that differentiates AI from other visioning or planning methodologies is that images of the future emerge out of grounded examples from the organization's past strengths. These images are compelling possibilities precisely because they are based on extraordinary moments from an organization's history.[4] These types of data can be compared with benchmarking studies of other organizations. In both cases, the "good news" stories are used the same way an artist uses materials to create a portrait of possibility. Without all of the colors (red, green, blue, and yellow), the painting is less beautiful. So, too, are many visions or reengineering programs that fail to take notice of organizational history.

---

3 The triple bottom line focuses on economic prosperity, environmental quality, and (the element business has tended to overlook) social justice and people. Refer to Elkington, J. (1998). *Cannibals with forks.* Oxford: Capstone Publishing.

4 "Ground theory" is the qualitative research methodology of choice. It is inductively derived from the study of the phenomenon it represents. It is discovered, developed, and provisionally verified through a process pertaining to the phenomena explored. For more information, refer to Strauss, A., & Corbin, J. (1998). *Basics of qualitative research: Grounded theory procedures and techniques.* Newbury Park, CA: Sage Publications.

The *Dream* phase is a time for key stakeholders to collectively share their stories of the organization's past and their historical relationship with the organization. As the various stories of the organization's history are shared and illuminated, a new historical narrative emerges. This narrative engages those involved in much the same way a good mystery novel engages a reader. As participants become energetically engaged in re-creating the organization's positive history, they give life to its new, most preferred future.

During the *Dream* phase, organization stakeholders engage in conversations about the organization's position and potential in the world. Dialogue about the organization's mission (present purpose) and the unique contribution it can make to global well-being catalyzes a furtherance of images and stories of the organization's future. For example, a sustainable development organization would seek to cocreate an organization that aligns it strengths and opportunities to best deliver economic, social, and environment benefits for the society in which it does business.[5] For many organization stakeholders, this is the first time to think "great" thoughts about and create "great" possibilities for the organization. The process is both personally and organizationally invigorating.

The *Design* Phase

Identify what should be the ideal.
Coconstruct the future design.

The *Design* phase involves creation of the organization's social architecture. This new social architecture is embedded in the organization by generating *provocative propositions* (also known as *possibility statements or design principles*) that embody the organizational dream in the ongoing activities. Everything about organizing is reflected and responsive to the dream, the organization's greatest potential.

A provocative proposition is a statement of the ideal organization as it relates to some important aspect or element of organizing: leadership, decision making, communication or customer service, and so on. Successful design involves identifying the elements of organizing that need to be designed and crafting the provocative propositions that integrate discovery and dream ideals into the elements.

---

5 To learn more about how to redesign your organization's strategy to focus on the triple bottom line and create a strategic framework that moves your organization to sustainability refer to Hart, S. (2005). *Capitalism at the crossroads.* Upper Saddle River, NJ: Wharton School Publishing.

By crafting the organization's social architecture, stakeholders define the basic infrastructure. This phase requires in-depth dialogues about the best strategies, structure, staff, and processes needed to support the new system. By analogy:

> *To construct a home, one must decide to include or not to include windows, doors, a cooking space, sleeping spaces, spaces to greet visitors, fireplaces, and/or walls, and so on.*

> *To construct an organization, one must decide to include or not to include leadership, strategy, structure, human resource management, customer relations, and/or culture, and so on.*

As provocative propositions are composed, the desired qualities of organizing and organizational life are articulated. To further illustrate:

> *To construct a home, one must, after deciding to have doors, determine the number and nature of doors to build.*

> *To construct an organization, after deciding to have collaborative leadership, one must describe the quality of organizational life, relationships, and interactions that are desired enactments of collaborative leadership.*

The *Design* phase involves the collective construction of positive images of the organization's future in terms of provocative propositions based on a chosen social architecture. These designs help move the system to positive action and intended results.

The *Destiny* Phase

Identify how to empower, learn, and improvise.
Sustain what gives life.

The *Destiny* phase delivers on the new images of the future and is sustained by nurturing a collective sense of purpose and movement. It is a time of continuous learning, adjustment, and improvisation (like a jazz group)—all in the service of shared ideals. The momentum and potential for innovation and implementation are extremely high. By this stage in the process, because of the shared positive image of the future, everyone is invited to align his or her inter-actions in cocreating the future.

During this phase, stakeholders are typically invited into an open-space planning and commitment session. Individuals and groups discuss what they can and will do to contribute to the realization of the organizational dream as articulated in the provocative propositions. Relationally-woven action com-mitments then serve as the basis for ongoing activities.

The key to sustaining the momentum is to build an "appreciative eye" into all of the organization's systems, procedures, and ways of working. For exam-ple, one organization transformed its department of *e*valuation studies to val-uation studies (dropping the *e*). Others have transformed focus group methods, surveys, performance management systems, merger integration methods, lead-ership training programs, and diversity initiatives. The areas for application of AI are far-reaching. Provocative propositions may require an organization to redesign its processes and system in this phase of inquiry.

Frank Barrett's four areas of competency development are central to sus-taining appreciative organizing.[6]

1. Affirmative Competence
2. Expansive Competence
3. Generative Competence
4. Collaborative Competence

These competencies are fully discussed in Chapter 7 in the *Destiny* phase.

The *Destiny* phase is ongoing and brings the organization back full circle to the *Discovery* phase. In a systemic fashion, continued AI may result in new affirmative topic choices, continuous dialogues, and continued learning.

Chapter 2 presented a basic understanding of how AI works, but AI is best learned by doing. Something as simple as a conversation with a colleague to move an issue forward or a team building initiative to get two areas within a department communicating is enough. It could be as simple as asking these questions at the end of a staff meeting: What do we do well as a team? What do we want to do more of as an effective team? To get started with an AI ini-tiative, a major change program is not required.

One of the wonders of AI is that it can be implemented after limited expo-sure to its theory base (**Chapter 1**) and process overview (**Chapter 2**). Those who want more formal training in AI will find a Bibliography at the end of this book.

One of the first challenges in planning an AI initiative is how best to intro-duce the concept, theory, and process to an organization. **Chapter 3** provides tips, suggestions, selected AI projects, and sample agendas to help prepare for an AI initiative. A good start usually leads to a good finish. An AI initiative is

---

6 See Barrett, F. (1995). *Creating appreciative learning cultures*. Organizational Dynamics, 24, 36–49.

no exception. The way AI is introduced to the organization sets the tone for the process that follows. Getting started involves three key activities: introducing AI; defining the project, purpose, and process; and creating a project plan. This next chapter includes an overview and examples of each of these three key activities.

3

Introducing, Defining, and Planning an Appreciative Inquiry Initiative

Introducing AI

For most organizations, AI is a new approach to organizational change. If some members of an organization have heard or read about AI, they generally have many questions. For example, how does it work, how might it fit with our culture, and how can we involve our people without closing down the business? The novelty of AI requires that successful AI engagements begin through the introduction of AI to key stakeholders. Some of the best experiences of introducing AI share the following characteristics.[1]

Involve the Whole System from the Beginning

AI is a high-engagement, high-performance process. The way it is introduced to an organization should be a demonstration of the way it will be carried out should the organization decide to go forward with it. This means that from the start, all relevant and interested people—all stakeholders—should be involved. When AI is introduced, as many informal opinion leaders (influencers) as possible should be involved, along with formal leaders, holders of the purse strings, and some of the many people who will be impacted by AI. At the very least, this action will create a sense of positive anticipation in the organization. Often it will begin the long-term process of transforming the organization's inner dialogue by demonstrating that people at all levels of the organization and in all functions have a valuable contribution to make.

Experience Is an Inspiring Teacher

AI can't be "sold" without giving people an experience of AI. What kind of experience do people need to become engaged by and attached to this new way of thinking, working, and being? First, they need to experience an appreciative interview that includes some variation of the four generic AI questions presented in **Chapter 2**, as follows:
- What would you describe as being a peak experience or high point in your life—personal or professional?
- What do you value most about yourself? your work? your organization?
- What is the core factor that gives life to your organization?
- Describe your vision of the future for the organization and your world.

This interview helps people taste the power, the effect, and what some people have described as the intimacy of the AI process. The interview begins to build relationships within the team that later become the driving force for a

---

1 Adapted from Whitney, D., & Trosten-Bloom, A. (2003). *The power of appreciative inquiry: A practical guide to positive change.* San Francisco: Berrett-Koehler.

whole-system inquiry. Each person finds a partner to interview. Each partner conducts an interview of the other person for at least 20 minutes. Then after the 40-minute interview session, the whole group reconvenes to discuss the experience. Depending on the size of the group, each person may introduce his or her partner to the group.

People must hear the story of AI, and its successes should be told. The powerful stories of personal transformation, community development, organizational change, and global organizing that have emerged from the extensive work in the not-for-profit and for-profit sectors are impressive and should be shared. These stories bring a level of inspiration, of "global relevance," to the process. They touch people's hearts in ways that elevate their decision making and assessment of AI as a viable tool for their organization. The details of the AI 4-D Cycle can be explained through stories, too, including testimonials to augment the presentation. Many of these testimonials are included in this handbook. You also can visit the AI Commons at http://appreciativeinquiry.case.edu. The AI Commons is a worldwide portal with the most complete and up-to-date academic resources and practical tools on AI. This site is hosted by Case Western Reserve University's Weatherhead School of Management.

AI is a process that speaks for itself when given the chance. As such, it calls leaders of change—consultants, scholars, students, and business managers—to new levels of humility. A successful AI engagement depends less on a single person's capacities to communicate and facilitate and more on the wisdom and insight that resides within the hearts and minds of people throughout every organization and community. The power of AI comes alive in the initial discovery interviews and continues in the group dialogues during the *Dream, Design*, and *Destiny* phases.

Use Alternative Media Whenever Possible

Talking and stories are effective, but pictures (and other media) speak a thousand words. Videos, music, and other methods can enhance the story of AI—its assumptions and its successes. The message of AI can be supported by inspirational quotes posted on walls. Excerpts from stories and poems can be read. Video clips may help demonstrate and describe the phases of the 4-D Cycle.[2] Interviews and outcomes may be quoted. To illustrate, in one introduction to a large workforce, video clips that had been shot in the company's production plants were shown of people talking about their peak experiences with the company. Visit the AI Commons where you can download video clips for your review. People must experience and be stimulated by AI on multiple levels.

---

2 The video produced by Amanda Trosten-Bloom, *The Appreciative Inquiry Approach to Whole System Change*, which is available at Amazon.com, is but one example.

Create Cultural Sketches Consistent with the Desired Outcome

As with any good organizational change effort, each step, including the introduction, should be consistent with the desired outcome. For example, if an outcome is to reduce organizational hierarchies, the process leading to a "flattened" organization can be introduced. The conversation or interview guide can start with a vision of a lean organization. If another organizational outcome is to build bridges across functions, cross-functional introductions must be created.

"Surprises" in an AI introduction can be a powerful signal that there will be no more business as usual. For example, several of the most compelling introductory sessions have included field trips to production sites or other business divisions or involvement of external stakeholders in an initial AI mini-interview. In the Hunter Douglas Case Clipping in **Chapter 7**, the business development and top management team were taken on a road trip to tour and interview employees working in the plants.

Include Impact and First Steps Conversations

As AI is introduced, participants need space and opportunity to discuss and imagine implementation possibilities and impact while they are still close to the first experience. If first steps or next steps are included in discussions in the introduction, imagining what AI might offer the participants' organization can be powerful. After a brief introduction and experience with an AI interview, participants should discuss why AI makes sense for the organization. People should have the opportunity to share how they see AI being used in their organization and to volunteer for upcoming activities. The key is to help people make the transition from the abstract to the practical while inspiration and insights are at a fever pitch.

Inspire a Team

If a team can be inspired, activities will move faster and enjoy greater organization-wide support. A small group of captivated and engaged people, even in nonleadership positions, can create a forward momentum for strength-based positive change. A cohesive group tends to be more creative, more insightful, and more enthusiastic than any one person alone.

Defining the Project Purpose, Process and Plan

In implementing an AI initiative, the authors have found it useful for organizations and consultants to be clear about the project's purpose, process, and overall plan for implementation. Each of those steps is discussed in the following paragraphs.

Purpose

AI can be used for a wide range of organizational initiatives—from transformation of a whole-system culture to strategic planning to retention to process redesign. Clarity of purpose is essential to successful large-scale AI work. The purpose of the effort usually affects the design of the AI process. For example, in the case of a merger or partnership between two organizations, the inquiry process would include cross-organization interviews, dialogues, and presentations. Once the purpose is established, the AI process is then designed. A simple statement should be articulated:

Our organization will use AI because we want to _____ in order to _____.

Process

Each AI process is designed to meet the needs and constraints of the organization(s) involved. Some organizations (as described in this handbook), such as Hunter Douglas and British Airways North America, have used AI processes that span a year and have been fully integrated into the organization. Other organizations, such as Nutrimental Foods and Roadway, have accelerated AI through a whole-system four-day summit. The following questions have been helpful in considering an AI change initiative. These questions are not intended to be comprehensive or to be used in any specific order. They are intended to prompt meaningful discussions and to remind you of people to involve and tasks to consider for leading successful positive change efforts.

Most likely you will not be able to ask or answer all of the following questions at any given time. If that is the case, consider including the unanswered questions in your discussions with the organization's or community's leaders, your core team, or others involved in the project and its success.

GETTING STARTED

Overview of the Situation

- What is the mission (purpose) of the organization or community?
- How many people are in the organization or community? Where is it located?
- Who are the organization's or community's most involved, interested, and influential stakeholder groups—internally and externally?
- Who are the people interested in AI? How much do they know about AI?
- Who are the people you hope to get interested in AI?
- Who is the change champion, sponsor, and group that will be directly impacted? What do you believe the expectations are?

Change Agenda (In asking these questions, define to whom or to what organization you are referring.)

- What change does the person or organization hope for?
- What is the person's or the organization's image of an ideal future?
- What results does the person or organization want to achieve?
- Why is the person or organization interested in AI?
- How would you *state* the person's or the organization's change agenda (or intended purpose) in inspiring language?
- Why do you believe AI is a good approach to achieving this purpose?

Leadership

- Who are the people who must be involved in leading this process? What will their role in the process be?
- Who else needs to be involved for the project to succeed? Why are they important, and what will be their role?
- How will you get them involved?
- In what ways will leadership stay involved, informed, and inspirational to others?

Core Team

- How many people need to be on your core team to ensure that the entire organization or community has a voice?
- What functions (i.e., Human Resources, Sales, Marketing, Engineering, Finance, Manufacturing, and so on.) need to be included to ensure success of the process?
- Who else would add to the creativity and effectiveness of the process?
- How will the core team be chosen?
- What will be the responsibilities of the core team? How often will the core team meet?
- How will the core team continue to communicate between meetings?

Introduction of AI to the Organization
- Is an introduction to AI needed for the leadership of the organization or community?
    Who needs to be included?
    What will you teach about AI?
    How will the leaders experience AI?
    When will you do this introduction?
- How will you introduce AI to the core team?
    What will you teach about AI?
    How will the team experience AI?
    When will you have this core team meeting?
- Will you have an organization- or community-wide kickoff for the change process?
    How will people be invited?
    Who will describe the purpose and process of the change effort?
    What will you teach about AI?
    What will be the experience of AI?
    What is the leaders' role in the kickoff?
    What is the core team's role in the kickoff?
    How will you make the kickoff a creative and fun event or series of events?
    When will the kickoff happen?
    How will you maintain momentum following the kickoff?

Form of Engagement: Design of the AI Process
- What do you think is the best form of engagement for the organization or community to achieve its change agenda? Why?
- Who will be involved in deciding on the form of engagement?
- When will the form of engagement and process design be determined? (Forms of engagement: summit, a whole systems inquiry, or a core team inquiry)

Preliminary Affirmative Topics
- Will the topics be "home-grown" or "preselected"?
- If preselected, who will select your topics?
- If preselected, given the change agenda, what topics do you think would be meaningful subjects for inquiry?
- How will you and the core team determine and finalize the selection of affirmative topics?

Interview Guide
- Who will create the draft interview guide? When?
- Who will finalize the interview guide? When?
- Will you pilot the interview guide? If not, who will do it? When?
- How will revisions and refinements be included? When?

DISCOVERY PHASE
Learning about the best of what has been and is currently being practiced

Interview Strategy
- Who will be interviewed? Who are all of the stakeholder groups—internal and external—that you will interview? Why is each group important?
- Who will do the interviews?
- How many interviews will be conducted?
- Over what period of time will the interviews be held?

Interviewer Training
- Will interviewer training be conducted?
- Who will lead it? When?
- What will the training include?

Story Collection, Sharing, and Meaning Making
- How will you collect and share stories of best practices, organizational excellence, success, and innovation? (Some ideas: reports, newspapers, videos, storyboards, books, and AI room)
- Who will be responsible for collecting and sharing stories?

Mapping of the Positive Core
- How will you gather and illustrate all of the organization's or community's strengths, resources, and abilities?
- Who will be involved in mapping the positive core?
- How will the positive core be communicated organization- or community-wide?

DREAM PHASE
Envisioning a better world, organization, or community

Envisioning of the Future
- How will you engage people in envisioning the future? When will this occur?
- What questions will you ask to stimulate bold dreaming?
- How will you inspire bold and playful dreaming?
- Who will you involve in envisioning the future?

Opportunity Mapping
- How will you collect and record opportunities embedded in the dreams?
- Who will determine which opportunities to pursue?

DESIGN PHASE
Determining the ideal organization or community

Provocative Propositions
- Who will be involved in writing the statements describing your ideal organization or community? When will this occur?
- How will these statements be shared with and validated by the organization or community? When will this occur?

DESTINY PHASE
Recognizing and sustaining positive change

Innovation Teams
- How many innovation teams will you establish and support?
- How will innovation team projects and membership be determined?
- Who will be the leadership champions for the innovation teams?
- How will you ensure the success of the innovation teams?
- What is the timeline for innovation teamwork?

Recognition of Innovation
- How will you identify and recognize creative expressions of positive change?
- How will you identify and recognize great examples of appreciative leadership?
- How will you identify and recognize people who are living the change?

Creation of an Appreciative Organization
- Are there people who can benefit by further training in AI?
  If so, who are they?
  How will they receive the training—internal workshop or public workshop?
- Will you conduct an Appreciative Leadership Development Program?
  If so, who will attend?
  When will it be held?
- Will you conduct an Appreciative Management Development Program?
  If so, who will attend?
  What topics will be covered?
  When will it be held?

- What Appreciative Human Resource Processes will you create?
  Hiring?
  New Employee Orientation?
  Performance Valuations?
  Others?
- How will you further develop an appreciative approach to customer relations?
- How will you create opportunities for appreciative team development?
- How will you ensure ongoing appreciative communication throughout the organization and/or community that has been impacted?

Plan

The plan must align with the purpose and process. In addition, a useful plan serves to order activities and to point people in a common direction. It specifies who will do what and when, providing guidance for the effort. It also must be flexible because AI is an emergent process, one that unfolds as success builds on success. As a result, organizations tend to be most successful when they combine long-term macro plans, which approximate the activities and time frame of the AI 4-D Cycle, with short-term detailed plans, which clearly specify times and outcomes for specific activities such as meetings, trainings, and interviews.

Samples

The remaining materials in this chapter are sample designs used to initiate an AI-based process. The five samples can be used independently or in combination with one another.

- **Brief Introduction to AI: One-Hour Agenda**
  This session can be used to acquaint members of the organization with the concept and value of AI. It can build interest in and demand for a more intensive session. It is typically used as a brief, yet formal presentation by the AI practitioner to a decision-making group.

- **Executive Overview to AI: Two-Hour Agenda**
  This session provides a little more time to explore the theory and process of AI as well as to engage in a set of mini-interviews.

- **Workplace Redesign Using AI: Four-Hour Agenda and Slides**
  This session reinforces concepts introduced in the Executive Overview to AI (the 2-Hour Introduction, developed in the following pages) and introduces more of the 4-D Cycle. It also includes more activities that allow participants to begin practicing AI techniques.

- **Values Project Using AI: Detailed Project Plan**
  This sample captures the same conceptual material as the other two options. In addition, it provides a concrete, detailed project plan that demonstrates the key elements of the AI process for the organization and an action plan to get the organization moving toward its destiny.

- **Two-Day AI Workshop, Agenda, Project Roles, and Interview Guide**
  This sample contains materials developed for The University of Kentucky Hospital/UK Children's Hospital. It begins with a project overview and includes a Core Team Kickoff agenda, the interview guide, an Appreciative Inquiry Workshop agenda, introductory remarks, and a summit agenda. It shows responsibilities of the core team and its organization divided into subteams focused on the interview guide, data collection and synthesis, and communication and the results.

The following materials can be modified or adapted to plan for and conduct an AI initiative for an organization.

Brief Introduction to AI: One-Hour Agenda

This outline for a brief informative introduction to AI was used for a global automotive manufacturer. The goal is to introduce the key concepts and highlight success stories appropriate for the organization. It should include a mini-experience so that people get a sense of AI's potential and its uniquely positive way of looking at the organization's future.

Agenda

1. AI—What's It All About? (10 minutes)
   - Define AI (theoretical and practitioner).
   - Introduce the Five Principles:
     - The Constructionist Principle
     - The Principle of Simultaneity
     - The Poetic Principle
     - The Anticipatory Principle
     - The Positive Principle
   - Highlight AI benchmark success stories.
   - Hand out success stories such as Roadway: AI Summit.[3]
   - Ask why we are here.

2. Opening Interviews—Using two of the four foundational questions (30 minutes)
   - Set up the process by reading the four questions:
     - What would you describe as being a peak experience or high point in your life—personal or professional?
     - What do you value most about yourself? your work? your organization?
     - What is the core factor that gives life to your organization?
     - Describe your vision of the future for the organization and your world.

   - State that time is only committed for the following two questions:
     - Think about a time when you were really engaged in and excited about your work. Tell me a story about that time. What was happening? What were you feeling? What made it a great moment? What were others doing that

---

3 See article by Hammonds, K. (July 2001). *Leaders for the long haul.* Fast Company, 56–58.

contributed to this moment? What did you contribute to creating this great moment?
– If you had three wishes for this organization, what would they be?
- Divide participants into pairs; allow 15 minutes per person.
- Return to the group and discuss how it went (e.g., sharing descriptive adjectives).

3. Sample Interview Guide Using Client's Choice Topics (10 minutes)
    - Review traditional problem-solving topics clients provide and rework these topics into affirmative topic choices.
    - Review the newly revised topics (based on group discussion) in the new AI protocol.
    - Discuss differences from traditional problem-solving questions.

4. Wrap-up—How can it help your organization? (10 minutes)
    - Go around the room and ask the following questions: How does this sound? Is it interesting enough to explore further?
    - Ask: What applications can you imagine for your organization? What does your organization want more of?
    - Discuss multiple ways to launch AI initiatives in a large organization.
    - Next step: Think of one AI project, big or small, with which you might like to experiment.

After a formal introduction, the decision-making team will want to engage in a planning session with the AI practitioner to set up an Executive Overview and/or a half-day to two-day workshop. The AI process is flexible enough to fit the organization's desired design and time frame.

Executive Overview to AI: Two-Hour Agenda

This outline is for a typical two-hour Executive Overview to AI. In a two-hour overview, the stage is briefly set and people begin interviews as quickly as possible, typically within the first 15 minutes. The keys to the success of a brief introduction of AI are the interview experience, stories of the impact of AI in other organizations, and the opportunity for participants to discuss applications of AI for their organization.

Agenda

1. Context Setting (10 minutes)
   - State that it's time to rethink human organization and change.
   - Describe it as something hopeful and heartfelt (in facilitator's own words).
   - Ask why we are here.
   - Define AI (theoretical and practitioner).

2. Five Principles of AI (5 minutes)
   - Introduce the Five Principles:
     - The Constructionist Principle
     - The Principle of Simultaneity
     - The Poetic Principle
     - The Anticipatory Principle
     - The Positive Principle
   - Acknowledge that these are abstract principles and explain how they work together.

3. Opening Interviews—Using the four foundational questions (35 minutes)
   - Set up the process by reading the following questions:
     - What would you describe as being a peak experience or high point in your life—personal or professional?
     - What do you value most about yourself? your work? your organization?
     - What is the core factor that gives life to your organization?
     - Describe your vision of the future for the organization and your world.
   - Divide participants into pairs; allow 15 minutes per person.
   - Return to the group and process how it went (e.g., sharing descriptive adjectives).

4. Introduction to AI (30 minutes)
    - Shift from deficit change to positive change.
    - Discuss the 4-D Cycle.
    - Describe a story of the AI process and success in another organization.
    - Discuss the importance of topics and questions.

5. A Sample Interview Guide (10 minutes)
    - Hand out a concrete example to participants.
    - Review two or three of the questions.
    - Discuss differences from traditional problem-solving questions.
    - Ask participants to imagine something like this for their organization.

6. The Choice Points: (15 minutes)
    - Decide what the topics are.
    - Decide who to include on the interview team and who to interview.
    - Decide how many interviews to conduct.
    - Discuss many possibilities for Dream and Design.
    - Make this point: "Our job today is not planning!"

7. Discussion: (15 minutes)
    - Go around room and ask these questions: How does this sound? Is it interesting enough to explore further?
    - Ask: "What applications can you imagine for your organization?"
    - Ask what the next steps are.

Workplace Redesign Using AI: Four-Hour Agenda and Slides

Once the purpose of an initiative is determined, it is often necessary to introduce AI to the people who will be leading the overall effort. The following agenda is an example of a four-hour introduction of AI in such a situation.

In this example, the decision had been made to use AI to study and redesign the workplace environments worldwide throughout the company. In this meeting, 30 people from around the world learned about AI and the project. They were invited to serve on the leadership team to help create the interview guide and to chart the course of the endeavor. This meeting was both an introductory meeting and a working session to get input and to clarify the project plan.

The slides that follow the agenda were used to support the introductory presentation. They provide background information about AI and specific information about the proposed project, including the stakeholders to be interviewed, the broad timeline for the project, and specific outcomes for various meetings. The two slides of assumptions (Slide 11 and Slide 12) are especially noteworthy because they highlight the conditions for success and the constraints that influenced the ultimate design of the AI process. They are a good example of how an AI process can be tailored to the needs and constraints of a specific organization and purpose.

This four-hour meeting illustration resulted in widespread support for the use of AI for the proposed project and numerous ideas for other ways the organization could use AI. Consequently, several informal AI initiatives have begun and are spreading best practices in areas related to customer service; employee morale; and, of course, work environment and productivity.

Agenda

1. Introductions and Stage Setting (5 minutes)
   - State the purpose for this meeting.
   - Introduce AI consultant or facilitator(s).

2. Brief Introduction to AI (15 minutes)
   - Discuss what it is—philosophy and methodology.
   - Discuss definitions—Appreciate and Inquiry
   - State where it's been used and with what results.

3. Mini-interview (45 minutes)
   - Set up the process by reading the following questions:
     - What would you describe as being a peak experience or high point in your life—personal or professional?

– What do you value most about yourself? your work? your organization?

– What is the core factor that gives life to your organization?

– Describe your vision of the future for the organization and your world?

- Allow 20 minutes for each person to interview his or her partner.

4. Debrief Interviews and Dream Question (20 minutes)
   - Debrief interview experience—descriptive adjectives? What was the experience like?
   - Debrief dream question—surprises? What new things did you learn?

5. More about AI (30 minutes)
   - Introduce the Five Principles:
     – The Constructionist Principle
     – The Principle of Simultaneity
     – The Poetic Principle
     – The Anticipatory Principle
     – The Positive Principle
   - Discuss the 4D Cycle; provide examples of how it has been implemented in other organizations. Share a video clip of another organization using AI.
   - Review the interviews just conducted and discuss their relationship to Discovery.

6. Break (10 minutes)

7. Proposed Process to Use for Workplace Redesign (45 minutes)
   - Discuss assumptions.
   - Discuss preliminary project plan.

8. Discussion and Decisions (45 minutes)
   - Discuss potential revisions to process.
   - Discuss timelines, including endpoint.
   - Discuss selection of core team.
   - Close with revisit of purpose and expectations.
   - Ask whether there are other issues.

9. Wrap-up—Next Steps? (15 minutes)

The following slides were used for the session.

Workplace Redesign Using Appreciative Inquiry—PowerPoint Slides

**An AI Approach for Designing
a Flexible Workplace**

"XYZ" Company

Intro Slide

Agenda

- Introductions
- So, what is AI?
- Mini-interviews
- Interview debrief
- More about AI
- The process we propose to use for this pilot
- Assumptions
- Wrap-up

Slide 1

What is Appreciative Inquiry?

"Ap-pre'-ci-ate, v."

". . . to value or admire highly; to judge with heightened understanding; to recognize with gratitude."

"In-quire', v."

" . . . to search into, investigate; to seek for information by questioning."

Slide 2

AI . . .

- Focuses organizations on their most positive qualities
- Leverages those qualities to enhance the organization

Appreciative Inquiry is the study of what works well.

Slide 3

What's *Different* About AI?

- Purposefully positive
- Builds on past successes
- "Grass roots" and "top down"
- Highly participative
- Nurtures a positive "inner dialogue"
- Stimulate vision and creativity
- Accelerates change

Slide 4

The *"4-D"* Cycle

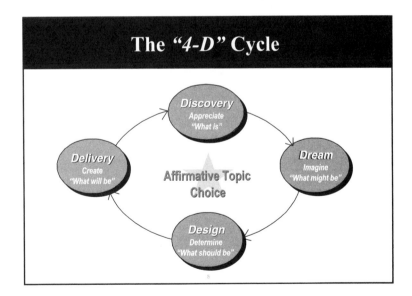

Slide 5

AI Success Stories

- **British Airways**
  Customer Service and Culture Change
- **Hunter Douglas Window Fashions Division**
  Culture Change and Strategic Planning
- **GTE Telecommunications**
  Union/Management Relations
- **United Religions Initiative**
  Organization Design
- **Green Mountain Coffee Roasters**
  Business Process Improvement

Slide 6

Questions to Start Us Thinking

- **Think back over your entire career, and all the work you've ever done – for pay, or for volunteer. Now, think about a peak experience or high point – a time when you experienced yourself as most successful and most satisfied.**

  - What was it like?

  - What were the conditions that contributed to that extraordinary level of success and satisfaction? In particular, what was it about the *physical space* that contributed to that experience?

Slide 7

Questions to Start Us Thinking cont.

- **Without being humble, what do you most value about . . .**

  - . . . yourself and your capacities to produce and contribute to your team and your organization?

  - . . . your team and its contribution to *XYZ company* and its clients?

  - What are the core factors that support your highest levels of success and satisfaction?

8

Slide 8

Questions to Start Us Thinking cont.

- **You fell asleep at work and you just woke up! You resume working and you are more successful and satisfied than you have ever been.**

  - Where are you working, and on what?

  - What is it like? (Details, please!)

  - What is it about you, the situation, and the task that makes you so successful and satisfied?

  - What type of support did *XYZ company* provide for you that contributed to this remarkable spike in your performance?

9

Slide 9

Purpose for the Inquiry

To engage XXX location stakeholders in a process of discovering "how we work at our best," in order to:

- Determine the necessary components of a *successful* and *satisfying* "new workplace."

- Generate relevant and meaningful insights related to the physical, technological, sociological, and organizational *design* of the new space(s).

- Create a *positive transition* to the new space(s) by building understanding, support, and buy-in for the change (and all that the change implies).

10

Slide 10

Assumptions

- We want the flexible workplace solution to reduce operational costs.

- We want to increase or maintain employee satisfaction and performance.

- We are limited in our ability to get blocks of committed time from employees serving clients.

- We need to be focused on the future in that the changes we make today are dynamic and flexible enough to meet future needs.

11

Slide 11

Assumptions cont.

- We have a broad population with differing needs and preferences. Not every group or individual employee wants or needs the same setting/services to be optimally productive and engaged.

- This will be a big cultural change and we need to work with other groups to make this successful.

- The flexible workplace solution will reflect the input of our stakeholders.

- The process we use for implementing the change should be inclusive.

12

Slide 12

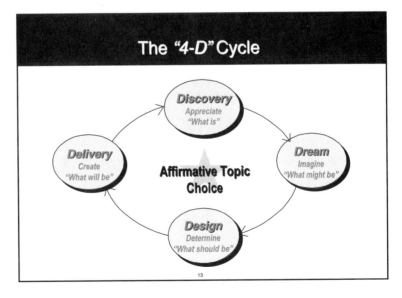

Slide 13

"Discovery"

- Getting Started

- Inquiry / Interviews

    - "When we are at our best, what makes work exciting, interesting, invigorating, motivating and productive?"

- Meaning Making / Reflections

- Preparation of report or presentation

14

Slide 14

Getting Started

- Hold an Initial Meeting:

    - 2-1/2-days

    - 17-20 participants (representatives from every related stakeholder group)

    - Early January

15

Slide 15

Meeting Outcomes

- Select Affirmative Topics

- Make Critical Decisions:

  - Who will conduct interviews?

  - Who will we interview?

    - Do we interview clients? Suppliers?

    - Do we benchmark other organizations? If so, which ones?

  - What are our timelines?

Slide 16

"Next Steps"

- Set up Sub-Groups

  - Finalize interview guides

  - Prepare interviewers

  - Prepare interview assignments / timelines

  - Make meaning of the "data"

Slide 17

Inquiry Process

- Conduct one-to-one interviews with stakeholders:
  - Internal "customers"
  - Clients
  - Vendors/suppliers
  - "Benchmark" organizations
  - Outside "experts" (architectural firms, consultants, other *XYZ company* offices, etc.)
- Answer the question: "When we are at our best, what makes work exciting, interesting, invigorating, motivating and productive?"

18

Slide 18

Meaning Making / Reflections

- Hold clusters of "synthesis" meetings
  - Keep interviewers *close* to their own data
  - Imagine *implications* and *possibilities*
  - Seek *inspiration,* not "common ground"

- Meeting outcomes
  - Broad sharing of interview insights
  - Creation of a small team which will meet to create the final report / presentation of interview data

19

Slide 19

The Summit
DREAM, DESIGN and DESTINY

- 1-1/2 days
- As many stakeholders as possible
- Meeting outcomes
  - Determine a variety of *organizing possibilities* that will build upon what we've learned works (from the Inquiry).
  - Agree to a set of *design principles* around which we will organize our "new workplace."
    - These principles will ensure that we will continue to operate at the highest possible levels of customer and client satisfaction and productivity - even as we realize savings in our overall costs.
  - Organize to *implement* the "next steps" that are suggested by our Design.

20

Slide 20

In other organizations, this four-hour topic selection process can be expanded into a longer workshop format that allows organizations to explore other potential topic areas. The next sample is a detailed project plan for a large-scale AI initiative at the American Red Cross.

Values Project Using AI: Detailed Project Plan

Following a two-day AI workshop, the emergent American Red Cross project conducted 5,000 appreciative interviews during a two-month period to discover the values implicit in the services the organization provides nationwide. Careful and detailed planning was one of many factors that supported the success of this effort. As one might imagine with an organization of this size, commitment was unquestionable and enthusiasm was high.

At the president's national conference presentation only three months after the Values Project began, the project plan showed milestones along the way. This plan showed in great detail all that goes into a mass mobilized inquiry, from creating the interview guide to identifying interviewers to conducting interviews to collecting data and stories to synthesizing the data and preparing a report. In this case, the final report was accompanied by a highly inspirational video showing various Red Cross employees and volunteers demonstrating the values in action as they provided service to people in need. The result of this extraordinary inquiry was the identification of "living values," the values that are embedded in the day-to-day activities of the American Red Cross.

The following project plan illustrates how effective project management techniques can be used to help an AI project arrive at various milestones. The American Red Cross, for example, had important deadlines for the AI interviews. A national convention was the place where the narratives of hope, courage, and excellence were shared. More than 2,000 people from American Red Cross chapters all over the country came together for this convention. In a case like this, the details and time frames can make or break the AI momentum. AI is powerful on its own, but it is even better when the best project management and other consulting and facilitating techniques are integrated to support the positive AI intentions.

Project Plan—Major Milestones

(**V**–Vince, **H**–Harry, **D**–David, **J**–Jan, **B**–Brian, **R**–Bob, **VT**–Values Technology)

Bold = Major Milestones

Italics = Values Technology

Standard = Appreciative Inquiry, combined activity or other activity

Week	Milestone	Date	Who	Notes	Complete = X
1	Project milestones and plan defined	3/2	V, H, B, R		X
	Interviewer criteria defined identified	3/2	V, H, B, R		X
	Major resource requirements	3/2	V, H, B, R		X
	Contracting with AI and VT vendors begins	3/3	CE&T		X
	Conference rooms reserved for training	3/4	B		X
	President's communication to ARC prepared and approved	3/4	J, B		X
	Chapters, blood regions, NHQ units supplying interviewers selected	3/5	V, H, B, R		X
2	Values project plan presented to OMC	3/8	President, V		X
	President's communication re: Values Project on Cross Link and by mail to board and key leadership	3/8	Comm.		X
	Hotel arrangements completed for AI training	3/9	CE&T	Hotel info and budget numbers needed for interviewer recruitment letters	X
	Interviewer recruitment letters completed and sent to execs.	3/9	J, B	Package contains cover letter specifying exec's recruitment job and due date and letter to interviewers describing process and admin. details	X
	Budget and account number assigned	3/9	B	Finance	X
	Execs. in chapters, blood regions, NHQ who are supplying interviewers are notified	3/10		Comm.	

Week	Milestone	Date	Who	Notes	Complete = X
	Determine requirements (if any) for customizing values inventory	3/10	V, H, VT		X
2	Print values inventory forms	3/12	VT		X
	Contract process completed with vendors	3/12	Contracts Office		X
3	Determine values inventory sample range	3/16	H, VT		X
	Mailing labels and cover letters sent to VT or mailing service	3/17	H		X
	Execs. send in names of committed interviewers	3/17	Field units	Send as e-mail to CE&T	X
	Interviewers sent notice of acceptance and travel details	3/18–3/19	CE&T	Phone or e-mail to CE&T	X
	Protocol for reporting stories and interview data determined	3/19	R	Demonstrate protocol for sending AI data during training; brief VT on interview reporting process	X
4	Mail values inventories	3/22	VT	Completed 3/19	X
	Determine date for values drafting meeting	3/22	V, H	Meeting date 5/5	X
	Develop participant list for drafting values statement	3/23	V, H		X
	AI training conducted	3/23–3/24	D, CE&T	Washington Marriott	X
4–6	VT inventories completed and mailed in	3/23–4/9	HQ and field units	Completed forms sent directly to VT. Forms processed as received.	
	Appreciative Inquiry interviews scheduled	3/25–3/28	Interviewers		
	Appreciative Inquiry interview protocol developed	3/25–3/28	D	Delivered to CE&T on 3/26, if possible.	
	Interview protocol sheets delivered to interviewers	3/29	CE&T		
4–7	AI Interviews conducted	3/29–4/12	Interviewers		
	Draft letter from president inviting senior leadership to values-drafting meeting	4/5	B, J	Meeting date 5/5	

Week	Milestone	Date	Who	Notes	Complete = X
5–7	Story compilation	3/29– 4/13	Interviewers	Interviewers send in story packages as completed; stories sent to VT for analysis	
5	Send invitation to senior leadership meeting to draft values statements	4/7	President, V, H	NHQ, BHQ, field representation	
	Determine convention broadcast options	4/8	V, H, Comm		
	Reserve satellite time for convention broadcast	4/30	Comm	If necessary	
6	All VT forms completed and sent in	4/9	ARC staff		
6–9	Analysis of VT forms	4/9– 4/30	VT		
7	All AI stories received by CE&T	4/15	Interviewers, CE&T		
	Electronic versions of stories sent to VT	4/17	R, CE&T		
7–9	Document analysis of stories	4/23– 4/30	VT		
7	Purchase (or release) satellite time for convention	5/1	V, H, Comm	Decision and purchase on same day. Might need decision sooner.	
10	Meeting to interpret data	5/3– 5/4	V, H, B, R, D, VT		
	Meeting to draft preliminary values statement	6-May	V, H, D, VT	Target date; key leadership from BHQ, NHQ, and field	
10– 12	Prepare convention presentation and related activities and materials	5/5– 5/20	V, H, B, R, Comm, et al		
	Preliminary values statement presented to president	5/6	V, H		
	Draft values statement revised as necessary	5/7	V, H, B, R		
10	Draft values statement sent to strategic planning comm. of board and appropriate senior leaders for comment	5/11	V, H, B	Involve strategic planning committee of the board	
10– 11	Comments on draft values statement received from board members and senior leaders	5/13– 5/19	CE&T		

Week	Milestone	Date	Who	Notes	Complete = X
12	Presentation of Red Cross Values at National Convention	5/21– 5/23	President, V, H, D		

Two-Day AI Workshop, Agenda, Project Roles, and Interview Guide

This sample contains materials developed by Susan Wood and Karen Stefaniak for an employee development project focusing on nursing excellence at The University of Kentucky Hospital. It begins with a project overview, the project scope, and sponsorship and funding. Included are the Core Team Kickoff Meeting Agenda, the AI Workshop Agenda, a Sample Introduction to use before starting a workshop, Core Team Roles, Core Team Kickoff Meeting Learnings & Results, the interview guide, brief project milestones, and an update with measurable results. The agendas show responsibilities for the core team and the organization into subteams focused on the interview guide, data collection and synthesis, and communication.

The University of Kentucky Hospital/ UK Children's Hospital

"Nursing Excellence – The UK Way"
By Karen Stefaniak and Susan Wood

Purpose and Overview

In 2001, University of Kentucky Nursing was designated a Magnet facility by the American Nurses Credentialing Center. The Magnet examination process (extensive documentation and a four-day on-site survey) validated nursing leadership's belief that the work environment facilitated autonomous professional nursing practice. However, a nurse satisfaction survey conducted in 2002 indicated the one area of nursing satisfaction that needed improvement: "professional autonomy." Although the result of this satisfaction survey was a surprise and puzzle to leadership, the staff's perception was taken very seriously. Further discussion with staff indicated frustration and powerlessness resulting from the need to solve the same or similar problems over and over again. Staff nurse councils' recommendations required far too much time to become reality, so the staff would "give up" and move on to another pressing issue. The time and commitment involved was draining the staff's energy. They needed to see their own successes and appreciate their contributions to patients, the organization, and the profession.

Two unrelated events occurred in late 2002 and early 2003. First, Karen Stefaniak, RN, PhD, the chief nursing officer (CNO), was introduced to AI by the nursing staff education director and immediately began reading everything she could find. She tested the approach with nursing leadership during an annual goal setting session. The positive approach was readily embraced as energizing and effective.

Second, Dr. Stefaniak was selected for a Robert Wood Johnson Executive

Nurse Fellows Program, which provided funding for a project. After consulting her colleagues, she began the search for an expert in AI to assist her in leading a culture change in nursing to one in which nurses appreciated themselves and each other. Further, it was hoped that the nurses would internalize their worth and appreciate the professional and autonomous work environment validated by the Magnet designation. AI was the method chosen to facilitate such a change because AI assumes that all organizations have past and present successes and encourages perpetuating those successes to create more successes. The AI 4-D Cycle would be the approach that nurses would use to share their stories, requiring reflection and self-insight.

Dr. Stefaniak conducted an online search; found the AI Commons Web site at Case; reviewed past projects of the consultants on the "Find an AI consultant" link; and located Susan Wood, who specialized in applying AI in healthcare. After a telephone conversation in which Dr. Stefaniak expressed the goals of her project and her vision of the future state of the nursing culture, Susan was interested in working with UK nursing to increase nurse and nurse manager satisfaction and retention, educate nursing leadership in the AI philosophy and methodology, and ultimately improve patient satisfaction.

Project Scope

Aim: Discover stories about nursing excellence, learn AI, and generate innovative ideas to reframe "Nursing Excellence – The UK Way." This would be communicated throughout the hospital with positive meaning for "The UK Way." Specific expectations included the following:
- Increase satisfaction of nurses and managers
- Improve problem solving skills and process improvement
- Amplify understanding of Magnet nursing
- Enhance teamwork and empathy for each other (know more about what everyone does)

"The project began 2003 and will last forevermore," stated Dr. Stefaniak. The purpose of the project was to develop nursing management and to move the nursing culture to one in which nurses at UK accepted nothing less than excellence in everything they did. The nursing department (1,600 nurses) initiated the inquiry, inviting pharmacy, nutrition, and other staff to participate in workshops and interviews.

Project Leaders
- Dr. Karen Stefaniak, RN, PhD, Associate Hospital Director/CNO, and Robert Wood Johnson Nurse Executive Fellow, UK Hospital/UK Children's Hospital

- Craig Casada, Nurse Recruiter, UK Hospital
- Susan O. Wood, Principal, Corporation for Positive Change
- Nurse Managers who taught 20 AI workshops at UK Hospital

Sponsorship and Funding

Dr. Karen Stefaniak holds a Robert Wood Johnson Executive Nurse Fellowship, a three-year program that includes a leadership project and professional development. She led "Nursing Excellence – The UK Way" with agreement and support from the UK hospital administration.

Core Team Kickoff Meeting

Forty-four staff members convened for 12 hours over two days to get the project started. What followed were meetings where nurse leaders and hospital administrators were introduced to AI and asked to support the initiative. They readily agreed, and a core team was invited to meet to select topics of inquiry and design the process. The core team was made up of 30 nurses from all units and stakeholders who work closely with nursing—pharmacy, nutrition, radiology, volunteer, rehab and respiratory, nurse recruitment, and quality improvement. Fourteen nurse managers who guided core team activities and led workshops joined these 30 people. Two-way interviews were done in 20 workshops over ten months, with a Story Collection Team gathering data.

UKH Core Team Kickoff Agenda

Purpose: Orient Steering Group to AI; plan and launch inquiry

Goals:
- Experience and understand Appreciative Inquiry
- Clarify purpose and desired outcomes of project
- Select topics for inquiry; draft interview guide
- Refine project plan, roles, and timeline

Products:
- Project plan, roles, and timeline
- Interview guide
- Workshop and interview schedule and process for interviewing
- Task teams—interview guide, communication, education, story collection, and summit planning

Day 1			
Activity	**Leader**	**Handout**	**Time**
Introductions/Purpose/Goals Introductions AI partners	Karen Stefaniak	1	5 minutes
Appreciative Interviews Pairs, quads, eights Mural (best stories/themes)	Karen	2	2 hours
BREAK – 15 minutes			
Appreciative Inquiry Briefing	Karen/Susan	3, 4	45 minutes
LUNCH – 45 minutes			

Topic Selection for Inquiry
    Debrief stories and mural
A "fateful act"
    What you want more of
	Susan/Karen		45 minutes

Topic Definition/Lead-ins
    Definition
    Ring bell for appreciative feedback
	Susan/Craig	5	1 hour

BREAK – 15 minutes			

Interview Guide Development
    Qualities of appreciative questions
    Sample guide/structure
	Susan/Craig	6	15 minutes

Round One: Subgroups Develop
Questions by Topic
    Refine lead-in
    Draft 3 or 4 questions
    Ring bell for appreciative feedback
	4 groups		1 hour

Round Two: Questions by Topic
    Improve questions
    Ring bell for appreciative feedback
    Assemble draft guide (computer for input)
	Susan/Craig		30 minutes

Review/Close/Questions	Susan/Karen/Craig		15 minutes

Day 2			
Activity	**Leader**	**Handout**	**Time**
Check In/Goals for Today	Karen/Susan		5 minutes

Brief Interviews 1/1
    2 questions
    Comments
	Craig		10 minutes

Pilot-test Interview Guide	Craig		45 minutes
BREAK – 15 minutes			
Visioning Activity for Project Draw a Picture of Success/Best-Case Scenario Name the Project—An Exciting and Evocative Name Refine Measurable and Immeasurable Outcomes	Susan/Craig	7	45 minutes

Project Planning
    Core team role
Timeline
    Stakeholders
    Workshops and interviewing—review design, guidelines
	Susan/Karen/
	Craig
		8	1 hour

Task Teams: Communication, interview guide, summit planning, story collection, and education/innovation (workshops)			
Teachable Moments—Lead with Affirmation	Susan +	9	15 minutes
Next Steps	Susan/Karen/Craig		15 minutes
Closing Comments	All		15 minutes

AI Workshops—Led by Nurse Managers

The following agenda was used by 14 nurse managers who led Appreciative Inquiry workshops. All staff and stakeholders were invited to enroll, and participation was deliberately mixed across nursing units and stakeholder groups. Interviewing partners sometimes took their conversations onto their units where they showed each other how things worked. This heightened understanding and appreciation of each other's roles. In one case, a nurse requested a transfer when she became intrigued with the work in the neonatal intensive care unit.

AI Workshop Agenda

Purpose: Illuminate the positive core of nursing through stories about nursing excellence.

Goals:
- Capture and contribute stories to the positive core of UK Hospital Nursing
- Develop expertise in Appreciative Inquiry interviewing
- Generate innovative ideas for bringing topics to life

Handouts:
- Interview guides with summary sheets (to be collected)
- 1-page summary of project
- Lead by affirmation

Materials Kit (AI bag):
- UK AI intro script, mural paper, tape, markers, graphic agenda, camera

Room Setup:
- Graphic agenda, 2 easels, blank mural posted with BESTS written at the top and WISHES at the bottom

Products from Each Workshop:
- Stories for story collection team (interview guides and summary sheets)
- List describing positive core
- List of innovative ideas
- Mural, which will be used at the summit (Take a picture and give mural to EF.)

Deliverables:
- Project timeline and plan
- Core team roster and role
- Draft interview guide
- Communication plan

This is the script the managers used to introduce the workshop:

First, introduce self: name, job title, and department

Suggested introduction: *I am here today to briefly speak with you about my experience with Appreciative Inquiry. I am part of the AI core team at UK Hospital, and we recently attended a workshop to introduce the concept to the nursing staff. Appreciative Inquiry (AI) is a process that helps participants remember and value what it is they do and why they do it. It facilitates positive change in an organization because looking for what works well is more motivating and effective than focusing on what is not working. By asking questions in a positive way, our thinking is geared more toward what works and what we want more of. Studies have shown that an organization will move in the direction of what they focus on!*

On a personal level, AI has been shown to have an overall beneficial impact on someone's life. At the AI core team meeting, we learned that from asking interview questions, we got stories. From stories, we got ideas on what works, leading to the question, What do we have that we want more of? We then brainstormed in small teams and identified our project title, the topics we believed were important and the questions that created the interview guide you will use today. So I invite you to be part of our journey, to share your stories. By doing so, you will begin the process of creating a positive change for all of us at UK Hospital!

Core Team Roles

The role of the core team (steering group) includes all of the following activities. Some have specific time frames for completion; others are ongoing for the life of the project. In addition, subteams have specific functions related to the interview guide, data collection and synthesis, and communication. It is very important to note who will complete what by when and to assign a lead coordinator to keep track of assignments/tasks.

- Articulate purpose and goals of project
- Identify and enroll stakeholders
- Select topics for inquiry
- Refine project plan
- Form necessary subgroups as specific "task teams" and assign responsibilities
- Design and test interview guide
- Invite others to interview
- Capture and document stories
- Plan and help design meetings and summit
- Track progress and outcomes during and after inquiry/measurement
- Communicate plans and progress

Task Teams
Following is a list of subteams and typical tasks.

Communication
Refine project title, purpose, and measures
Generate communication about the project to encourage involvement
Spread stories
Create a summit invitation

Interview Guide
Refine and test interview guide
Identify stakeholders and design interview guides

Story Collection
Collect stories using summary sheets from interviews
Read and organize stories, identifying key stories to share in summit
Pass interesting stories to communication team to share

Education and Innovation
Lead AI workshops
Capture ideas/innovation from workshops (via summary sheets/murals)
Prepare ideas to bring to summit

Summit Planning
Advise on whom to invite and how to invite and design of summit
Act as host at summit

Core Team Kickoff Meeting Learnings & Results
Purpose: Orient core team to AI; plan and launch inquiry to discover affirmative topic choices; write interview guide

During the core team launch, someone said, "Oh, that's just the UK way," referring to times when problems resurfaced and were not fixed. "The UK Way," with all of its negative connotations, had become a catch phrase. Nurses and stakeholders (pharmacy, nutrition, and so on.) decided right then to change the meaning of "The UK Way" from "when things go wrong" to reflect "nursing at its best." From the stories the team members told, five topics became the focus of inquiry for "Nursing Excellence – The UK Way." The topics were as follows:

1. Art of Nursing
2. The UK Quilt of Teamwork
3. UK Magnet Nursing

4. Celebrate Life as UK Nurses

5. Humor—A Vital Sign of Life

Another moment of truth occurred when the core team talked about how newly hired nurses were treated. "We eat our young," one of them said with some embarrassment. Susan asked, "What would it be if you did the affirmative opposite of eating your young?" After several moments of silence, someone said quietly, "We embrace our own." Mentoring and assimilating new staff became an important part of the inquiry.

The inquiry culminated in two one-day summits held in October 2004. In January 2005, an **Appreciative Inquiry Summit** convened to refine the vision and develop action plans to engage others in making the bold ideas come to life. Four themes emerged for action:

- Interdisciplinary Excellence
- Technology, Equipment, and Facility
- Quality of Work Life
- Our Public Image

AI Interview Guide

The following interview guide was created by the core team at the kick-off meeting:

The University of Kentucky Hospital/UK Children's Hospital
"Nursing Excellence – The UK Way"

Date: _____

Name: _____

Unit: _____ Phone: _____

Thank you for participating in this interview. I am an interviewer for this nursing project. We are inquiring and learning more about "Nursing Excellence – The UK Way." Nurses and related staff will be interviewed directly to collect the "best-case" stories on which to build the future. Your input will be an important contribution to generate meaningful ideas and actions.

Many times in the interviews, we ask questions about things that aren't working well so that we can fix them. This time we are going to approach things from a different angle. We are going to find out about your experiences of success so that we can find ways to create more of those types of experiences at UK Hospital and UK Children's Hospital.

Over the next few months, we will interview as many nurses as possible, primarily in workshops. We also will interview others who have a stake in quality nursing care. When the interviews are complete, everyone's input will be synthesized to identify qualities of nursing care that make UK Nurses unique. With those qualities as a foundation, we will create specific future steps to build on our strengths.

During our interview, we will be exploring your experiences in five areas: (List topics below)

1. Art of Nursing
2. The UK Quilt of Teamwork
3. UK Magnet Nursing
4. Celebrate life as UK Nurses
5. Humor—A Vital Sign of Life

I want you to listen like you have never listened before. The following series of questions will be very thought-provoking. Please listen carefully about each question and allow yourself time to think about your answer. Remember, there are no right or wrong answers.

Before we begin, do you have any questions?

1. What were your initial hopes and dreams when you first joined the UK Hospital?
2. What has been your most positive experience since you've been here?
3. Without being humble, explain what you value most about:
    – Yourself?
    – The people you work with?
    – Your department? your work?

Topic One: Art of nursing

Nursing care is an art at its very best. What we do with our minds, hearts, and hands is truly beautiful. We paint with brush strokes of compassion, weave tapestries of comfort, and sculpt an environment of caring beyond technology for our patients, their families, and often for one another. At UK, this is the art of nursing.

Question 1: What does the art of nursing mean to you? Describe a time when you or someone else demonstrated the art of nursing.

Question 2: Imagine the perfect painting of nursing at UK. What does it look like? Where do you picture yourself in it?

Topic Two: Nursing, the common thread that unites a patchwork of disciplines into a quilt of teamwork

Question 1: Tell me about a time when you accomplished more than expected by working together as a team. What was it about the team that made it work?

Question 2: What three wishes do you have for fostering teamwork and collaboration at UK?

Topic Three: UK Magnet nursing—a strong force pulling out the best in people through:

> Mentoring—embracing our own
> Autonomy—achieved through independent Nursing Practice
> Growing—always learning something new
> Nurturing—focusing on patients, their families and each other
> Excellence—exceeding expectations/above and beyond
> Teamwork—being a good fit/always being the insider

Nursing in a Magnet-status hospital provides improved patient outcomes, offers a better working environment, supports autonomous nursing practice, and encourages professional development. The infrastructure provides avenues for nurses to fully use their knowledge and expertise to deliver exceptional patient care. We believe in the value of superior nursing care and the way it can transform lives—we recognize the power of what one nurse can do for himself or herself and the patients he or she cares for.

Question 1: Tell me about an experience you had when you knew you were having a "Magnet Moment" (high point) (e.g., a specific situation or event of nursing excellence you have been part of).

Question 2: What three wishes do you have that could make UK Hospital and UK Children's Hospital more "magnetized"?

Topic Four: Celebrate life as UK nurses

Sail the 7 Cs

Celebrate our camaraderie, compassion, caring, commitment, and collaboration through complimentary words and actions.

Question 1: Tell me about an event or a situation in which you felt appreciated as a nurse. What did you value most about that experience?

Question 2: Describe a moment or example when you recognized a colleague by words or actions that conveyed a message that indicated "I could not have gotten through this without you." What were the circumstances surrounding this experience, and how did you and others feel afterward?

Question 3: What ideas do you have for celebrating success and expressing appreciation at UK?

Topic Five: Humor is a vital sign of life. Laughter sometimes is the best medicine. Humor allows us to deal with sad situations and job stress and enables us to relax and enjoy our patients, their families, and each other.

Question 1: Describe a specific work experience in which humor eased a painful, stressful, or tense situation or enhanced a positive one.

Closing: I'd like to ask you two final questions:
1. In your opinion, what was the highlight of this interview?
2. What do you hope comes of this process?

Project Milestones (what was accomplished; what AI topics/themes emerged)

One goal was to transfer knowledge and skill in AI to staff and leaders at UK Hospital so that the positive perspective would last beyond the initial project scope. This happened in several ways:

Craig Casada and Karen Stefaniak went with Susan Wood to an AI workshop to learn the principles and to create an effective project plan.

Managers learned AI and led workshops that accelerated permeation of AI.

Beyond nursing—Stakeholders were invited to participate with nurses in workshops, which strengthened relationships and generated innovative improvements.

Environmental Services (a UK vendor) picked up on AI and used it for conversations to define customer expectations with UK Hospital!

A nursing and materials management team designed its own inquiry to improve efficiency, cleanliness, and teamwork.

Vision Statement

Here is the vision statement that came from the summits held in October 2004 and January 2005.

The vision of Nursing Services at the University of Kentucky Hospital is as follows:

> *To be the premier nationally and internationally recognized leader in professional practice, patient care, education, and research thereby advancing our institution's pursuit of achieving top 20 academic health center status.*

The participants added the following "In 2004, Nursing Services discovered its Positive Core, using Appreciative Inquiry. We selected 5 topics to study. Then we told each other stories about our best moments in patient care, what we love about our work and our colleagues, what excellence looks like, and what makes our work fun and enjoyable. We are permeating the entire hospital with positive meaning for 'The UK Way.' Through *planned osmosis*, we invite our colleagues in all disciplines to join us in a positive revolution so that UK Hospital/UK Children's Hospital will be changed forevermore, building on our strengths and what we do well."

"The UK Way" means:
– We exceed expectations.
– Safe and efficient.
– Cutting edge.
– Respectful.
– Considerate.
– Visionary.

Reflections from participants about "Nursing Excellence – The UK Way" included:
– This process helped me rediscover the joy of nursing.
– The strongest thing at UK is the teamwork.
– We have a new understanding of one another.
– It's nice to "live outside my area" for a while.
– The experience has been a big boost.
– I may now be able to deal more effectively with negative people.

– This needs to go on indefinitely.

– "Nursing Excellence –The UK Way" stimulated me to come up with new ideas to brighten my patients' days.

– Positive energy is better than negative—it's more fun to make it work.

– So many changes! Nursing is stepping forward in a positive way now—not just waiting.

Project Update

Although the introduction of AI into nursing at UK began as a solution to a perceived negative attitude among nurses and to fulfill a Robert Wood Johnson project assignment, ultimately the goal was for AI to be part of the fabric of nursing and to become integrated into nursing management. It would be employed as a strategy for process improvement, recruitment and retention, morale enhancement, and strategic planning. This has been accomplished, and examples of the goal accomplishment are regularly visible.

Quantifiable results that improved: RN vacancy rate decreased from 6.2% to 4.1%. RN turnover rate decreased from 10.35% to 8.42%. RN staff autonomy score increased from 46.93 to 50.89 over the year after implementation. Manager satisfaction was unchanged.

A more impressive outcome that speaks to the versatility and the compelling nature of AI is the frequency with which the nurses spontaneously approach a problem and/or project with a simple question: What and/or where does it work well? That question has surfaced repeatedly during the planning and designing of a new hospital. Certainly, ineffective processes and systems are not to be moved to a new building. On the other hand, those systems that work well are being used as a model for the desired operations in the new facility. During recent preparation for one of the first unannounced Joint Commission on Accreditation of Healthcare Organizations (JCAHO) surveys, those units working well were used as models for process improvement of less prepared units.

Another pressing issue at UK today is patient satisfaction. The nursing managers of those units with the best scores are actively utilized in assisting other managers with their efforts. Although not always identified as AI, the philosophy is leading positive change in the organization. AI is now a major influence in recruitment activities, creative marketing copy, exit interviews, new employee interviews, performance improvement projects, and shared governance council operations. In 2005, UK nursing received Magnet redesignation with no recommendations for improvement. In fact, AI was central to most of the written materials. During the survey, the nurses repeatedly referred to their AI work and met the surveyors with, "I want to show you and tell you what we do." The pride was overwhelming, and the entire visit was a celebration of Nursing Excellence the UK Way.

From the beginning, nurses at UK Hospital talked about how to measure change. They developed the following list at the core team launch. In every core team meeting, they talked about "what's already changing" using these measures. The following measures remain topics of focus today:

Quantitative measures
– Nurse satisfaction
– Manager satisfaction
– Patient satisfaction
– Retention and recruitment tool
– Increase occupancy/capacity (beds) by virtue of staff available
– Affirmative problem solving (solve and resolve, not repeat)
– Inclusion (how many elect to be interviewed, attend workshops, and go to summit)

Qualitative measures
– Increase in positive thinking
– More appreciative mind-set
– Shared ownership
– Increase in self-confidence, self-image
– A "blame-free" culture

Other desired results
– "The UK Way" described in positive terms
– "Benefit of the whole"
– Greater nursing leverage
– Confirm and renew articulation of values for UKH
– Market ourselves in the community and improve image
– Capitalize on providing service to all, including indigents and under-served

A Final Note

The agendas, interview protocols, and methods provided in this chapter have been successfully modified and used with hundreds of organizations (large and small; for-profit and nonprofit) and governments to accomplish their respective organizational strategies and structures. The purpose of these samples is to provide different ways to launch an AI initiative for key organizational leaders and their stakeholders.

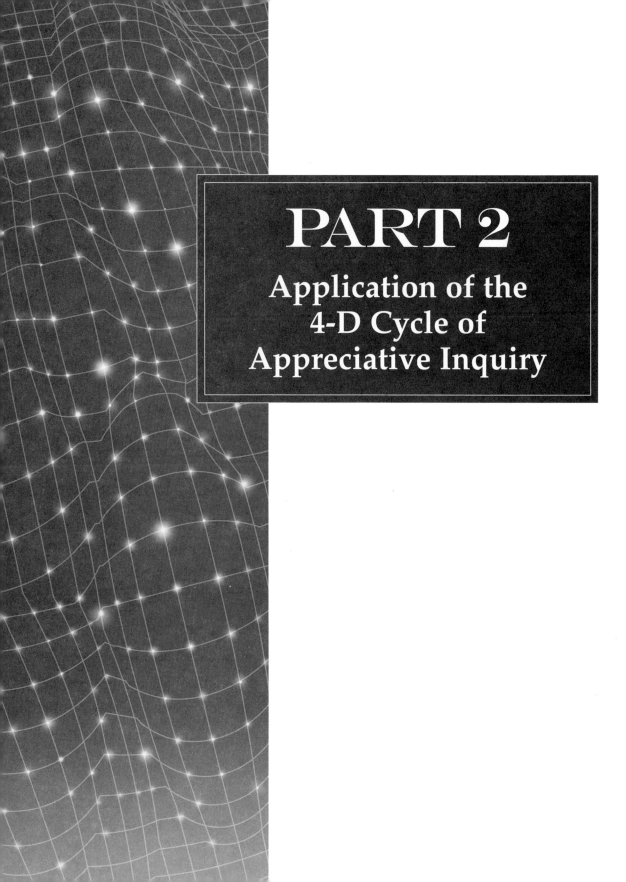

PART 2

Application of the 4-D Cycle of Appreciative Inquiry

AI is a process for positive change. It may be applied to whole organizations, teams, or departments. It may be used for strategic planning, merger integration, culture transformation, or leadership development. Whatever the purpose or change agenda for using AI, it is most often addressed through the AI 4-D Cycle of *Discovery*, *Dream*, *Design*, and *Destiny*, introduced here as Part 2.

The AI 4-D Cycle may be as formal as a year-long, whole-system process involving hundreds of employees and other stakeholders in interviews, dialogue, and decision making. Or it may be as informal as a conversation between a manager and an associate. While the hallmark of AI is organization-wide interviews using a set of unconditionally positive questions, AI is more than crafting questions, conducting interviews, and gathering data. It is a process for engaging all relevant and interested people in positive change.

Successful change requires new relationships to be formed along with large amounts of energy, enthusiasm, and creativity. To do this, AI engages people throughout the organization in discovering, sharing, and building on inspiring accounts of peak experiences, successes, and strengths—their positive core. When individuals, organizations, or communities tap into their positive core and link it to their change agenda, personal, professional, and/or organizational transformations never thought possible can emerge.

The AI 4-D Cycle is a dynamic iterative process of positive change. The 4-D Cycle, along with supporting information, is presented in the next four chapters.

- *Discovery:* What gives life? (Chapter 4)
- *Dream:* What might be? (Chapter 5)
- *Design:* How can it be? (Chapter 6)
- *Destiny:* What will be? (Chapter 7)

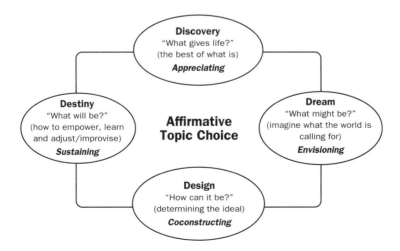

This brief overview of the 4-D Cycle provides the context for the next several chapters. During the first phase, Discovery, interviews are conducted to uncover success stories from the company's past and present. These stories include not only organizational successes but also individual successes. To capture these positive life-giving events, the interview questions will be designed intentionally to solicit positive affirming answers.

Chapter 4 provides examples of engaging AI interview questions that might surface during the *Discovery* stage. Once the interviews are completed, the stories are shared and discussed in an attempt to create a shared vision, or dream, of the future for the company. As an example of the latter, the Case Clipping at the end of Chapter 4 is an interview guide from an insurance company.

Chapter 5 illustrates the movement from discovery to the *Dream* stage through an application of AI at the Roadway Express Summit; this second edition also includes an update on Roadway's continued AI applications. The chapter ends with an introduction to Design, which takes the vision of what the organization can be and creates specific action-oriented provocative propositions, also called possibility statements or design statements.

Chapter 6 contains Tendercare, Inc.'s "+1 Census Development Campaign" case study to demonstrate how an organization and its key customers move together from discovery to dream to create a set of possibility statements in the *Design* phase. This chapter includes an update of the Tendercare story and two new powerful additions to the ways the design phase can unfold to allow for creativity and enhance speed of innovation in reaching the marketplace. A new application from Fairmount Minerals demonstrates how AI can be used to create new products and business processes based on the ideal of sustainable development. (In Section 3, Chapter 8 provides a new illustration on how Fairmount Minerals is using AI 15 years later.)

Chapter 7 concludes Part 2 with the *Destiny* phase in which organizational members can declare intended actions and ask for organization-wide support from every level. The chapter also uses the updated Case Clipping from Hunter Douglas Window Fashions (one of the longest sustained applications of AI) to describe how the company has changed and sustained its appreciative corporate culture. Hunter Douglas was awarded the honor of one of the "Top Ten Places to Work" in Denver, Colorado, in 2004 and in Colorado in 2006.

4

Discovery:
What Gives Life?

Perhaps, the most important thing we do as leaders and consultants is inquiry. We read situations; we do organizational analysis and diagnosis. It all starts with inquiry. The key point is that the way we know is fateful. The questions we ask, the things that we choose to focus on, and the topics we choose to ask questions about determine what we find. What we find becomes the data and the story out of which we dialogue about and envision the future. And so the seeds of change are implicit in the very first questions we ask. Inquiry is intervention.

—David Cooperrider

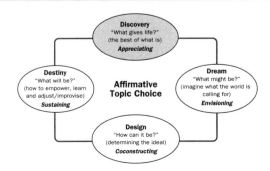

The task in the *Discovery* phase is to uncover, learn about, and appreciate the best of "what is." This is done by focusing on one's highpoint experiences and successes. In this phase, stakeholders share stories of exceptional accomplishments and explore the "life-giving" factors of the organization. Recognizing that the organization is not always at its best, AI seeks to discover rich accounts of when it is at its best and use those accounts as a foundation for the future.

During *Discovery*, interviews are conducted, stories are shared, and themes are identified that cut across the many stories and high-point experiences. The data collected during the interviews help the AI team identify, illuminate, and understand the distinctive strengths that lend the organization life and vitality when it is functioning at its best.

Data collection and narrative exploration represent the core of the inquiry process in this phase. They serve as the jumping-off point for dialogue and the application of learning to a unique theory of organizational innovation and change. In traditional research processes, data are collected as an objective reality. Such data are assumed to stand apart from the people involved and the process through which they are generated. In the AI process, collecting objective data is not the goal. It is not the goal because interviewers assume an active role in order to explore and enliven the interview process through their stories of the organization.

When data are collected, an important goal is to stimulate participants' excitement and delight as they share their values, experience, and history with the organization and their wishes for the future. In addition, thinking and dialoguing about positive possibilities are invited into the process. To lead the *Discovery* phase interview, the interviewer must actively listen and learn. Data collection and its associated narrative exploration are mutual learning processes. Both the interviewer and interviewee learn as they explore the participants' values, peak experiences, and aspirations for the organization's future. In this phase, participants are sharing and creating newly emergent strengths and possibilities.

This chapter begins by exploring the key steps in *Discovery* data collection. Considerations for data collection are presented. Instructions are provided to create the interview protocol and guidelines for effective AI questions. Tips for conducting AI interviews are included. This chapter ends with a Case Clipping of a completed interview guide from an insurance company. Chapter 8, in Part 3, provides several more sample interview guides and a sample AI Report.

Key Steps in Data Collection

Discovery: At this point, inquiry begins. Management genius rests on the ability to craft and ask the unconditional positive question—a powerful, penetrating question that mobilizes an organization-wide inquiry and draws out the best creativity and vision from all. As already stated, by transcending problem- and deficit-based approaches to change management, AI opens a new path to affirmative growth in human systems. This path begins with a person discovering who he or she is when at his or her very best.

Collecting appropriate, useful, strength-based, and future-focused data is the key to the *Discovery* phase. Data collected at this stage serve as the basis for the next stage of creating the organizational dream and possibilities in support of that dream. Table 4.1 summarizes the key steps.

Table 4.1 Key Steps in Data Collection

1. Identify stakeholders.

2. Craft an engaging appreciative question.

3. Develop the appreciative interview guide.

4. Collect and organize the data.
   - How will the findings be used?
   - How will the findings be recorded?
   - How will the team's data be compiled?
   - How will the data be reported?
   - Who will be responsible for collecting and organizing the data?

5. Decide how and when interviews will be conducted and who will conduct them.

6. Conduct interviews.

7. Make sense of inquiry data.

Step 1. Identify Stakeholders

Successful *Discovery* data collection requires identifying key stakeholders in the organization and deciding who will interview whom and when and where to conduct interviews. Stakeholders are typically people who have a vested interest in and/or a strong impact on the organization's growth and future and who can supply valuable insights into selected topic areas. These members become the core AI team or the steering group. Chapter 2, Table 2.3, Potential Representatives for Topic Team Selection, provides a list of possible stakeholders.

Once key stakeholders have been identified, this core team (sometimes referred to as the steering committee) creates the interview guide and develops the inquiry architecture. This team can be as small as four people or as large as twenty-five. Ideally, this team involves a microcosm of the whole organization and includes a variety of voices to encourage diversity. The goal is to seek out stakeholders who offer unique viewpoints and experiences from many levels and perspectives in the organization. This is why the list of potential participants is not limited just to employees; the list also can include customers, suppliers, and community representatives.

Inclusiveness also is the reasoning behind the statement that "more is better." Larger representation allows for a stronger base of dialogue. In an AI initiative with the Girl Scouts, the organization cocreated the statement "Don't do anything about me without me!" The authors' advice is to make sure to include those members (mentioned above) who may be impacted by the change initiative.

Step 2: Craft an Engaging Appreciative Question

As stated previously, the heart and spirit of the AI process starts with the crafting of engaging questions in the *Discovery* phase. The questions asked are fateful in that they ultimately determine the change of direction for the organization. The following guidelines generally produce engaging appreciative questions:

- State questions in the affirmative.
- Begin with a leading question that builds on the affirmative topic choice.
- Give a broad definition to the topic.
- Invite participants to use storytelling and narratives.
- Phrase in rapport talk, not report talk.
- Allow ambiguity because it gives room to "swim around."
- Value "what is."
- Spark the appreciative imagination by helping the person locate experiences that are worth valuing.
- Convey unconditional positive regard.
- Evoke essential values, aspirations, and inspirations.

AI is based on the premise that the *art of inquiry moves in the direction of evoking positive images that lead to positive actions*. Therefore, every question must begin with a positive preface. This plants the seed of what is to be studied. It deliberately tells the interviewee what will be learned. Each question has a Part A and a Part B.

Part A: The question must evoke a real personal experience and narrative story that helps participants see and draw on the best
learnings from the past.

Part B: This part of the question allows the interviewer to go beyond
the past to envision the best possibility of the future.

This premise (positive image—positive action) explains the need for engaging appreciative questions, as shown in the following question:

**U.S. Navy Illustration: Organizations Developing Bold and Enlight-
ened Leadership:** Think about the best organization you have seen,
heard, read about, or directly experienced outside your own organization. We are looking for exemplary, even radical, models or places
that attract great people because of the positive culture or enlightened
leadership at every level. Please share what you have heard or know
of this organization and its approaches to leadership or leadership
development. What is its story? What characteristics do you most
admire about this organization and its leaders? Why? What is it doing?
How is it doing it? What are the benefits? Where can we take this
model? Share what you think an organization would look like if bold
and enlightened leadership was at every level. What does the organizational culture and climate look like? What is happening?

Step 3: Develop the Appreciative Interview Guide

Once the stakeholders are identified, the core team must arrange, develop, and
distribute an interview guide. Creating the interview guide is an exciting task.
A complete **interview guide** incorporates a formal introduction to explain the
project and the purpose of the interview, the desired questions to be asked,
and a summary report sheet. This process includes three types of questions:

1. Opening questions:
    - Describe a "peak experience" or "high point."
    - What are the things valued most about:
      - Yourself?
      - The nature of your work?
      - Your organization?
2. Questions centering on three to five affirmative topic choices
    selected by the core team.

3. Concluding questions:
    • What are core factors that "give life" to organizing?
    • Operating at its "best from it strengths," where do you envision this organization five years from now? How can you and/or your team contribute to its success?
    • What are your three wishes to heighten the vitality and health of your organization?

1. Opening Questions

The first and second opening questions capture the tone, energy, and direction that set the stage for the entire inquiry. For example:

• Let's start with something about you and your work—and a larger sense of purpose. What is it that you do now and what most attracted you to your present work that you find most meaningful, valuable, challenging, or exciting?

• One could say a key task in life is for everyone to discover and define his or her life purpose. Think back over important times in your life. Can you think of a story to share about a moment or a milestone where clarity about your life purpose emerged for you? For example, perhaps you experienced an important event or the gift of a special mentor or teacher or perhaps you were given unexpected opportunities or faced difficult challenges.

2. Topic Questions

The second set of questions relate to the affirmative topic choices. They should be in the form of questions with lead-ins that assume the subject matter in the question already exists. A helpful resource for creating these questions is the *Encyclopedia of Positive Questions* (see the Bibliography).

• We have all been part of initiatives, large and small, where we joined with others to create positive change, that is, change that brought into being ideas and dreams of a better world. As you think about the years of your work, you will likely recall ups and downs, high points and low points. For the moment, we would like you to reflect on a high-point experience, a time that is memorable and stands out, a time when you felt most engaged, alive, challenged, or effective as part of a positive change initiative.

    – Please share the story of the experience. Where was it? What happened? What were your feelings and insights about change?

   – Now beyond this story, let's imagine I had a conversation with people who know you quite well. I asked them to share the three best qualities they see in you and the qualities or capabilities you bring to the leadership of change. What would they say?

   – As you continuously seek to develop into the best leader you can be, would you be willing to share with me how you generate your own inspiration to lead positive change initiatives? What are the personal, spiritual, and developmental practices you have found most useful?

This second set of topic questions is the heart of the inquiry and allows the participants to collect the data that are necessary to advance the human system or the organization being studied in order to achieve the desired objectives.[1]

For example, another possible topic choice is enhanced learning:

- People learn in different ways and experience the joy of learning in a variety of settings, both in and out of the classroom.

   – Describe a learning or mentoring experience that was particularly meaningful for you. When and where did it occur? Who was involved? Why was this experience so effective and memorable?

   – In your experience, what are one or two of your organization's most effective tools or techniques for enhancing student learning and success?

   – What two or three wishes do you have to further enhance learning?

Concluding Questions

The concluding question is most effective when it incorporates and follows the third and fourth foundational questions. For example:

- It is now 2015. We are able to preserve our core strengths, and we have innovatively transformed our ways of doing business to best serve our customers. We are an organization you want to be part of and others want to join. How would you describe this division's relationships with

---

1 These questions were selected from the "Business as an Agent of World Benefit (BAWB)" Interview Guide. This is a project cosponsored by The Weatherhead School of Management at Case Western Reserve University, Spirit in Business, The Society for Organizational Learning and Appreciative Inquiry Consulting, LLC.

its business partners? How does this business work to achieve strategic business objectives? What are people doing? How are you working differently in 2015? What was the key to your success and the organization's success? How did you get there?

- What was the smallest change the division made that had the most significant impact?

The following two options for a generic concluding question have often been used to good effect:

- Looking toward the future, what are we being called to become?
- What three wishes do you have for changing the organization?

Each Case Clipping in this chapter and in each of the following chapters offers complete interview guides. Additional sample interview guides are provided in Chapter 3 and Chapter 8.

At a minimum, an interview guide should contain the purpose of the inquiry (why we are coming together to complete this and what will be done with the data gathered) and instructions for preparing, conducting, and reporting the interview. Table 4.2 provides tips for creating an AI interview guide. Many complete AI interview guides are offered throughout the Handbook.

Table 4.2 Tips for Creating AI Interview Guides

AI Interview Guides should include:

- Project background and description.
- Interview instructions.
- List of questions to ask.
- Instructions to collect and record data.
- Information summary sheet.
- Demographic summary sheet if applicable.
- Interviewee/respondent consent form.
- Description of follow-up activities.
- Thank-you to the interviewee/respondent.

Step 4: Collect and Organize the Data

Designing appreciative questions requires some thought regarding how the data will be collected, organized, and used. Careful consideration is needed because the design entails the discovery of the life-giving forces. Table 4.3, Data Collection and Organizing Considerations, highlights information that must be taken into consideration in order to discover, re-create, and understand the positive core of the organization.

Table 4.3 Data Collection and Organizing Considerations

Methods of data collection	Interviews
	Participant observations
	Focus groups
Agents of data collection	Outside party
	Core team or steering committee
	Everyone—the interview chain
Information that is meaningful to collect	Best quotes and wishes
	Best stories and practices
	Exemplars
	Illustrations of the positive core
The AI Report	Rich narratives
	Exemplary stories
	Description of the positive core
	Multi-media presentations

Finally, there are some side benefits to the process of inquiry beyond the content. A typical question is, How many interviews should we conduct? The answer: Do as many interviews as possible. Why? For one thing, it is clear that inquiry and change are a simultaneous event and the changes begin at the moment of inquiry. It makes sense to involve all relevant and affected parties in any change effort. This fact has been reinforced and documented by many years of change research. Second, the methods make it easy to engage everyone.

The cascade interview approach works well. For example, 30 or so people are trained in AI and they each interview three others in their system. After their interviews, they ask the person interviewed how the interview went and whether he or she would be willing and interested in conducting three interviews. Many people instantly say yes, and the process is off and running. The first 30 people interview an additional 90 people. Those 90 then interview 270. The whole process builds momentum quickly. At the Red Cross Values Project (presented in Chapter 3), 5,000 people shared their hopes and dreams for the future within two months.[2]

Another major benefit is observed in what happens to the interviewers. As

2 Refer to Chapter 3, "Introducing, Defining, and Planning an Appreciative Inquiry Initiative," for the American Red Cross Values Project.

they sit down with people from different departments and with different functions and meet with stakeholders at every level, they often report how their own visions of possibility expand. It is often exciting for people to experience this view, and the resulting networks become major resources. These people begin to see the organization much as any CEO would—by taking in the big picture. In the early stages of AI work, the careers of people doing the interviews are often accelerated.

To illustrate, at Touche Ross, a financial services firm in Canada, John Carter conceived the *Discovery* phase as a leadership development process. Thirty or so of the high-potential junior partners conducted the interviews, first with each other as a training exercise and then with 400 senior partners of the firm. These junior partners then analyzed the themes and stories and kicked off the partnership's strategic planning process. The junior partners played a prime-time role. They learned the industry's trends and opportunities. They developed a consciousness of the whole, and they built relationships. At the same time, "the elders" were valued. The younger people showed the deepest kind of respect: listening to the best of history and recording insights, acquiring hard-won wisdom, and helping to transmit values. The elders not only felt valued but also felt like teachers. This created a positive atmosphere of trust and regard; and, of course, many of the junior partners became senior partners in due course.

Whereas many change initiatives are a threat, this kind of AI generates positive feelings. Consider Margaret Mead's observation about the intergenerational nature of societal learning. The best learning, she argued, was always intergenerational, with the young people alongside the elders and together with the middle generation adults.[3] Bringing people together in these kinds of natural ways, across the whole system, quite simply brings out the best in human behavior.

These examples illustrate a key point: there are tremendous developmental benefits for organizations in the *Discovery* phase alone. All of this is missed if one simply thinks of the data collection in scientific "sampling" terms. Again, inquiry and change are a simultaneous event and the system can benefit as much from the process as it can from the succeeding content.

---

3 To learn more about Margaret Mead and her work on intergenerational learning, visit the Mead Centennial 2001, The Institute for Intercultural Studies, at http://www.interculturalstudies.org/Mead/2001centennial.html.

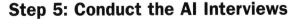

Step 5: Conduct the AI Interviews

The final section provides helpful tips for conducting the AI interviews. The following tips should be reviewed before the first interview begins.[4]

1. **Explaining Appreciative Inquiry:** Like anything new, appreciative interviewing may seem different at the beginning. It may be equally awkward for the interviewee. He or she may be caught up in looking at the organization as a problem to be solved and may not immediately understand this positive, strength-based inquiry approach. Saying something like the following may help:

   Before we start, I would like to explain a little bit about what we are going to do because it may be a little different from what you are used to. This is going to be an appreciative interview. I am going to ask you questions about times when you saw things working at their best in your workplace. Many times we try to ask questions about things that aren't working well, the problems, so we can fix them. In this case, we try to learn about things at their best, the successes, so we can find out what works and find ways to infuse more of the positive core into the organization's performances. It is much like what we do with children and athletes when we affirm their smallest successes and triumphs so they will hold a positive image of themselves and envision even greater possibility. The end result of the interview will help me understand the life-giving forces that provide vitality and distinctive competence to your organization. Do you have any questions?

2. **Respecting Anonymity:** Tell the interviewees the information will be kept anonymous. The data from this interview and others will be compiled into themes. No names will be associated with the overall summary or report. Stories and quotes from interviews will not have names associated with them.

3. **Managing The Negatives:** Sometimes people work with individuals and places they don't like. An explanation like the one above can generally get a person to identify things at their best. However, people should feel free to talk about things they believe require fixing. Depending on the interviewer's empathic understanding of the interviewee, this can be managed in several different ways:

---

4 See Johnson, P. (1992). *Organizing for global social change: Toward a global integrity ethic.* Unpublished manuscript, Case Western Reserve University, Cleveland, OH.

- *Postponing:* Tell the interviewees you would like to make note of what they have said and come back to it later. The question What would you change if you could change anything about the organization? is a place to collect this "negative" data. Make sure you come back to it at the appropriate time.

- *Listening:* If someone feels real intensity about what he or she wants to say about issues, let the person say it. If it is "up close and personal," you are not going to get any appreciative data until the person speaks his or her mind. This may mean muddling through quite a bit of organizational "manure," and the biggest threat is that you will absorb it and lose your capacity to be appreciative. You must be empathic, but remember that you cannot take on that person's pain. You cannot be a healer if you take on the patient's illness. Maintain a caring and affirmative spirit.

- *Redirecting:* If you have listened sufficiently to the seemingly negative issues, find a way to redirect the interviewee back to the task at hand. "I think I understand some of the problems . . ." and paraphrase a few you've heard. "Right now, however, I would like to focus on times when things were working at their best. Can you think of a time, even the smallest moment, when you saw innovation (for example) at its best?" If the interviewer says it never happened where he or she works, before giving up, find out whether the person ever had the experience in any organization or work context.

4. **Using Negative Data:** Everything people find wrong with an organization represents an absence of something they hold in their minds as an ideal image. What organizational processes, if present (rather than absent), might create the ideal organization, which the negatives imply? Data are data. Use the information, but use it affirmatively. One could argue that there is no such thing as negative data, for every utterance is conditioned by affirmative images.

5. **Starting With Specific Stories—The Interview Rhythm:** There is a rhythm to these interviews. When you begin to address your topic, start with specifics relevant to the person interviewed. Try to get him or her to tell a story. A useful beginning might be this: Tell me a story about a time when you experienced *cooperation* (the topic) at its best. Probe deeply and intently—not like a dentist or like a pira-

nha going after the bait, but like an interested friend hanging on to every detail. *Be genuine.* Listen and learn from this experience. Try to find out "who did what when" and "what were you thinking" and "what you did then." Be an active listener. Your goal is to learn not only what the person did (behavior) but also what the person thought or felt (values) while he or she was doing it.

6. **Generalizing About "Life-giving" Forces:** After you have thoroughly heard the interviewee's story, go for the generalizations: What is it about this organization—its structure, systems, processes, policies, staff, leaders, and strategy—that creates conditions where cooperation (for example) can flourish? If your topic (e.g., *cooperation*) was a plant, you would be trying to find out what kind of soil, water, and sunlight conditions nourish it. Sometimes people will not understand what you mean by organizational conditions, factors, or forces. Give examples: Are jobs designed a certain way, for example, to foster cooperation? How does the culture or climate of the organization foster cooperation? Try to get the person to think a bit abstractly about what is present in the organization when peak experiences have occurred relative to the topic (i.e., cooperation).

7. **Listening For Themes—"Life-giving" Factors:** To get a sense of some of these factors, listen for information about what the structure was like, as well as the systems, rewards, and so on. It may not be necessary to ask systematically about the factors; the stories may contain information about them. If the stories do not, gently probe. Listen for a theme, an idea, or a concept presented or defined in the stories being told during the interview. Present these themes in the dialogue session during the *Dream* phase to see if the group thinks these are important.

8. **Keeping Track of the Time:** An interview typically has a fixed schedule, so keep track of the time. If more time is needed, ask the person if he or she has more time. It is best to pace questions appropriately to the time scheduled.

9. **Having Fun And Being Yourself: It's A Conversation:** Try not to approach the interview as a piece of drudgery; otherwise, the interview may be lost before it has begun. Welcome each interviewee as if he or she is a special person. Take time to listen and value the

best of whom he or she is. Be humble; the interviewee is the teacher. Be yourself. Do not put on an expert role or pretend that every word in the interview protocol must be exactly right. Be a learner. Realize that everyone likes to share his or her knowledge and wisdom with people who genuinely want to listen and learn. If you have an affirmative spirit going into the interview, mistakes in wording will not impede the collection of data. Finally, have fun. This is an opportunity to get to know someone new and hear some fascinating and important stories.

Following these guidelines will help ensure that the appreciative interview has the key characteristics shown in Table 4.4, Key Characteristics of the Appreciative Interview.

Table 4.4 Key Characteristics of the Appreciative Interview

- Assumption of Health and Vitality
- Connection through Empathy
- Personal Excitement, Commitment, and Caring
- Intense Focus through "Third Ear" and "Third Eye"
- Generative Questioning, Cueing, and Guiding
- From Monologue to Dialogue

Creating the interview guide, collecting the data, and locating the themes that appear in the interview stories represent the key activities of the Discovery phase. It is where the dialogue begins in the AI process.

Step 6: Sense-Making from Inquiry Data

After the interviews are completed, it is time to make sense of the data. **Sense-making** is an umbrella term used to explain how people make sense of conversations and events based on their experiences in the world. Sense-making is making sense of the themes and patterns discovered in the interviews, lifting up meaningful metaphors and stories that give momentum to organizational success. As it relates to AI, one asks, What is the best way to capture and transform the stories from the interviews in order to be able to understand the positive core of the organization? What does one want to learn more about?

In sense-making, a diversity of approaches has been used—from formal narrative analysis to narrative forms of best stories and moral tales.[5] Data can

---

5 See A. Coffery, A., & Atkinson, P. (1996). *Making sense of qualitative data.* Newbury Park, CA: Sage Publications.

be reduced and displayed in diagrams, charts, tables, pictures, storybooks, newsletters, and other visual aids. The search for one perfect method to make sense of data is not the point. There is no single right way to analyze the data. What is important is to find creative ways to organize, listen, and understand what is being said from multiple perspectives, both during and after the interviews. Look for common threads and anomalies in the data. Specifically, what are the best stories, practices, and wishes that came out of the interviews? The goal is to identify themes to discover how to do more of what worked well in a situation. Focus on the meaning of the data. The meaning of these data forms the foundation of dialogues that inspires the dreams based on the best stories told (continuity) and the best of what will come (novelty). The *Design* and *Destiny* phases transform (transition) the data into the desired future.

AI is a method, a type of action research, that attempts to discover "the best of what is" in any organizational/human system. In completing the interviews, the objective should be to understand *when* and *why* organizations are operating at their best and *what* are the core capabilities to allow the organization to perform well. The process seeks to identify the positive core that contributed to such operation (continuity) and that can transform itself to the new vision (novelty).

In managing the information and structuring it in a meaningful analysis, the data collection step outlined earlier coincides with data interpretation and narrative reporting and writing. Code the data under key themes. It also may require recoding under new, emerging themes based on the conversations around the original themes.

A primary goal is to reduce and interpret the meanings and, through dialogue, confirm that these are the interviewees' meanings. That is why Interview Summary Sheets are helpful. An example of a generic AI Interview Summary Sheet is shown here.

Interview Summary Sheet

Please use whatever space you need to answer each question.

1. What was the most appreciative quotable quote that came out of this interview?

2. What was the most compelling story that came out of this interview? What details and examples did the interviewee share? How were the interviewee and/or others changed by the story?

3. What was the most life-giving moment of the interview for you as a listener?

4. Did a particularly intriguing "golden innovation" emerge during the interview? If so, describe what you learned about it, including who is doing it and where.

5. What three themes stood out most for you during the interview?

6. What small steps toward positive change emerged as being possible?

7. What broader steps of positive change emerged?

The *Discovery* phase is both exploratory and descriptive. It allows for an open-ended discovery of an organizational system at its best. The objective is to generate themes, descriptors, a dream, the vision, and key ingredients for dialogue and design of possibility propositions. The topics of dreaming and design will be covered in more detail in Chapter 5 and Chapter 6.

Case Clippings: Texas Insurance

The Texas Insurance Company employed an AI approach to facilitate the transformation of its information technology (IT) organization, approximately 2,000 employees, from a traditional internal IT function to a business/client-facing operating model. The goal of the transformation was threefold: (1) to create a culture of service, (2) to demonstrate the strategic value of IT, and (3) to ensure high levels of productivity and effectiveness during the transformation to the new operating model. Central to this transformation was the strategic inquiry (Discovery) into the life-giving factors of the organization and three positive transformation themes. Of primary importance were the affirmative topic choices to guide the successful design of the new operating model: Revolutionary Partnerships, Continuous Transformation, and Innovative and Adaptive Environment.

The following interview packet illustrates affirmative topic choices and meets the criteria for an engaging AI question. It includes the following:

- *Purpose of the interviews*
- *Overview of the interview process*
- *Tips for conducting interviews*
- *Interview guide*
- *Interview summary sheet*

The Discovery phase was carried out over a three-week period and included approximately 130 interviews across a broad cross section of the IT organization and key clients. The Discovery outputs were used extensively as input into the design of the three-day Dream and Design Summit that followed. In alignment with the intent of the Discovery process, the goal of the interview guide was to obtain information on the three factors that give life to organizations—continuity, novelty, and transition. (Refer to Mini-lecture VIII in Chapter 1.) The following outcomes resulted from the Discovery phase:

- *Quotable Quotes wall*
- *Texas Insurance's Positive Core (continuity)*
- *Individual visions of a best-performing IT organization (novelty)*
- *Positive Deviant Profile (novelty/transition)*
- *Positive Transformation Themes (transition)*

Purpose of the Interviews

Thank you very much for participating in this information-gathering process. The Application Services group is actively involved in a business transformation that will focus on the design and development of a business/client-facing operating model that will accelerate time and results. In this way, Application Services will better serve our internal business partners and strengthen Texas Insurance's overall competitive position. To this end, we will be gathering specialized input from colleagues across the organization. These interviews are part of an intense effort to discover our internal best practices and high points, to use this rich experience as leverage for the Application Services Transformation, and to apply this learning to the development and implementation of our future-state operating model. In addition, the results of the individual and group IT fact-finding discussions, along with information and research on external best practices, will be integrated into our design process.

As part of this process, we will look at:
- What core factors enable success in our organization.
- What we can learn from our experiences, especially when we closely examine those moments when we have been at our best.
- What our most effective practices, strengths, and best qualities are—what we need to preserve as we transform.
- What important lessons we can draw from our experiences.
- What kind of organization we want to create in the future—the organization that we and others want to be part of.
- How our positive past, the best of our experiences, can help us become more daring and innovative as we think about our true potential as an organization.
- In the context of Texas Insurance, what our specific hopes and images are for the future of Applications Services.

Application of Interview Feedback
- All interviews will be reviewed and summarized for thematic content.
- Themes will be shared and discussed based on relevance to the Application Services Transformation.
- At a three-day off-site design session, Accelerated Solutions Environment (Design Shop), in August, which multiple Texas Insurance participants will attend, these themes will be used as key input in designing the Application Services future-state operating model.

- An additional output from the Design Shop is an implementation road map, which will outline key activities and workstreams to support our new operating model. Interview themes will be applied directly to some of the resulting workstreams and indirectly to many of the other workstreams.
- All comments from the interviews will be anonymous. Names will not be attached to any of the stories, suggestions, or examples.

Overview of the Interview Process

Part I—Completing Four to Six Interviews
- You will be provided a list of the names of four to six colleagues to interview. You typically will be assigned individuals with whom you may not interact on a regular basis. This is a good opportunity to get a fresh perspective.
- The Transition Team will notify your interviewees that they have been selected as participants. Contact your interviewee to schedule the interview. Explain that each interview will take approximately one hour to complete.
- Complete your interviews and post your summary forms to the Phase I-Interviews folder in the Transition Team Folder as soon as they're completed, but no later than July 18.
- Assure your interviewees that all comments are anonymous but not confidential. In other words, stories and quotes will be shared but no names will be attached to them.
- If you're having difficulty scheduling an interview, call so we can help you by supporting scheduling of the interview or by providing an alternative interview participant.

Part II—Returning the Interview Summaries
- Please use the space after each question for taking notes during the interviews. (Note taking is usually very individualized, but we want you to be able to recall your interview to best assure your summarization.)
- It is recommended that you summarize the interview immediately after the interview session. Use the attached two-page summary template at the end of this guidebook.
- Remember to note your name, the date of the interview, and the interviewee's organizational group and service date on the summary page.

- Post the electronic summary forms to the Phase I-Interviews folder in the Transition Team Folder no later than July 18.

Try not to wait until July 18 to send all of the interview summary forms. Please post them as you complete them.

Part III—Leveraging the Interviewing Feedback: Next Steps
- All interview summaries will be reviewed and integrated. In this way, we will document major themes to better understand our internal best practices, high-point moments, and images of the future.
- These internal best practices and positive transformation themes will be shared and leveraged during the August off-site Design Shop to support the development and implementation of our Application Services operating model. In addition, the results of the individual and group IT fact-finding discussions, along with information and research on external best practices, will be integrated into our design process.
- Following the Design Shop, the new operating model, the benefits of the new model, the positive transformation themes, and the general timeline for implementation will be shared.
- We will make a special effort to share positive transformation themes with all interview participants in late July.

Tips for Conducting Interviews

Use the interview question section for script guidelines and note taking.
- Use these questions to probe further:
  - Can you tell me more?
  - Why was that important to you?
  - How did that affect you?
  - What was your contribution?
  - How did the organization/business area/team support you? (e.g., information systems, leadership, resources, and structures)
  - How has it changed you?
- Let the interviewee tell his or her story.
- Take notes and listen for great quotes and stories.
- Be genuinely curious about their experiences, thoughts, and feelings.
- Some people will take longer to think about their answers. Allow time for silence.
- If somebody doesn't want to or can't answer any of the interview questions, that's okay. Let it go.

- Use the questions as guidelines. You may choose not to use of all the questions or to adapt the questions to what works best for your interviews.
- Allow the interviewee to interpret whether the questions apply to work or to personal situations.

Interview Guide

Suggested Opening

I'm (name). Thank you for meeting with me and participating in this process of gathering information from colleagues across the organization. These interviews are part of an intense effort to discover our internal best practices in key strategic business areas. These best practices will be leveraged by our Application Services Transformation project to develop our future-state operating model. In addition to these interview findings, we will be leveraging information related to external best practices and the individual and group IT fact-finding discussions.

This interview is divided into three sections:
- Celebrating Texas Insurance's Rich Heritage and Past Successes
- Carrying Forward What We Value Most
- Wake Up. It's 2010: Your Vision of a Best-Performing Application Services

Before we start, I would like to explain what we are going to do because it may be a little different from what you are used to. I am going to ask questions about times when you were at your best in your work. You may be more familiar with interviews that ask questions about things that aren't working well—the problems—so we can fix them. In this case, we are going to find out about your work and the organization at its best—the successes—so we can find out what works and find ways to integrate what we learn into the Application Services Transformation moving forward. This positive-change approach has been widely researched and proven effective in a variety of situations; for example, transformation efforts, education, building learning organizations, parenting, athletics, increasing team and organizational effectiveness, and healthcare. The end result of the interview will help us understand those positive factors that will increase our vitality, effectiveness, and success going into the future together. Specifically, we are gathering information on what we are calling Positive Transformation Themes. To surface these themes, the interview questions focus on areas that we believe are critically important to the successful design of our new Application Services operating model:

- Continuous Transformation
- Revolutionary Partnerships
- Innovative and Adaptive Environment

What questions do you have?

OK. Let's begin.

I. **Celebrating Texas Insurance's Rich Heritage and Past Successes**
   To start, I'd like to learn about your beginnings at Texas Insurance. When did you come to the organization, and what attracted you to Texas Insurance? What keeps you at Texas Insurance? What sets us apart and makes the difference for you?

   In your work at Texas Insurance, you have probably experienced ups and downs, twists and turns. For a moment, I would like you to think of a time that stands out to you as a high point at Texas Insurance—a time when you felt energized, passionate about your work, and most effective and a time when you were able to accomplish more than you imagined.

   Please describe in detail the situation and the people involved and what made it a high-point experience for you. What actions did you and others take? How did those actions translate into business results?

   Let's talk about some things you value most—specifically, about yourself and Texas Insurance as an organization.
   - Without being humble, what do you value most about yourself as a human being? What are the most important qualities or strengths you bring to Texas Insurance?
   - What is it about the nature of the work that you do here that you value most? What is most interesting or meaningful?

   Continuous Transformation:
   Organizations today must continually change and evolve to remain ahead of the competition and to thrive in this rapidly changing

economy and business environment. Organizations that have passion and energy for continual transformation display business excellence and are distinguished from their peers—leading the way and creating their future instead of reacting to it.

Tell me about a time when you were involved with a significant transformation or change effort, a time when you positively influenced the results. What was exciting about the transformation? What did you and others do to make it effective?

Revolutionary Partnerships:
The mark of a revolutionary partnership is doing things together radically different—not only different, but quicker, with a common focus, leveraging each other's diverse strengths. It is also establishing new ways of doing business that are based on trust, mutual respect, and a shared vision.

Think of a time when you were part of a revolutionary partnership, a time in your life (at work or in your personal or community life) when you not only met another person or other people halfway but also met and exceeded needs on both sides. Describe the situation in detail. What made it feel radically different? Who was involved? How did you interact differently? What were the outcomes and benefits you experienced?

Innovative and Adaptive Environment:

"Nature has been learning to adapt for four billion years; maybe we need to pay attention." – Stuart Kauffman, molecular biologist

As this is true in nature, it is also true in the business world. An effective environment enables risk taking, empowers leadership throughout the organization, is agile, and thrives on change. These powerful environments can balance speed and discipline, are liberating yet standards-based, and support growth and innovation.

Think of a time when you were in an innovative and adaptive environment. Describe how the environment supported your success—that is, leadership, creativity, tools, recognition, and/or resources. How did it feel? What were the keys to success? What were some of the significant breakthroughs you achieved? Again, this could be personal, community-oriented, or work life-based.

II. Carrying Forward What We Value Most

Good organizations know how to "preserve the core" of what they do best and are able to let go of things that are no longer needed. In transforming Application Services, what are three things—core strengths, values, qualities, ways of working—you want to see preserved and leveraged moving into the future?

III. Wake Up. It's 2010: Your Vision of a Best-Performing Application Services

Fast-forward. It is now 2010, and we were able to preserve our core strengths and transform Application Services. Revolutionary partnerships, continual transformation, innovation, and adaptability are how we do business. It is an organization you want to be part of and others want to join.

- How would you describe Application Services' relationships with business customers? How do they work together differently in 2010 to achieve Texas Insurance's business objectives?

- What are people doing? How are you working together differently in 2010? What was the key to your success and the organization's success? How did you get there?

- What was the smallest change Applications Services made that had the most significant impact?

This is the end of the interview. Thank you very much for your time. Your input will be summarized and used to design the Application Services Operating Model.

Interview Summary Sheet

Complete and post by Wednesday, July 18, to the Application Services Transition Team shared drive in the Phase I-Interviews folder. Save the document using the filename Interviewerlastname-interview#.doc (e.g., Smith-interview3.doc).

Name of Interviewer (your name): _____

Date of Interview: _____

Interviewee's Organizational Division: _____

Interviewee's Service Date (year is optional):_____

What was the most quotable quote that came out of this interview?

What was the most compelling story that came out of this interview? (Use as much space as you need.)

Overall, what was your sense of what was most important to this individual?

What three positive themes related to each of the following stood out most to you during the interview?

Revolutionary Partnerships	Continuous Transformation	Innovative and Adaptive Environment
1. _____	1. _____	1. _____
2. _____	2. _____	2. _____
3. _____	3. _____	3. _____

Carrying Forward What We Value Most

- _____
- _____
- _____

Vision of the Future

1. _____

2. _____

3. _____

5

Dream:
What Might Be?

"One of the basic theorems of the theory of image is that it is the image which in fact determines what might be called the current behavior of any organization. The image acts as a field. The behavior consists of gravitating toward the most highly valued part of the field."

—Kenneth Boulding

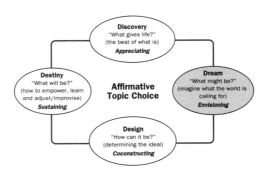

Once an organization discovers its positive core, the next step is to imagine and envision its future. The *Dream* phase of the AI 4-D Cycle accomplishes this step.

The *Dream* phase is an invitation for an organization to amplify its positive core by imagining the possibilities for the future that have been generated through the Discovery phase. During the *Dream* phase, the participants are encouraged to talk about (and dream about) not what is, but what might be a better organization and a better world. The *Dream* phase is practical in that it is grounded in the organization's history and generative in that it seeks to expand the organization's true potential. It is the time to challenge the status quo of the organization. It is intended to create synergy and excitement. Once the group gets into the spirit and acknowledges the possibility of greatness, the positive core can be channeled, focused, and used to design how it will be and create the destiny of the envisioned dream.

The primary goal of the *Dream* phase is twofold. First, it is to facilitate a dialogue among stakeholders in which they begin to share positive stories in a way that creates energy and enthusiasm. This is accomplished by asking those who participated in the Discovery phase to share their stories with the entire group. These stories are the vehicles for bringing out the positive core of the organization. Therefore, those who are telling the stories must be encouraged to share the essence of the stories, not a bullet point description of events. Giving the storyteller the latitude to share the story in full and rich detail generates more data for theme building. Therefore, the job of the facilitator is to gently probe for details in order to continue identifying themes. One tool used to encourage these conversations is dream dialogues. The dream dialogue is often integrated into appreciative interviews with questions about wishes, hopes, and dreams for a better organization and world. Some interview guides probe for best practices and peak experiences from outside the organization in question. Thus, interviewers might learn through discovery of positive possibilities that have existed elsewhere and that might be transported into their system.

The second goal of the *Dream* phase is to allow participants to begin to see common themes. At this point, it is important to encourage the group to observe and value the stories rather than critique, judge, or analyze them. Unlike other organizational change methodologies, AI does not focus on solving a problem. Dreaming is a journey of mutual discovery, not an analytical journey. Therefore, dreaming does not emphasize identifying one best idea. Instead, participants look for broad themes or **life-giving forces** that contribute to the organization's success. Those positive themes are the building blocks for the rest of the AI process. They are the short answers to the question What do people describe in the interviews as the "life-giving" forces of this organization?[1]

---

1 See Watkins, J., & Mohr, B. (2001). *Appreciative inquiry: Change at the speed of imagination.* San Francisco: Jossey-Bass/Pfeiffer.

Accomplishing those two goals helps participants imagine the organization as they would like it to be. By building energy, excitement, and synergy and by extracting the common themes or life-giving forces, participants can begin to envision an organization of the future; an organization that embodies the images, hopes, dreams, and visions of its people.

The remainder of this chapter deals with creating the *Dream* activity, introduces the concept of dialogue that creates vision consensus, and provides an example of the Roadway Express AI Summit. A complete project plan for the Roadway Express AI Application is available at the end of this chapter.

Creating the Dream Activity

Organizations tend to move in the direction of what they study. The crafting and asking of questions and activities during the *Discovery* and *Dream* phases possesses strategic significance to eliciting the information needed to identify the themes that will become the starting point for the next phase of the 4-D Cycle.

Many of the best Dream activities share common components:[2]

- They take place on the heels of some sort of brief Discovery process, one that brings the spirit of the original inquiry into the room in personal and creative ways.

- They often involve large groups of people—anywhere from a couple dozen to hundreds at a time.

- They begin with some kind of energizing activity (e.g., guided visualization, a walk, a high-energy activity, or yoga).

- They use a focal question that "primes the pump" for rich, creative dream dialogues. (Facilitators select the question, along with an appropriate time frame for individual and group discussions.)

- As participants complete their individual dreaming reflections, they move into groups (ideally, no more than 12 people per group) to talk about what they've seen, heard, and experienced in this world of the future during the Discovery interviews. This dream dialogue takes up to an hour. The dialogue is finished when people have had a chance to

2 See Whitney, D., & Trosten-Bloom, A. (2003). *The power of appreciative inquiry: A practical guide to positive change.* San Francisco: Berrett-Koehler.

share fully what they have seen and imagined and to create a collective verbal picture of the desired future.

- The group creatively depicts what they have seen. The more playful the depictions, the better. The facilitator (whose role was introduced in the organizational overview) can offer a variety of ways in which to depict the dream. Some examples include a picture, a story, a skit, a commercial, a newspaper, a song, or a poem. The facilitator should be ready with a variety of supplies and props to aid in this creative process.

- Each dream team prepares a brief Appreciative Report from its dream session (often less than five minutes each). Although each team has a spokesperson, everyone on the team is included in the presentation. All presentations are made to the entire group.

- Small-group discussions of common themes and common threads often follow these presentations.

The *Dream* phase is the time to push the creative edges of positive possibilities and to **wonder** about the organization's greatest potential. To illustrate, an AI initiative was launched with Roadway Express at the Akron, Ohio, terminal. Roadway is one of the largest trucking companies in America, with about 30,000 employees. The company is unionized, and the relationship between Roadway and the Teamsters is strong. Roadway's goal is to create an organization with leaders developing leaders at every level, a "high-engagement organization." The inquiry started with this opening question:

When did you feel most alive, most engaged, in your job at Roadway?

The *Dream* phase began on Day 2 when participants were divided into small groups (teams) to envision the organization's potential for positive impact. The next foundational question was asked:

Imagine you've awakened after being asleep for five years. What does Roadway look like? What will be happening in the world outside? What is the best outcome you can imagine?

The *Discovery* was about the positive core and valuing the best in Roadway's history. The *Dream* phase, about the future and the possibilities, includes two activities. The first activity is a collective conversation on "images of the future." The second activity is the creation of possibilities. Roadway did this in the form of an "opportunity map." In moving from *Discovery* to *Dream*, employees at the Akron terminal focused on the following purpose:

"To begin to build a future you want, an Akron Roadway team that is truly dedicated to "maximizing throughput with unsurpassed speed, driven by employee pride and involvement."

Roadway's dream dialogue focused on the following three statements:

- Share your wishes and dreams from the interviews you did yesterday morning (Question 3). Add any ideas or thoughts about changes or improvements you think will have a major impact on improving our throughput.

- Brainstorm a list of opportunities to improve throughput at the Akron complex.

- As a group, choose the three to five opportunities your team believes will have the greatest impact on throughput.

From this opportunity map, each team created aspirations and visions of the future. For example:

Roadway Aspiration Statement
Measurement, Technology, Procedures, and Equipment Team

"Roadway is #1 because employees take pride and are engaged in ensuring that customers are receiving unsurpassed service and error-free delivery that is unequaled by any other carrier.

Employees know and understand cost impacts of all decisions and information is shared through technology so all employees are empowered to make customer-focused and profitable decisions."

The *Dream* activity gave team members the opportunity to summarize key success factors collectively and preserve the past. Together they mapped the highest impact opportunities. More details on the *Dream* activity are available at the end of this chapter.

Dreaming is a strategically significant activity that leads to higher levels of creativity, commitment, and enthusiasm for the organization and its future. It is this new level of enthusiasm and images embedded in the dreams that facilitate the creation of specific actions and propositions for the future (*Design* phase).

Evolution of Dialogue to Create Vision Consensus

A vision is a direction for an organization. It is what the organization wants to be. It expresses a desire by the organization to be more than what it is. It is strategic in providing a focal point for direction and movement. It is fateful in defining what an organization holds dear and creating excitement for ways to move forward and achieve it.

Sometimes a vision is a statement created by senior management that is passed down to employees. If so, it is at best a sneak preview of what the leaders of the company believe is important, providing some indication as to why decisions are made. At its worst, it is ink on paper without significance or meaning for or without connection to stakeholders. The power of AI lies in its ability to collectively breathe life into a vision; to make it speak to all stakeholders; and to provide some value, consequence, and direction in stakeholders' daily lives.

Through the *Discovery* and *Dream* phases, participants have been asked to share times and events during which they operated at their peak, felt most alive, and were inspired to push beyond the mundane. Now, while riding on the enthusiasm and energy created by sharing these high points, the group should be asked to imagine an organization in which these sporadic glimpses at brilliance are the norm. What would this organization look like?

Once the group begins to create a shared vision of the new and improved organization, the power of AI becomes apparent. Unlike other visioning exercises, AI creates a shared vision for the future that is grounded in examples from the organization's past. It is the greatness demonstrated in the past that allows stakeholders to achieve their vision for the future. In short, there is no question as to whether the new vision is achievable; the participants have already demonstrated their desire, willingness, and ability to make it possible. This most preferred future, along with the accompanying energy and synergy, is what will carry the group to the *Design* phase. The *Design* phase is where the key stakeholders regroup and work to transfer the dreams into a concrete plan of action.

Sample Dream Questions

The following Dream questions may prove helpful in shaping the dialogue to achieve the vision for the future of the organization.

- It is the year 2015, and you have just awakened from a long sleep. As you look around, you see the world just as you always wished and dreamed it would be.

- What is happening? How is the world different? How is your organization contributing to this new world? What are you doing that makes a difference?

- As you reflect on the industry and business environment in which your organization works, what do you see as the two or three most significant macro trends emerging? How might they change the way your industry and business operate? In your opinion, what are the most exciting strategic opportunities on the horizon for your organization?

- Imagine that it is 2015 and your organization has just won an award as the outstanding socially responsible business of the year. What is said about your organization as the award is dedicated? What are customers saying? What are employees saying? What did it take to win the award?

AI Summit: Using Large Groups to Mobilize Positive Change

The **AI Summit** is a large-scale meeting process that focuses on discovering and developing the organization's positive change core and designing it into the organization's strategic business processes, systems, and culture.[3]

Participation is diverse by design and includes all of the organization's stakeholders. The duration is generally three to four days and involves 50 to 2,000 participants or more. AI serves as the framework for an AI Summit. The AI Summit can be used to conduct the *Dream* and *Design* phase if data are available from the *Discovery* phase. Many variations are possible; therefore, planning, creativity, and flexibility are required.[4]

---

3 We want to acknowledge the important role Marvin Weisbord and Sandra Janoff played. Their pioneering work with Future Search impressed us most with the principle of the whole system in the room as well as the clarity of worksheets and some of the exercises in a typical Future Search. For more on Future Search, refer to *Future Search: An Action Guide to Finding Common Ground in Organizations and Communities*, 2d ed. (San Francisco: Berrett-Koehler, 2000).

4 Material contributed and adapted from *The Appreciative Inquiry Summit: A Practitioner's Guide for Leading Positive Large-Group Change*. The book details the strategies for whole system participation and activities before, during, and after an effective summit. (Available from Berrett-Koehler, Spring 2003, by Ludema, Mohr, Whitney, and Griffin.)

The AI Summit is designed to flow through the AI 4-D Cycle of Discovery, Dream, Design, and Destiny in real time. Figure 5.1 illustrates the Akron Roadway Summit AI 4-D Cycle.

Figure 5.1 Akron Roadway Summit's 4-D Cycle

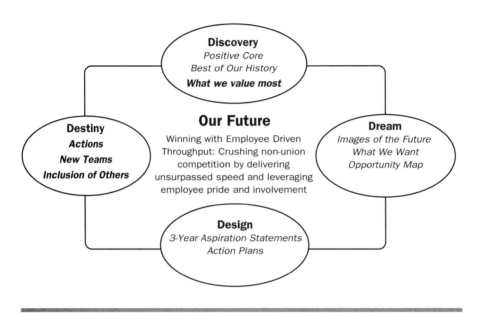

Day 1—*Discovery*: Participants discuss the organization's positive core, which was discovered in earlier interviews. Participants look at characteristics of which they are most proud and discuss those characteristics that create success and build a competitive future for Roadway. They are asked the questions Who are we? Whom do we represent? As a group, they dialogue about why they are here and what they hope for.

Key activities include defining the context and purpose of the summit, conducting more AI interviews, highlighting stories from prior AI interviews, mapping out the positive core, and launching a continuity search. A **continuity search** is seeking out and preserving what the organization does best. For example, Roadway wanted to build optimal margins; therefore, it first wanted to learn what things Roadway did best organizationally.

Day 2—*Dream*: This phase builds on the outcomes of the *Discovery* phase. Participants break into small groups and envision their organization's potential for positive influence and impact. The discussion is centered around developing ideas of what the future can be. What will the company look like in 2015? What is happening? What is better? What positive things are the stakeholders saying? After the small breakout discussions, the groups report back to the entire summit to share their stories.

Key activities include sharing of dreams; enlivening the dreams; and enacting, imaging, and defining the dreams.

Day 3—*Design*: Participants focus on cocreating an organization (that includes the positive core and dreams in every element possible). The design results for Roadway were called "Aspiration Statements," describing the organization participants hoped Roadway would become, and "Action Plans," describing how the organization would function.

Key activities include creating the organization's architecture, selecting high-impact organization design elements, and crafting possibility propositions (possibility or aspiration statements without conditions).

Day 4—*Destiny*: This is where the energy is channeled into action planning to understand what needs to happen to deliver on the possibility statements defined in the Design phase. Participants craft the newly created organizational design into a list of inspired action-oriented tasks. Task groups emerge around each Aspiration Statement. Then each group establishes principles for working together after the AI Summit and agrees on immediate steps they will take next.

Key activities include generating possible action steps, selecting possible action tasks, forming task teams, and closing the large-group summit.

Little, if any, AI training occurs during a summit; the summit is about enacting AI. After a summit, organizations may decide to develop their capacity in AI by conducting a training program for key employees in leading organizational change. In this situation, AI is taught as a process for management, leadership, and organizational development and change. The result is sustainability of AI beyond the initial initiative into the everyday actions of members.

From start to finish, the AI Summit process invites the whole organization to participate. A successful summit takes time, careful planning, and attention. The task must be clear. The summit is usually a three- or four-day event that can include from 50 to 2,000 participants, as stated. The typical results from a summit are:

- More informed and ultimately more effective change efforts.
- A critical mass of people making changes in which they all believe.
- A total organization mind-set.
- Simultaneous change.
- A perception of change as "real work."
- A fast-change organizational network.

The following example from Roadway illustrates an AI Summit, the results, and an update on how AI has been sustained in Roadway's culture.

Case Clippings: Roadway Express[5]

The work at Roadway has been very powerful. Again, Roadway's goal was to create an organization with leaders developing leaders at every level, a high-engagement organization. An important part of this goal was building a strong financial literacy at every level, where everyone was thinking and acting as owners of a business. As a result, the main topic in one of the early AI statements at Roadway had to do with "optimizing margins." While topics on AI interventions can concern human, technical, environmental, or financial issues, nonetheless, the same principle still holds true: human systems move in the direction of what they most persistently, actively, and deeply ask questions about. When reviewing the questions below on optimizing margins, think about potential changes that might take place in the future.

In this case, something remarkable did happen at the Akron terminal of Roadway. In 2002, a few years after the start of the AI work at Roadway, one of the AI teams came up with a $10 million-per-year-cost savings idea. When this happened, the excitement was understandably quite high. This illustrates the principle that the seeds of change are implicit in the first questions asked. Keep that in mind while reading the interview questions that follow.

The Case Clipping includes the following:

- *Interview Guide*
- *Summit Preworksheets*
- *Summit Working Agenda*
- *Summit Agenda Overview*
- *AI Organizational Summit*
- *Discovery Worksheet #1*
- *Discovery Worksheet #2*
- *Discovery Worksheet #3*
- *Dream Worksheet #1*
- *Dream Worksheet #2*
- *Dream Worksheet #3*
- *Design Worksheet*

---

5 http://appreciativeinquiry.case.edu/practice/toolsFilmDetail.cfm?coid=585

The following resulted from the Dream phase:
- *An Opportunity Map of needs and priorities*
- *Identification of which needs and priorities were most pressing*
- *Action teams formed to address organizational trust, drivers as strategic sales representatives, employee communications, performance measurements, and monitoring and education.*

The most surprising learning was that it did not matter what your job was; everyone wanted the same thing—to win.[6] Shared goals included sustained growth, happy customers, and job security. Within two years, stock rose from $14 to more than $40 per share, resulting in a sale to an even larger firm, Yellow Trucking. Other measures have steadily improved: operating ratios, throughput, overtime changes, increased morale and levels of trust, clarity in mission and vision, and job functions.

Sustainability

Over time, Roadway has conducted more than 60 AI Interventions with more than 10,000 employees. During this time period, Roadway has improved its performance and union-management relationships. Measurable results: improvement in throughput increased 47% to 64%, average transit speed was reduced from 2.3 days to 2.1 days, average production efficiency increased 59% to 64%, and more.[7]

Today Roadway is one of the largest carriers in the nation and is one of the most stable LTL employers, one that offers seamless service in 50 states. It merged with Yellow to form Yellow Roadway Corporation. As a testimony to the perceived value of the AI change process, the AI Summit was selected as the approach to bring the two organizations together. The synergistic savings from this merger are estimated at $300 million.[8]

---

6 For more information on this story, see Hammond, K. (July 2001). Leaders for the long haul. *Fast Company*, 56–58.

7 For more detailed information on how Roadway applied the 4-D Cycle and results, see Barrett, F., & Fry, R. (2005). *Appreciative inquiry: A positive approach to building cooperative capacity.* Chagrin Falls, OH: Taos Institute Publishing.

8 For more information on this continued success of Roadway, see Cooperrider, D., & Whitney, D. (2005). *Appreciative inquiry: A positive revolution in change.* San Francisco: Berrett-Koehler.

Interview Guide

A Roadway Inquiry into Optimal Margin
Opening Dialogue

(In diverse pairs complete an interview. [across functions and levels])

- **Results you want:** With revenues, tonnage, and sales at record levels, one of the most important opportunities we face is to engage everyone in increasing positive margins now. To do so will call on discovery of new strengths, build on old strengths, and carry us to higher levels financially.
  A. As you look at Roadway from the perspective of our capabilities and as you think about the business context and opportunities, how do you define "optimal margin" for us? What is the positive margin you want and believe we have the capability to create right now? What is a moderate time frame looking at the long term?
  B. What results do you want from this meeting? What would make this day a good one for you?

- **Insights from your work:** We all pride ourselves on the things we do that add the most value in terms of creating margin. Some of our work activities add a great deal of value, while others do not. Likewise, some things we do as leaders—our style, our approaches to managing people—engage everyone else in increasing margins. Let's reflect using the essential things you do that you believe add the most value.
  A. When you think of your precious time and how you spend it, what are the things you do that, in your view, add the most value in terms of creating margin? Any examples?
  B. In the ideal, if you were able to recraft what you do, what parts of your work (from the perspective of creating margin) would you want to keep doing, let go of, or do new and differently?
    - Keep doing?
    - Let go of (things that are not really needed)?
    - Do new or differently?

C. As you reflect on your leadership role here at Roadway—times when you have mobilized or helped develop others—there have been high points and low points and successes and failures. Please describe one situation or change initiative you are proud of, an achievement in which you believe you had an impact in realizing better margins. What happened? What were the challenges? What was it about you or your leadership style? What lessons were learned?

D. Let's think about other leaders or successful stories of change—situations you have heard about or seen here at Roadway as they relate to engaging people to achieve good margins. Is there a story or an example that stands out for you—something that exemplifies the kind of leadership approaches we should aim for more often? Can you describe the leadership and insights?

- **Continuity search:** Good organizations know how to preserve the core of what they do best and are able work out or let go of things that have built up or are no longer needed. Preserving the right things is key. Letting go of other things is the next step.

    A. In relationship to building optimal margins, what are the things we do best organizationally—for example, measurement systems, leadership systems, ways of developing others, accountability systems, ways of delegating and building trust, and technologies—things that should be preserved even as we change in the future?

    B. Assuming that things do build up, there is a need to "work out" and streamline. There is a need to let go of things that, given precious time constraints, are not needed. Assuming that very few things are sacred, what things (small or large) do you think we should consider letting go of?

- **Novelty:** Novelty is imagining new possibilities for optimal margins. If anything imaginable were possible, if there were no constraints whatsoever, what would the ideal Roadway organization look like if we were delivering optimal margins? Imagine that you had a magic wand to use. Describe what we would be doing new, better, or different? Envision it happening. What do you see happening that is new, different, or better?

- **Transition:** Transition is moving from A to B, asking how we get from here to there.
  - A. What is the smallest step (an action, a decision, an initiative) we could take that would have the largest impact?
  - B. What is one thing we have not even thought of yet—something that could have a payoff?

Summit Preworksheets

During the summit meeting, we will be creating a shared history of Roadway's strengths and best past experiences to help in deciding the future we all want to be part of. It is important that all of the different participants are heard and appreciated so we truly work from a shared sense of what we already do well and why.

Please take 5–10 minutes to fill out the two attached sheets. Bring them with you to the summit. We will use them on the first day.

Preworksheet #1

How Are Our Industry and Company Changing?
What is Our Story? Our Competitive Strengths?
Key Moments In Our History?

Purpose: To develop a collective picture of our changing world, the industry, and the core of our history (strengths, achievements, challenges, changes, and so on).

- Make notes below about memorable industry events and changes in society that have had an impact on Roadway—things you believe are notable milestones, trends, and/or turning points. (At the summit meeting, you will use a magic marker to add your notes or pictures to timelines on the wall.)

INDUSTRY/SOCIETAL Events, Changes, and Trends
What happened in the trucking and transportation business? (Why was it important?)

1930s–1950s _____

1960s _____

1970s _____

1980s _____

1990s _____

2000– _____

The future you think is coming:

Preworksheet #2

How Are Our Industry and Company Changing?
What is Our Story? Our Competitive Strengths?
Key Moments In Our History?

- Make notes below on notable achievements, changes, events, trends, or turning points here at the Akron complex. (At the summit meeting, you will use a magic marker to add your notes or pictures to timelines on the wall.)

COMPANY Changes, Events, Trends, and Accomplishments
What happened at Akron Roadway?

1930s–1950s _____

1960s _____

1970s _____

1980s _____

1990s _____

2000_ _____

Where is our company going (the future changes you see coming)?

Summit Working Agenda

Day 1	DISCOVERY	PRESENTERS
8:00–8:15	Welcomes and comments on topic	Mark O. & Jim B.
8:15–8:45	Why doing this/using AI	Terry G.
8:45–9:00	Intro facilitators and topic more	Pete & Ed
9:00–9:20	Community-building activity	Ed
9:20–10:00	AI Introduction (Time to rethink. What is a summit? Prep for 1:1 interviews)	Dave & Ron
10:00–11:00	AI interviews (including break)	
11:00–11:45	Max-mix subgroups: Themes and Expectations	Pete
11:45–12:30	Group reports (only some tables)	Pete
12:30–1:30	Lunch (customer panel)	
1:30–2:00	Map timelines on walls and convene in stakeholder groups	Cindy & Ed
2:00–2:45	Stakeholders: Proudest Moments and Key Success Factors	Cindy & Ed
2:45–3:00	Break	
3:00–3:45	Group reports: Story and Factors to Keep	Cindy & Ed
3:45–4:45	Positive Image —> Positive Action	Dave & Ron
4:45–5:00	Summary of day and close	Dave & Ron

Summit Working Agenda

Day 2	DREAM	PRESENTERS
8:00–8:30	Community activity: Labeling Positive Core Freight to be shipped to the future….(stakeholder groups)	Pete
8:30–9:30	Mix/max groups: Generating Opportunities for Improving Throughput	Dave
9:30–10:15	Opportunity mapping (and dot voting)	Ed & Pete
10:15–10:30	Break (facilitators cluster and label action groups)	
10:30–10:45	Self selection into opportunity groups	Ron
10:45–12:00	Dream: 3-year aspiration draft and skits	Ed
12:00–12:45	Working lunch	
12:45–2:15	Presentations of aspirations and visions	Ed
2:15–2:30	Gallery Aspiration Statements for feedback	Ed
2:30–2:45	Break	
2:45–3:00	Task for new groups: 3-year and 1-year statements	Pete
3:00–4:30	Group work: new opportunity groups	Pete
4:30–5:00	Community: Loading our aspirations for shipping	Pete

Summer Working Agenda

Day 3	DESIGN AND DESTINY	PRESENTERS
8:00–8:30	Community: Naming the Destination for our Positive Core and Aspirations	Pete
8:30–10:30	Design and action planning (ready for reports)	Pete
10:30–10:45	Break	
10:45–12:00	Presentations (3 x 15 minutes: 10 min to present + 5 min discussion)	Ron & Dave
12:00–1:00	Lunch (prep/coach for closing comments in community session)	
1:00–2:30	Continue presentations	Ron & Dave
2:30–3:00	Teams reconvene for last minute detail and next steps	Ron & Dave
3:00–3:15	Break	
3:15–3:45	Community: 1:1 interviews re personal commitments – One message I'd take back… – One thing I can do on my own… – My commitment to my team, going ahead	Ron
3:45–end	Community: Open microphone forum	Dave + all

Summit Agenda Overview

Akron Roadway

Winning with Employee-Driven Throughput: Crushing nonunion competition by delivering unsurpassed speed and leveraging employee pride and involvement.

Day 1
- Welcomes and overview
- Introduction to topic
- Community-building exercise

Discovery: 1:1 appreciative interviews
Mixed groups of pairs search for themes and factors that "give life" to our topic

Lunch (customer panel)

Creating our shared-history stakeholder groups: Identifying proudest moments and what we want to keep

Input: Where does positive change come from?
- Summary and closing

Day 2
- Summarizing key success factors and practices to preserve

Dreaming: Mixed groups: Improvement possibilities for our topic
Mapping highest impact opportunities
Images of our future around opportunities of most interest
(New self-selected groups)

Lunch

Presentations of images
Declaring aspirations for the future: five-year, goal and one-year steps

- Summary reflections and closing

Day 3
- Summarizing our five-year aspirations

Design: Work on one-year, targets and action steps
Prepare presentation of "yes-able proposals for action"
Community forum:
Presentations from 3 or 4 action groups

Lunch

Presentations from 3 or 4 action groups

Delivery: Team formation: Action groups convene to agree on
(immediate next steps the will take next.)

- Personal commitments to act on after this Summit
- "Open microphone" to entire community for comments/reflections
- Closing

NOTE: All sessions will begin and end on time. There will be breaks with refreshments each morning and afternoon. All sessions will be videotaped so a summary of deliberations and action plans can be communicated (if we want) to the whole organization.

AI Organizational Summit

ROADWAY
What is an "AI" Organizational Summit?
This is not your typical planning meeting!

- The **WHOLE SYSTEM** participates—a cross section of as many inter- ested parties as is practical. That means more diversity and less hier- archy than is usual in a working meeting and a chance for each person to be heard and to learn new ways of looking at the task at hand.

- Future scenarios—for an organization, a community, or an issue—are put into HISTORICAL and GLOBAL perspective. That means thinking globally together before acting locally. This feature enhances shared understanding and greater commitment to act. It also increases range of potential actions.

- People **SELF-MANAGE** their work and use **DIALOGUE**—not prob- lem solving—as the main tool. That means helping others do the tasks and taking responsibility for our perceptions and actions.

- **COMMON GROUND**, rather than conflict management, is the frame of reference. That means honoring our differences rather than having to reconcile them.

- **APPRECIATIVE INQUIRY (AI)** is a combination of the following: to appreciate means to value—to understand those things worth valuing. To inquire means to study, to ask questions, to search. Therefore, AI is a collaborative search to identify and understand the organization's strengths, its potentials, the greatest opportunities, and people's hopes for the future.

- **COMMITMENT TO ACTION** involves the whole system, allowing for more rapid decision making and committing to action in a public way—in an open way that everyone can support and help implement.

SELF-MANAGEMENT and GROUP LEADERSHIP ROLES

Each small group manages its own discussion, data, time, and reports. Here are useful roles for self-managing this work. Leadership roles can be rotated. Divide up the work as you choose.

- **DISCUSSION LEADER**—Assures that each person who wants to speak is heard within the time available. Keeps the group on track to finish on time.

- **TIMEKEEPER**—Keeps the group aware of the time remaining. Monitors report-outs and signals the time remaining to the person talking.

- **RECORDER**—Writes the group's output on flip charts, using the speaker's words. Asks a person to restate long ideas briefly.

- **REPORTER**—Delivers a report to the large group in the time allotted.

Discovery Worksheet #1

Interview Conversations
(Turn to person next to you…. Complete by _____ o'clock)

Our Current Reality

Today's transportation environment is characterized by fierce competition in the one- and two-day regional markets. Every day we lose market share as current and former Roadway customers give more and more freight to nontraditional nonunion carriers who beat us at the game we "invented"—service! Why? How? Because they get the freight to its destination faster than we do. We are better at rating bills and building "high-'n-tight" claim-free loads. We have better computer systems and more dock doors. We have the best-trained and most-skilled employees. On price, our base rates are better than the regionals. Yet they still beat us out of market share because they get the goods delivered quicker. But by leveraging the pride and involvement of our people, we can respond and recapture lost business as well as establish new business. Our key to success in this arena is as follows:

Throughput

Throughput is the measure we use to monitor how quickly we can process the freight through our facility. We win the battle for the one- and two-day market when we accelerate the processing of freight from pickup, through the 211 gate, across the dock, and down the road. System speed—that's our need. If we achieve maximum throughput, we can crush the nonunion regionals and dominate the market.

Question 1:

Think back to a time at work that you recall as a high point, an experience, or a moment you remember as having left you with an intense sense of pride, excitement, or involvement in having been a part of something that was meaningful, a time when you truly believed you had contributed to the betterment of a fellow employee, the customer, or the organization.

Describe that experience. What was going on, who was involved, and what made it so memorable?

Question 2:

Tell me about a time when you thought throughput (speed) was at its best at 211 or when you were involved in moving a shipment quickly through the facility to a final destination in order to meet a customer requirement.

- Tell the story of what was going on, who was involved, and what happened.
- What did you do? What did you value most about your involvement in that story?
- What do you value most about the contribution of others in that story?

Question 3:

Tomorrow's reality. Imagine that you have awakened from a deep sleep and three years have passed. It is 2010, and the landscape of regional LTL is different. Roadway dominates the nonunion regional carriers in the marketplace! Wall Street is buzzing over the dramatic success Roadway has had in the regional markets! Articles in Transport Topics describe how Roadway—by tapping into the pride and involvement of its employees—has leveraged a dramatic improvement in speed at the 211 complex! This muscular yet agile system has catapulted Roadway Akron to the forefront in reducing costs while establishing unparalleled levels of customer service and employee satisfaction. For customers, it's now imperative that they do their one- or two-day regional business with 211/Akron! For employees, 211 is the preferred location over other Roadway locations!

- What happened to allow for this kind of success?
- What part did you play in this success?
- What three wishes do you have to help Akron Roadway reach and sustain this success?

Discovery Worksheet #2

Discovery at Roadway:
Discovering the Resources and Strengths in This Community
Group reports will begin at _____ o'clock.

Purpose: To appreciate and welcome each other and to learn about the special experiences, commitments, capabilities, and resources people bring to this conference.

Self-Manage: Select a recorder, reporter, timekeeper and discussion leader.
- **Introduce the person you interviewed.** Go around the table. Introduce your interview partner to the group and share one highlight from your interview (high-point story and vision of Roadway).

- As a group, talk about (each person shares):
  - What interests or excites you about being here? What results are you hoping for?
  - From the stories you have heard, what stands out as key factors or themes that cause effective throughput with unsurpassed speed that is driven by employee involvement here at the Akron complex?

- Recorder/reporter listens for and prepares a two-minute summary on:
  - Hopes we have for this meeting and results we want.
    - Three to five key factors that give life to throughput with unsurpassed speed that is driven by employee pride and involvement.

Discovery Worksheet #3

Discovery at Roadway:Root Causes of Success:
When Are We Most Effective and Why?
Reports are due at _____ o'clock.

Purpose: To look at the things we are doing of which we are most proud and to understand the things that create success and build competitive advantage.

Self-manage: Select a reporter, recorder, timekeeper and discussion leader.
- On a flip chart, list what you and this stakeholder group are doing (or have done) of which you are most proud in relationship to the task—Achieving Maximum Throughput with Unsurpassed Speed, Driven by Employee Involvement and Pride: "We are most proud of . . ."   (Use the historical timelines to remind the group of significant moments, turning points, achievements, and so on.)
- Select your "proudest prouds" and come up with two examples/stories of successful "high-throughput moments."

  NOTE: These might be stories you told or heard in your opening interviews in pairs this morning.

- Now do an analysis of the two stories. Have someone tell the story and listen for patterns. What were the root causes of success? What happened that was new or different? What was it about the people and customers that stood out? What was it about the work group that led toward positive outcomes? What was it about the organization (e.g., procedures, resources, equipment, leadership, communications, and/or training) that seemed to elevate the whole enterprise of positive question asking?

- Recorder: List 5–10 root causes of success, things we want to keep doing or do even better no matter what else changes.

- Reporter: Prepare a three-minute summary. Choose one story to tell to the whole group and review the list of the root causes of success.

Dream Worksheet #1

Roadway Moving from Discovery to Dream
Mapping the Opportunities for Improvement
Summaries are due at _____ o'clock.

Self-Manage: Select a discussion leader, recorder, and timekeeper.

Purpose: To begin to build a future you want—an Akron Roadway team that is truly dedicated to "Maximizing Throughput with Unsurpassed Speed, Driven by Employee Pride and Involvement."

1. Share your wishes and dreams from the interviews you did yesterday morning (Question 3). Add any ideas or thoughts about changes or improvements you think will have a major impact on improving our throughput.

2. Brainstorm a list of opportunities for improving throughput at the Akron complex.

3. As a group, choose 3–5 opportunities you all believe will have the greatest impact on throughput.

Dream Worksheet #2

Dreaming the Future Roadway Wants
Ideal Future Scenarios
Presentations are due at _____ o'clock.

Self-Manage: Select a discussion leader, recorder and timekeeper.

Purpose: To imagine and define the future you want to work toward— an Akron Roadway team that is truly dedicated to "Crushing the Nonunion Competition by Maximizing Throughput with Unsurpassed Speed, Driven by Employee Pride and Involvement."

- Put yourselves three years into the future. It is 2010. Visualize the Akron complex you want from the perspective of the opportunity area you have chosen. What is happening?
    - How did this come about? What helped it happen?
    - What are the things that support this vision— leadership, structures, training, procedures, and so on?
    - What makes this vision exciting to you?
    - How does this vision maximize throughput with unsurpassed speed?

- Capture this dream in a three-year aspiration statement draft on one flip-chart page: "By 2010, what we most aspire to in terms of (your chosen opportunity area) is . . ."
    (See two examples on next page.)
    - Use vivid language.
    - Be positive.
    - Be bold and provocative. Make your statement a stretch that will attract others.

- Choose a creative way to present your vision to the rest of us in a five-minute "portrayal," as if your vision existed now. Use as many members of your group as possible in the presentation.
            Examples: * A TV News Report * A Song or Poem * A Day in the Life * A Skit * A Hiring Interview *

Dream Worksheet #3

Dreaming the Future Roadway Wants
Ideal Future Scenarios

Example Aspiration Statements:

Opportunity Area: Delegation and Trust

> "Roadway 2010: Roadway is an organization that is world-class in terms of its leaders developing leaders at all levels. We are known throughout the industry for our core competency of delegation. People want to work at Roadway because all employees are trusted and empowered to create value."

Opportunity Area: Career Opportunity/Training/Mentoring

> "Roadway is a proactive organization that enables employees to achieve their personal career goals by taking advantage of career opportunities, centrally administered and personally initiated training/education, and mentoring."

> "Career opportunities are provided by vehicles such as internal job fairs, intranet job postings, use of a skills database, career assessment inventories, and a formalized mentoring process—with a key emphasis on promoting from within. All employees are provided time for various training where tuition reimbursement for continuing education is "boundary-less" (i.e., all departments, job levels, and interest levels), fully supported, budgeted, and funded."

> "Training includes soft skills for all employees, leadership training, and advanced and technical training using experienced personnel as a training asset."

Design Worksheet

Designing for Optimal Throughput at Roadway

Self-Manage: Select a discussion leader, recorder, and timekeeper.

Purpose: To begin translating your three-year aspiration statement into one-year goals and steps to be taken in the next 6–12 months.

- Using the feedback and comments from other groups, take 10–15 minutes to revise, edit, or improve your aspiration statement.

- Begin formulating one-year targets or goals that can be achieved and demonstrated showing we are on our way to your three-year aspiration.
    - Brainstorm ideas about specific things that can occur or be changed in the upcoming year that will put us on a course to realize your vision for 2010.
    - Agree on key targets and scenarios for how to get there. Who would need to do what by when?

Guidelines for Action Steps:
- Is it a "yes-able" idea (likely to get support)?
- Does it address/reflect the underlying principles in our aspiration statement?
- What are we already doing (key success factors from yesterday) that can be continued or enhanced?
- What new actions would create an impact?

6

Design:
How Can It Be?

"Organizational transformation is much more than the critical mass of personal transformation. It requires macro level changes in the very fabric of organizing, the social architecture."

—Diana Whitney

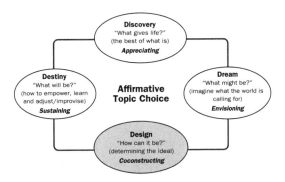

The *Dream* phase articulates the strategic focus, such as a vision of a better world, a powerful purpose, and a compelling statement of a strategic intent. In the *Design* phase, attention turns to creating the ideal organization so that it might achieve its dream. Future images emerge through grounded examples from an organization's positive core. Good-news stories are used to craft **provocative propositions**[1] that bridge the best of "what gives life" with a collective aspiration of "what might be." This is where the organization's social architecture is designed.

The *Design* phase of the 4-D process is the crucial stage in sustaining positive change and responding to the organization's positive past. Grounded in the best of what has been, good appreciative designs address all three of the elements necessary for effective organizational change—continuity, novelty, and transition—discussed in Mini-lecture VII in Chapter 1. The positive core identified and expounded in the first two phases begins to take form.

The design starts by crafting provocative propositions. Sometimes referred to as *possibility propositions*, they bridge "the best of what is" (identified in Discovery) with "what might be" (imagined in Dream). They are written in the present tense. They re-create the organization's image of itself by presenting clear, compelling pictures of how things will be when the positive core is fully effective in all of its strategies, processes, systems, decisions, and collaborations. In this way, provocative propositions redirect daily actions and create future possibilities and a shared vision for the organization and its members. It is important that the design fully integrate the "best of past and possibility" and that it be consistent with the intended outcome of the inquiry.

The following pages present the concept of social architecture and its relationship to AI-based design. The elements of a good provocative proposition are defined. This chapter includes additional provocative propositions to stimulate imagination and creativity. The Case Clippings at the end of this chapter are from a long-term healthcare organization, Tendercare, Inc. They illustrate how this organization incorporated AI into its "+1 Census Development Campaign" at an assisted-living center. The clippings demonstrate how Tendercare's Core Care Team moved from Discovery to Dream and through the *Design* phase. This second edition describes what's new and institutionalized at Tendercare, leading to sustainable organizational development and a revamped corporate culture.

In the context of moving forward to present new developments in the AI *Design* phase, this chapter offers some concluding thoughts on the social architectural approach by looking at the related fields of fashion design, graphic design, art and architectural design, and product design. These correlative disciplines contain lessons about the spirit of AI design. The authors' colleagues

---

1 Provocative propositions also have been referred to as possibility propositions, possibility statements, and design statements. The different wording depends on the language preferred by the organization.

Richard Boland and Fred Collopy have written a separate text on what they call the "design attitude," which will be highlighted later in this chapter.

IDEO, one of the top design firms in the world, has teamed up with leading AI practitioners to combine the AI Summit methods with its unique product design methods for sparking innovation. IDEO helps organizations create and innovate through design.

After a complete overview of the social architecture approach to organization design, this chapter will point to several more advanced variations, including an example of Fairmount Minerals, one of the fastest growing companies in America. Fairmont is a leader in the field of sustainable ecological design focused on "doing good and doing well." Fairmount Minerals has been using AI as an organizational development tool for more than ten years.

Social Architecture for Organizing

When creating a building, an architect considers many elements in the design, as previously stated. A building requires certain key elements: foundation, roof, walls, windows, doors, and floors. But within the constraints of those necessary elements, the architect and client have a number of choices, ways in which to accommodate their unique preferences. For example, they may choose a brick or adobe exterior, a flat roof or a roof with a pitch, a glass or solid wall, and a traditional or cathedral ceiling.

In many ways, a set of provocative propositions is a kind of social architecture for the ideal organization. The **social architecture** is the basic infrastructure that allows the organization to make the dream a reality (from concept to action). It addresses the **design elements** critical to an organization (e.g., leadership/management structure, systems, structures, and strategies) for supporting the positive core. For example, "socio" refers to the following social system components:

- The set of job functions and reporting (formal) and building (informal) relationships
- The management systems, processes, and policies

The design steps are outlined in **Table 6.1**.

Table 6.1 Four Design Steps

- Select design elements.
- Identify internal and external relationships.
- Identify themes and engage in dialogue.
- Write provocative propositions.

Step 1: Select Design Elements

The first step in AI Design is to select design elements. Organization members may choose to articulate their own social architecture; or they may choose to write provocative propositions based on other common models, such as Marvin Weisbord's Six Box Model, Watkins and Mohr's process, or McKinsey's 7-S model.[2] In Tendercare's situation, the Core Care Team selected those elements that best fit the organization's architecture for each affirmative topic choice, as illustrated in Table 6.2.

The *Design* phase defines the basic structure that will allow the dream (or vision) to become a reality. Like the other phases, the *Design* phase requires widespread dialogue about the nature of the structure and processes. This is what is meant by coconstructing the organization's future.

Table 6.2 Design Elements

Design elements to Consider When Designing a Social Architecture

Alliances and Partnerships	Market Opportunities
Beliefs about Power and Authority	New Products
Brand Identity	Policies
Business Models	Practices and Principles
Business Processes	Relationships
Communication	Results
Competencies	Shared Values
Culture	Social Responsibility
Customer Relations	Societal Purposes
Distribution of Wealth	Staff/People
Ecological/Environmental	Stakeholder Relations
Education (Training)	Strategy
Governance Structure	Structure
Knowledge of Management System	Systems
Leadership	Technology
Management Practices	Vision and Purpose

For example, if "leadership" is the element selected, cogent questions might be as follows: What kind of leadership structure is needed? What is the preferred behavior of the leaders?

---

2 For more alternative approaches on whole-system design, see McKinsey's 7-S framework in DeKluyver, C. (2006). *Strategic thinking: An executive perspective.* Upper Saddle River, NJ: Prentice Hall; Weisbord, M., & Janoff, S. (1994). *Collaborating for change: Future Search.* San Francisco: Berrett-Koehler; Weisbord, M. (1994). *Discovering common ground.* San Francisco: Berrett-Koehler; and Mohr B., & Watkins, J. (2001). *Appreciative inquiry: Change at the speed of imagination.* San Francisco: Jossey-Bass/Pfeiffer.

In the Tendercare example ("+1 Census Development Campaign" project), the Core Care Team created a unique business operating environment and culture based on an image of three rings (Figure 6.1). Tendercare's architecture placed the residents in the center ring, the stakeholders in the second ring, and the design elements in the outermost ring.

Step 2: Identify Internal and External Relationships

In the second step, staff and residents worked from the inside out to identify those relationships that helped build the positive core. They listed those key relationships that affected "resident loyalty," as shown in the two boxes labeled "Internal" and "External" in Figure 6.1. Therefore, when designing the provocative proposition, these key relationships had to be considered.

Figure 6.1 Tendercare's Business and Social Architecture

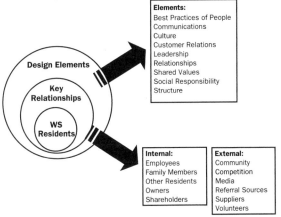

Step 3: Identify Themes and Engage in Dialogue

The third step was to go back to the AI analysis report and the Interview Summary Sheets to identify those key themes that supported resident loyalty. The Core Care Team called those themes "the key ingredients needed to build and sustain resident loyalty." These key ingredients were listed on a large sheet of newsprint. During this step, a great deal of open dialogue took place and stories were told about what contributed to resident loyalty.

Looking through the data and listening to the conversations, the team attempted to pick out statements and/or stories that seemed to exemplify the essence of resident loyalty. The following examples were included:

- Building relationships between staff and residents, staff and family, staff and community, and residents and community
- Providing caring and consistent follow-through on residents' requests
- Showing genuine interest and compassion toward the residents (staff acted like an extended family)
- Knowing each resident by name and knowing something special about him or her
- Taking time to do something helpful for a resident, such as tying his shoe or putting on her makeup
- Developing trust through the managing of a resident's finances, such as monthly budgeting for amenities or balancing a checkbook
- Keeping the physical grounds looking nice
- Helping residents keep their dignity and independence

From those statements, the team selected the best words and created new concepts they believed captured their meaning of resident loyalty. Words such as *positive relationships, nurturing, listening, understanding, trust, compassion, quality care, service,* and *independence* were listed. Then the group took time to reflect on the list and make changes, additions, and alterations. At this point, a deeper conversation took place, ensuring that just the right words were listed. For instance, the word *communication*, which was initially listed, was changed to *understanding* because the group believed *understanding* better captured what the staff and residents wanted in their relationship in order to enhance resident loyalty.

Step 4: Write Provocative Propositions

Next, each member of the Core Care Team worked independently to write a preferred possibility statement about resident loyalty.[3] At this point, the group was quiet and reflective as each member attempted to use the words the group identified as significant. The themes and key ingredients were posted to capture resident loyalty in their version of a possibility statement. The participants were instructed to incorporate these ingredients into the possibility statements, as well as to include the key relationships that were identified earlier. After adequate time was allotted, each team member read his or her statement aloud. As each statement was read, it was transcribed and posted for everyone to see.

This resulted in ten affirmative possibility statements for further dialogue. Many statements were similar, yet each had a unique offering. For example, several statements helped develop the framework of the possibility statement.

---

3 For this Case Clipping, Tendercare used the term *possibility statements* instead of *possibility propositions*

Other statements provided key ingredients to make the dreams a reality. Another possibility statement provided the concluding sentence that captured the essence of resident loyalty.

Resident Loyalty Possibility Statement:

At Wayne Seniors, residents are our lifeline. We maintain this lifeline by building relationships with our residents and their families to ensure a caring, consistent, and positive living experience.

We strive to nurture relationships by creating an environment of listening, understanding, and trust.

Residents trust us with their lives—a responsibility we hold sacred. We earn trust through unwavering commitment to superior care tempered with compassion and respect.

To provide superior care, we provide knowledge to residents, staff, and families to ensure consistent and compassionate service delivery.

With dedication to these ideals, our center for seniors nurtures resident loyalty, thereby effectively serving the community.

Typically, the core team or steering group coordinates this effort; but it is important to incorporate the feedback of all affected stakeholders. Once the design elements and stakeholders have been selected and most stakeholders identify with the dream, the provocative propositions can be written. The next section covers suggested criteria for writing a provocative proposition. These propositions articulate the desired organizational qualities, processes, and systems (created in the *Dream* phase) to help guide the organization to its higher purpose.

To get buy-in from the entire organization, a process must allow everyone affected to make a contribution. In the Tendercare example, a dietary aide later suggested creating a dining committee made up of residents and staff to explore how to improve the residents' dining experience. This suggestion resulted in a flexible meal program with more menu choices and different meal times, while also providing the residents with a greater sense of independence and control over their surroundings. This fostered greater resident loyalty. Such contributions move the provocative propositions forward to implementation of the dream in the *Destiny* phase.

Criteria for Good Provocative Propositions

A provocative proposition is a statement that bridges the best of "what is" and "what might be." It is provocative to the extent that it stretches the realm of the status quo, challenges common assumptions or routines, and helps suggest desired possibilities for the organization and its people. At the same time, it is grounded in what has worked in the past. It conveys the positive images (from the Dream phase) of the ideal organization.

The following questions serve as a guideline or checklist for crafting engaging provocative propositions:

- Is it *provocative*? Does it stretch, challenge, or interrupt the status quo?

- Is it *grounded*? Are examples available that illustrate the ideal as a real possibility? Is it grounded in the organization's collective history?

- Is it *desired*? Do *you* want it as a preferred future?

- Is it stated in *affirmative* and bold terms?

- Does it follow a *social architecture* approach?

- Does it expand the *"zone of proximal development"*?[4]

  – Used with a third party (outside appreciative eye)

  – Complemented with benchmarking data

- Is it a *participative* process?

- Is it used to stimulate *intergenerational learning*?

- Is there balanced management of *continuity, novelty, and transition*?

Provocative propositions provide a clear, shared vision for the organization's destiny. The following samples of provocative propositions focus on a specific design element and theme or topic of the organization's social architecture.

---

4 The Zone of Proximal Development (ZPD) was developed by Lev Semenovich Vygotsky (1896–1934). He suggested that the mind is not fixed in its capacity, but provides a range of potential possibilities. For more information on ZPD and how it relates to AI, refer to Stavros, J. (1998). *Capacity building using an appreciative approach: A relational process of building your organization's future.* Unpublished dissertation, Case Western University, Cleveland, OH.

Sample Provocative Propositions

DESIGN ELEMENT: Culture

THEME/TOPIC: Recognition and Celebration

The AI Advocates Standing Committee understands and honors the pivotal role of recognition and celebration within the formation of a true "appreciative organization." Therefore, frequent and visible recognition and celebration of the value of life, people, and ideas are an integral part of the AI Advocates' philosophy and practice.

We value diversity of people and ideas. We nurture and support people to express who and what they are. We begin all meetings and gatherings with positive storytelling and recognition. Whenever we are engaged in a discussion or decision-making process, we consciously use "appreciative feedback" with one another and with coworkers outside the team. We collect and publicly disseminate stories that communicate the richness of individual and collective contributions within the community. We purposefully recognize and celebrate those individuals in the community who regularly recognize and celebrate other people, ideas, and accomplishments.

DESIGN ELEMENT: Human Resources Management System

THEME/TOPIC: Performance Appraisal

Our organization acts on its value of high-level trust in the belief that people are committed to personal accountability by using appreciative performance appraisals. It focuses on employee competence and exemplary service to our stakeholders. Our employees are valued.

DESIGN ELEMENT: Shared Values

THEME/TOPIC: Authenticity

Authenticity in human relationships is a key foundation for true organizational transformation and excellence. When we are authentic, we recognize and share our thoughts, feelings, and experiences with others in the spirit of deepening relationships and in service of collaborative achievement. This dialogue allows us to:

- Unleash the best of who we are.
- Become energized and unite around our heartfelt focus.
- Meet the goals of the business.
- Contribute to the greater good.

Being authentic is a shared individual, interpersonal, and organizational responsibility. In practical terms, we:

- Each commit to reflecting and contributing openly.
- Seek out other's viewpoints so we can get the best of everyone's thinking.
- Build in pauses to allow people to know their own thoughts.
- Embrace the philosophy of slowing down so we can finish sooner.

DESIGN ELEMENT: Organizational Purpose

THEME/TOPIC: Shared Vision

Partners in all regions share a basic common vision of the firm's core mission, intent, and direction. It is an exciting, challenging, and meaningful direction, which helps give all partners a feeling of significance, purpose, pride, and unity. The firm uses whatever time and resources are needed to bring everyone on board, thus continuously cultivating the thrill of having "a one-firm feeling," of being a valued member of one outstanding national partnership.

DESIGN ELEMENT: Structure

THEME/TOPIC: Ownership

We have created an organization where everyone experiences himself or herself as an owner of the business. People at all levels believe the organization is theirs to improve, change, and help in order to reach its potential. We recognize that there is a big difference between owners and hired hands. Ownership happens in three ways: (1) on an economic level, where everyone is a shareholder and shares in the profit; (2) on a psychological level, wherein people are authentically involved; and (3) on a business level, when the big-picture purpose is shared by all and all take part at the strategic level of business planning.

The Spirit of Designing: Recent Developments

Finally, mentioned at the outset of this chapter is the goal of addressing the "spirit of designing" and several exciting additions to the ways the *Design* phase can unfold—building on and going beyond the basic social architectural approach. In terms of the spirit of designing, this chapter looks to the fields of fashion design, graphic design, art and architectural design, and product design for new lessons about the AI *Design* phase.

First, as previously mentioned, the authors' colleagues Richard Boland and Fred Collopy have written a book on what they call the "design attitude." In brief, their book is about approaching the world like an artist—with a great deal of improvising, iterating, sketching and mapping visually, creating connections and cross-pollinations across seemingly disparate domains, and moving iteratively between liquid (very open) and more crystallized (convergent) stages in the design process. Designing in this view is often visual, taking concepts—for example, verbal or descriptive elements of the ideal organization—and giving them three-dimensional form or making them into "prototype" models or storyboards.[5]

Secondly, in their work at Appreciative Inquiry Consulting (AIC), David Cooperrider and his colleagues teamed up with one of the top design firms in the world, IDEO, to combine their large group AI Summit methods with IDEO's unique product design method for sparking innovation. IDEO employs design thinking to help clients navigate the speed, complexity, and opportunity areas of today's world. IDEO calls its method the "deep dive," and it involves a powerful brainstormer method and a process of rapid prototyping.[6]

Sustainability: The Triple Bottom Line

In Chapter 8, you will find the participant workbook for an exemplary AI Summit design session, one that utilizes these new design options. Held at Fairmount Minerals in 2005, the focus of the summit was on designing new products and business processes based on the sustainable development and triple bottom line concepts. Chuck Fowler, the CEO and president of Fairmount Minerals, and Bill Conway, Fairmount's founder and chair, had introduced the approach of AI to the company in 1991. From 1991 to 2005, the company's revenues increased dramatically—from $48 million to more than $250 million. During this period, Fairmount became the second largest sand mining operation in America.

Next on the OD agenda was to become a "**sustainable enterprise**"[7] focused on the **triple bottom line** of people (social), prosperity (economic), and planet (environment).[8] Once again, the AI Summit was selected as the way to bring the entire company as well as external stakeholders such as environmental NGOs, watchdog groups, and community citizens into the strategic planning process to advance the company as a sustainable value creator.

Three hundred people came together for three full days, and one goal was to come away with actual prototypes of new products and "green design" busi-

---

5 See Boland, R., & Collopy, F. (2004). *Managing as designing*. Palo Alto, CA: Stanford University Press.

6 For a good, simple overview of IDEOS brainstormer and rapid prototyping methods see Nussbaum, B. (2004, May 17). The power of design. Business Week. Also see the IDEO Web site at http://www.ideo.com.

7 Hart, S. (2005). *Capitalism at the crossroads*. Upper Saddle River, NJ: Pearson Education, Inc.

8 Elkington, J. (1998). *Cannibals with forks*. Gabriola Island, BC: New Society Publishing.

ness opportunities that would allow the organization to take account of the "entire life cycle from the sourcing of raw materials and energy from the earth to the reuse, remanufacture, or return of materials to the earth." In her opening talk at the AI Summit, the chief financial officer of the company spoke to the tremendous opportunity:

> *Not since the days of the Great Depression has there been such a severe decline of public trust in business and in our economic system—nor has there been a better opportunity to build a new era of business-led excellence and leadership in our industry and beyond. We believe that doing good and doing well go hand in hand and that economic prosperity, environmental stewardship, and empowerment of people can, in an integrated way, become a source of innovation and competitive advantage for the long term.*

As you will see in the *Fairmount Minerals Sustainable Development AI Summit Participant's Workbook*, the *Design* phase was broken down into two parts. Following the *Dream* phase, "opportunity areas" were identified and people were asked to vote with their feet by moving to the opportunity area named on flip charts located around the room. Opportunity areas, unlike many OD summits, were focused largely on new product opportunities (socially responsible and green design). For example, one dream was to create a new business using recycled or "spent" sand; another dream was to create a low-cost sand filter product that could be used to purify contaminated drinking water in parts of the world where billions of people survive on less than $2 per day and where many childhood diseases and deaths could be averted with clean water.

In each case, the goal was to come out of the summit with more than an aspiration statement or possibility proposition and action plan for creating something later; indeed, the goal was to prototype and model the product design on the spot—even in the case of the group that was working on a less tangible piece. (They were working on a draft of the corporate sustainability principles or "constitutional beliefs," as in "We hold these truths to be self-evident.") This group was asked to create a prototype of the new corporate principles, complete with symbolism and the visual effects of the complete packaging of the principles.

Can you imagine 300 people designing new sustainable, green products—progressing from discovery of strengths and dreams to actual market opportunities and product designing? After the focus or "possibility proposition" was created, Part One of the design session involved a "deep dive brainstormer" process, an intense idea-generating session (with sticky notes going up on large blank walls). The following IDEO tips were included:

- Defer judgment.
- Encourage wild ideas.
- Be visual.
- Go for quantity.
- Hold one conversation at a time.

It was exciting to see the "hot teams" and the energy, with each opportunity group averaging more than 150 ideas in the hour-long brainstormer session.

Part Two of the design phase included a five-hour "rapid prototyping" session. Here the best of the best of the brainstormer ideas were selected for mock-ups to be brought into visual existence as 3-D models, storyboards, or skits of the emerging products or processes. The idea is that once a person starts drawing or making things, he or she opens up new possibilities of discovery, like trial balloons. Effective, rapidly created prototypes also do something more: they persuade and they help move the ball forward for real-life experimentation. In that sense, they provide a business edge, a jump start. What is going to be more effective—a five-page wordy report of a possible new sand filter for cleaning water or a cardboard mock-up of the water purifier together with a skit demonstrating its use in a part of the world where many children suffer from lack of clean water? There is something inspiringly tangible about a prototype. Ending the group meeting or summit with this kind of visual mock-up, instead of just descriptive words, gives the project added impetus.

"Takeaways" from the Summit

As a result of the three-day Fairmount Minerals Sustainable Development Summit of 2005 and the methodologies that were employed, the following "takeaways" emerged:

- More than 850 stakeholders identified and surveyed on the subject of sustainability
- Increased emphasis on reclamation projects in areas where Fairmount was mining resources, resulting in, for instance, efforts to increase diversity of flora and fauna in those areas
- Initiatives toward the recovery, recycling, and reuse of resources utilized in the mining process, including use of biodiesel fuels and the "cradle-to-cradle" use of natural resources such as "spent" sand
- Increased philanthropic sponsorship of community development programs with school districts and Habitat for Humanity, for example
- Development of a low-cost sand and water filter (producing clean drinking water), embodying "doing good and doing well"
- An overall increased awareness of the importance of sustainable development throughout the company and with stakeholders

For more information on this initiative in addition to quotations from the company officials and employees/stakeholders involved, go to http://media.mindgrabmedia.com/fairmount/Minerals/Fairmount%20Minerals.html.

Summary

You are learning that the *Design* phase can be taken beyond organizational design work into the innovative design of new products and other tangible prototypes for action. Another related point is instilling the spirit of design—the design attitude—into the establishment of the new organization, which is what AI is all about. AI is not a process that throws all of its attention and energy at yesterday's problematic patterns. It is a process of creating positive change, which, in turn, is about establishing the "new"—that is, focusing on what people want instead of what they don't want. That is also what design is and why change, in this approach, can be so much fun and so easy to facilitate.

The following Case Clippings illustrate the more commonly used foundational and fundamental ways of carrying out the *Design* phase within the traditional AI framework. At the same time, you are encouraged to consider investigating and applying some of the new design options presented previously.

Case Clippings: Tendercare

This AI project was designed and adapted to discover the positive core of one of Tendercare, Inc.'s assisted-living centers to enable the staff to focus on projects, process improvements, and rewards that were aligned to increase the residents' occupancy (census).[9] At the same time, it was designed to build a team spirit, thereby creating a better environment for the residents and staff.

Since 1990, Tendercare, Inc., has become Michigan's largest provider of long-term care services. It has 39 health centers located throughout the state and more than 3,400 employees. In an effort to build census, the marketing department created the "+1 Census Development Campaign" and invited the center's staff and residents to participate in this project. This campaign had three primary goals:

---

9 Assisted-living organizations generate their revenue by increasing resident occupancy levels. As another company works to increase sales, long-term care providers work to increase census.

- *To educate the entire staff as to the importance of increasing occupancy and how having more residents positively impacts them on a daily basis*

- *To educate the staff as to how they can help with the census development efforts*

- *To establish a census goal and create an environment of energy and excitement toward the center's census goal*

An AI intervention was designed and combined with the "+1 Census Development Campaign" to enhance the education and participation of the staff, while identifying and sustaining the positive core of the center.

Four topics were selected as the focus of this project: Provider of Choice, Resident Loyalty (stated earlier in this chapter), The Excellent Team, and Appreciation. The other three possibility statements created by the Core Care Team with the input of the entire staff and residents were as follows:

Provider of Choice

We are the provider of choice because we have a high-quality, trained, experienced, and caring staff to meet the needs of our residents. We create a positive culture that radiates energy and life through a superior dining experience and activities that encourage participation and increase the quality of our residents' lives. We offer a fun, clean, and friendly community that caters to the individual's needs.

The Exceptional Team

We are proud to be an exceptional team. Our team is driven by our commitment and ability to communicate with those we are privileged to work with and care for.

Our respect for each other is a value that is carried to every aspect of service delivery. Through appreciation, we build strong connections that result in a fun, high-energy work environment that supports friendship and loyalty to our Wayne Seniors community.

Appreciation

At Wayne Seniors, EVERYONE is appreciated. We take the time to make our residents, families, staff, and community feel welcome. We listen, care for, and support each other by:

- Greeting each other.
- Remembering special moments.
- Celebrating holidays.
- Getting to know residents.
- Sending gifts and cards.
- Sharing time.
- Valuing daily contributions.
- Recognizing accomplishments.
- Seeking out the best in one another.
- Asking if anyone needs help.
- Giving heartfelt thank-yous.
- Taking care of our environment.

Appreciation is a gift we give each other every day.

Outcomes of the Tendercare Project

The center used these possibility statements as guiding philosophies to make the center the provider of choice by building an excellent team through appreciation and development of resident loyalty, thereby creating a better environment for the residents and staff. The Case Clippings for this initiative include:

- *Project Proposal*
- *Interview Guide and Summary Sheet*
- *Project Summary*
- *Sample Master Wish List*
- *Agenda: AI Discovery and Dream*
- *AI: Discovery and Dream Minutes*
- *Agenda: AI Design and Destiny*
- *AI: Dream and Design Minutes*

The AI approach was favorably received by the staff and residents, and it yielded highly insightful information about how the staff related to each other and to the residents and how the residents related to each other. Later four managers at Tendercare remarked how drastically the culture had changed. They observed that the culture had gone from negative to very hopeful and positive in a matter of weeks. Three individuals who were reported to be skeptical and to have the most negative of the employees' attitudes shifted during their AI interviews and offered excellent ideas for improvement. They felt respected and hopeful that someone would care enough to ask what they thought could happen to turn this facility around.

The Master Wish List became an action plan that management and employees used to implement the ideas for improving the overall quality of work life and living conditions. The positive core of the staff lies within the genuine compassion and sincere caring for the residents and for each other.

The center experienced several noticeable outcomes. First, within a six-week period, the center experienced an increase in census of 12%. Second, monthly in-service meetings for the staff were reinstated. Third, the staff worked with management to develop an ongoing marketing action plan. Six months after the intervention took place, the staff voted to remove the union that had represented them to management for many years. Finally, and in perhaps the most significant demonstration of the new spirit of cooperation, 18 months after the AI intervention, government reimbursement for this type of health center changed—making it no longer financially profitable to operate this facility. Management and staff again used the AI principles and approach to develop a closing plan that included the relocation of all residents and the placement of the staff at other centers. Not one employee left the facility during this time to pursue outside employment interests until the residents were safely placed somewhere else. To this day, the company considers the closing of the center to be a model of cooperation, participation, and efficiency.

The following outcomes resulted from the *Design* phase:
- Creation of the social-technical architecture
- Crafting of the possibility propositions
- Dream becoming a reality in these statements

The original Project Proposal is outlined in the following section.

Project Proposal

Tendercare Assisted Living
"Discovering the Positive Core to Best Achieve Census Growth"

Purpose and Overview
Our vision is "to be the provider of choice for both our residents and our staff." Our team is committed to our residents and to each other.
    "Caring people, caring for people"

The "+1 Census Development Campaign" is a six-week census development program designed to accomplish three goals. The first goal is to educate the entire staff as to the importance of census and the way it impacts them on a daily basis. The second goal of the campaign is to educate the staff on how they can help with the census development efforts. The third goal is to create an environment of energy and excitement toward the center's census goal. It is expected that by creating this air of enthusiasm, teamwork, and synergy and by educating the staff as to the importance of census and the way they can help increase the center's census, that census (and revenue) goals will be greatly enhanced.

This campaign will be combined and enhanced by integrating it within an Appreciative Inquiry (AI) intervention. The project will consist of completing an AI interview at the assisted-living center to identify and sustain the positive core of the center. This positive core will help to achieve census growth while placing the resident in the center of the circle of quality care. This change process will incorporate the entire staff. The results of the AI intervention will be specific actions targeting elements that help increase census.

Identifying these attributes will enable the staff to focus on projects, process improvements, and rewards that are aligned to increase census while building a team spirit.

Expected outcomes include:
- An increase in average daily census of 8 (from 92 to 100).
- Qualitative findings that articulate elements of the positive core.
- Identification of specific tactics that will enhance teamwork and cooperation.

Evaluation

It is anticipated that the AI process will generate positive feedback and goodwill as measured by the Interview Guide. Other evaluation measurements will include turnover levels, customer satisfaction scores, and identification of what is working well within the center, as well as strategies designed to repeat and amplify success.

Primary Participants
Champions—Census Care Team (CCT):
- Vice President of Marketing
- Marketing Development Consultant
- Administrator
- Director of Care

- Community Relations Representative
- Dietary Manager
- Activities Coordinator
- AI Coordinator and AI Facilitator
- Direct Care Staff (5)
- MBA Student Interns (2)

Project Scope

The scope of this project is to learn about and use an AI process to discover and sustain the qualitative elements of the positive core, identify specific tactics that will enhance teamwork, and report findings to all participants for the purpose of increasing the daily average census. A series of meetings to train a core team of participants on the AI techniques will be conducted, as will interviews and additional meetings to collect, theme, analyze, and interpret the data sets (or outcomes) of the interviews. The final deliverable will be a report of the key findings and outcomes of this project.

The AI process will be integrated with the "+1 Census Development Campaign." It will begin with the *Discovery* phase to learn about the positive core of the group. The following key topic issues/themes will be addressed:

- Provider of Choice—"Best in Care"
- Resident Loyalty
- The Exceptional Team: Working and Winning Together
- Appreciation

An AI Interview Guide will be designed around these core topics, and each team member will be interviewed to help determine the positive care core and identify what is most valued. The *Dream* phase begins with a visioning dialogue among the team members to identify the key themes. As a team, we will create images of the future, relating to what everyone wants and requires.

These themes will be designed into possibility statements based on the center's organizational architecture. The final phase will be creating the Destiny in the form of census action plans to implement these design elements to ensure continued success of the campaign. In addition, the Census Care Team (CCT) will learn about a change process called AI to use throughout their work at the center.

Interview Guide and Summary Sheet

Tendercare Assisted Living
Discovering the Positive Core to Best Build Census
Interview Guide

Thank you for participating in this interview. I am an interviewer for "Discovering the Positive Core" in our "+1 Census Development Campaign." We will be asking questions to learn more about why we choose to work here and why residents choose to live here. We want to learn about the positive core of our people and identify ways to increase the positive aspects of the work life.

Staff and residents will be interviewed to collect the "best-case" stories on which to build the future. The goal is to move forward in achieving the vision "to be the provider of choice for both staff and residents." Your input will be an important contribution to generate meaningful ideas and actions.

Many times in interviews, we ask questions about why things don't work well. This time we are going to approach things from a different angle. We are going to find out about your experiences of success at Tendercare so we can build on those experiences.

We will interview everyone who works and lives here. When the interviews are complete, everyone's input will be reviewed to identify the positive core that makes us unique. With those qualities as a foundation, we will create specific steps to build on our strengths and to build census.

The conversation will take an hour or so. I'm going to take notes as we talk. During our interview, we will be exploring your experiences in several areas:

- Provider of Choice—Best in Care
- Resident Loyalty
- The Exceptional Team—Working and Winning Together
- Appreciation

Shall we begin?

Introduction: The Privilege of Caring

Our profession is based on caring with compassion and understanding. The privilege to participate in the aging and healing relationship is what creates and maintains the passion for healthcare providers. We would like to acknowledge that passion and explore with you how to acknowledge and develop this in all of the people who work here.

First, I would like to know what attracted you to our center? What were your initial excitements and impressions when you joined this center?

Can you recall a high point when you felt most alive, most involved about your work at the center? What made it exciting? Who was involved? Please tell me the story.

- What were your hopes and dreams when you chose to work here?
- What is it about caring for others today that keeps you involved?

Before we get into our interview topics today, can you tell me what is it that you value about yourself, the nature of your work, and the center?

Topic 1: Provider of Choice

Provider of choice means that we are the place where residents want to live and employees want to work. We can be the provider of choice by identifying and nurturing the "best-in-class" qualities within our departments and job responsibilities.

The provider of choice means that we demonstrate levels of caring and excellence that are beyond the reach of other "good" assisted-living centers. It consists of the way we need to do things to allow us to accomplish exceptional results, along with high levels of care and employee satisfaction.

Please tell me what it is about you and the way you do your job that's "best in class"? What effect do those skills or behaviors have on you and your sense of belonging to the team? What effect do they have on your coworkers and the residents?

Topic 2: Resident Loyalty

Today's best companies create and maintain exceptional levels of customer loyalty. Loyal customers are great customers. They provide information, which, in time, helps us give them what they need. They share great ideas. They invite new customers.

Resident loyalty is something we must earn. We can earn it by listening to what our residents and their families or referral sources tell us they want. If possible, we can exceed our residents' expectations by treating them with genuine respect and care and by creatively anticipating ways we can provide the services they want more of in order to be happy, safe, and cared for.

By earning resident loyalty, we build ourselves a caring, competitive edge that puts each of us in a position of being the provider of choice for our residents.

1. Think of a time when you were a very loyal customer (to a large organization or, for example, to a neighborhood babysitter).
   • What were the most significant things this company or person did to earn your loyalty in the first place?
   • How did this company or person learn about what was important to you? How did this company or person stay current with what you needed?
   • Describe a time when this loyalty was tested. What did your "provider" do to keep you as a loyal customer and, if necessary, rebuild the relationship?

2. Put yourself in the place of one our most loyal residents or referral sources.
   • How would this person describe us to a new resident?
   • Why would this person say he or she is so committed to our center?

3. Suppose we could choose just three things to do more of or do differently to dramatically enhance our resident loyalty. What would they be?

Topic 3: The Exceptional Team—Working and Winning Together
An exceptional team is built on individual expertise and excellent cooperation. Cooperative teamwork, clear communication, and wisdom are essential elements in delivering superior patient care.
   1. Describe a time when you participated as a team member where your expertise truly made a difference to the team.
   2. Imagine that you are working with an exceptional team. Describe the team.
   3. What do you value most about this team?

Topic 4: Appreciation
All of us want fulfillment through meaningful work. The most gratifying appreciation is that which is expressed from the heart by active communication, a kind gesture, or written words.
   1. Describe a time when you felt extremely appreciated.
   2. What is the most meaningful way your contribution is recognized and appreciated?

Excellence in Long-Term Care Award
Imagine that you are representing our center in accepting a national award for "Excellence in Care" in 2010.
    1. Describe what you admire about working here.
    2. What makes caring for our residents unique?

Three Wishes
What three wishes do you have to make our center the best place to give care and the best place to receive care?

Reflections on This Interview
In closing, I would like to ask you two questions about this interview:
    1. What did you like most about this interview?
    2. Would you be interested in conducting this interview with one of your residents?

Appreciative Interview Summary Sheet

Interviewer: _____

Interviewee: _____

Years of Experience in Caring _____

Years Employed _____

What are the best quotes that came out of this interview?

What were the best stories that came out of this interview?

What were the best wishes that you heard in your interview?

What were the best practices or specific recommendations that you heard reflected in your conversation?

What contributes to the positive core?

What do residents and staff want more of?

Length of Interview _____

Project Summary

A "+1 Census Development Campaign" kick-off meeting was held at the assisted-living center with the following three goals as its focus:

1. To educate the entire staff as to the importance of census and the way it impacts them on a daily basis
2. To educate the staff as to how they can help with the census development efforts
3. To establish a census goal and create an environment of energy and excitement toward the center's census goal

This AI project coincided with the "+1 Census Development Campaign" in an effort to build on momentum and to discover and sustain the positive core of the group to enable the staff to focus on projects, process improvements, and rewards that are aligned to increase census while building a team spirit, thereby creating a better world for our residents and staff.

Four topics were chosen as our project focus: Provider of Choice, Resident Loyalty, The Excellent Team, and Appreciation. Our main goal in using AI was to obtain constructive information as to what is working well today and to learn what we can do to improve with regard to the four focus topics.

Outcomes
The following key objectives were met:

- Learned and used AI to discover the qualitative elements of the positive core at the center
- Identified specific tactics that will enhance teamwork
- Conducted a series of meetings to train a core team of participants on AI
- Conducted interviews with the staff and residents
- Collected, themed, analyzed, and interpreted the data sets (or outcomes) of the interviews
- Reported findings to all participants for the purpose of increasing the daily average census

The initial training of AI with the core team (identified as the Census Care Team (CCT) in the proposal process) was conducted on April 29. The significant outcome of this meeting was 11 AI staff interviews and an introduction of the Discovery, Dream, Design, and Destiny concepts of AI to the CCT team.

The next meeting on May 6 discussed the common themes of the 11 interviews and provided an in-depth overview of the *Dream* and *Design* phases. The significant outcome was the development of possibility statements for the Resident Loyalty and Provider of Choice topics. At this point, each member of the CCT was given a list of staff and resident names to interview. The next two weeks were spent conducting interviews.

Method

A combination of qualitative and quantitative methods was used in the process of data collection and data interpretation. A comprehensive survey relating to the four focus topics was designed to identify attributes of as many staff and resident respondents as possible. The survey information was collected over a two-week period using a face-to-face interview format with the individuals. This method was used to build an environment of trust and openness and received very favorable feedback, as it gave each individual an opportunity to talk about what was important to him or her.

The total number of AI interviews conducted was 74 (24 staff and 50 residents). All staff and resident interviews were collected, themed, and summarized. From this information, a Master Wish List was created.

Sample Master Wish List

Master Wish List:

Wish	Ideas/Solutions	Time frame	Resource	Cost
More Activities: Give everyone a chance to do more around here. They just want to have more options and do and go places. Get out more—more activities instead of just smoking. Group activities outside. You're only as old as you feel; activities schedule keep their minds going. More outings. Have more family-oriented activities. Get staff more involved in resident activities. More field trips for the residents. Have more games. More outings. More family-oriented activities that involve the families. Should have the most awesome activities in the world. More entertainment. More outings for residents. To have more family-oriented events. More functions with residents and staff.	Exercise Program 1. Square dancing or some kind of dancing 2. Resident picnic 3. Go to a ball game 4. "Ask" program—Volunteers: recruit agencies, churches, and schools 5. Tabletop bowling 6. Vegas Night, Black Jack Night, Roulette 7. Shopping: dollar store or mall walking 8. Call day camps to have children come in, do activities at WS 9. Create Resident Recreation Committee: need buttons			
Facility: When someone walks in the front door, the facility should smell clean, look and feel cozy and inviting. Just make it a nice place for the residents and us. Pride in physical plan—building itself. More private areas.	1. Fresh flowers from weddings, churches 2. Put air-conditioning in the halls; some are very hot 3. Why isn't our bathroom as nice as their bathroom up front? Air freshener in employee's bathroom 4. What about new lockers? 5. Photographs of staff and residents in halls 6. A more comfortable place to sit outside (lawn chair) 7. Call landscape companies, funerals, flower shops to send overflow to center 8. Create a gardening club 9. Create Historical Room or Century Wall			
Appreciation: More appreciation from each other and corporate office	1. Send letters or certificates based on corporate calendar. Give facilities funds to recognize their employees (e.g., employee of the month)			
More training/communication	1. New employee orientation 2. Customer service 3. White board to communicate supplies needed			
Food: Do something with the menu; give a choice or two. Get a list of things residents like to eat.	1. Survey residents on food preferences 2. Coffee all day 3. Create Food Committee: Have residents volunteer to cook their specialties with the staff 4. Presentation and serving of food			

Agenda: AI Discovery and Dream

AI Discovery and Dream Meeting
9:30 a.m. – 1:30 p.m.

Facilitators: Jackie Stavros and Anne Meda
Purpose: Orient CCT to AI, plan and launch inquiry

Goals:
- Understand AI as an integral foundation of this project
- Complete AI interviews
- Explain Project Plan and Timelines

Deliverables:
- Complete the *Discovery* and *Dream* phases
- CCT group roster and role

Project Stakeholders:
- Tendercare
- Residents
- Marketing Team

Activity	Leader	Time
Introductions/purpose How we got here? Why AI?	VP Marketing	10 minutes
Agenda/roles	Jackie	15 minutes
Appreciative Interviews Mural (best stories/themes)	Jackie	1.5 hours
Discovery and Dreaming (Working lunch)	Jackie/Anne	1 hour
Report-Outs	Jackie/Anne	30 minutes
Interview Plan – Define – Rotate subgroups/refine – Need a list of employee shifts for the interviews and how to best set up interviews with the residents	Jackie/Anne	15 minutes
Review/Close	VP Marketing/Jackie	15 minutes

AI: Discovery and Dream Minutes

---

10 a.m.— Introductions: "If I owned the company, I would...."
Ideas:

- Hold classes for new employees (new employee orientation)
- Invite family of residents and family of workers to functions
- Hold monthly in-services with each department; mandatory staff meetings
- Hold an Appreciation Day
- Pay overtime
- Keep employees
- Ensure accountability among staff
- Change budget, build census, make sure residents are well cared for
- Add staff—lighten workload and provide better care
- Move into the twenty-first century and have more technology (would like to see residents using e-mail to stay in contact with family members living far away)
- Provide more social activities for employees and residents
- Build teamwork

96% full to break even

10:15 a.m. — Handout: Develop an Appreciative, Caring Environment "What do we do really well?"

Core Team—Whole-System Representation

Focus on common ground.

Interview Guide—Intro (question walk participants through the Interview Guide)

10:15 a.m. – 12:15 p.m.— Interviews

Debrief:

Fun, informative, more commonality—we're after the same thing; we need to know the person better; it's nice to be listened to.

12:15 p.m. – 12:30 p.m.— The Unconditional Positive Question
　　　　　1. Discovery ⇒ 2. Dream ⇒ 3. Design ⇒ 4. Destiny

Today we covered the *Discovery* phase wherein we interviewed each other. The next step is to dream. Based on the stories you heard in your initial interviews, select 3–5 positive topics. We will discuss them in our next meeting. We also will cover the *Design* and *Destiny* phases in our next meeting.

12:30 p.m.— "How are the rest of the folks going to be interviewed?"
- Try talking about things from the other side; for example, What works well here?
- Create a shared dialogue, stop and listen to people, create positive intent to trust each other.
- Make a difference in the attitude of people you work with; build self-esteem.
- Create a course of action—capture the rich, thick dialogue of what people say.
- During interviews, listen and TAKE GOOD NOTES!
- CCT is responsible for its interviews.

12:55 p.m.— Read first question and state the answer that was given.
Common themes:
- Tendercare cares about employees
- Culture
- Family feeling
- Elderly care and support
- Acceptance
- Rapport with residents
- Staff (care group)
- Activities
- Appreciation
- Tenure of staff
- Likes to solve problems and impart knowledge
- Likes to help seniors, especially those who don't have family
- Extended family—residents ask employees about their weekends
- Likes to listen to residents
- Likes to be treated as his or her family is treated

Focus on what is good, not on what is wrong. What will give life to your center, what should it be, what energizes you about your well-being? Next meeting is Monday, May 6, 9:30 a.m. – 2:30 p.m.

Agenda: AI Design and Destiny

AI Design and Destiny Meeting
9:30 a.m. – 2:00 p.m.

Facilitators:　Jackie Stavros and Anne Meda
Purpose:　　　Create Possibility Statements

Goals:
- To make "dream" themes a reality
- To learn how to create an appreciative learning culture

Deliverable:
- Defined Possibility Statements

Project Stakeholders:
- Staff
- Residents
- Marketing Team

Activity	Leader	Time
Welcome Back	VP Marketing	5 minutes
Explain Design Phase	Jackie	30 minutes
Theme Selection	Anne	15 minutes
Design Team Activity	Jackie/Anne	2 hours
Destiny Discussion (Working lunch)	Jackie	1 hour
Report-outs	Jackie/Anne	30 minutes
Review/Close	VP Marketing/Jackie	10 minutes

AI: Dream and Design Minutes

9:40 a.m.— Debrief from last week's meeting

+1 Blitz went very well, heard nothing negative, made a good connection; eight people got pins that day. Picnic appears popular. Hard to choose a good time that people will attend. Just purchased a grill, can make a lunch for employees. Did you notice/get feedback from last week?

Nothing in particular, other meetings were scheduled all week, ratifying contract today. Marketing consultant is getting together with group on Thursday to brainstorm, has received great ideas. The attention from corporate has been great. Have always felt neglected; impressed to meet upper management.

9:48 a.m.— Question posed to the group by VP Marketing: If you had one superpower, what would it be?

BC: Photographic memory
BS: The ability to mind-read and know what other people are thinking
DC: Five minutes to ponder the impact of the decision you just made (see into the future)
LJ: The ability to see into the future
TF: Time travel—observe and get actual/real perspective
TS: Wants a magic wand
JP: Wants super energy
JS: The power to be in two places at the same time
AM: Wisdom
PS: The ability to control other people's minds
MH: To also be in two places at the same time
FG: To have perfect employees
JH: To control time: stop and have enough time to do everything and then start time back up again

9:54 a.m.— Agenda overview

Handed out schedule of all interviewers/interviewees. Everyone is to call Terry or Mabel to obtain information about assigned interviewee's schedule and availability.

Shift hours run: 7 a.m. – 3 p.m., days
3 p.m. – 11 p.m., afternoons
11 p.m. – 7 a.m., midnights

Copies of the Staff and Resident Interview Guide will be provided, and a master copy of both was given to Tony.

10 a.m.— Handed out meeting notes from 4/29 meeting
Reviewed notes

A table of "wish list" items will be created and quantified so we can see each wished-for item and the number of times it was mentioned in the interviews.

DESIGN PHASE
A handout was given to the group. We are trying to do a positive revolution of change. There are things we can do now that do not cost money. When we hit census, a $200 census incentive will be added to the monthly budget. When we exceed census, we will be able to do more things. Looking at the data, (JS) came up with eight things—four can be implemented next week, and four will need help.

DISCOVERY
Appreciating—critical to people. We have chosen four topics that we discovered and turned into possibility statements. Take an idea and turn it into a possibility statement. The four topics are as follows:
1. Resident Loyalty
2. Provider of Choice
3. The Exception Team—Teamwork
4. Appreciation

Making everyone understood—take time to be an active listener.

Design ⇒ What should be the ideal? Construct possibilities.

Destiny ⇒ After we leave, how do you continue to keep this going? Cycle—every six months conduct another discovery/inquiry, find consensus.

Getting to transformational topics:

Ideas: Extra care, shoe untied, customer service: What specifically is this? Define and demonstrate. How do you change mind-set? Develop happier employees (via appreciation programs) to change culture. By doing things for the employees, leading by example. Change starts one step at a time. Have policy for employees to use.

10:30 a.m.— Two ways to deal with things (after we finish):

1. Focus on problem
2. Ask what possibilities exist that we haven't thought about yet. The smallest change makes the biggest impact.

Four Fundamental Questions (from handout):

Discover optimal margins—census.

DESIGN PHASE
The social-technological architecture:

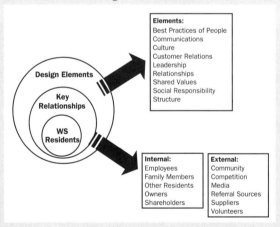

Ingredients: The themes from the interviews.

Key Relationships—Who's affected? How does it affect the center?

You design what you want and then make it happen in *Destiny* phase, creating a grand possibility statement.

Department heads are part of the core team, must extend to a larger group and get rid of the "us versus them."

**Idea: Stress Call: pick up page—"meet me in the dining room," play the Hustle.

11:15 a.m. – Noon— Theme Exercise

Topic: Provider of Choice

As a group we:
1. Identified the inner circle: family, residents, responsible party (guardian, lawyer, and so on), and staff. This is whom we are providing care for.

2. Identified the next outer circle: Key Relationships: community, corporate office, referral sources, FIA and hospitals, transportation (taxis, bus pickups), and volunteers.

3. Identified outer circle components: Elements that affect the center and being a provider of choice: training (i.e., CPR, new-employee orientation, consistent care), culture, leadership, strategy (continuous), energy/life, activities, stability, and so on.

What makes our center the provider of choice? What is it that people would say makes us the best provider of care? What does our "ideal" center consist of?

We brainstormed the following list to answer the last question. Each team member got to vote for the four top elements on the list that he or she thought most significantly impacted the center's ability to become the provider of choice. The chart illustrates the number of votes each item received. (Items in bold were the top picks.)

Ideal Environment	Team Members				
Physical Plant					
Clean	•	•	•		
Fun	•	•	•	•	
Friendly	•				
Services (i.e., medical, nonmedical)	•				
Security/Comfort	•				
Delicious food	•	•	•		
Highly Trained Staff	•	•	•	•	•
Empathetic Staff					
Mentor System					
Concierge/Amenities (i.e., massage therapy, cable TV, and so on)	•				
Energy/Life	•				
Activities	•	•			

We also brainstormed what makes the "ideal" food environment so great. We came up with the following:

- Taste
- Quality and quantity
- Variety and choice
- Presentation
- Ambience/atmosphere
- Special meals/themes
- Salad bar

We then constructed the possibility statement using the elements that were the most frequently selected.

Provider of Choice Possibility Statement:
. . . We are the provider of choice because we have a high-quality, trained, experienced, and caring staff to meet the needs of our residents. We create a positive culture that radiates energy and life through a superior dining experience and activities that encourage participation and increase the quality of our residents' lives. We offer a fun, clean, and friendly community that caters to the individual's needs . . .

Topic: Resident Loyalty
- Identified the inner circle: Wayne Seniors residents
- Identified the components of the next outer circle: Key Relationships: referral sources, guardians, families, staff (food), volunteers, and RA
- Identified the outer circle components: social responsibility, follow-up, follow-through, culture, systems, customer relations, education, and community

The following was the result of a brainstorm session on the definition of resident loyalty: What makes a resident loyal?

Resident Loyalty:
- Relation building, show loyalty to family members, referrals
- Consistency—same-grade service (temp/resident), what? Follow-up and through
- Genuine vested interest, how? Know thy resident, know what is important (by listening)
- Compassion—staff residents (extended family)
- Knowledge—(staff), why? In what they do (e.g., tie shoe, mash potatoes); level of service
- Finance—(trust), at ease; What are we doing with their money? Budgeting, amenities, balance checkbooks, manage money, keep independence; demonstrate by staff being members
- Physical plant

Common Parts among the Group
- Trust
- Compassion
- Interest
- Knowledge
- Dedication
- Listening
- Relationships (effective)
- Respect

Each member of the group wrote an individual possibility statement based on the definition brainstorm elements of resident loyalty. The combined possibility statement is as follows:

Resident Loyalty Possibility Statement:

At Wayne Seniors, residents are our lifeline. We maintain this lifeline by building relationships with our residents and their families to ensure a caring, consistent, and positive living experience.

We always strive to nurture relationships by creating an environment of listening, understanding, and trust.

Residents trust us with their lives—a responsibility we hold sacred. We earn trust through unwavering commitment to superior care, tempered with compassion and respect.

To provide superior care, we provide knowledge to residents, staff, and families to ensure consistent and compassionate service delivery.

With dedication to these ideals, Wayne Center for Seniors nurtures resident loyalty, thereby effectively serving the community.

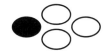

7

Destiny:
What Will Be?

"Allow yourself to dream and you will discover that destiny is yours to design."

—Jackie Stavros

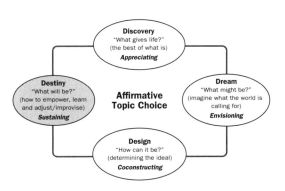

The final phase of the 4-D Cycle is known as *Destiny* (sometimes called Delivery). The goal of the *Destiny* phase is to ensure that the dream can be realized. The AI perspective looks at the role of improvisation in building appreciative management into the fabric of organizational culture. The design team publicly declares intended actions and asks for organization-wide support from every level. Self-selected groups plan the next steps for institutionalization and continued vitality. This is where the dream becomes reality.

Like the other phases, *Destiny* is systematic in terms of accommodating and continuing dialogue. Provocative propositions can be revised and updated. Additional AI interviewing may take place with new members in the organization and/or new questions posed for existing members.

The *Destiny* phase represents the conclusion of the *Discovery*, *Dream*, and *Design* phases and the beginning of the evolving creation of an "appreciative learning culture." This chapter explores both aspects of the *Destiny* phase:
- Aligning the actual organization with the provocative propositions created in the Design phase
- Building AI learning competencies into the culture

The techniques associated with the final phase of the 4-D Cycle spring from self-organized groups. They often resemble Open Space processes. Individuals and small groups self-organize to implement the Design statements (provocative propositions). This approach involves neither prioritization of needs nor an imposed sequence of concerns. Instead, people who are passionate about implementing a particular aspect of the design step forward and join with like-spirited collaborators. It is a time of continuous organizational learning, adjustment, and improvisation.

As a result of the extensive involvement of large numbers of people in the *Discovery*, *Dream*, and *Design* phases, collective focus is centered on actions to be taken. The often massive number of people engaged in interviews, large-group meetings, and critical decision making help participants get a strong sense of what the organization is about and how they can contribute to the future through their personal actions. It is a time of continuous innovation and inquiry, which continues on to the implementation stage within the newly created social architecture.

The chapter begins with the rationale of this phase's name change—from *Delivery* to *Destiny*. Following this, a summarization of Frank Barrett's material on appreciative learning cultures helps organizations and change leaders learn how to build AI-based learning competencies. The chapter also highlights GTE in its Destiny phase and concludes with *Destiny*-phase Case Clippings from the Hunter Douglas story. Excerpts from this study illustrate the outcomes that were experienced upon completion of the initial *Destiny* phase of inquiry and illustrate how the organization continues to use AI concepts and applications ten years later. The connections between the four phases, along with the outcomes that such an approach can deliver, are quite apparent and are sustainable over time.

Rethinking Destiny

In the early years of AI work, the fourth *D* was called *Delivery*. This phase emphasizes planning for continuous learning, adjustment, and improvisation in the service of shared ideals. It was viewed as a time for action planning, developing implementation strategies, and dealing with conventional challenges of sustainability. But the word *delivery* did not go far enough. It did not convey the sense of liberation that AI practitioners were experiencing. A perfect example is the well-documented hotel case *The Medic Inn*, where an organization transformed itself from a one-star to a four-star hotel by using AI and literally putting a moratorium on all the traditional problem-solving efforts it had been using.

AI practitioners soon discovered that momentum for change and long-term sustainability increased as traditional "delivery" ideas of action planning, monitoring progress, and building implementation strategies were abandoned. In several of the most exciting cases, the substitution was to focus on giving AI away to everyone and then stepping back.

The GTE (now Verizon) story told in the Introduction of this handbook (refer to the AI Insight) is still unfolding. It shows that organizational change needs to look more like an inspired movement than a neatly packaged or engineered product. Dan Young, the head of organizational development at GTE, and his colleagues Maureen Garrison and Jean Moore call it "organizing for change from the grassroots to the frontline." It can be considered the path of positive protest or a strategy for positive subversion. Whatever it is called, it is virtually unstoppable once it is up and running.

GTE calls it the Positive Change Network (PCN). GTE trained 2,000 people in AI so anyone could use it anywhere in the organization to launch a positive change initiative. One especially dramatic moment gives the sense of improvisation.[1]

> The headline article in GTE Together described what was spreading as a grassroots movement to build the new GTE. Initiated as a pilot training to see what would happen if the tools and theories of Appreciative Inquiry were made available to frontline employees, things started taking off. All of a sudden, without any

---

1 See Cooperrider, D., & Whitney, D. (2000). *Collaborating for change: Appreciative inquiry.* San Francisco: Berrett-Koehler.

permission, frontline employees are launching interview studies into positive topics like innovation, inspired leadership, revolutionary customer responsiveness, labor-management partnerships, and "fun." Fresh out of a training session on AI, one employee, for example, does 200 interviews into the positive core of a major call center. Who is going to say "no" to a complimentary request like, "Would you help me out? I'm really trying to find out more about the best innovations developing in your area, and I see you as someone who could really give me new insight into creating settings where innovation can happen. It is part of my leadership development. Do you have time for an interview? I would be glad to share my learnings with you later!"

Soon the topics are finding their way into meetings, corridor conversations, and senior planning sessions. In other words the questions, enthusiastically received, are changing corporate attention, language, agendas, and learnings. Many start brainstorming applications for AI. Lists are endless. Ever done focus groups with the 100% satisfied customer? How about changing call center measures? What would happen if we replaced the entire deficit measures with equally powerful measures of the positive? How can we revitalize the TQM groups, demoralized by one fishbone analysis after another? What would happen if we augmented variance analysis with depth studies that help people to dream and define the very visions of quality standards? How about a star stories program to generate a narrative-rich environment where customers are asked to share stories of encounters with exceptional employees? How about a gathering with senior executives so we can celebrate our learnings with them, share with them how seeing the positive has changed our work and family lives, and even recruit them to join the PCN?

The pilot had acquired a momentum all its own. The immediate response, an avalanche of requests for participation, confirmed that large numbers of people at GTE were ready to be called to the task of positive change. To grow the network by the hundreds, even thousands, GTE decided to do a ten-region training session, all linked and downloaded by satellite conferencing. A successful pilot of three sites confirmed that the same kind of energy and response could happen through distance technologies. Quite suddenly, the power of a thousand-person network caught people's attention. Very rapidly, by connecting and consistently noticing breakthroughs, new patterns of organizing could become commonplace knowledge. Changes could happen not by organized confrontation, diagnosis, burning platforms, or piecemeal reform, but through irresistibly vibrant and real visions. PCN was becoming a lightning rod for energy and enthusiasm that was previously underestimated.

Then the unions raised questions. There were serious concerns, including the fact that they were not consulted in the early stages. The employees were told the initiative was over. There was to be a meeting of the unions and GTE at the Federal Mediation Offices in Washington, DC, to put the whole thing to rest.

But at the meeting, leaders from both groups recognized something fresh and unique about AI. They agreed to bring 200 union leaders together for a two-day introduction. Their purpose was to evaluate AI to see if it should have any place in GTE's future. A month later as the session began, the room was full of tension and overt hostility. During the course of the two-day session, the group of 250 went from polarized hostility to appreciative dialogue. Then there was the moment of decision. Thirty tables of eight were instructed to evaluate the ideas and cast a vote as a group: "Yes, we endorse moving forward with AI" or "No, we withhold endorsement." For 30 minutes the groups deliberated. Tensions were high. The vote was called:

> Table 1, how do you vote? The response was ready: We vote 100% for moving forward with AI and believe this is a historic opportunity for the whole organization.
>
> Then the next table: We vote 100% with a caveat that every person at GTE have the opportunity to get the AI training and that all projects going forward be done in partnership with the unions and the company.

On and on the vote went. Thirty tables spoke. Then thirty tables voted. Every one voted to move forward. The outcome was stunning. Eight months later AI was combined with the "conflictive partnership" model of the Federal Mediation Services at the kickoff session announcing a new era of partnership. The historic Statement of Partnership stated:

> The company and the unions realize that traditional adversarial labor-management relations must change in order to adapt to the new global telecommunications marketplace. It is difficult to move to cooperation in one quantum leap. However, the company and the unions have agreed to move in a new direction. This new direction emphasizes partnership.

This story boldly illustrates how AI can accelerate the nonlinear interaction of organizational breakthroughs. Putting historic, positive traditions together with strengths creates a "convergence zone," facilitating the collective repatterning of human systems. At some point, apparently minor positive discoveries connect in an accelerating manner. Suddenly, quantum change, a jump from one state to the next that cannot be achieved through incremental change alone, becomes possible.

The *Destiny* phase of AI suggests what is needed: the networklike structures that liberate not only the daily search into qualities and elements of an organization's positive core but also the establishment of a convergence zone for people to empower one another to connect, cooperate, and cocreate. Changes never thought possible are suddenly and democratically mobilized when people constructively appropriate the power of the positive core and simply "let go" of accounts of the negative.

Creating Appreciative Learning Cultures

An important task for an organizational leader is to create cultures in which members can explore, experiment, extend capabilities, improvise, and anticipate customers' unspoken needs. Frank Barrett has called such cultures **appreciative learning cultures**.

Organizations need to innovate and strive to create new ideas and new products. The push for innovation requires a different kind of learning, one that goes beyond adapting to challenges and solving problems. Instead, such learning focuses on imagining possibilities and on generating new ways of looking at the world. Innovation requires willingness to think outside the box. It involves an appreciative approach, an ability to see radical possibilities, and a willingness to go beyond the boundaries of problems.

The challenge in the *Destiny* phase is to do just that. Whether trying to create a radically new, innovative organization or tweaking an already well-run organization, appreciative learning cultures nurture innovative thinking by creating a positive focus, a sense of meaning, and systems that encourage collaboration.

To review: AI begins with the assumption that something in the organization is working well. When engaged in appreciative learning, managers attempt to discover, describe, and explain those exceptional moments in which the system functioned well, those moments when members were highly motivated and their competencies and skills activated. The art of appreciation is the art of discovering and valuing those things that give life to the organization, of identifying what works well in the current organization. This positive approach creates what Peter Senge calls "generative conversations" as the dialogue expands from valuing the best of "what is" to envisioning "what might be." While problem solving emphasizes a dispassionate separation between observer and observed, appreciation is a passionate, absorbing endeavor. Appreciation involves the investment of emotional and cognitive energy to create a positive image of a desired future.

Likewise, appreciative learning cultures accentuate the successes of the past, evoke images of possible futures, and create a spirit of ongoing inquiry that empowers members to new levels of activity.

Destiny: An Improvisational Capacity

AI has achieved remarkable results in the areas of productivity improvement, efficiency, and performance. However, the "goal" of the process is to create highly improvisational organizations. These are organizations that, according to Frank Barrett, demonstrate consistent strength in four key kinds of competence: affirmative, expansive, generative, and collaborative.[2] In the end, these four areas of competence are expanded through ongoing application of the skills applied during *Discovery, Dream, Design*, and *Destiny*.

- *Affirmative Competence.* The organization draws on the human capacity to appreciate positive possibilities by selectively focusing on current and past strengths, successes, and potentials. In nurturing affirmative competence, leaders of a high-performing organization celebrate members' achievements, directing attention to members' strengths as the source of the organization's vitality.
- *Expansive Competence.* The organization challenges habits and conventional practices, provoking members to experiment in the margins. It makes expansive promises that challenge members to stretch in new directions, and it evokes a set of higher values and ideals that inspire members to passionate engagement. High-performing organizations create a vision that challenges members by encouraging them to go beyond familiar ways of thinking; these organizations provoke members to stretch beyond what have seemed to be reasonable limits.
- *Generative Competence.* The organization constructs integrative systems that allow members to see the results of their actions, to recognize that they are making a meaningful contribution, and to experience a sense of progress. High-performing organizations inspire members' best efforts. These systems include elaborate and timely feedback so mem-

---

2 Refer to Barrett, F. (1998). Creativity and improvisation in jazz and organizations: Implications for organizational learning. *Organization Science*, 9(5), 605–622.

bers sense that they are contributing to a meaningful purpose. In particular, it is important for people to experience progress, to see that their day-to-day tasks make a difference. When members perceive that their efforts are contributing toward a desired goal, they are more likely to feel a sense of hope and empowerment.

- *Collaborative Competence.* The organization creates forums in which members engage in ongoing dialogue and exchange diverse perspectives to transform systems. Collaborative systems that allow for dialogue promote the articulation of multiple perspectives and encourage continuous, active debate. The high-performing organization creates the environment that fosters participation and highly committed work arrangements.

Injecting appreciation and inquiry into the way work is completed requires some of the same "design elements" that were central to the original crafting of provocative propositions. High-impact systems into which AI can be integrated can make this way of working "everyday and ordinary" rather than a distinct cultural or change program that fades away. Table 7.1 identifies areas in which AI and the 4-D Cycle can be integrated into business operations.

Table 7.1 Areas for Integrating AI into Business Operations

Organization Design	Employee Satisfaction	Process Improvement	Learning & Development	Measure-ment	Customer Satisfaction	Planning
Communication Architecture	Employee Orientation	Work Process Redesign	Supervisory Development	Performance Management	Focus Groups & Surveys	Strategic
Joint Ventures	Staffing & Development	Continuous Quality Improvement	Leadership & Management Development	Metric Standards	Customer Feedback	Business
Strategic Alliances	Coaching	Benchmarking	Team Development	Reward & Recognition	Supplier Feedback Systems	Operations
	Diversity Initiatives	Innovations	Training	Surveys	Public Relations	Marketing

There is no one best way to carry out the *Destiny* phase. Each organization has chosen a different approach to implementing and sustaining the design from the dream that it discovered. One example is still unfolding in the *Destiny* phase of the Hunter Douglas story. In 1993, Hunter Douglas Window Fashions Division (HDWFD) embarked on a whole-system AI process. Branded "Focus 2000," the purpose of the process was to enhance employee engagement in creating the future of the organization. In addition, it aimed to build leadership bench strength needed for the fast-growing, highly successful organization. The entire workforce of 950 people was involved in discovering best practices and creating the future. They interviewed employees, customers, vendors, and members of their local community. They hosted a 100-person AI Summit. From the *Design* to *Destiny* phase of this event, 14 action teams were launched as "innovation teams" to coconstruct their future. The results were **transformative** for the organization and its employees.

The following Case Clipping is a snapshot of the Hunter Douglas sustained and continuous applications of AI—delivering its destiny. This is a seminal case that undeniably demonstrates the power of AI to mobilize a system in an ongoing process of sustainable positive change. Many years after the company's original exposure to AI, Hunter Douglas's stakeholders recognize and continue to acknowledge its "unique" approach to organizing—that it has at its foundation the affirmative, relational, and inspirational core of the AI 4-D Cycle. Hunter Douglas's extraordinary ten-year commitment to the AI philosophy is described in depth in the *The Power of Appreciative Inquiry* (Berrett-Koehler, 2005) by Diana Whitney and Amanda Trosten-Bloom.

Case Clippings:
Hunter Douglas Window Fashions Division[3]

Hunter Douglas Window Fashions Division is the largest and most profitable division of the Hunter Douglas Group. Innovating, manufacturing, and fabricating high-end window covering products, the division experienced a ten-year period of off-the-chart growth and leadership transitions during the late eighties and early nineties, before the "growth pains" set in. On the heels of so many changes, people were suddenly challenged with a multitude of directions and conflicting priorities when attempting to define the future. Communication gaps between leadership and the general workforce, between business units, and across functions made it difficult for people to act in service of overall organizational goals. Not surprisingly, employee satisfaction scores began to drop, turnover increased, and employees felt overloaded to a level that reduced their initiative and ability to contribute.

*Hunter Douglas leaders were looking for a change, which led to the launch of an AI process they branded "Focus 2000." Targeting **whole-system culture transformation**, they designed a process where the intended outcomes were to:*

- *Create a collective vision that could engage and excite the entire organization and its stakeholders.*

---

3 Special thanks to Rick Pellet, president of Hunter Douglas Windows Fashion Division, and Mike Burns, vice president of Human Resources, for embracing AI and to Diana Sadighi, director of Human Resources, for carrying its legacy forward.

- *Re-instill a sense of creativity, flexibility, intimacy, and community throughout the organization.*
- *Enhance the skills of existing leadership and build bench strength by identifying and training future leaders.*
- *Build communication and collaboration between management and the general workforce, across business units, and between operations and support functions.*
- *Create a company culture based on values that challenged the organization and the employees to achieve higher levels of involvement, responsibility, and community.*

In the first wave of AI work (1998), more than half of the 1,000-person workforce participated in a six-month discovery that was transformational. For example, a line employee discovered a best practice in a sister business unit that he felt empowered to transport into his own organization. The practice, when adapted, eliminated the need to purchase three new fabric printing machines, which dropped $350,000 from the company bottom line. Similarly, a third-shift fabricator positively affected relationships with a group of third-shift immigrant employees and ultimately volunteered to coordinate an English as a second language (ESL) program that would enable her colleagues to gain the tools needed to access personal and professional advancement opportunities.

The Window Fashions Division's initial period of Discovery concluded with a 100-person summit involving employees, customers, suppliers, and community members. The immediate outcome of this summit was the initiation of 14 action groups, including a group that eventually created one of the most comprehensive and accessible corporate universities in Colorado. Indeed, a number of culture- and employee-focused initiatives birthed at the first Focus 2000 summit reduced turnover from 42% to 29% over a two-year period and ultimately contributed to the Window Fashions Division being named one of the top ten places to work in Denver for 2004 and in Colorado for 2006.

But Hunter Douglas leaders weren't yet satisfied. They chose to move beyond their original culture transformation objectives and apply the AI process to the business of the business. Six months after the original summit, they organized a whole-system strategic planning conference, engaging large segments of the workforce in discovering the organization's core capabilities and strategic opportunities and crafting a ten-year vision for the company's future. As a direct result of this conference, the company leveraged its core technology into a new arena, eventually spinning off a sister organization specializing in an acoustical product for commercial establishments.

And then, beginning in 2000, they combined AI with a more traditional approach to process improvement, engaging the entire workforce in quality improvement initiatives that helped fulfill the promise of one of their original provocative propositions: "Customers eagerly do business with us because we are easy to do business with." Six years later these improvement projects have increased productivity, improved product quality, dramatically reduced workplace injuries, and yielded more than $25 million dollars in cost savings and waste reduction between 1996 and 2006.

The following pages demonstrate how the 4-D Cycle unfolds by showing how a single topic (education) evolves from the initial topic selection through action. In addition, samples are provided for the Leadership and Employee Introductory meetings that demonstrate how to build whole-system commitment to an AI process from start to finish. This case study shows how affirmative topic choices led to discovery, organizational learning, dream, design, and innovative actions.

The Case Clippings include:
- *Initial Topic Selection from Concept to Design*
- *Employee Interview Guide*
- *Interview Summary Sheet*
- *Design Statements*

Initial Topic Selection: From Discovery to Destiny: AI Full Cycle

Topic Selection—Education: Given that Hunter Douglas was seeking to build the informal leadership capacities of its workforce, education was of prime interest to the 90-person topic selection team. It was selected as one of five affirmative topics.

Appreciative Interview Question: Two weeks after the selection of the topics, a ten-person subgroup finalized the interview guide and published the following question related to the topic of education.

Education: Knowledge empowers people, and people power Hunter Douglas. We each contribute to Hunter Douglas's position of market leadership through personal knowledge of our jobs and equipment, other functions in the company, our customers, our competition, and the industry.

To maintain our position as market leaders, we must continue to invest in each employee's training and education through individual coaching, challenging work assignments, cross training, tuition assistance, on- and off-site classes, and family scholarships for our children.

1. If knowledge empowers people and people power Hunter Dou-
    glas, what kind of learning opportunities would turbo-charge
    Hunter Douglas?
2. If you could learn more about our customers, our competitors, the
    industry, and all functions of our company, how would that infor-
    mation help you take ownership in your role for continued suc-
    cess at Hunter Douglas?
3. What is the best training you ever experienced? Why? How did
    it influence your development as a professional? How did it influ-
    ence the training you passed on to others?
4. Reflecting on your past and where you are today, what types of
    training have proven most beneficial to you?
5. Robert Fulghum wrote a book entitled *All I Really Need to Know I
    Learned in Kindergarten*. If this were kindergarten, what would you
    like to learn for the future?

Sense-Making: Three months and 500 interviews later, hundreds of people had responded to this and four other questions. A group of 30 people
gathered for two days of sense-making. Sticky notes were everywhere,
and conversations were energetic.

The Report: Two weeks later a written report went to press, the Inquirer
2000 Special Edition. It was a newspaper-like report distributed to the
entire workforce, including 100 people who would attend the upcoming
three-day summit.

Dream: The following excerpts from the Inquirer 2000 reflect the dreams
shared in the interview process.

HD WFD Supports People Through Training and Education

In a series of discussions, Synthesis team members exploring the topic of
education made two important discoveries:

First, Hunter Douglas employees, customers, suppliers, and community members are committed to enhancing their work performance,
career potential, and relationship with Hunter Douglas through job-relat-
ed training.

Second, and perhaps more striking, employees look to the company
to support their development as human beings. Some of the richest comments, stories, and dreams referred to people's desire for education, for

skills that will help them not only live their lives better but also become stronger on the job. Many interviewees shared a dream that HD would help educate them for higher levels of personal as well as professional success.

Those who gave details suggested classes and programs that would help them in their personal lives as well as at work. These offerings would include a wellness program on how health is essential to a good attitude and good performance. Others asked for classes in stress and money management. Still others shared dreams for access to experts in career and life counseling, including an on-campus career guidance center or counselor. They believed this resource would help people understand the steps needed to better themselves at work and at home.

Possibility Design Statement: Turn the clock forward again by a month. It's the second day of the summit. Participants are self-organizing into "design teams." Not surprisingly, one of the seven design statements is on the topic of education. Here is the Education Design Statement:

> Education and training are cornerstones of Hunter Douglas. Individuals partner with the company to achieve a sense of inner purpose, direction, and continuous growth. This, in turn, nurtures the strength and confidence people need to achieve their full personal and professional potential.
>
> Hunter Douglas sponsors a learning center, Hunter Douglas University (HDU), which provides such things as mentoring, customer training, career counseling, and skills development.

The *Design* phase interprets the organization's dreams about the future. It is the collective commitments, principles, processes, actions, programs, structure, and tasks necessary to make the dream come alive.

Destiny: It is now the third day of the summit. All 100 participants have self-organized into groups that have been inspired by the seven Design Statements. Several of the 14 groups deal with issues of education, training, and development.

Fast-forward now in the still-unfolding *Destiny* phase. Beginning six months later, the following are implemented within the HDWFD:

- **A formal mentorship program.** With an advisory team consisting of both leaders and floor staff, this program solicits mentors and matches them with people requesting mentoring. It offers formal "accreditation" for people's personnel files. More than 30 people completed the program within the first year.

- **Appointment of a half-time career planning professional.** This person—a latecomer to the AI effort—bids for and is awarded a job transfer. He or she goes through formal training in career planning and moves to spending half of his or her time at this activity, with the other half dedicated to internal communication (in response to one of the other Design Statements).
- **Establishment of an "English as a Second Language" program.** One of the original third-shift employees conducted interviews during the original inquiry with some of the Laotian refugees who were employed on her shift, people she had seen but had never spoken to. Shocked and saddened by some of what she learned in her conversations, she informally committed herself to teaching English on her lunch hour in order to "make right" on the wrong that fate had done to her colleagues.

  She approached the vice president of Human Resources about her intention. He talked her into serving as on-site coordinator for the local community college's professionally developed ESL classes. Human Resources had been trying to get these classes under way for more than two years, having been unable to get a critical mass of non-English speaking employees to sign up for the classes.
- **Initiation of a state-of-the-art "new-hire orientation" program.** This is yet another program that the Human Resources Department had tried unsuccessfully to design for more three years. Following the summit, it becomes a regular monthly event. A year or so after its initial implementation, long-time employees begin rotating through the program. The innovation team that designs this program commits that every employee will develop a sense of his or her relationship to the entire business.
- **Establishment of a Hunter Douglas University.** Initially launched as a virtual university, it becomes the clearinghouse for all on- and off-campus classes available to HD employees. A year later the company breaks ground on an on-site learning center, dubbed Hunter Douglas University (HDU). A year after that, HDU contains two classrooms (each seating up to 50 people and fully equipped with sound and visual equipment and a breakdown wall between rooms), two conference rooms, a computer laboratory, and a library. It has a kitchen and a serving area for on-site training programs.

  In its first two years of existence, HDU hosted hundreds of training and planning meetings, several of which included 100 or more people. Its regular schedule now includes training classes in focus on excellence (continuous improvement), English as a second language, interaction management for supervisors, Dale Carnegie, personal financial planning, and Toastmasters training for presenters.

Results: A year after the initial inquiry, HDWFD conducted a mini AI interview. The first question in the inquiry solicited people's input on what is best within the division . . . most worthy of holding on to . . . with the greatest capacity to influence the organization positively as it grew. Almost to a person, the response was "this company's commitment to employee and customer training and education is second to none."

This story is a clear reminder that organizations move in the direction of the things they study. Therefore, it is necessary to continue to seek ways to gain a deeper understanding of those things that give life to an organization and its people. Finding ways to tell the stories, to build the conversations, and to enhance the relationships and dialogue will bring the best to life.

Employee Interview Guide

Hunter Douglas Window Fashions Division
Interview Guide

Name: _____ Phone Ext. (if available):_____

Position: _____

Business Unit/Function: _____

Years of Service: _____ Date: _____

Interviewed by: _____

OPENING

Thank you for participating. I'm looking forward to what I'll be learning from this conversation, and I hope it will be a rewarding experience for you as well. As Rick Pellett explained in his letter to you, these interviews are critical to the future of our company.

Many times in interviews, we try to ask questions about things that aren't working well so we can fix them. This time we are going to approach things from a different angle. We are going to find out about your experiences of success here at Hunter Douglas or in other parts of your life so we can find ways to create more of these types of experiences in our organization.

Later in the summer, everyone in the Window Fashions Division will have been interviewed. At that time, everybody's input will be compiled to identify the qualities that make Hunter Douglas a rewarding place to work. With those qualities as a foundation, we will dream about our vision for the year 2000 and beyond.

There are just a few more things you'll want to know about this process. Our conversation will last between 1-1/2 and 2 hours. I'm going to take notes as we talk. Sometimes if you tell a really great story or say something in a way that's especially striking, I might write down what you say word for word. But the information I collect will still be confidential and anonymous unless you ask to have your name attached to it. I am the only person who will see the detailed notes from this interview. A summary of our conversation will be turned into an independent consultant, who will work with a group of people later in the summer to pull together all of our results.

Now before we begin, do you have any questions? Okay, then. Let's get started.

1. What were your initial excitements and impressions when you first joined the company?

2. What has been your most positive or pleasurable experience since you've been here?

3. Without being humble, explain what you value most about:
   - Yourself.
   - The people you work with.
   - Your business unit or functional area here at Hunter Douglas.

PEOPLE

The foundation of any great organization lies in the strengths of its people. The experiences and diverse backgrounds are assets that any organization must utilize to be successful. When we look at Hunter Douglas, it is obvious why it has been so successful. Looking back, we have grown from a small company to a worldwide market leader. How have the people contributed to this success? Hunter Douglas has fostered personal growth through teamwork, two-way respect, communication, and creativity.

When employees have the freedom to express themselves openly and to be involved in the decisions that affect their future, they gain confidence and authority to perform at their best.

1. Describe the most memorable event that illustrates your contribution to the success of a team or an organization. What strengths did you bring to that success?
2. Reflect on someone in your life you have admired and describe his or her qualities. How do you feel those qualities have influenced your growth?
3. If you could look into a crystal ball and see the haute of Hunter Douglas and its employees, what would you like to see? How do you think we can get there?

EDUCATION

Knowledge empowers people, and people power Hunter Douglas. We each contribute to Hunter Douglas's position of market leadership through personal knowledge of our jobs and equipment, other functions in the company, our customers, our competition, and the industry. To maintain our position as market leaders, we must continue to invest in each employee's training and education through:

- Individual coaching.
- Challenging work assignments.
- Job cross training.
- Tuition assistance.
- On- and off-site classes.
- Family scholarships for our children.

1. If knowledge empowers people and people power Hunter Douglas, what kind of learning opportunities would turbo-charge Hunter Douglas?

2. If you could learn more about our customers, our competitors, the industry, and all functions of our company, how would that information help you take ownership in your role for continued success at Hunter Douglas?

3. What is the best training you have ever experienced? Why?
   - How did this influence your development as a professional?
   - How did it influence the training you passed on to others?

4. Reflecting on your past and where you are today, what types of training have proven most beneficial to you?

5. Robert Fulghum wrote a book entitled *All I Really Need to Know I Learned in Kindergarten*. If this were kindergarten, what would you like to learn for the future?

QUALITY OF LIFE

Quality of life is achieved, in part, through a balance of work and family. By ensuring personal and professional well-being, employees can reach their highest level of performance and self-satisfaction.

Throughout the past, Hunter Douglas has been sensitive to its employees' changing personal and professional needs through flexibility and awareness. We can ensure success today and in the future by continuing to acknowledge this need for balance.

1. Describe your definition of what a perfectly balanced personal and professional life is.

2. Envision a time when you were able to balance the personal and professional aspects of your life.
   • Describe how this balance was achieved.
   • What was it about the experience that made you feel this balance?

3. If you could travel over the rainbow, what do you think the quality of life would be like there?

COMMUNICATION

An ongoing and productive exchange of information and creative ideas is vital to the success of Hunter Douglas. Information about how our business is doing, our customers and competition, our plans for the future, and business processes in other parts of the company allows each of us to make the most effective decisions possible. As we grow, this kind of complete communication ensures our continued success in delivering innovative and quality products to our customers.

By exercising active listening and two-way communication, we secure our future as a fair and open organization where every voice is heard.

1. Describe the best example you have experienced of open two-way communication?
   • What did you learn from that experience?
   • How have you applied this to your daily interactions (for example, with your supervisor, coworkers, other business units, customers, and suppliers)?

2. What do you believe would be the ideal situation in which your questions, concerns, or ideas could be heard and responded to?

3. What do you foresee as the most effective process of receiving Hunter Douglas information concerning products, employees, competitors, and the Window Fashions industry?

MORALE

We, as a company, appreciate the importance of each individual's contributions to our success. Recognition, commitment to excellence, and a sense of being stretched or challenged provided the motivation to do our best and go beyond our realm of responsibility. This, in turn, creates:
- Job satisfaction.
- Self-worth.
- A sense of value.
- Ownership.

Continuous focus on positive morale ensures a fun and appreciative work environment.
1. When you reflect on your own experiences, tell me about a high point in your life that gave you a sense of ownership and value.
2. Think of someone who brings a sense of value and pride to his or her job and how he or she projects this level of ownership toward his or her peers. Tell me about it.
3. How do you think receiving recognition from your leadership and others and having the resources and equipment needed to get the job done would contribute to morale?
4. How can we continue to improve morale, build camaraderie, and have fun in the workplace?

CLOSING

In conclusion, I'd like to ask you just a few final questions.
1. What direction would you like to see yourself going with Hunter Douglas in the future?
2. Five years from now, your best friend wants to work for Hunter Douglas. What would you like to be able to tell him or her?
3. If you had three blank memos signed by Rick Pellett, the general manager of Window Fashions, that would become company policy, how would you use them?

4. In your opinion, what was the highlight of this interview? What do you hope comes out of this process?

5. Would you like to become a future Focus 2000 interviewer? If so, it will involve meeting with between two and five people over the next month or so using the same process you and I just used.

   (Interviewer Note: Fill out the Future Interviewer Notice at the end of this packet for those who say yes to this question.)

Interview Summary Sheet

Information requested from each interviewer

- Complete in full after each interview.
- Be sure to gather information from *each section* of the Interview Guide.
- If possible, review your notes with your interviewee before submitting.

What were the best quotes that came out of this interview?

What were the best stories that came out of this interview?

What were the best practices or specific recommendations that you heard reflected in your conversation?

Interviewer Name _____

Interviewee Name (optional) _____

Date of Interview _____

Please complete this summary sheet within 30 minutes of your interview and send it promptly to the Focus 2000 mailbox in Building One.

Design Statements

Hunter Douglas Design Statements
Possibility Propositions

CREATIVITY

Hunter Douglas thrives on creativity. It is the source for new ideas, the lifeblood of the company, and the catalyst for positive change. It is the basis for leadership in products and processes that are both proprietary and innovative.

Hunter Douglas leads the industry in creative ideas that involve all of the company's stakeholders, including employees, customers, and suppliers. We vigorously promote a creative culture to help reinvent and improve products, services, and organizational and business processes. We actively solicit, implement, and reward ideas generated by all people.

We foster an environment that inspires unique ideas, and we provide resources and opportunities for people to develop their creativity and bring their ideas to fruition. Decision makers actively listen to all ideas to enhance creativity and enable people to realize their dreams.

LEADERSHIP

Visionary leadership permeates Hunter Douglas and is the catalyst for our success. Leadership exists in three areas: individual, managerial, and industry. We seek out and develop leadership qualities among our employees. Leadership strongly supports hands-on involvement and mentoring; defines leadership opportunities; and actively listens to all voices, all opinions, and all ideas with fairness and impartiality.

PEOPLE

HDWFD's success as a company is built on the ideas, dreams, and diversity of our people and business partners.

We encourage, challenge, and support people in the pursuit of their ideas, dreams, and aspirations through (1) utilizing and participating in the AI process, (2) enhancing the quality of life through the balance of work and personal life, (3) providing opportunities and resources for continuous personal and professional growth and, (4) providing a safe and open work environment while honoring and rewarding individual and team accomplishments.

The future of the company is dependent upon employees' participation, ownership, integrity, and respect for others. Commitment to people and their ideas ensures continued success, enhanced profitability, and product quality for Hunter Douglas and its partners, while resulting in happier, more productive people.

EDUCATION

Education and training are cornerstones of Hunter Douglas. Individuals partner with the company to achieve a sense of inner purpose, direction, and continuous growth. This, in turn, nurtures the strength and confidence people need to achieve their full personal and professional potential.

Hunter Douglas sponsors a learning center, Hunter Douglas University (HDU), which provides such things as:
- Mentoring.
- Customer training.
- Career counseling.
- Skills development.

COMMUNICATION

Hunter Douglas demands open, honest, high-quality, and ongoing communication among its employees, business partners, and communities. We provide all stakeholders the opportunity to express and be actively listened to on all ideas and opinions.

The organization:
- Promotes continuous two-way exchange of information and ideas across all cultures and languages.
- Actively shares the big picture through open access to all appropriate information about the company, its history, and its business environment.
- Maximizes use of the most effective communication tools.
- Expects individual ownership of and responsibility for effective communication.

CUSTOMERS

Customers are Hunter Douglas's lifeblood and future. We delight customers (fabricators, dealers, consumers, suppliers, employees, and the community) by understanding and exceeding their expectations in the areas of:
- Product quality and innovation.
- Customer service and technical support.
- Customer relations.
- Training and education.

- Community involvement.
- Promises kept.

We provide professional and seamless service, create strong partnerships, and significantly contribute to customer success. The Hunter Douglas family embraces customers through commitment to excellence, innovation, imagination, dreams, and "small company values." Our culture demands an atmosphere of respect, trust, integrity, honesty, reliability, and responsibility. We expand our customer base by nurturing current and new relationships. Customers eagerly do business with us because "we are easy to do business with." We set the benchmark for others to follow!

PRODUCTS

HDWFD's market leadership is built on the strong foundation of its products. Critical driving forces behind our market leadership are product innovation, improvements, quality, and marketing. We create high-fashion, high-function, and reliable branded products. In addition, we are committed to:

- Continually reinvent our business through the creation of profitable, new, proprietary products.
- Extend, defend, and continuously improve our existing products.

Our challenge is to develop and deliver "whole" products that provide total satisfaction for our fabricators, dealers, and consumers through:

- Creation of new products that are imaginative, fashionable, and robust.
- Thoughtfully designed and engineered products, with processes that have high yields, zero defects, and minimal return rates—and that are easy to install and fabricate.
- Products that are positioned and marketed effectively so their place in the market is easily understood by dealers and consumers.
- Supportive sampling and sales efforts that effectively communicate product features and benefits.
- Low-maintenance products that require minimal care and cleaning.

This results in products that consumers display with pride and enthusiasm.

Hunter Douglas Today

Ten years after the first AI initiative was launched, Hunter Douglas Window Fashions Division remains the largest, most profitable division in Hunter Douglas worldwide—and the leading window coverings innovator and manufacturer in the world. Now this division manufactures six different products (up from one in 1985), increasing revenues by 40 percent, yet with only a 13 percent increase in head count over the past ten years. How? The company continues to reap the benefits of the positive culture, strategic gains, and efficiencies imagined and implemented in the early years of its work with AI.

In the 1998 strategic planning summit, employees' vision was to leverage the proprietary technology in a new market: interior design. The company achieved this goal in 2003 when it developed and launched TechStyle Acoustical Ceilings. According to plan, it maintained focus on its "positive core" by spinning that business off and continuing to do what it does best—window coverings. Hunter Douglas Specialty Products currently manufactures and distributes innovative acoustic ceilings for the commercial market from a new Hunter Douglas campus in Thornton, Colorado.

If you wandered into a Hunter Douglas Window Fashions Division production facility today, what would you see or hear of Appreciative Inquiry? You would see or hear very little of the phrase itself. But of the essence, you would see and hear a great deal. The *Hunter Douglas Way*, as it's sometimes known, is to regularly engage mixed groups of people in studying what has worked in the past, imagining what might happen, and creating from there . . . in leveraging strengths, in changing the world through conversation. These AI-based patterns are permanently imprinted on the hearts and minds of Window Fashions Division employees—even those who were hired after the first several years of Appreciative Inquiry-based transformation and training.

Appreciative Inquiry has enabled Hunter Douglas to build on its positive core and to maintain its leadership through a decade of industry changes. It will continue to do so in the years to come.

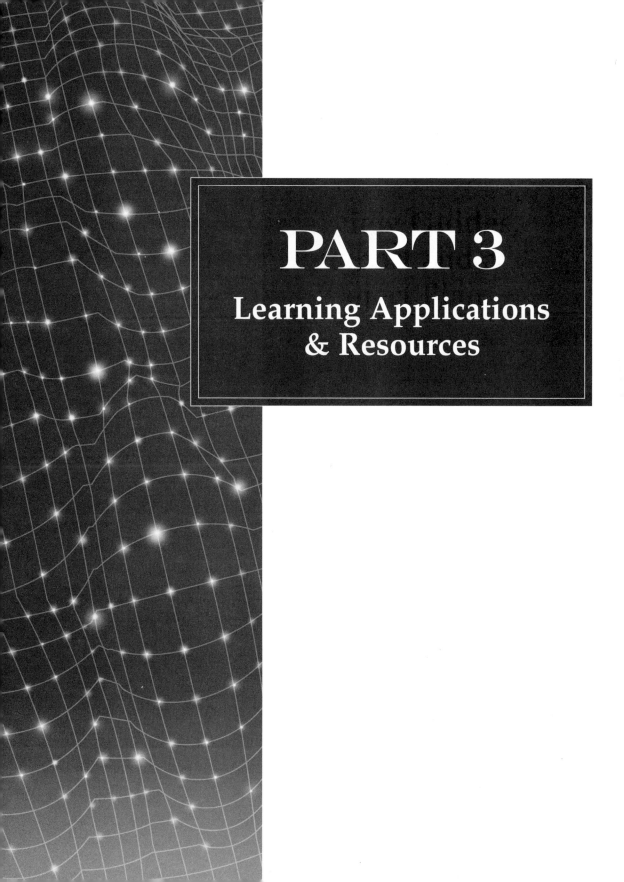

PART 3

Learning Applications
& Resources

Since the first edition of the *Appreciative Inquiry Handbook*, case applications continue to emerge all over the world. AI has been applied in a variety of environments, industries, cultures, and ways. This final section has been updated to provide a rich collection of sample materials and resources. These resources are offered not as a formula for success, but rather as guides for your AI learning and initiative. Many of these resources are contributed by the organization or consultants who worked extensively and collaboratively with their clients to tailor AI to their needs and context. Examples range from services, manufacturers, retailers, and government to not-for-profit organizations.

Chapter 8 offers six interview guides to a sample AI Summary Report and a Detailed Project Plan. This chapter offers a range of formats, affirmative topics, and interview summary sheets.

Sample Interview Guides
- First American National Bank (service)
- North American Steel, Inc. (manufacturer)
- World Vision Relief and Development (not-for-profit)
- Canadian Tire (retail)

AI Summary Report and Summit Workbook
- Fairmont Minerals (formerly Fairmont North America)

The second edition offers a new resource, *The Fairmount Minerals Sustainable Development Appreciative Inquiry Summit Workbook*. It includes a summit agenda, an interview guide, and several worksheets. It builds on more than 15 years of AI work with Fairmont to bring the organization into a sustainable global development enterprise. The workbook is preceded by an AI Summary Report that resulted from the original inquiry.

Chapter 9 is a new chapter with a selection of nine case studies from a variety of areas in for-profit, government, and not-for-profit sectors. Each case application provides the story, project scope, AI application, project milestones and outcomes, summary of learnings, and contributors' contact information. These cases were selected based on the successful, sustained AI change efforts. Each application involved participants in a meaningful way with stated objectives and outcomes. The following cases are included:
- BP Castrol Marine
- BT Global Services
- Nielsen Media Research
- Pennsylvania Community Hospitals and Medical Centers
- Alice Peck Day Health Systems

- Environmental Protection Agency's (EPA) Office of Research and Development (ORD)
- Boulder County, Colorado Aging Services Division
- Head Start Program
- Metropolitan School District

The complete interview guides are available on the CD-ROM accompanying the Premium Edition of the Handbook, available at http://www.crowncustom publishing.com. (The web site also contains a complete table of contents for the CD-ROM.)

Chapter 10 contains an updated set of 11 worksheets for use in AI-related training sessions or workshops. New to this edition is an application of how you can use these worksheets to create your own AI project or summit from the EPA/ORD Leadership Summit: Igniting Leadership at all Levels. The secondary theme of this summit focuses on "working together to ensure the earth's vitality."

Chapter 11 concludes this handbook with a request from readers of the first edition to keep two of the four original AI classic articles (most widely referred to and read) and includes a popular and often-requested classic article called "Strategic Inquiry with Appreciative Intent: Inspiration to SOAR!" The articles in Chapter 11 are reprinted by permission of the respective publishers and are copyright-protected. In addition, the classic and popular article "Positive Image, Positive Action: The Affirmative Basis of Organizing" by David Cooperrider is available on the Handbook's accompanying CD-ROM (www.crowncustompublishing.com).

You can obtain more information about these case studies by contacting their contributors or by visiting the AI Commons at http://appreciative inquiry.case.edu. The AI Commons is a worldwide portal that offers academic resources and practical tools on AI and the rapidly growing disciplines of strength-based change and positive organizational scholarship. This site is hosted by Case Western Reserve University's Weatherhead School of Management. Many of the case studies presented in this handbook have complete sets of tools and materials related to ongoing AI projects. The AI Commons has a case site that pulls together all materials used with ongoing AI projects, several of which are included in this handbook. Feel free to adapt these resources and materials to your own projects.

The case contributors work with organizations around the world to introduce, apply, and provide coaching on the AI process and principles to create communities in which people want to work and live in. The authors want to thank the contributors in helping to create this new chapter by sharing their stories.

8

Sample Interview Guides, Summary Report and a Detailed Project Plan

SAMPLE INTERVIEW GUIDE—Service
First American National Bank
Appreciative Inquiry Questionnaire

Name _____

Title_____ Date_____

Group/Department _____

Years of Service_____ Phone _____

Interviewed by _____

OPENING:

As part of a special study, we are conducting interviews with employees about their work experience. In particular, our goal is to locate, illuminate, and understand the distinctive values, management practices, and skills that lend the organization its organizational vitality. In other words, we are interested in understanding more about what is happening when we are at our best.

The information you provide in this interview will be used to help prepare a corporate vision statement as seen and valued by members at all levels of the corporation. Our interest is in learning from your experience. The collected comments, experience, and suggestions from all of the employees interviewed will be summarized and reviewed with senior management.

The interview takes about one hour. The interview will tend to focus on the organization when it is operating at its best in the following (preliminary) topic areas:

1. Being the Best   4. Integrity
2. Shared Ownership Commitment   5. Empowering People
3. Cooperation

QUESTIONS:

EXPERIENCE OF ORGANIZATION
   1. First, I'd like to learn about your beginnings with the organization.
       • What attracted you to the organization?
       • What were your initial feelings and impressions when you joined the company?

2.   Looking at your entire experience, can you recall a time when you felt most alive, most involved, or most excited about your involvement in the organization?
     • What made it an exciting experience?
     • Who were the most significant others?
     • Why were they significant?
     • What was it about you that made it a peak experience?
     • What were the most important factors in the company that helped to make it a peak experience? (Probe—leadership qualities, structure, rewards, systems, skills, strategy, and/or relationships?)

3.   Let's talk for a moment about some things you value deeply— specifically, the things you value about (1) yourself, (2) the nature of your work, and (3) the organization.
     • Without being humble, what do you value most about yourself as a human being, a friend, a parent, a citizen, or a son or daughter?
     • When you are feeling best about your work, what do you value about the task itself?
     • What is it about the organization that you value?
     • What is the single most important thing the company has contributed to your life?

BEING THE BEST

4.   The organization builds on "proven strengths" and has a history of being a pioneer in a large number of areas. In your opinion, what is the most important achievement you can recall that illustrates this spirit of being the best?

5.   What is the most outstanding or successful achievement you have been involved in pulling off—a piece of work or project of which you are particularly proud?
     • What was it about you (unique qualities you have) that made it possible to achieve this result?
     • What organizational factors (e.g., leadership, teamwork, and/or culture) fostered this determination to excel or achieve?

SHARED OWNERSHIP AND COMMITMENT

Organizations work best when people at all levels share a basic common vision in relation to the company's core mission, intent, and direction. When people know the big picture, they often experience a feeling of purpose, pride, significance, and unity.

6. In your mind, what is the common mission or purpose that unites everyone in this organization? How is this communicated and nurtured?

7. Think of a time you felt most committed to the organization and its mission. Why did you feel such commitment?
   - Give one example of how the organization has shown its commitment to you.

COOPERATION / TEAM SPIRIT

A cooperative team spirit is important to our company. Important initiatives usually depend on the support and goodwill of others within work groups and/or between groups that cross department, specialization, and hierarchical levels. Cooperation requires trust, open channels of communication, responsiveness to others' needs, and interpersonal competence.

8. Can you think of a time when there was an extraordinary display of cooperation among diverse individuals or groups in the company?
   - What made such cooperation possible? (Explore planning methods used, communication systems or process, leadership qualities, incentives for cooperation, skills, team development techniques, and others).

9. Give an example of the most effective team or committee you have been part of. What are the factors/skills that made it effective?

EMPOWERING PEOPLE

Our organization's strength rests with its people. It has a tradition of providing structures or opportunity for members of the corporation to excel. This requires considering individual goals, ideas, and aspirations as well as providing developmental opportunities to learn, to grow, and to take risks.

10. What individual qualities are most valued in this organization?

11. What qualities are necessary for people to excel?
    - In empowered organizations, people feel significant. People believe they have a chance "to make a difference." They believe that what they do has significance, and they are recognized. What does the organization do best (at least three examples) when it comes to empowering people?

12. How do people develop these qualities?

IN CONCLUSION

13. What is the core factor that gives vitality and life to the organization (without which the organization would cease to exist)?
    - If you could develop or transform the organization in any way, what three things would you do to heighten its vitality and overall health?

SAMPLE INTERVIEW GUIDE—Manufacturer

North American Steel, Inc.
Learning from 40 Years of Experience

INTRODUCTION

Thank you very much for agreeing to be interviewed for the organization study we are conducting in preparation for North American Steel's 40th-year celebration. As you may know, the majority of organizations in our society die before they reach the age of 40. But there are exceptions. North American Steel is one of them. Even more important, North American Steel is stronger than ever. Over the years, North American has proven itself resilient. In good times and bad, it has provided a stable base of employment for many people. It has adapted, changed, and grown with the times. And its future looks positive and promising. The question is why?

What are the core factors that give life to this organization? What can we learn from our history, especially when we examine closely those moments when we have been our best? What are North American Steel's most effective practices, strengths, or best qualities — things we should try to preserve about our organization even as we change? What important lessons can we draw from our history? Building on all of this, what kind of organization do we want to be in the future? What is our potential? Can our positive past, the best in our past, help us become more daring as we think about our true potential as an organization? What is your dream for North American Steel? What ideas do you have for helping us move to a whole new level as a business?

The information you provide will be used to help accelerate our continuous improvement as an organization and to help us prepare for our 40th-year anniversary celebration in September 1994. The important thing is learning from everybody's experience. The collected comments will provide the basis for a report to be reviewed by all. Your comments will be put together with others anonymously. Your name will not be attached to any of the stories, suggestions, examples, or comments you make. The interview will take about 30 to 45 minutes.

    A. Experience with North American Steel, Inc.
        1. To start, I'd like to learn about *your* beginnings at NAS.
            a. When did you start at NAS, and what were your first impressions?
            b. Why have you stayed with NAS?

        2. What is one of the most rewarding experiences you have had at NAS, something that was a *real high point*? Can you

tell me about a time when *you felt best*, most alive, most effective, proud, and so on?

3. Let's talk a moment about some things you value most specifically about (1) yourself and (2) the organization.
   a. What do you believe is the strongest, most important asset you offer to NAS? What are your best qualities?
   b. What is it about NAS as an organization that you value the *most?*

4. Brief History of NAS: From what you have experienced or heard of NAS's history since 1954, name two or three key events, decisions, innovations, achievements, or challenges that were important turning points in the life of the organization.

B.   Exploring Best Qualities and Hopes for the Future
   1. **Team Mind-set:** Organizations work best when team spirit and enthusiasm are high and everyone is a valued member of a group where his or her ideas are heard. To be effective over time, organizations need cooperation within groups as well as between groups that cross department lines, jobs, and levels in the hierarchy. Teamwork requires trust, open channels of communication, appropriate business information, responsiveness to others' needs, good training, and interpersonal skills.

      Think of an example of the most effective team or group effort *you* have been part of at NAS. Tell the story of what happened. Who was involved? What made the teamwork effective? What were the important lessons?

   2. **Customer Satisfaction and Market Responsiveness:** Central to the vision statement of NAS is an organization that is market driven and totally responsive to customer satisfaction, which time and time again is the lifeblood of the business.
      a. Think of a time when NAS was most effective in terms of customer responsiveness or market innovation? Tell me a story of what happened. What was most noteworthy?
      b. Possibilities for the Future: What things could NAS do to improve or even revolutionize its responsiveness to and connection with its customers?

3. **Continuous Learning:** In a changing world, the competitive edge goes to the company that is able to change, grow, or learn faster than any of its competitors. When at its best, NAS is a "learning organization" in which people are continuously challenging themselves to move out of their comfort zones, think in new ways, acquire new knowledge and skills, and experiment with new management and production methods.

    a. Describe a time at NAS when you believed you were learning something new, meaningful, and helpful to the business. More importantly, what lessons can be drawn from your example? What does NAS do *best* as it relates to building good learning opportunities or strengthening the learning spirit of the whole company?

    b. As you look to the future, describe one thing you think NAS could or should do more of to strengthen the learning capacity of the company.

4. **Shared Vision and Ownership:** Organizations work best when everyone thinks and acts as though they are an owner of the business. That sense of ownership is highest when a shared vision exists for the direction the business is headed in the future, when people are involved in major decisions that are relevant to them and their work, when appropriate information about the business is shared openly, when people know the whole picture in terms of others' tasks or jobs, and when people believe they are at the center of things rather than on the outside.

    a. Describe a time when you felt most involved in the big picture of the organization, a time when you felt most like a partner or even an owner of the business. What can we all learn from this experience?

    b. Thinking about the future, what could NAS do *more of* to create a shared vision of the future and a heightened sense of ownership at all levels?

5. **Resiliency and Managing Change:** Over the years, NAS has proven its resiliency and its ability to manage change when small and large challenges have confronted the organization. Many of the changes introduced (for example, in the early 1990s) were positive, healthy, and successful.

a. Thinking of all the changes you have seen, what changes have most positively affected you, your work, or the company?

b. What could NAS do more of, less of, or the same in the future to become more resilient, more flexible, and more able to manage change?

SAMPLE INTERVIEW GUIDE—Not-for-Profit

World Vision Relief and Development
Interview Questionnaire for Appreciative Inquiry

GENERAL INFORMATION

Name:_____

Title: _____

Group/Department: _____

Years of Service: _____

Extension: _____

Interviewed by:_____

Date: _____

INTERVIEW PROTOCOL

As part of a special study, we are conducting interviews with employees and other individuals about work experience and perceptions of our organization.

The information you provide will be used to prepare a corporate vision statement as seen and valued by members at all levels in the organization. Our intent is to learn from your experience. The collected comments, experiences, and suggestions from all of the employees and others interviewed will be summarized and reviewed with senior management. We assure you that your name will not be attached to any of the final data.

The interview will take about one hour. The interview will tend to focus on the organization when it is operating at its best in the following topic areas:

1. Integrative Process
   a. Partnership
   b. Programs
   c. Holistic Communication
2. Innovation
3. Empowerment
4. Quality
5. Diversity
   a. Transnational
   b. Faith
   c. Specialization
6. Organizational Ethos (Sharing and Learning)

A. **Experience with WVRD**
    (The following three questions are stage-setting.)

    1. To start, I'd like to learn about your beginnings and/or
        awareness of WV/your organization.
        a. What attracted you to WV/your organization?
        b. What was your initial excitement/impression when you
            joined/participated with WV/your organization?

    2. Looking at your entire experience, can you recall a time
        when you felt most alive, most involved, or most excited
        about WV/your involvement?
        a. What made it an exciting experience?
        b. Who were the most significant people involved?
        c. Why were they significant?
        d. What was it about you that made it a peak experience?
        e. What were the most important factors in the organiza-
            tion that helped make it a peak experience? (Probe—
            leadership qualities, structures, rewards, systems, skills,
            strategies, and/or relationships.)

    3. Let's talk a moment about some things you value deeply;
        specifically, the things you value about (1) yourself, (2) the
        nature of your work, and (3) WV/your organization.
        a. Without being humble, what do you value most about
            yourself as a human being, a friend, a parent, a citizen,
            and so on?
        b. When you are feeling your best about your work, what
            do you value about the task itself?
        c. What is it about WV/your organization that you value?
        d. What is the single most important thing WV/your
            organization has contributed to your life?

B. **Communication**
    Global organizations often create a special feeling of alignment among
    their members wherein individuals believe that they "live" the values
    and goals of the organization in their work and personal lives.
        a. What does your organization do to heighten a sense of
            understanding, alignment, or attunement among its
            members?

b. When new members enter the organization, what does WV/your organization do particularly well to educate them about the mission and values of the organization?

c. Does your organization provide its members with meaningful opportunities so they can consider how their personal values fit with organizational values?

C. Empowerment

Global organizations need members who can act and make decisions that are aligned with organizational values and goals. People who are empowered are given latitude to make decisions related to their position and work. They are also given information and support to carry out these decisions and actions.

a. When have you felt most empowered by WV/your organization?

b. What does your organization do to encourage members to take action in whatever ways they can?

c. How does your organization succeed in empowering its members?

d. What factors in WV/your organization serve to empower people outside of the organization to help themselves?

D. Quality

Global organizations often face the strategic issue of an effective transition from a "Growth" model to a "quality" model of organizational development for all aspects of programmatic, fund-raising, and organizational activities.

1. How does your organization face the challenges of donor relations and demands in light of shifting from a northern-dominated international partnership to one of engagement with southern participants as full partners?

2. How does your organization shift from resource quantity to resource quality?

E. Diversity (Transnational, Faith, and Specialization)

Global organizations encounter incredible diversity among their members—diversity in cultures, goals, backgrounds, experience, age, sex, religion, and values.

1. What does your organization do to embrace the diversity among its members?

2. What does your organization do to create common goals and beliefs that allow diverse people to work together effectively?

3. What does your organization do to prevent diversity among its members from becoming divisive or interfering with the success of its overall efforts?

4. How does your organization respond to the need for local groups to determine their own approaches to accomplishing tasks?

F. **Sharing and Learning Organization**
   An effective global organization must always be in a state of evolution in order to remain effective in the current world's rapidly changing political, technical, and economic paradigms.
   1. What does your organization do to maintain a "current" perspective?
   2. What does your organization do to help its members think about the global perspective of their work and to encourage reflective thinking?

G. **Conclusion**
   1. What is the core factor that gives vitality and life to this organization (without which the organization would cease to exist)?
   2. If you could envision, develop, or transform this organization in any way, what would you do to heighten its overall vitality and health? (List three things in order of priority.)

SAMPLE INTERVIEW GUIDE—Retail
Canadian Tire
An Inquiry into What Our Customers Value Most

PURPOSE OF INTERVIEWS
Thank you very much for participating in this process of gathering information from colleagues across Canadian Tire. These interviews are part of an intensive effort to connect all parts of Canadian Tire to become truly **the best at what our customers value most.**

A robust customer value is not only strategic but also fundamental to our success and central to Canadian Tire's statement of purpose. It is a journey we are in for the long term.

What do our customers want? At the top of the list, studies show our customers want:

- Enthusiastic, knowledgeable help from our people.
- Us to deliver on our promises.
- To be respected (for their time, caring, and rapid service).
- To trust in our quality and price.
- To work with people who are empowered (people who are resourceful and able to think, act, and serve with enthusiasm).
- To have an exciting shopping experience (a memorable experience that leaves a lasting impression).

This Appreciative Interview Guide forms the start of our conversation. On the following pages, you will find a set of questions that invite you and your interview partner to reflect on and look with an appreciative eye to the topics we will address during this meeting.

The questions are offered to engage you in the best thinking you can do about customer values. Give your partner your full attention and draw out the richness of the stories and images that he or she shares with you. After the first interview, simply thank your partner and shift roles.

To begin: First, some things about you and your background at Canadian Tire…

1. Think back to the moment in your career at Canadian Tire when you were offered a position at Canadian Tire and you said yes.
   - What were some of the attributes that attracted and excited you?
   - What set us apart and made the *difference* for you?

2. In your work at Canadian Tire, you have probably experienced ups and downs, twists and turns, high points and low points. For a

moment, I would like you to think about a time that was a high point for you. This is a time that stands out when you felt most engaged, alive, effective, or really proud of your involvement in the organization. It might have been a special change or innovation, a great team, or even a special year.

- Please tell me the story about a high-point experience for you?
- What made it a high-point experience?
- What was it about *you* that make it successful; more specifically, *what are your best skills or qualities* as a leader, manager, or change agent.?

Now let's shift specifically to an exploration of Canadian Tire's customer values.

3. **Enthusiastic, Knowledgeable Help For Every Customer:** Central to Canadian Tire's statement of purpose is to be the best at delivering what our customers value and want. One of those values is **"to have enthusiastic, knowledgeable help"** from every person at Canadian Tire.

   a. To begin, I would like you to think about *your own work*—times when you have best served or responded to your valued customers. Can you share with me one story, something you were involved with, that best illustrates what it means **"to deliver enthusiastic, knowledgeable help"**? Please share with me the whole story. What did you or your group do, and what was the impact?

   b. Now let's build on that story and think about the future and what you would most like to see at the Canadian Tire stores. Let's fast-forward into the future; it is 2010. What is your vision of "enthusiastic, knowledgeable help"? Please describe it. What does it look like?

4. Now let's take a look at another value our customers say they are looking for, **"an exciting shopping experience"**—an experience that is enjoyable, exciting, different, or fun. We all know stories that make us proud and show us what we can be when we are at our best. Learning from these stories is important. A famous proverb says "stories have wings and they fly from mountaintop to mountaintop."

   a. From something you observed or heard about (from any store or dealership at Canadian Tire), can you share a story of a place or person delivering "an exciting shopping experience"? Where does the story take place? When? Why does it stand out for you?

b. In a changing world, the competitive edge goes to the company that is able to change, grow, or learn faster than any of its competitors. We need to become great at sharing and amplifying stories like the ones we have been talking about—helping them fly "from mountaintop to mountaintop" all across Canadian Tire. *As you look to the future, describe one thing you think we as a whole could do more of to strengthen our learning capacity and our ability to replicate new "customer value" successes all across the company?*

5. **Continuity Search:** Good organizations know how to "preserve the core" of what they do best and are able to work out or let go of things that have built up or are no longer needed. Preserving the right things is key. Letting go of other things is the next step.

    a. With regard to being the best in our industry at providing customers with what they value and want, what are three things we do best *at the stores* today that we should keep, things that should be preserved or amplified even as we change in the future?

    b. What are three things we do best *at the corporate level* that we should keep, things that should be amplified or preserved even as we change in the future?

Wrap-up and looking to the future...

6. **Images of the Canadian Tire of the Future:** Let's assume that tonight, after this session, you go to sleep and don't wake up until ten years from now. The year is 2015. While you were asleep, significant and exciting changes happened. Canadian Tire became exactly as you wanted to see it. It is No.1—*the best at delivering what our customers value most.*

    a. Imagine you wake up and it's 2015. You go into the Canadian Tire stores and the corporation. What do you see and feel happening that's new and different and better? How do you know? Describe the Canadian Tire of the future.

    b. What is the smallest step (an action, a decision, an initiative) we could take today that would have the largest impact on creating the future you want?

    c. What is one thing have we not thought of yet—something new we could do that would improve or even revolutionize, our ability to become **the best at what our customers value most?**

SAMPLE AI SUMMARY REPORT
Fairmount North America
Our Future Begins with Our Strengths

Teaching note: This Appreciative Inquiry Report goes on to describe eight "Ideal-Type" Themes with illustrative quotes and stories. It ends with a compilation of all the visions for the future. We are including only one "Ideal-Type" Theme here for review.

    This kind of report is useful as background material for building provocative propositions. Reports like this have been distributed prior to people coming to a Future Search conference. Before an artist paints a picture, he or she assembles his or her colors: green, blue, yellow, and so on. The Appreciative Inquiry Report serves exactly the same purpose, it is the material that will help the collective imagination come alive.

Overview

On behalf of all the people at Fairmount North America, the Committee on Appreciative Inquiry (AI) is pleased to present its first report: **"Vision 2000: It Begins with Our Strengths."**

    Our hope is that this report serves as both a catalyst and an invitation. The invitation: To participate in an organization-wide process where everybody at each location has the opportunity to think strategically and imaginatively about "our common vision for the organization of the future." As a catalyst: The report provides inspiring snapshots of many of the strengths of the organization "when it is working at its very best." There is, it must be acknowledged, an undeniable positive quality about this report. Some of it stems from the nature of the questions that were asked of you in the interviews. But equally important, much of it comes from the real sense of optimism people feel about the company and its prospects for the future. We, too, as a committee, found ourselves energized and excited about the organization's future when we began letting our imaginations go.

> What will Fairmount North America look like in 2000? What will it look like if all of its best qualities are magnified, extended, or multiplied, let's say, by a factor of ten? Are we really ready, as many have said in interviews and private conversations, to jump to a whole new level as an organization? What is our dream? What do we really want this organization to be in the future?

How This Document Was Put Together

We constructed this analysis from interviews with 329 of you, comprising all locations and all levels of personnel. The questions used in the interviews (which lasted from one to two hours each) were generated in several three-day workshops on Appreciative Inquiry held in August and September. During those workshops, several topics were identified: **care and respect for people, teamwork, leadership, empowerment, common goals and direction, commitment, and recognition**. The interviews were designed to explore these topics in several ways. When, for example, have people felt really empowered in this organization? What supports or strengthens empowerment? What are the organization's "best practices" when it comes to good people management or empowerment? What would we like to do more of to build a more empowered organization?

On the basis of the interviews, the data was put together first by location and then as a whole corporation. This particular report is a summary overview for the whole of Fairmount. It draws on information from each site report, attempting to discover those ideals that are common throughout the company.

In terms of analysis, we first typed up all the interview responses and grouped them together by question. The next step was to code each comment to discover, for example, what the most important factors are that create, maintain, or strengthen **empowerment**? We then grouped examples (and quotes) of empowerment together and attempted to put words to the **topic ideals**. What do people really mean when speaking about empowerment? What are people really saying is **ideal**? We figure if we did our homework well, the topic ideals, as written, will resonate strongly with what people **want** the organization to be. Two things are important to keep in mind when reading through the report. First, these topic ideals are fashioned from people's actual experiences. There are examples, many examples, of each of the ideals (see actual quotes). Thus, the topic ideals express the corporate culture of Fairmount as we understand it from appreciation of our proven strengths. But the statements go a step further. They also, hopefully, represent a bold extension of those strengths—focused vision to which people are saying they aspire to as an organization. Therefore, the topic ideals are stated in the present tense not because they have been attained, but because people are saying this is their present "ideal" based on experiences when they/we have been at our best. We invite you to think of this document as a resource, as a catalyst, to help you think seriously about what you want this organization to be like in the future.

How to Use This Document
The most thorough approach we have in mind is as follows:

1. Read the **summary** at the beginning of each section to get a feeling for the topic ideal. Ask yourself: If we could be this way all the time, would I want it?

2. Read each of the **sample quotes** to get an idea of what people actually talked about. Ask yourself: Do these quotes illustrate the topic ideal? Do you have other examples from your own experience that help illustrate the way things could be like in the ideal? What are those illustrations?

3. Read through the **analysis**. Ask yourself: Does the analysis sound plausible? What else would you add to the analysis?

4. Remember: A future does not arrive uninvited. It is built. Organizations begin in the imagination. And when an organization as a whole takes time to give voice to its preferred future, it is all that more likely to bring about that future. Put simply, it is easier to do things together when there is common focus.

Next Steps
Over the next several weeks, meetings will be held to discuss the report. We hope these meetings will serve three purposes:

1. As a vehicle for discussing the discoveries — to confirm, restate, debate, and elaborate.

2. As an opportunity to appreciate the organization for what it is today and to expand our thinking about what it can be in the future.

3. As an invitation for people at each location to become part of a Vision 2000 team.

We believe the Appreciative Inquiry approach is a powerful way of building a common focus. One management thinker, Peter Senge, calls it building "a learning organization." He writes:

> If anything, the need for understanding how organizations learn, and accelerating that learning, is greater today than ever

before. The old days when a Henry Ford, Alfred Sloan, or Tom Watson learned for the organization are gone. In an increasingly dynamic, interdependent, and unpredictable world, it is simply no longer possible for anyone to "figure it all out at the top." The old model "the top think and the locals act" must now give way to integrated thinking and acting at all levels. While the challenge is great, so is the potential payoff. "The person who figures out how to harness the collective genius of the people in his or her organization," according to former Citibank CEO Walter Wriston, "is going to blow the competition away."

It has been an exciting task thus far. We look forward to the feedback sessions.

Ideal-Type Theme #1: A Team-Based Organization

Fairmount North America has become a multifaceted business where the mindset of teamwork has become a critical success factor in continuous innovation and responsiveness to customers (internal and improvement). Said one person, "There are hundreds of examples of positive impact and innovation because of teamwork. Our history keeps teaching us that none of us is so smart as all of us."

More than a set of empty slogans or words, the call for teamwork has been a call for fundamental change. Fairmount is an organization that has, in fact, dared to experiment with advanced organizational changes and management approaches. It is an organization that has shown its change efforts even when there are inevitable setbacks and learning pains. The movement to a team-based organization at Fairmount is not cosmetic. "It is inevitable," said one person.

But it is not just the spirit or mind-set of teamwork. When working at its best, the organizational structure eliminates unnecessary hierarchy and division and engages people as partners. At Fairmount, the so-called organizational chart, with its hierarchy of reporting relationships and separation of jobs, reflects only one reality. The "other structure," not generally shown on the chart, is an overlay of person-to-person networks, cross-functional project groups, teams, information-seeking meetings, new-business planning groups, and the like. While this kind of "ad-hoc teamwork" often seems a bit confusing (from a standard organizational-chart perspective), it can be argued that it is precisely this— the ability to create fast, focused, free-formed, flexible (even fun) teamwork—that has brought Fairmount so much success in recent years. Through the use of this "parallel" organizational form (i.e., the nonhierarchical team-based organization), Fairmount fosters the cross-fertilization of ideas, minimizes the building of empires, harnesses the synergy of group cooperation, and cultivates the pride of being a valued member of "one outstanding corporation."

Sample Quotes:

1. *Early last year we had a serious situation in California. It was a dangerous situation where the product could jeopardize someone's safety. We never had an experience like that. We never had a recall before. Lives could be at stake. Liability laws in California were strict. It put us in an unbelievable pressure-filled situation. Some of our customers were afraid for their business. The negative situation grew darker. Our customers became adversarial. But we dug down deep. I remember sitting in the room when we made the decision to respond. People were shouting, arguing, searching for what to do. Gerry stepped forward and made the decision. We acted immediately, came up with a war pla,n and launched a campaign. A team went to Escardo, California, hunting down all the big tanks. Bob at our Ontario warehouse was a hero, helping to make everything happen in California. Millions of dollars were at stake. At home, FRP was heroic. They made 700 replacement tanks in a matter of months. It probably cost us a half million dollars to do what we did. But we were taking the long-term view.*

2. *Teams: This is what the place is really all about. It's about people working with one another. Why have an organization if people don't need other people? We are what we are because of our teamwork, and not just individual parts. It's how the parts fit together. You see, you could try to make a car from all the best parts: engine of a Mercedes, body of a Corvette, brakes from a Cadillac, and so on. But you know what? The car won't work. It is how the parts mesh, how the parts act as a team. The same is true here. Teamwork is not an option. It's got to be a way of life.*

3. *The most effective team effort was on an integrated product development team. It was about large tanks. We were working out the concept of flanges and various ports. Fifteen people were involved. The group was too large but worked OK. To make these teams work really well we need to (1) involve only six to eight people, (2) recognize people's contributions, (3) recognize people in written minutes and (4) utilize democratic leaders who are dynamic and positive and give people the recognition they deserve.*

4. *I felt most involved when we redid the whole back on the FRP line. We cut the water bath down, re-arranged equipment, figured out how to run it with six people instead of sixteen — and we did it together. It was fantastic. We met once a week. Tim was a great listener. All of our ideas were used. There wasn't anybody in the area not involved unless a person chose not to be. This is a model of how we can be all the time. We need more of this.*

5. *Great teamwork happened when the marketing group decided to introduce a new product. We were all kind of intoxicated !! It was a universal tank concept. We had all the pieces and parts, and it cost no money. A team took the ideas from concept to production in less than six months. We had twelve people from every part of the company. We can draw three lessons: (1) The goal was sold to the team—everyone agreed 100%. (2) Everyone wanted to make it a success. (3) We had lots of communication—lots of meetings. At times, we met once a week for a couple of hours. We also had good leadership.*

6. *I've been here almost twenty years, and I'm really sure that my high point was the beginning of the teams and the team training. But it was also a low for me. The high point was being in the training session with the managers. Just being in the same room together broke down lots of negative stereotypes we had for each other. I wish this would continue. The company needs it. A low point was not being accepted by coworkers anymore. Lots of people were negative about the team idea, saying it wouldn't work. As it turns out, maybe their predictions were right. But we shouldn't let the thing die. Sure, there were mistakes with two steps forward and three back for a while. But the team idea is critical for our future. Nobody wants to go back to the authoritarian style where workers are to "leave their brains at the time clock."*

Commentary:

Fairmount North America is an organization that has dared to experiment with advanced organizational changes and management approaches. The most controversial, and arguably the most productive, has been the idea of teams. My reading is that the organization has been overly hard on itself as it relates to inevitable "learning pains." The idea of a more group-based, less hierarchical or paternalistic form of management is a major change; and Fairmount is not alone in its love-hate affair with complex transformation like this. In my reading of the sentiment of the organization, there is no going back to more authoritarian management relations ("where people check their brains at the time-clock").

The question is not whether to have team-based processes, but how to persist and work through inevitable learning pains even when there are voices of cynicism. In this case, even the cynicism should be valued. The cynical voice puts into words the doubts we all have. We have no doubts only about things we do not care about. That's the point. People care. They see a promise in the team idea that they really want. The idealism in this area is extremely high at Fairmount. In my more adventurous moments, I find myself wanting to suggest a giant step forward with the team idea, much like the examples given in an important new book, *Real Time Strategic Change*. With recommitment, the team idea can and will thrive at Fairmount; and making it work will be a big key to the company's success in the future.

The Fairmount Minerals
Sustainable Development
Appreciative Inquiry Summit

August 29–August 31, 2005
Itasca, Illinois

Participant Workbook

Summit Task

Fairmount Minerals, An Empowered Family:
Building on our proud past, designing an exceptional today with a
responsible focus on everyone's tomorrow.

Summit Objectives

- Discover Fairmount's core strengths and valued past—the "positive core" of Fairmount we want to keep and build upon as we create a sustainable future that delivers stakeholder value, including value for shareholders, employees, customers, and supply chain members as well as social and environmental value.

- Dream and envision the shared future we want to create—our vision for becoming a sustainable company on each of the 3 *P*s of sustainable development: *people, profits,* and *planet*.

- Design sustainable development into our organization's purpose and principles and into our day-to-day business products, services and operations, as well as into our personal lives.

- Deploy a set of actions—value creation initiatives and follow-up learning processes (with metrics)—to actively move us in the direction of our shared aspirations and commitments.

Summit Agenda

Summit Day One (Monday): Discovery

Timeframe	Task
8:00–2:45	Welcome and opening address

- Focus for summit: topic statement, objectives, stakeholders
- The business case for becoming a sustainable company

Overview of the AI Summit method and how we will work

- A time to rethink . . .
- 4-D Cycle and our agenda

Set up and conduct 1:1 interviews
Table share (max-mix groups) and report-outs
What is sustainable development?

- The global context and business logic of sustainable value
- Sustainable business leadership examples—video

12:45–1:45	Lunch
1:45–5:15	Identifying "proudest prouds" and success factors

Two benchmark companies—stories and opportunities
Future expectations of our stakeholders: toward an integrated economic, social, and environmental approach to creating value

Summit Day Two (Tuesday): Dream and Design

Timeframe	Task
8:00–11:45	Welcome and overview for day

Positive image/positive action
Images of the future: our dreams of the Fairmount Minerals we want—ten years into the future

- Groups create their visions and aspirations
- Presentations

11:45–12:45	Lunch
12:45–4:30	Discovery of opportunity areas (those that have most impact on summit topic statement)

Introduce design and prototyping methods
Build new groups around opportunity areas

- Brainstorming
- Rapid prototyping

Summit Day Three (Wednesday): Design and Deploy

Timeframe	**Task**
7:30–11:45	Check in and task for morning

- Prepare for presentation of prototypes
- Present prototypes of value initiatives

11:45–12:45	Lunch

12:45–3:00	Work in groups to refine prototypes

- Presentations/commitments
- Next steps to build momentum and organizational learning

Open microphone reflections

Closing

NOTE: All sessions will begin and end on time. There will be breaks each morning and afternoon, with refreshments. Sessions may be recorded so a summary of deliberations and action plans can be communicated to the whole system.

Fairmount Sustainability Summit
Opening Appreciative Inquiry

It is an exciting time to be an employee and stakeholder with Fairmount Minerals. While many companies simply talk about becoming socially and environmentally responsible, Fairmount, because of its proud past and present capabilities, is ready to exceed standard practices and expectations in each of the 3 Ps of becoming a sustainable company: people, profit, and planet.

Not since the days of the Great Depression has there been such a severe decline of public trust in business and in our economic system—nor has there been a better opportunity to build a new era of business-led excellence and leadership in our industry and beyond. We believe that doing good and doing well go hand in hand and that economic prosperity, environmental stewardship, and empowerment of people can, in an integrated way, become a source of innovation and competitive advantage for the long term. Ensuring the preservation of our environment and the responsible use of our natural resources is the right thing to do. Building trust through socially responsible practices with our employees, their families, and our host communities is the right thing to do. Building economic strength and prosperity for our company and all of our stakeholders is the right thing to do.

This summit is about all of us taking a great organization and moving it toward becoming an even better one—where all of our stakeholders, anyone who can impact our business, can see the value of our operations as a sustainable company.

In the following activity, we are looking for your ideas. For example, What things from our past—the best things and strengths—do you want to keep at Fairmount even as we move into a new and changing future? What new and bolder innovative things should we consider doing (for example, in the areas of environmental stewardship, empowerment of people, elimination of waste, building of trust and goodwill with host communities, and creation of new products and services that are profitable and that build a better world)? How can we make this idea of sustainability and the focus on people, profits, and planet part of our day-to-day mind-set and operations? When you look to the future of Fairmount (let's say ten years from now in 2015), how would you finish the following sentence?

> *I will be most proud of our Fairmount family in the future when . . .*

These are examples of things we want to explore. Your ideas are critical. Now let's look at the questions that will launch our work and move us to the task of this summit.

What Is an Appreciative Inquiry Summit?

This is not your typical planning meeting!

The **WHOLE SYSTEM** participates—a cross section of as many internal and external stakeholders as possible—people and groups that care about and have a stake in the future of the organization. This means more diversity and less hierarchy than is usual in a working meeting and a chance for each person and stakeholder group to be heard and to learn other ways of looking at the task at hand.

TASK FOCUSED—A summit is task-focused, not simply an educational event or a conference. We are here to accomplish the task of building our vision and plan of action for becoming a sustainable company in ways that benefit the business and our society—creating new sources of shareholder value, employee and customer value, and societal value.

Future scenarios—for the organization, community, or issue—are put into **HISTORICAL** and **GLOBAL** perspectives. That means thinking globally together before acting locally. This enhances shared understanding and greater commitment to act. It also increases the range of potential actions.

People **SELF-MANAGE** their work and use **DIALOGUE and INQUIRY**, not problem solving, as the main tool. That means helping each other do the tasks and taking responsibility for our perceptions and actions.

COMMON GROUND rather than "conflict management" is the frame of reference. That means honoring our differences and then discovering areas for action where we have strong common ground.

APPRECIATIVE INQUIRY (AI)—To **appreciate** means to value—to understand those things worth valuing. To **inquire** means to study, to ask questions, to search. **AI** is, therefore, a collaborative search to identify and understand the organization's strengths, the greatest opportunities, and people's aspirations and hopes for the future.

COMMITMENT TO ACTION—Because the "whole system" is involved, it is easier to make more rapid decisions and to make commitments to action in a public way—in an open way that everyone can support and help make happen.

The AI Sustainability "4D Cycle"

Questions for Reflection

1. **High-Point Experience:** As you look over your experience with this organization, there have obviously been ups and downs, peaks and valleys, high and low points. We'd like you to reflect on one of the memorable high-point moments. Think about a time that most stands out as a "high point" for you—a time when you felt most effective, alive, most engaged, or really proud?

   A. Please share the story. What happened? when? where? feelings? challenges? How were they overcome? What are you insights?

   B. Based on this story and others like it, if we had a conversation with people that know you the very best and asked them to share *the three best qualities that they see in you, the best capabilities or qualities that you bring to Fairmount Minerals,* what would they say?

2. **Things We Should Continue—Fairmount's Strengths and Distinctive Capabilities:** Every organization today must change—constantly. But great organizations know how to preserve the core of what they do best, *and* they know how to innovate and change at the same time.

    A. If you could keep three things about Fairmount Minerals—even as it moves into a new and changing future—what three strengths would you most want to keep?

    B. When you look at the marketplace and the industry, at what could Fairmount Minerals be best in the world—its signature strength or capability?

Please share one example of Fairmount's strengths in action:

3. **Doing Good and Doing Well:** Fairmount wants to exceed standard practices and expectations on each of the 3 *P*s of sustainability—people, profit, and planet.
    * **Economic Prosperity**—providing value to customers and the company and value for all stakeholders
    * **Social Responsibility**—including employee empowerment and responsibility to families and our communities
    * **Environmental Stewardship**—ensuring the preservation of our environment and eliminating waste and promoting good use of our natural resources

Please share one example in which doing good and doing well became a source of innovation and success for Fairmount rather than simply an added cost. In your view, what is the best example of benefiting from the 3 *P*s of focusing on people, profit, and planet?

4. **Images of the Future: Fairmount Minerals in 2015:** Assume that tonight you fall into sound sleep, a great sleep, that lasts for ten years. During those ten years, many positive innovations and changes happen throughout Fairmount Minerals. Fairmount becomes the organization and the business you most wanted to see—a system creating great customer value, employee value, societal and environmental values, and profitability. During the ten years, Fairmount Minerals becomes the company you most wanted—some miracles even happen—and it becomes the place you are most proud to be part of.

Now you wake up, and it is 2015. You get a tour and a panoramic view of the whole company—its people and operations; its products and services; its standing in the industry; and its reputation with customers, business partners, the government, and communities.

A. As you wake up and see the future Fairmount you most wanted, what does it look like? What are you seeing in 2015 that is new, different, changed, or better? Please describe what you see.

B. Now with this future in mind, what is one step, the smallest step, we could take today to become the future company you want?

C. What is one big and bolder step we might consider, something we may not have considered yet?

Self-Management and Group Leadership Roles

Each small group manages its own discussion, data, time, and reports. Here are useful roles for self-managing this work. **Leadership roles can be rotated.** Divide up the work as you choose.

- **DISCUSSION LEADER**—Assures that each person who wants to speak is heard within the time available. Keeps group on track to finish on time.

- **TIMEKEEPER**—Keeps the group aware of the time left. Monitors report-outs and signals the time remaining to the person talking.

- **RECORDER**—Writes group's output on flip charts, using the speaker's words. Asks a person to restate his or her long ideas briefly.

- **REPORTER**—Delivers a report to the large group in the time allotted.

Discovering the Resources in Our Community

Purpose:
To appreciate and welcome each other and to learn about special
experiences, visions, capabilities, and resources people bring to this summit

Self-Manage:
Select a discussion leader, timekeeper, recorder, and reporter.

Steps:
1. Share highlights from what you learned about the person *you
    interviewed*. **Focus on question 1.**

    Go around the table. Each person introduces *his or her* interview partner.
    Focus on highlights from his or her high-point story and the best
    qualities people see in the stories (interview question 1).

    A place for your notes as you listen

Question 1 High-Point Experiences/Stories	**Themes** You Hear in the High Points: What are the "root causes of success"?

Reporter Note: Please be ready to present a report of high-point story
themes and be ready to retell to the large group **one** of the special-high
point stories from your table—a story that helps illustrate the themes.

2. Share your discoveries about **one** of the other interview questions
    assigned by tables.
    *   Tables 1–9 focus on the continuity question—number 2.
    *   Tables 10–18 focus on the examples of sustainability question—
        number 3.
    *   Tables 19–28 focus on the images of the future question—number 4.

    Reporters: Prepare a 3–4 minute report-out to the large group.
    *   Include themes from the high-point stories and choose one of the
        stories to share.
    *   Include themes from the second question assigned to your table.

What Is Sustainable Development?
Overview by Chris Laszlo, Sustainable Value Partners, Inc.

Key Messages and Themes:

Discovery
Root Causes of Success: When Are <u>We</u> Most Effective and Why?

REPORTS ARE DUE AT _____ O'CLOCK

Purpose:
To look at the things we are doing—from the perspective of our stakeholder group—that we are most proud of, our strongest strengths

Self-manage:
Select a recorder, timekeeper, discussion leader, and reporter.

Steps:
1.   List what YOUR STAKEHOLDER GROUP is doing (or has done) that you are most PROUD of and/or the strengths that you bring in relationship to becoming a sustainable company involving the 3 *P*s of sustainability—people, profit, and planet.

     • **Economic Prosperity**—providing value to customers and the company and value for all stakeholders

     • **Social Responsibility**—including employee empowerment and responsibility to families and our communities

     • **Environmental Stewardship**—ensuring the preservation of our environment and eliminating waste and promoting good use of our natural resources

     What is your stakeholder group doing in one of more of these areas that you are proud of?

2.   Select your "PROUDEST PROUDS" or "STRONGEST STRENGTHS" as a group.

3.   Identify and record your top two "PROUDEST PROUDS" or "STRONGEST STRENGTHS" and the root causes of success.

4.   Identify one story to share with the group—one story to illustrate your stakeholder group's "PROUDEST PROUDS" or "STRONGEST STRENGTHS."

Stories and Opportunities from Benchmark Companies
Presentation by Cindy Frick
Vice President, Organizational Development, HR & Engineering
Roadway Express, Inc.

Key Messages and Themes:

Stories and Opportunities from Benchmark Companies
Presentation by Bob Stiller
President and CEO
Green Mountain Coffee Roasters

Key Messages and Themes:

Discovery

Stories of Sustainability from Other Companies
Focusing on People, Profit, and Planet

Purpose:
To identify the key themes from the presentations on sustainability

Self-manage:
Select a recorder, timekeeper, discussion leader, and reporter.

Steps:
1. **Go around your table and share** your thoughts about the:
   - Key messages that resonated most with you.
   - Points most critical as you think about our summit task. Why might these issues be important as we begin to think about creating the future of Fairmount Minerals?

2. **As a group,** arrive at a consensus on the most compelling themes to emerge from the presentations.

3. **The recorder/reporter listens and prepares a two-minute summary** on the three or four most compelling themes or company examples. He or she should be prepared to share with the whole group.

Positive Image → Positive Action

Powerful Placebo and Positive Health

Pygmalion

What Good Are Positive Emotions?

Unbalanced "Inner Dialogue"

Rise and Fall of Cultures

Affirmative Capacity

Questions for Discussion

What in all of these areas is most interesting to you?

Do you have illustrations or examples of any of these? Is there other research you know about? If so, discuss them.

What are the implications?

The Future Fairmount Minerals

Dreaming the Future We Want to Create: Ideal Future Scenarios

PRESENTATIONS ARE DUE AT _____ O'CLOCK

Purpose:
To imagine and define the future you want to work toward—a Fairmount Minerals family that is truly dedicated to being a leading sustainable company involving the 3 *P*s of sustainability—people, profit, and planet
  • **Economic Prosperity**—providing value to customers and the company and value for all stakeholders
  • **Social Responsibility**—including employee empowerment and responsibility to families and to our communities
  • **Environmental Stewardship**—ensuring the preservation of our environment and eliminating waste and promoting good use of our natural resources

Self-manage:
Select a recorder, timekeeper, discussion leader, and reporter.

Steps:
1. Put yourselves ten years into the future. It is 2015. Visualize the Fairmount Minerals Organization you really want to work toward. Be bold. It's the company you want to see. **Everyone shares his or her vision based on questions such as these:**
    • In 2015, I will be most proud of Fairmount Minerals when what occurs?
    • What do you see in the future—things that are new, better, and sustainable?
    • How did this come about? What are the things that support this vision—providing new ways of engaging stakeholders and communities; reducing energy, waste, and other process costs; creating safety and reducing risks of lawsuits or regulatory audits; providing new ways to empower people; discovering new markets and developing new business products based on sustainability; building reputation, brand identity, and culture for being a good company; providing new education and learning programs; designing sustainable facilities; impacting the industry or suppliers and partners?
    • What makes this vision exciting to you? What results do you envision?
    • How does this vision help us unlock hidden value and generate otherwise missed opportunities (new processes, products, and services; new business opportunities; cost savings; better

partnerships; an enhanced reputation; the ability to attract and retain great people; a sense of purpose; and pride, trust, and a competitive advantage)?

2. Choose a creative way to present your vision to the rest of us in a three-minute "portrayal" as if that future vision existed right now. Use as many members of your group as possible in the presentation; for example, a TV news report, a TV show, a day in the life, a skit, headlines in *The New York Times*, a panel presentation.

Moving from Discovery and Dream to Design

What We Are Learning from Designers

Observation
- Shadowing—observing people using the product or service
- Behavioral Mapping—photographing people within a two- to three-day time span
- Consumer Journey—tracking all of the interactions a consumer has with a product or service
- Camera Journals—keeping visual diaries of activities/impressions relating to the product or service
- Extreme User Interviews—talking to people who really know (or know nothing) about a product or service and evaluating their experience using it
- Storytelling—prompting people to tell personal stories about their consumer experiences
- Unfocus Groups—interviewing a diverse group of people

Brainstorming
- Defer Judgment—Don't dismiss any ideas.
- Build on the Ideas of Others—Do not use *buts*; use only *ands*.
- Encourage Wild Ideas—Embrace out-of-the-box notions because they can be the key to solutions.
- Go for Quantity—Aim for as many new ideas as possible. (In a productive session, up to 100 ideas may be generated in 60 minutes.)
- Be Visual—Use yellow, red, and blue markers to write on big sticky notes that are displayed on a wall.
- Stay Focused on the Topic—Keep the discussion on target.
- Hold One Conversation at a Time—Do not interrupt or dismiss; show no disrespect or rudeness.

Rapid Prototyping
- Mock Up Everything—It is possible to create models not only of products but also of services.
- Use Videography—Make short movies to depict the consumer experience.
- Go Fast—Build mock-ups quickly and cheaply; do not waste time on complicated concepts.
- Provide No Frills—Make prototypes that demonstrate a design idea, but don't worry about the details.
- Create Scenarios—Show how a variety of people use a service in different ways and how various designs can meet the people's individual needs.
- Bodystorm—Delineate different types of consumers and act out their roles.

Refining

- Brainstorm—in rapid fashion to weed out ideas and focus on the remaining best options.
- Focus Prototyping—on a few key ideas to arrive at an optimal solution to a problem.
- Engage the Client—actively in the process of narrowing the choices.
- Be Disciplined—and ruthless in making selections.
- Focus—on the outcome of the process, reaching the best possible solution.
- Get Agreement—from all stakeholders; the more top-level executives who sign off on the solution, the better the chances of success.

Implementation

- Tap All Resources—Involve a diverse workforce to carry out the plans.

Creating New Value through the Lens of Sustainable Development:

Sustainable Development Opportunities

"How might we ... ?"

Levels of Focus	*Sources of Value*
Business Context	Changing the "rules of the game" to provide a competitive advantage for sustainability strategies
Reputation/ Brand	Gaining stakeholder recognition and preference, such as attracting and retaining talent and aiding in employee productivity
Market	Entering new markets driven by customer and societal needs
Product	Creating product differentiation based on technical *and* environmental/social features
Process	Reducing energy, waste, and other process costs
Risk	Instituting the compliance-oriented management of risks and protecting the license to operate

Design

Part One: Holding a Brainstormer on Sustainable
Development Opportunity Areas

Purpose:
To brainstorm as many ideas as possible related to your group's opportunity area—ideas that can move us in the direction of our future visions and dreams. Here is the key question:

Assuming anything imaginable was possible for creating a sustainable company in relation to your opportunity area, how might we . . . ?

Brainstormer Rules
- Defer judgment—don't dismiss any ideas.
- Encourage wild ideas—be radical.
- Build on the ideas of others; don't use *buts*; use only *ands*.
- Stay focused on the topic.
- Hold one conversation at a time.
- Be visual.
- Go for quantity.

SELF-MANAGEMENT AND GROUP LEADERSHIP ROLES

Each breakout group manages its own discussion, data, time, and reports. Here are useful roles for self-managing this work. Leadership roles can be rotated. Divide up the work as you choose.

- **BRAINSTORMER RADICAL**—Assures that the group is challenged to contribute wild, "out there" ideas.

- **BRAINSTORMER TIMEKEEPER**—Keeps the group aware of the time left.

- **BRAINSTORMER FACILITATOR**—Facilitates the brainstormer by upholding the brainstormer ground rules and raises questions to keep the brainstorming moving. Challenges the group to go for quantity; tries to get as many ideas (and sticky notes) as possible on the wall.

Design
Part Two: Rapid Prototyping

Purpose:
To take the three to five most promising areas from the brainstormer and build and design a prototype or model that can be brought into Fairmount Minerals to help us realize our visions. The goal is to begin prototyping an initiative that has strategic value for the company.

Self-manage:
Select a recorder, timekeeper, discussion leader, and reporter.

Steps:
1. Do a quick read of the promising ideas or combination of ideas from the brainstormer. Think about ideas that can be designed into something that is tangible—a value creation initiative. It might be a new business product or service, a training manual, the redesign of a facility or structure, a new communication program, tools for eco-efficiency, a new process design, or a program for customers.
2. For the sake of building at least one prototype, narrow and prioritize the brainstormed list. One way to do this is to use colored dots. Have each group member take five dots and place them on the items they most want to work on. (Someone could put all five dots on one item or could vote for five different items.)
3. If the prototype has several discrete elements, you might want to form subgroups to work on different pieces.
4. Build the prototype and make it visual; for example:
    *   A drawing
    *   A storyboard
    *   A model
    *   A headline story on CNN
    *   A bodystorm (a skit with props)
    *   A business proposal format

Presentation:
1. Be prepared to five a three- to five-minute presentation of the prototype to the whole group.
2. After your demonstration, we'll ask you to name the discrete design elements or big ideas you included. Be ready to make the case—the business case for the sustainability initiative you are prototyping.

Deployment

Purpose:
To refine the prototype and build an action plan to find the quickest, cheapest, and least riskiest ways to put the prototype into practice

Self-manage:
Select a recorder, timekeeper, discussion leader, and reporter.

Steps:
1. Name your prototype.
2. Clearly describe what your initiative is and what it is intended to accomplish, that is, key objectives.
3. Determine at what level of strategic focus it is intended to create value.
4. Whose input or partnership (some structure or group in the organization or external stakeholders with whom we should collaborate) would be most valuable at this stage of development?
5. Assess business/ financial logic.
6. Identify challenges and requirements for execution.
7. Create an action plan: what, when, and who.
8. How will you communicate to help the prototype succeed?
9. By what criteria will you evaluate the success of your prototype—30-day milestone? 60-day milestone? 90-day milestone?
10. Identify the group members who will continue with this initiative and their contact information.

Reporters: Please use the PowerPoint slide template for your final presentation. The group joins for the final presentation to the large group (three- to five-minute presentations).

Deployment

Moving to Action
Ambassadors for Success at Fairmount Minerals

Instructions: With your original interview partner, discuss the following:

1. Name the three most exciting or important things that happened at this summit.

    _____

    _____

    _____

2. What one message will you communicate to ensure the success of Fairmount Minerals?

    _____

3. What are your personal commitments and to-dos?

    _____

    _____

    _____

    _____

    _____

    _____

9

AI Case Applications

From Turnaround to Cultural Transformation: Delivering Business Results in BP Castrol Marine

The Story

When David Gilmour was appointed managing director of Castrol Marine, a number of key business areas lacked clarity: customer segments, brand positioning, disappointing financial results, declining customer satisfaction, and an unclear strategic direction of the business for employees. The business was on the BP "sick list."

This case study highlights key activities in the two-year period from 2004 to 2006.[1] However, these improvements did not happen in a neat or traditionally planned way. Armed with the set of principles that underpin the positive change approach, Gilmour took an iterative and emergent approach that gradually developed a culture of commitment and delivered financial success and greater employee satisfaction. At the same time, market conditions were very difficult, with a shortage in marine lubricants and several increases in oil price.

Castrol Marine is a performance unit operating within the International Marine Business unit within Refining and Marketing in BP. Castrol Marine is a $300–$500 million turnover global marine lubricants marketing business that sells and markets in more than 70 countries and has sales, marketing, and technical teams resident in more than 40 countries.

Project Scope

Gilmour was trained in AI and used it in several situations, although this would be his largest and most complex project to date. He knew the approach had delivered results in other companies; he could draw on a network of practitioners; and he wanted Castrol Marine people in the same location, across regions, and throughout the business to work together.

He also was aware that he would need to adjust his leadership style to be more inclusive and to develop leadership skills throughout the business. This was when he contacted Anne Radford (an experienced AI consultant in Europe) to work with him in this area.

---

1 More detailed information on this case study can be found in Gilmour, D., & Sutton-Cegarra, B. (November 2005). Enabling the easy business transformation in Castrol Marine. *AI Practitioner*.

AI Application

His appointment was on July 1, 2004; and a new management team was in place by September 1, 2004. From 2004 to 2006, the key changes were carried out in Castrol Marine. The process started with applying AI to leadership with the managing director, his direct reports, and regional sales teams. This took place in one-on-one meetings and AI Summits.

Six months into his role as leader of Castrol Marine, Gilmour reflected that the business needed to be easier for staff to work in and easier for customers to interact with. He asked this question: How can we make life easier for ourselves and our customers? The answer to that question was crucial for the organization to be able to deliver the rapid and flexible response to changes in the business environment that rising oil prices were causing. This question generated the Easy Business project.[2]

From January to April 2005, a group from sales, marketing, trade, accounting, and finance attended a pilot workshop in Madrid to discover the core factors and to envision the "ideal contract." Improvements were made; and further workshops were held in Athens, Singapore, and the United Kingdom. These workshops involved all regions and functions in the business unit. The *Design* and *Destiny* phases for Easy Business were completed from April to mid-June 2005. Marketing, customer service, trade accounting, and finance agreed on a clear design specification. Senior managers in Castrol Marine and the supporting BP Marine organization committed to delivering and implementing Easy Business in the marketplace by the end of 2005. Each regional team also committed to developing a workshop for all staff members in its region to work with the Easy Business concept and tools.

Project Milestones (Outcomes)

In mid-August 2005, the first Easy Business contract was established with an important Taiwanese customer. Further contracts followed. However, as the new year approached, there was clear recognition that although prices had increased by some 20%–30%, the business was still making poor returns. A step change in profitability was needed, yet the cost of goods continued to rise as oil hit $60–$70 a barrel. The focus expanded to achieving outstanding financial performance. This resulted in two price increases, and a price increase by some 50% was implemented successfully in the first half of the year. Significant investment in people capabilities, especially value selling, ensured that profitability improved significantly and the financial turnaround was complete. Castrol Marine had emerged as a top-quartile business delivering outstanding financial performance. The results included the following:[3]

---

2 Sutton-Cegarra, B., & Gilmour, D. (May 2005). Taking an 'easy business' approach. *Project Management Today.*
3 Source: Internal BP documents.

The Customer

Satisfaction with Castrol Marine improved by ensuring improvements in delivery performance

The Financial Performance

- Significant turnaround recognized at the group level
- Costs stabilized and overhead gotten under control

Internal Processes

- Well-defined contracting processes implemented and embedded in the organization
- United team approach being built
- Clear segmentation and understanding of customer needs taking place

Organizational Climate

- Business serving as a reference for excellence in business marketing
- Due to scale, organization currently being established as a separate business unit away from the umbrella of International Marine
- Pride in performance that resulted in rising employee morale
- Major investment in people capability (leadership and sales and marketing)

Today Castrol Marine is sustaining its growth with a Global Strategic Inquiry to review progress, to see where future opportunities lie, and to identify ways forward. Also recognized was the fact that sustaining growth would require more leaders and, perhaps, a different type of leadership from those who initiated the turnaround.

Summary of Learnings

An inclusive, positive approach may seem slow at first; but it delivers fast results as everyone is on board from the start of implementation. Management of change began at project conception, which enabled its success. There was inclusiveness, inquiry, and adaptability from the start of the project. Stakeholders believed that clear structure and project management would ensure that each stage of the project would be prepared properly and executed successfully.

We learned that senior management must empower and enable the organization to deliver the changes. Management teams also need to trust the judgment of those who do the work on a daily basis. Catching best experiences and learning how to share and reproduce them is an uplifting and motivational experience.

Contributors

David Gilmour, Managing Director, Castrol Marine, BP PLC, david.gilmour@bp.com

Anne Radford, Consultant and Publisher, AI Practitioner, editor@aipractitioner.com

The authors would like to acknowledge the significant involvement of the consultants, Robbie Macpherson robbie@mcweb.co.uk and Benita Sutton-Cegarra benita@bjc-europe.com in bringing about the results highlighted in this case study.

BT Global Services: An Appreciative Inquiry into Learning Solutions

The Story

In July 1998, BT Global Services (GS) (a division of Syntegra Benelux in the Netherlands, which is part of BT worldwide with 125,000 employees) with its 100 employees was facing a serious situation due to its former director having left the company and the unit rapidly losing its competitive edge in the market. The management style used up to that moment could be described as directive with poor delegation. In July, a new director (one who was familiar with AI) was appointed and a management team of five people was formed to turn this division around.

Project Scope

The new director had two primary objectives in applying AI:

1. Turn the organization around, whereby the products and services would be regarded as added value to BT GS's product lines and a profitable, sustainable business would be created.

2. Create an environment in which people feel empowered and valued for their contributions.

Basically, the new director had to reinvent the division into something that would fit the larger BT Syntegra picture (becoming a leading system integrator), while at the same time maintaining profitability and retaining staff (knowledge and experience).

AI Application

In July 1998, the newly appointed management team brainstormed themes that needed to be addressed. Four key themes emerged:

1. Teamwork
2. Trust within the division
3. Communication between the various groups within the division
4. Reward and recognition

In September 1998, an interview guide was developed with the help of two external consultants. A full day of interviewing was planned for October 1998.

The total group was split into four smaller groups, each covering one of the four themes above.

In October 1998 at an off-site location, a full-day AI intervention was organized and the full AI 4-D cycle was covered. During the storytelling in the *Discovery* phase, remarkably, very few stories came from within the organization. The surprise was that people who had been working for that division for years could not come up with best stories from the work environment. They had to draw on stories from other environments in the past that would help cocreate this new working environment. During this full-day event, special attention was paid to the issue of how to ensure that the results of the day would be sustained. Among other concrete actions, Provocative Propositions were placed in frames together with photographs of the groups.

Other actions included producing a booklet with names, addresses, and other personal information that people wanted to share. This booklet helped create a sense of community in a group that had lost much of its identity in the period before the AI interventions started. Also, *The Thin Book Of Appreciative Inquiry* by Sue Hammond was distributed to all employees a few weeks after the event to help sustain the momentum around AI.

In July 1999, the second AI, day was organized with 100 employees. Two major themes needed to be addressed:

1. Teams/teambuilding
2. Service to both internal and external clients

The people of Arts in Rhythm began the day by dividing the group into six smaller groups, each equipped with its own simple rhythm instrument. (Arts in Rhythm is a group of professional musicians that, through the use of music produced by simple instruments, involves people in creating a sense of teamwork beyond what they normally believe to be possible.) Within 45 minutes, Arts in Rhythm got the whole group performing as an orchestra capable of producing a harmonic piece of music, including variations in tempo, volume, and loudness. The people of Arts in Rhythm made the comparison to a dynamic organization. This activity had a positive influence on the AI process that followed, as it clearly demonstrated what people are capable of achieving and set a positive stage for the life-giving stories that each person had to tell.

In April through June 2000, AI played a major role in two activities. The first activity involved applying AI to a project where the groups of planning, project office, and sales had to move and redesign their departments. The group of six drew up an interview protocol with questions, trying to determine by what workspace people felt most empowered. Interviews involving some 40 people were conducted over a two-week period. The interviewers processed the results of the interviews and put them before the interviewees. The end result was that the departments would have a new workspace that largely met their requirements in terms of space, light, quietness, and openness.

The second activity was a day spent with the management team trying to develop a vision for the next two to three years in terms of where the training market in Learning Solutions was headed and what its role might be. AI was applied in a group process to come up with a provocative statement that could serve as a mission/vision statement for the division. As a result of this day, the following statement was created: *Learning Solutions is the leading expert and inspiring innovator in learning with a focus on practical solutions facilitating change and bringing out the best in people.*

From 2001 onward, AI was used as a "standard approach" in many different situations; a couple of examples are as follows:

- Learning Solutions merged with BT in 2004. A major AI intervention addressed the key identity issues that people thought needed to be secured. The result was a triptech. A triptech is a "picture" consisting of three separate frames—in BT's case, the three questions and the three provocative statements pertaining to the merger. BT considered the triptech its identity. The framed picture with a provocative statement outlined the vision. The picture was handed to the executive to whom the group reported when it became part of the BT family.

- AI has been introduced as a way of engaging with customers and identifying the strength and value of the relationship. In most cases, this lifted the relationship to a more engaging level and resulted in a drastic reduction of escalations.

Project Milestones (Outcomes)

The division successfully mastered a dramatic change in leadership/follower styles as well as in organizational structure. Within a 14 month time frame, the people in the organization managed to embrace a totally different perspective on how the market should be approached as well as how their views and personal responsibilities made the difference.

The division saw significant growth over the course of five years; from 2000–2005, average annual revenue growth was 18% and profit growth was over 20%. The turnover of staff in the division fell from 35% to less than 14% in a market where it is hard to find the right employees. (This statistic is of great importance.) After departures, people usually stayed in touch and contacts remained very good; in general, the result was positive relationships with new organizations. A dramatic change in market approach took place in the whole unit, which resulted in each department in the division taking on a more customer-friendly approach.

Summary of Learnings

After eight years of consistently applying AI, all members believe AI has largely contributed to the positive spirit and dynamic relationships within the division. In applying AI as an approach for organizational change, continued active facilitation is necessary for an organization to operate in an **appreciative paradigm**. The belief is that when AI is not actively facilitated, the tendency is for rapidly changing organizations to fall back on "old complaining styles" and/or deficit behaviors.

This success is noticed by other groups within and outside the division. Today outside parties frequently ask the division to share its experiences with AI. In the past 12 months, the BT Learning and Development community has extended three invitations to this division to share its views on AI with groups of newly appointed managers.

Case Contributor
Joep de Jong, Director Learning Solutions, BT GS Learning Solutions, joep.dejong@bt.com

Enhancing Leadership and Communications Skills through the AI Core Principles

The Story

Local Products (LP), a business division of Nielsen Media Research, is focused on delivering television ratings products and data to its 210 TV markets across the United States. LP division had recently implemented the product development methodology known as Agile, specifically the Extreme Programming (XP) version. Agile XP is a real-time, iterative, and collaborative means for developing software. Although this changeover was moving forward, there were undercurrents of discord and a focus on problems, which highlighted communication issues across departments, and there were concerns that employees might resist the XP effort.

Nielsen's LP management team felt this undercurrent might be less about XP and more about the conversational and relational dynamics across all divisional sections. It was believed that if employees took the time to know, understand, and appreciate one another better, communication would improve, allowing for more open and effective conversations. LP's vision for the division was a sense of unity—all one team—with shared leadership, mutual trust and respect, and the capacity to have open and honest conversations, especially about tough issues, in order to support Agile practices. Specific outcomes management desired included (1) shared understanding for where and how decisions were made and (2) well-defined, communicated, and shared strategic targets. Pamela Skyrme of Skyrme & Associates, Inc., and Cheri Torres of Mobile Team Challenge partnered with LP to support its vision.

Project Scope

LP's leadership team was made up of approximately 17 management leaders across the department: senior management (3), product management (7) and IT (7). The total department size was 180, and initial plans were to roll out AI throughout the organization. It was decided first to focus heavily on relationships among leaders to ensure greater understanding and practice of AI. This would ensure that through follow-up activities, the remaining teams would achieve greater success in implementing the principles of AI, thereby generating positive relationships and enhancing communication.

AI Application

During the first meeting, after senior management voiced their concerns and dreams, Skyrme and Torres asked each leader to interview several of his or her department members regarding XP and Agile. AI interviews were used. Senior leadership was surprised to discover how positive people felt about the changes that had been made. Despite the grumblings that had bubbled to the surface, everyone thought that the new strategy would better serve customers. This was the perfect introduction to the notion that *how* we inquire makes all the difference. To deepen their understanding of AI and to develop a foundational understanding of the principles of AI and the way they influence relationships, senior leaders and directors/managers read *Dynamic Relationships: Unleashing the Power of Appreciative Inquiry in Daily Living*.[4]

The first meeting was followed by a series of weekly individual reflections (refer to the AI in Daily Working Relationships Weekly Reflection Form, see page 291) and a weekly small-group coaching call with the Senior Leaders. The focus of these calls was to reflect on the application of AI principles in working relationships. In addition, a two-day retreat was designed for the directors and managers of the two departments: product management and IT. This retreat integrated Experiential Learning (EL) activities and AI, focusing on teamwork, communication, trust, shared leadership, and continuous learning. This resulted in a pivotal conversation in which participants experienced their capacity to have honest conversations and effective teamwork. During this retreat, the group members developed principles for their working relationships. Like senior management, they decided to engage in weekly reflections and small-group coaching calls to facilitate their capacity to live their principles and practice the principles of AI in their daily interactions. Cycles of action and reflection for individuals and for working teams lasted approximately nine months for senior management and five months for product management and IT directors.

A third training day was sponsored for a larger team of approximately 15 IT project managers and 15 product planners to generate shared understanding and increase a sense of teamwork and communication. This brought the practice of AI, trust, and collaboration deeper into the LP division.

Project Milestones (Outcomes)

In just nine months, the division saw marked improvements in energy and overall relational dynamics. Individuals found ways to address issues by focusing on the outcome and recognizing one another's value to the overall project. Language changed to include greater inquiry into what was of value. Their

---

4 For more information, see Stavros, J., & Torres, C. (2005). *Dynamic relationships: Unleashing the power of appreciative inquiry in daily living*. Chagrin Falls, OH: Taos Institute Publishing.

focus shifted to what was working and how to achieve goals. Ways of handling conflict were transformed as issues were addressed without linking them to personalities; and overall communication was more open, honest, and respectful. AI influenced the approach taken in planning meetings, making decisions, and handling difficult topics. Developing positive *dynamic relationships*[5] shifted the way people engaged in conversation by allowing them get to know one another at a deeper level. This enabled them to actively listen to be influenced, ask questions, and question assumptions in order to understand one another.

The following comments from LP team members capture the highlights of their progress:

- You heard me even if you disagreed with me.
- We challenge issues and assignments together to form a collaborative plan.
- When I needed information, you took the time to give it.
- You trusted us when we said, "Trust us, we'll fix it." And we did.
- Meetings are where everyone shares information, comes together, and rolls decisions out as a unit.
- We recognize the tough position someone else is in and acknowledge it.
- We are better at iteration planning: setting weekly goals for projects, establishing priorities, and making sure we all know them; everyone has full awareness.
- Communication improved, especially with the external stakeholders.
- Trust has improved; the team hears what the user wants and understands what is needed.
- Day-to-day is better; overall interactions are improved, we know everyone better, and retrospectives are beneficial.
- Instead of us versus them, the team works to incorporate all new requirements.
- Empowerment as a team: people feel responsible and accountable; less bureaucracy.

An ending provocative principle that guides them: *We develop and maintain mutual respect across our teams, focusing on trust, honesty, and a shared vision for success, which encourages (a) open communication, (b) awareness and appreciation of individual styles, (c) opportunities to contribute in all ways, and (d) positive controversy so that everyone arrives at a shared vision.*

---

5 "Community members are self-reflectively aware of the richness of their relationships with and to other. This awareness extends to understanding that relationships are dynamic: any action taken on the part of any member will result in changes for other members and potentially the community as a whole." Stavros, J., & Torres, C. (2005). *Dynamic relationships.* Chagrin Falls, OH: Taos Institute.

Summary of Learnings

Organizations interested in generating positive dynamics among organization members will find that the principles of AI support collaborative and open relationships when combined with reflective practice. This case study demonstrates the power of individuals to shift organizational culture by focusing on the dynamics of their interpersonal relationships. The LP division of Nielsen Media Research set out to create a more positive, open, and collaborative interdepartmental team. Using practices from *Dynamic Relationships: Unleashing the Power of Appreciative Inquiry in Daily Living* and focusing on constructing relationships that supported best practices, it dramatically changed the way the division worked together and generated a more positive working environment.

Change doesn't happen overnight; but with the right approaches and tools, significant change can occur in a short time period. This entire project was nine months in duration. The combination of AI, EL, and coaching was very powerful, creating an atmosphere of hope and movement. Gradually changing habits of thought and feeling reinforced and strengthened the shifting culture. The strong commitment of the employees of the LP division to one another and its vision for what was possible were essential to its success.

Contributors
Cheri Torres, Mobile Team Challenge, cheri@mobileteamchallenge.com
Pamela Skyrme, PhD, Skyrme & Associates, Inc., Pskyrme@tampabay.rr.com.
Todd Hillhouse, Vice President, Nielsen Media Research, Local Products, Todd.Hillhouse@nielsenmedia.com

AI in Daily Working Relationships Weekly Reflection Form

My vision for who I am and how I relate when I am at my best on this team

(Make sure you write this in the present tense and it describes your thinking, feeling, and acting in relationships; this is about you-in-action.)

Personal Leadership Goal(s) for This Week

1.
2.
3.

Reflection-on-Action This Week

Shining examples of living my **vision in meeting my goals** this week. (Be specific in offering an example of how you actually lived your vision. See yourself in a situation where you were achieving "the dream." How did your thinking/feeling/acting help create the kinds of relationships and business success that you desired?)

- Challenges I faced this week in fully living my goals; questions I have.

- How those challenges would be experienced if I were living my vision.

- What needs to be done to achieve that experience?

- What I most appreciate about myself and my colleagues this week.

- What is a pressing concern for next week?

Catching My Team and Colleagues

Share one story of catching your team or a colleague working at its/his or her best and living its/his or her shared principles. (Let the team or your colleague know you are highlighting this story this week!)

Building Capacity for Better Work and Better Care: Pennsylvania Community Hospitals and Medical Centers

The Story

What happens when a nurse researcher, a state hospital association executive, and an AI consultant pool their collective talents and networks to enhance nurse retention and the quality of patient care? In this case, Donna Havens from The University of North Carolina at Chapel Hill, Lynn Leighton of the Hospital & Healthsystem Association of Pennsylvania (HAP), and Susan Wood of Corporation for Positive Change organized a five-year project to enhance nurse retention and quality of patient care.

Pennsylvania is one of 30 states experiencing an escalating nursing shortage. By 2020, the national nurse shortage is expected to be as high as 29%. Eighteen of Pennsylvania's 67 counties are designated by the Health Resources and Services Administration (HRSA) as "Nurse Shortage Counties," where nurses are older, report higher levels of dissatisfaction with jobs and career, and have a higher level of intent to leave nursing in the next five years. Data suggest that the nursing shortage will increase and further threaten access to healthcare for vulnerable populations in the future in Pennsylvania.[6]

Project Scope

The six participating hospitals are in rural locations or in areas designated by the HRSA as nurse shortage areas. Six hospitals recognized by the American Nurses Credentialing Center (ANCC) as Magnet Hospitals are acting as mentors.[7] The project began on July 1, 2004, and will end on June 30, 2009, with three years of study and activity and five years of data collection. The premise is that it will take five years or more to generate measurable change in the following three project objectives:

- Increase collaboration and communication among nurses and other healthcare professionals

---

6 This project is supported by funds from the Division of Nursing (DN), Bureau of Health Professions (BHPr), Health Resources and Services Administration (HRSA,) and Department of Health and Human Services (DHHS) under D66HP03170 (Donna S. Havens, Principal Investigator). The information or content and conclusions are those of the author(s) and should not be construed as the official position or policy of, nor should any official endorsement by inferred by, the DN, the BHPr, the HRSA, the DHHS, or the U.S. government.

7 *Magnet Hospitals*: The ANCC establishes standards of excellence and bestows recognition on healthcare organizations that demonstrate sustained nursing care excellence.

- Increase nurse involvement in the organizational and clinical decision-making processes
- Increase cultural sensitivity and competency

Based on partner hospitals' statistics for fiscal year 2003, this project has the potential to impact 1,937 RNs and 55,647 patients in designated "Nurse Shortage Counties" or rural counties in Pennsylvania.

As a researcher, Donna Havens has studied work environments and the organization of nursing work in hospitals for 20 years. More than two decades of research shows that communication, collaboration, and involvement in decisions about nursing work and patient care are features of the work environment that positively impact nurse recruitment, retention, and quality patient outcomes. Thus, it is not surprising that the Institute of Medicine (IOM) has called for implementation of these features to *transform the nursing work environment to keep patients safe.*[8] The HRSA funded *Building Capacity for Better Work & Better Care* through the University of North Carolina. Donna S. Havens, PhD, RN, FAAN, is the project director. HAP has been a collaborating partner, as has Corporation for Positive Change principal Susan Wood.

Each of the six hospital partners—Sewickley Valley Hospital, Meadville Medical Center, Lewistown Hospital, Susquehanna Health, The Good Samaritan Hospital in Lebanon, and DuBois Regional Medical Center—is paired with an ANCC Magnet mentor hospital. The Magnet hospitals participating in the program are Fox Chase Cancer Center (Philadelphia, Pennsylvania), Abington Memorial Hospital (Abington, Pennsylvania), Lancaster General Hospital (Lancaster, Pennsylvania), Johns Hopkins University Hospital (Baltimore, Maryland), Lehigh Valley Hospital and Health Network (Allentown, Pennsylvania), and Englewood Hospital & Medical Center (Englewood, New Jersey).

AI Application

AI was used to define the project objectives (topics) and inquiry, then to locate and build on the best ideas and practices already existing in each hospital. Appreciative interviews conducted in each hospital were tailored to its priorities. For example, one hospital immediately focused on decisional involvement to accelerate formation of staff nurse councils and shared decision making. Another hospital focused on deepening its understanding of cultural awareness and sensitivity by broadening its views on what "differences" entail. A third hospital immediately went to work in the emergency department (ED), finding the interfaces between the ED and other departments to improve interfaces—moving from "push to pull" to improve patient flow and the quality of care.

All of the hospitals studied the three objectives in ways that provoked

---

8 Page, A. (2003, November 4). Keeping patients safe: Transforming the work environment of nurses, *Institute of Medicine.*

growth and learning. Nurse surveys conducted each year illustrate the measure of change occurring by unit and by hospital and in the project overall.
Several participating hospitals and mentors experimented with a strength-
based framework for strategic planning—SOAR (strengths, opportunities, aspirations, and results).[9] SOAR was used as a framework to conduct focus groups
for designing a professional practice model with staff nurses and to develop
the first strategic plan for nursing.

Three times a year hospitals and their Magnet mentor hospitals come
together for a two-day face-to-face learning collaborative. Hospital teams share
what they are doing and learning and work together to meet project objectives.
This sharing among the hospitals has been one of the most exciting parts of
the project. Collaboratives are two-day meetings where nurses and others from
the six-partner and six-mentor hospitals come together to share what they are
learning and doing regarding the three project objectives. Based on what works
best, they plan how to continue. Because of the value of learning, one hospital brought 14 people. Attendance at the collaboratives grew from 40 to 80 by
the third year.

Project Milestones (Outcomes)

At the last collaborative (the seventh in the project to date), each partner hospital described the work they were doing with respect to each of the project's
objectives. This included:

- Development of professional practice councils at the unit and hospital
  level.
- Creation of leadership tools for registered nurses who are chairing the
  councils.
- Use and adaptation of SBAR (Situation-Background-Assessment-Rec-
  ommendation), a standardized communication technique to enhance
  the quality of care.
- Nurse strategic planning using SOAR (strengths, opportunities, aspirations, and results).
- Unique adaptations of AI to hard-wire the technique into the culture of
  the organization, including meetings, process improvement, performance feedback, employee interviews, and exit interviews.
- Adjustment to manager roles.
- Use of brainstorming rules to involve staff in idea creation and decision
  making.
- Staff nurse accountability and involvement.

9 See the article "Strategic Inquiry with Appreciative Intent: Inspiration to SOAR" by Jackie Stavros, David Cooperrider, and Lynn Kelley. This new framework for strategic planning was edited and originally published in the November 2003 issue of *AI Practitioner*, pp. 10–17. The complete article is provided in Chapter 11 of this handbook.

- Creation of behavioral norms and codes of conduct.
- Use of courageous conversations to develop better relationships between nurses and others.
- Exploring and understanding of diversity.
- Sharing of procedures and processes, especially related to communication hand-offs.

Between collaborative sessions, project team members visit partner hospitals and information is shared between facilities. Collaboratives have been supplemented by conference calls on topics of interest to the group. A call on "Crucial Conversations to Enhance Communication and Collaboration" drew more than 90 people from both partner and Magnet mentor hospitals.

Hospitals also receive input from content experts in communication, cultural diversity, shared governance, and professional practice. A topic of particular interest was "Positive Deviance" to discover uncommon and successful practices and behaviors.[10] A "Crucial Conversations" book was provided as personnel looked more deeply to explore the need to establish civil behavior.[11]

Summary of Learnings

Sustainability was the focus of the project during 2006–2007. Partner hospitals were planning ways to meet and talk with each other when the official activity ended in July 2007. The comfort level and trust to share needs and ideas grew over three years, and differences between partners and Magnet hospitals decreased. Initially, some partner hospitals were intimidated by the prospect of working with Magnet-recognized hospitals. One sign of change was that as a group, the Magnet mentors recently reported, "The partner hospitals are no longer in awe of us. We are learning as much from them as they are from us." The project team published a paper on AI in *The Journal of Nursing Administration*, describing the use of AI in this initiative.[12]

Case Contributors

Susan O. Wood, Principal, Corporation for Positive Change, Susanowood@comcast.net

Donna S. Havens, PhD, RN, FAAN, Professor, The School of Nursing, The University of North Carolina at Chapel Hill, dhavens@email.unc.edu

Lynn G. Leighton, VP, Professional and Clinical Services, The Hospital and Healthsystem Association of Pennsylvania, lgleighton@haponline.org

---

10 Sternin, J., & Choo, R. (2000, Jan–Feb). The power of positive deviancy, *Harvard Business Review*, 14–15.

11 Patterson, K., Grenny, J., McMillan, R., & Switzler, A. (2002). *Crucial conversations: Tools for talking when stakes are high.* New York: McGraw-Hill.

12 Havens, D., Wood, S., & Leeman, J. (2006). Improving nursing practice and patient care: Building capacity with appreciative inquiry. *The Journal of Nursing Administration, 36*(10), 463–470.

AI in Healthcare—Whole Systems Change at Alice Peck Day—Creating the Best Patient Experience in the World, Right Here at Home

The Story

Alice Peck Day Health Systems (APDHS) is a community-based healthcare system that has provided healthcare services through the continuum of life in Lebanon, New Hampshire, for 75 years. Its services include primary care with approximately 40,000 patient visits annually, a birthing center, surgical services with approximately 3,300 patients annually, a 20-bed hospital, 72 assisted living apartments, and a 50-bed nursing home. APDHS is supported by approximately 550 employees, physicians, and allied health professionals.

Early in 2005, Harry Dorman, president and CEO of APDHS, initiated a five-year organizational change process with an overarching goal of providing the best service possible to patients. The initiative focused on three main objectives: creating a high-performing organization, increasing improvement capability, and developing an opportunity-focused workforce engaged in positive change. These objectives built on the strengths of APDHS and the strong loyalty of the community and staff to the organization.

Project Scope

The AI change process is systemwide, involving all stakeholders of the patient, resident, and staff experience. It has consisted of three primary phases from 2005 to date:

1. Introduction of AI to the organization
2. AI leadership development and systems improvement
3. APDHS summit on the task of "Creating the Best Patient Experience in the World, Right Here at Home"

During the first phase, board of trustees' support for the AI change process was achieved and AI was employed in several departmental improvement initiatives. Harry Dorman and Alex Jaccaci, Director of Performance Improvement, also were trained in the AI Summit methodology and facilitated an AI-based board retreat on "Leading APD in Excellence," which set the direction for the initiative.

The second phase of work focused on developing the leadership and organizational systems required to lead APDHS through a five-year change process.

This phase included a three-day AI Leadership Summit focused on "The Heart of Leadership Fostering a Healthy APDHS—Creating an Environment of Positive Change." The 75 participants included all senior administrators, managers, physicians, and members of the board and 12 informal leaders. The summit launched eight Innovation Teams that had advanced leadership and several organizational systems, which, in part, established the readiness for the systemwide APDHS Summit. Leadership Summit Innovation Team members also were surveyed, and the results informed improvements that were integrated into the planning for the APDHS Summit Innovation Teams.

The third phase of work included a systemwide summit on the task of "Creating the Best Patient Experience in the World, Right Here at Home." Three identical two-day summit sessions took place during September 2006, engaging 394 stakeholders. Ninety-one percent of the employees took part along with 28 physicians; 25 residents; and 22 members of the patient, volunteer, board, and affiliated communities. The summit generated the Positive Core of the APDHS Best Patient, Resident, and Staff Experience; a vision for 2011 that is guiding strategic planning; and organizational, departmental, and individual improvement actions.

AI Application

AI was employed throughout the organization in a variety of capacities including summits, team building, curriculum design, coaching, meeting redesign, new process design, and advancing of innovation projects. For example, in the *Design* phase of the APDHS Summit, the participants focused on the "four levels of change at APDHS" (individual, departmental, interdepartmental, and organizational).[13]

The first activity involved designing at the two levels of organizational and interdepartmental change. This resulted in 64 proposals for Innovation Projects and 24 ideas for improvement from the residents of the nursing home and assisted living facility. A process called the Innovation Team Prioritization Process (ITPP) was created to address all proposals and suggested improvements. The ITPP occurred five days after the last summit session and created an implementation plan for all proposed projects and improvements in the form of "First Round," "Second Round," and "Departmental/Functional Team-Led Initiatives."[14]

The second activity in the *Design* phase of the APDHS Summit involved "At-Home Groups" designing the other two levels of change: intradepartmental and individual change. This work launched the YES! Program, a pro-

---

13 Jaccaci, A, Coburn, K., Peyton, A., & Wood S. (2006). Levels of Change at APDHS.
14 Jaccaci, A. (2006). Innovation Team Prioritization Process.

gram promoting departmental-level improvement by empowering individual staff members to conceive and implement improvement ideas. Within a month of the summit, all departments began participating in the YES! Program and 38 YES! Champions received training.

Project Milestones (Outcomes)

An evaluation of the APDHS Summit demonstrated high workforce engagement in the change process. The participant's responses showed that:

- 99% are committed to improving the APDHS patient/resident/staff experience.
- 98% feel supported to make positive change at APDHS.
- 97% are aware of available tools and resources to support positive change.
- 99% stated that the AI method was effective to begin positive change.

The Positive Core and Vision data generated in the APDHS Summit is being developed into a four-year action plan of strategies and metrics in each of the four topics of study: Our Best Service, Our Best Quality, Our Best Environment, and Our People at Our Best.

In the first month following the APDHS Summit, the YES! Program yielded 62 proposed ideas and 27 implemented projects within departments. Innovation Teams launched from the Leadership Summit implemented systems including Shared Leadership Expectations; organizational-wide Time for Improvement; the Follow-Through Tracking System, a project and knowledge management resource; and Leadership Education Series 2006.

In 2006, indirect improvements included becoming the number one performing hospital in New Hampshire for nationally recognized quality standards of surgical care and pneumonia care, improving patient satisfaction scores in the Immediate Care Center by 37%, and the Birthing Center being ranked in the 99th percentile in the nation for patient satisfaction.

Summary of Learnings

Healthcare, by design, is a profession that is deficit-focused. AI is a powerful way to initiate positive change as people have demonstrated commitment to sustain an appreciative focus in their work and relationships. APDHS found that a blend of process improvement tools is needed in the *Destiny* phase to support the implementation of desired change. APDHS is becoming a learning organization, and the iterative cycles of AI have enabled the organization to improve the way it improves.

Contributors:

Alex Jaccaci, Director of Performance Improvement & Medical Staff Relations, Alice Peck Day Memorial Hospital, jaccacia@apdmh.org

Harry Dorman, President/CEO, Alice Peck Day Memorial Hospital, dormanh@apdmh.org

Fostering Cultural Change in a Federal Research Organization: (EPA/ORD)

The Story[15]

The mission of the Environmental Protection Agency's (EPA) Office of Research and Development (ORD) is to provide the EPA with sound scientific support for regulatory decision making. In 1994, a Congressionally mandated assessment concluded that "the discipline-based organization of ORD's laboratories was not optimal to support the mission-based organization of the rest of the agency" and recommended a functional reorganization.[16] Also, the challenges of increasingly complex environmental issues, severe resource constraints, political pressures, and impending wave of retirements demanded that ORD become more flexible and more accountable for demonstrating results. After trying several deficit-based approaches to change, in 2002, ORD's senior management assembled a Leadership Coalition that investigated using AI.

Project Scope

ORD's nearly 2,000 researchers, managers, and administrative personnel operate in nine consolidated organizational units in 14 locations around the country. To effect cultural change in this hierarchical, geographically distributed, knowledge-based organization, the Coalition developed a two-level strategy: (1) engage the larger organization in AI Summits to identify common values and images of a successful future and (2) foster application of AI concepts to important local issues; for example, instituting strategic research planning, improving the organizational climate, and/or overcoming conflict.

AI Application

Experiential Learning (EL) involves presenting a group with a challenging task and then reflecting on the experience to explore how to work together more effectively. Having previously experienced the positive effects of EL on learning and group dynamics, the Coalition decided to incorporate EL exercises[17]

---

15 This article has been reviewed by the Office of Research and Development, U.S. Environmental Protection Agency and approved for publication. Approval does not signify that the contents necessarily reflect the views and policies of the Agency, nor does mention of trade names or commercial products constitute endorsement or recommendation for use.

16 For a retrospective, see National Research Council. (2000). Strengthening science at the U.S. Environmental Protection Agency: Research-management and peer-review practices. Washington, DC: National Academy Press.

17 For examples, see Rainey C., & Torres, C. (2001). *Mobile team challenge: Low ropes course facilitator's manual.* Maryville, TN: MTC Associates, LLC.

into the AI planning meetings for the second summit to assess whether EL would enliven the meetings and add value to the summit.[18] Also, ORD partnered with Mobile Team Challenge (MTC) to bring to the EL experience its AI-based Appreciative Facilitation™ (AF) methodology,[19] which focuses on identifying and building on strengths and applying the resulting insights to the workplace in meaningful ways.

EL had a tremendous effect on the planning meeting: tensions quickly melted, and participants spontaneously erupted in applause and laughter when their innovative approaches helped them complete the tasks successfully. Consistent with Frederickson's "Broaden and Build" theory,[20] the resulting infusion of positive emotions stimulated creativity and increased receptivity to new ideas. Accordingly, the Coalition decided to incorporate EL into the summit design to expand thinking in advance of critical dialogues. For example, prior to the *Dream* phase, a "balloon-tower" exercise was used to promote awareness of the synergies that can result from sharing resources (a practice not ordinarily embraced in the "stove-piped" organization).

Project Milestones (Outcomes)

Using EL to Expand Thinking Capacity and Increase Energy at AI Summits

At the August 2004 Summit, 300 participants (in 34 small groups) were guided through EL exercises from the stage and, to leverage the few facilitators, were provided appreciative questions in a summit workbook to help the groups self-manage their discussions. While the questions helped frame conversations, they were no substitute for the probing questions, reflective comments, and group-management skills that a dedicated skilled facilitator could have brought to the interactive discussion. As such, there was no observed expanded awareness to the extent hoped for. However, everyone was surprised by EL's capacity to increase participant energy and reduce frustration following intensive small-group discussions. It was concluded that carefully designed, well-facilitated EL exercises substantially broaden thinking during an AI summit.

---

18 For details on the two summits, see McCarthy-O'Reilly, M., Elstein, K., Torres, C., & Weisenberger, C. R. (May 2005). Igniting leadership at all levels in the federal workplace: An experiment for organizational change at US EPA's Office of Research and Development (ORD), *AI Practitioner*.

19 Torres, C. (2001). *The appreciative facilitator: A handbook for facilitators and teachers.* Tulsa: Learning Unlimited.

20 Frederickson, B. L. (2001). The role of positive emotions in positive psychology: The broaden-and-build theory of positive emotions. *American Psychologist, 56,* 218–226.

Sustaining an Appreciative Mind-Set through Follow-up Workshops and Participatory Action Research

While ORD's two AI summits created a "global" vision of a better future, employees did not yet possess the tools needed to implement the vision at the local level. To address this need, ORD staff developed a workshop that (1) introduced participants to a simple philosophical model of an appreciative, continuous learning environment (Figure 1, right column, Excellence); (2) used EL activities and AF concepts to enable employees to conduct productive, reflective discussions about a task regardless of whether the task was completed successfully; and (3) included workplace-relevant role-plays on how to initiate constructive conversations with those who might resist change by helping them envision and explore new possibilities.[21]

After one year of workshops, the expanding Facilitators Community of Practice, a participatory action research group, engendered important changes in how ORD did business, including restructuring staff meetings to enable all participants to lead energizing, appreciative discussions; opening strategic-planning meetings to internal and external stakeholder groups to enable participative decision making; fostering closer cross-organizational collaborations; and promoting stronger team dynamics. In turn, decision making became faster and better informed and had greater stakeholder support, reducing the conflict-promoting dialogues that stifled progress in the past.

Summary of Learnings

The primary learnings were ways to integrate EL into AI Summits for real-time learning and action and the importance of developing follow-up training to develop and sustain an appreciative mind-set.

Integrating EL into AI Summits

Based on ORD's experiences, the following steps helped ensure an effective integration of EL into AI Summits:

- Incorporate brief EL exercises after intensive small-group discussion sessions to increase energy, expand thinking, and reduce frustration.
- For large groups, from the stage, provide clear oral instructions and use slides projected onto large screens. For some exercises, it is helpful to demonstrate the setup on stage.
- Provide skilled facilitators in each group to ask probing questions, stimulate reflective comments, and manage the group dynamic.

---

21 For details, see Elstein, K., & Driver, K. (Spring 2007). Fostering a continuous-learning mindset in a federal research organization. *Organization Development Journal.*

- If skilled facilitators are not available to debrief each group after an activity, frame conversations with carefully worded appreciative questions in a Summit handbook.

Fostering an Appreciative Mind-Set
- A simple model contrasting the existing culture with the desired end-state (Figure 1 on the following page) fosters mutual understanding at an intuitive level.
- Helping employees apply the model to important local issues greatly facilitates cultural change.

In addition to the workshop, ORD promotes local application of the appreciative mind-set through coaching and retreat-design/facilitation services.

Contributors

Cheri Torres, MBA, MA, and Carolyn R. Weisenberger, BS, LPN, Mobile Team Challenge, Maryville, TN; cheri@mobileteamchallenge.com, Rainey@mobileteamchallenge.com

Ken Elstein and Kathy Driver, US EPA/ORD, Research Triangle Park, NC, Elstein.kenneth@epa.gov, driver.kathy@epa.gov

Figure 9.1: Contrasting the Pursuit of Perfection and of Excellence
as Two Approaches for Progressing through Uncertainty, Ambiguity,
and Change

Pursuit	Perfection	Excellence
Definition of success	No errors	An inspiring and evolving state of knowledge
Dominant motivator	Fear of making mistakes, of being wrong	*Anticipation* of acquiring new skills, gaining insights about oneself and others
Underlying assumption	- I should know all I need to. (Also, I may fear I can't learn what I don't know.) - There is only one perfect answer; and by extension, there are limited possibilities and resources.	- Life is continuous learning, and I will learn in the way most useful to me. - There are infinite possibilities and resources I have yet to uncover.
Basis for self-esteem	Internal (pathological) critic. If I'm right, I'm a wonderful person; if wrong, I'm a flawed person.	An explorer's sense of wonder, awe, and humility at life's complexity.
Consequences of mistakes	Feeling of failure resulting in negative emotions/actions (e.g., defensiveness, blame attribution, contrition, anger, and/or resentment).	Realization that whatever happens is a result of people's knowledge and awareness at the time; hence, a deep interest in exploring ways to increase knowledge and awareness.
Interpersonal manifestations	- Advocate our opinions; seek to persuade. - A need to judge others relative to ourselves; eagerness to point out others' mistakes; pleasure in others' misfortunes (schadenfreude).	- Inquire about others' opinions; seek to understand. - Anticipation that I will learn something from everyone with whom I interact; an appreciation for the value of diverse perspectives.
Consequence for us and for others	Us: Self-esteem depends on whether we are right or wrong. We don't seek others' opinions/ideas. Little, if any, learning occurs. Others: Win/lose outcomes. Our actions breed resentment; our negativity infects others.	Us: We learn and therefore maintain a healthy self-esteem. We seek out and appreciate the goodness, skills, and talents in others. Others: Win/win outcomes regardless of "success." Our appreciative approach infects others. We help others achieve the three universal needs: to be heard, to feel essential, and to be seen as unique and exceptional.
Organizational manifestations	Fear of failure and unwillingness to take on any risks.	Fascination with outcomes; willingness to take on reasonable risks as learning opportunities.
Which lead to . . .	Excessive controls to prevent undesirable outcomes.	Informed spontaneity; cocreation.
Which in a rapidly changing world, results in . . .	Untimely responses, isolation, irrelevance, and obsolescence.	Responsiveness, connectedness, and continuous evolution.
And that creates a work environment that is . . .	Stressful, painful, and difficult.	Fun and exciting.

Greeting Our Future:
An Appreciative Inquiry into Aging
Well in Boulder County, Colorado

The Story

Nestled in the Rocky Mountain foothills northwest of Denver, Boulder County, Colorado, boasts stunning natural beauty, outdoor recreation, world-class technological and academic resources, and strong networks of community services. For these and other reasons, it is a prime spot for aging baby boomers and retirees. In fact, shortly after the turn of the millennium, Boulder-area statisticians and service providers predicted a coming "silver tsunami" that would radically increase the number of older adults available to contribute to the community as volunteers, board members, community leaders, employees, and caregivers—as well as the number of frail, vulnerable elders and caregivers requiring service and support.[22]

With this backdrop, Boulder County Aging Services Division and its community partners committed to developing a countywide strategic plan for aging services to proactively address the coming challenges, while harnessing and leveraging the growing resources that would be available in this aging community. Knowing that it was important to engage a broad cross section of the community in the process, they asked themselves:

- How do we meaningfully engage large, diverse groups of participants in this process?
- How do we create a *shared vision* that will draw people together in service of its implementation?
- What kind of system might we use that will be *congruent* with our strengths-based approach to service for older adults and caregivers?

Michele Waite, manager of the City of Longmont's Senior Services, and Rosemary Williams, division manager of Boulder County's Aging Services Division, had heard about AI as a large-systems change process. Intrigued, they enrolled in a Foundations workshop, which convinced them that AI was a process that could answer all three of their questions. Consultant Amanda Trosten-Bloom joined the project team. Together they launched the Greeting Our Future initiative.

---

22 The number of people 60 and older in Boulder County increased by 32% between 1990 and 2000 and by another 19% between 2000 and 2004. The number of older adults is projected to increase by 30% between 2004 and 2008 and by an additional 30% by 2012.

Project Scope

Their overall purpose was "to engage the passions, creativity, and life experiences of all generations and cultures in Boulder County in transforming the aging experience and creating vibrant communities in which we all age well." Specifically, they were charged with crafting a strategic plan that clearly reflected the vision of the community and that would build momentum for grassroots implementation. Thus, the specific focus of the Greeting Our Future initiative was to:

- *Identify and lift up* best practices in the aging services (the best in aging services) that already existed in Boulder County.
- *Envision* a future in which aging services would be even stronger than they already were.
- *Generate enthusiasm* for (*and participation* in) the Greeting Our Future initiative and its implementation.

Taking place from early 2005 through the summer of 2006, their appreciative process was guided by a ten-person Strategic Visioning Leadership Team (SVLT) consisting of the directors of senior services from municipalities throughout the county.

The SVLT's first act was to form a 50-person Coordinating Team (SVCT). The SVCT developed and refined an AI Guide, created a plan for conducting several hundred interviews, and initiated a first "wave" of 157 interviews to catalyze community involvement in the process.

Over the course of the coming months, approximately 400 more community members participated through a variety of venues including:

- **Community Conversations**—local gatherings that expanded on the one-on-one interviews and engaged elders, caregivers, service providers, and others in Discovery and Dreaming activities.
- **Community Summit**—a two-day summit focused on validating the positive core, establishing strategic goals for aging well in Boulder County, and designing principles to guide future decisions and actions.
- **Strategic Planning Meetings**—half-day regional gatherings to articulate and prioritize plans for implementing the strategic goals.

AI Application

The project began with AI training and facilitation at the SVCT level. Subsequently, AI guides were developed that served as the foundation for the Community Conversations. The Community Summit was designed on the AI 4-D Cycle, and the Strategic Planning Meetings were developed using the AI principles as a backdrop. AI was the backbone of the strategic visioning process. It continues to inform the *Design* and *Destiny* phases that are still unfolding. AI complemented the strengths-based approach to aging services in Boulder County and fostered the involvement of a large number of people in moving from a common vision to community action.

Project Milestones (Outcomes)

In July 2006, a countywide strategic plan called Creating Vibrant Communities in Which We All Age Well: Moving from Common Vision to Community Action was approved by the county commissioners and returned to the community. The plan included a set of Strategic Design Principles by which Boulder County would design, develop, deliver, fund, and evaluate aging services in the future. Seventy community members attended the meeting during which this plan was delivered, leading the county commissioner to comment:

> *The presence of so many stakeholders here today clearly shows that this plan reflects the community's vision. And, it ensures that the plan will not just gather dust on a shelf somewhere. We will move forward together to implement it.*

The involvement of a large, diverse group of volunteers generated excitement, ownership, and broad community commitment to the change process. For example, the city of Lafayette, Colorado, adopted a "visitability" ordinance to ensure that a percentage of all new homes built in the community could be accessed by people using assistive devices (wheelchairs, walkers, and so on). An intergenerational festival in spring 2007 brought together people of all ages in celebration of community.

In late 2006, a Countywide Leadership Team (CLT) formed to oversee the plan's implementation. This team continues to plan, design, and organize activities using the AI 4-D Cycle.

Summary of Learnings

This vital initiative was rich with learnings about AI and about its application to large-scale social change. Following are a few of the most important learnings:

- It is not only possible but actually *preferable* to engage a broad cross section of the community in a strategic change process, provided the community is highly relational, positive, and focused on possibility.
- Such a process (particularly at a community level) requires a well-trained infrastructure and administrative support in order to succeed.

- The appeal of AI is seductive. A wide range of people will want to be involved in the process; and the more opportunities for inclusion over the life of the initiative, the more effective and contagious the change effort.

The most exciting learning was actually more of a reminder than a new insight: that a well-conceived and well-executed AI process takes on a life of its own. It generates the energy needed to sustain itself and reach completion; yet it may do so in unexpected ways. Leaders of the process must be prepared to continue to guide and support a process that moves in directions they'd not initially imagined. In other words, AI yields positive *and unexpected* results.

Contributors

Amanda Trosten-Bloom, Principal, Corporation for Positive Change, amanda@positivechange.org

Rosemary Williams, Division Manager, Boulder County Aging Services Division, rtw@perfx.net

Michele Waite, Manager, Senior Services, City of Longmont, michele.waite@ci.longmont.co.us

Funk to Fervor: Small Steps Result in Big Dreams–A Head Start Program

The Story

A small community of 4,000 residents in Louisiana was noted for being one of the ten poorest areas in the country. Racially divided and economically depressed, it struggled to maintain community identity in the face of out-migration of young people. Citizens lived with little hope and a few memories of a bygone era when the East Carroll Parish was comparatively prosperous. Fortunately for the town of Lake Providence, what began as a small AI effort in one nonprofit, played a major role in rekindling community spirit.

A local Head Start agency lost federal funding after years of mismanagement and deteriorating services. As the designated national interim management entity, Community Development Institute (CDI) enters such failing programs with the mission of enhancing their program operations and services, establishing fiscal integrity, expanding partnerships with other local service agencies, and restoring Head Start's reputation in the community.

The assigned site manager recognized immediately that the organization was a microcosm of the whole community—depressed, resentful, and backward-looking. Staff members felt powerless to make the changes necessary to fulfill their mission. Traditional team-building techniques had proven ineffective: they produced no permanent change in attitudes or interactions; and when staff members talked, no one appeared to listen.

Project Scope

After eight months of traditional staff and OD efforts that showed little lasting improvement, CDI's lead manager began a series of positively focused inquiries into the "best of" for the staff over the next year to revitalize a failing education program. Initially, topic questions focused on their best memories of their community history and their hopes for their children and themselves. The next set of strength-based inquiries zeroed in on staff skills in communications, meetings, teamwork, facilities, and program operations. The results were profound for the children, the families, the staff, and the community.

There were approximately 30 staff members; and of those, 8 were managers in the program. For most of the AI sessions, all personnel were present. The managers were present for the "Being Heard" session, which they shared in the form of a commitment to all staff. This resulted in the implementation of simple appreciative acts within the program.

AI Application

The new manager had experienced AI through CDI. Although she did not initially possess formal training in AI, she saw the possibility of using it to animate her disheartened organization. Arranging a staff retreat, she used positive questions to encourage staff members to talk about what really mattered to them. The staff retreat was held away from the rural parish, and all employees were invited to participate. The site manager's sole intention of the day was to cocreate a powerful transformation in which the past was released and space and energy were created for something new.

A few simple questions were asked:

1. Think back over this past year and all of your accomplishments as a group of individuals who stepped up to make a difference for children and families in the parish. What was the highpoint experience for you? When did you feel most successful, happy, and confident about your role and the group's accomplishments? Tell me about that time. What about that experience made it so special for you?

2. If I were to ask a friend about you, what special gifts would that person say that you have—those gifts that you bring to the Head Start program? What qualities do you bring to the program—to the children and families?

3. Imagine that you are granted three wishes for the upcoming year. What three wishes would you ask to be granted that would make the greatest change in this program?

The energy generated was infectious. Subsequently, other AIs were introduced as part of an overall plan to continue the organizational culture shift.

Several inquiries were held over the next few months with all staff present. One inquiry was held to generate a foundation and framework for the work by identifying the underlying values of the organization and its individuals. This quick session generated a shared ownership as well as individual commitments to forward the quality of the program.

Following a complaint by a parent that she was not feeling welcomed by a teacher in the classroom, a session was held with all staff members to create how they wanted to interact with parents and children. Following simple interview questions, participants explained how they wanted to welcome children, parents, and others into their classrooms and the program: with spoken words, by smiling, by being approachable, by using pleasant facial expressions, by making eye contact, through interaction, by being helpful, and by being considerate and having a welcoming attitude. In addition, the teachers created specific statements about what parents would be saying about them at the end of the year as being a wonderful teaching staff.

One of the staff's biggest complaints—"people aren't being heard"—was, in fact, shorthand for a style of communication characterized by rumor, gossip, innuendo, and complaints. Provocative propositions—statements of possibility—were developed to ensure that positive communication, shared commitment, and resiliency became the norm. Examples of these possibility statements follow:

1. Clear and open communication is an essential component of any successful organization, team, or family. Mutually supportive and respectful interactions among all staff increase our positive energy and foster a productive environment where service excellence and individual satisfaction and even delight are the norm everyday.

2. Organizations perform exceptionally well when employees are attracted to the work, not just as a job to earn a wage, but as a way to connect to a higher purpose aligned with the mission. An organization at its best is made possible by everyone having a shared commitment. Working together inspired by a sense of shared purpose, we are energized, productive, and focused on high-quality services in support of the overall goals of this organization and each other.

3. Webster's dictionary defines resiliency as "the capacity to spring back, to recover quickly, especially from an illness or setback; to possess elasticity, the ability to stretch, especially mentally." The vitality of our organization depends on our ability to bounce back quickly from adversity. We support one another to focus on what can be done today to move forward, even a little bit. We have more to contribute to those we serve, more satisfying work and a greater role in shaping our own futures in a positive manner as we strengthen our capacity for resilience.

Project Milestones (Outcomes)

The site manager described the resulting change this way:

> When I came to the organization, one of the first things I noticed was silence, uncanny silence, as if people had given up talking to one another. Now when I walk around, I hear the hum of conversation in every corner of our offices and in the classrooms. To me, it's the sound of happiness from people engaging in activities that make a difference.

The program director explained how this change process touches the lives of the customers:

> *"It was truly amazing to me to observe the impact of a renewed connection to one another and commitment to their Head Start program. People displayed enjoyment working together on projects, took pride in their accomplishments, and wanted it to be known in the community that they were providing high-quality services in the program."*

A mental health consultant who worked with this children's program over a number of years recently reported compelling accounts showing significant positive changes in staff interactions with children and in children's scores on developmental outcomes since AI was embraced into the organization's culture. A precipitous drop in problem behaviors in the classrooms occurred as teachers became happier working there and enthusiastically sought out classes to increase their professional skills.

From the start, the organization's connection to the community was an issue due to the many years it neglected its clients. A case in point: broken and unsafe equipment installed in the 1950s made up a dilapidated playground adjacent to the agency. Through community organization and donations, an architect created a site plan; hazardous equipment was removed; and a "yard party" cleared the ground, built a sandbox, installed a barbecue, and brought in movable playthings: tricycles, wagons, and outdoor building blocks. Eventually, permanent and safe playground equipment was installed. While the playground was being created, the staff seemed resistant to the concepts of outdoor play as an extension of the classroom and topics such as sand and water play raised teachers' concerns. The site manager and architect crafted a few simple questions about the highpoints of outdoor play when the participants were children themselves, which created a shift in their willingness to plan for an outdoor play space that was more child-oriented.

Unexpectedly, an opportunity to benefit the community at large arose. A new billboard reading *New Voice—New Vision* appeared one day: the newly elected mayor's promise to the people. Recognizing another application for AI, the site manager told the mayor how her organization was reinventing itself and asked to collaborate with him on applying these ideas toward community renewal. The mayor enthusiastically accepted her partnership and convened a small group of 20 civic leaders for an AI session at a town meeting. As a result, the racially mixed group of participants meeting together for the first time discovered they wanted the same thing—to restore their community. Residents were enthused. One result is a new coffee shop sponsored by a local church, conceived of as a cozy place for townsfolk to gather and have conversations—many of them about exciting possibilities for the future.

Summary of Learnings

The primary learning in this experience was the importance of a champion to keep positive conversations alive and expanding over time while the capacity of staff to be their own resource was strengthened. The structure of the AI intervention was loose and emergent as the philosophy became embedded in the staff's thinking and behaving. Staff members successfully transitioned to the new local sponsoring agency and brought with them the spirit of appreciation and positive action.

Contributors

Patti Smith, Nila Rinehart, and Carolyn Miller at Community Development Institute, psmith@cditeam.org, nrinehart@cditeam.org, cmiller@cditeam.org

Appreciative Inquiry at Metropolitan School District

The Story

A new superintendent and a new school board wanted to find a way to change the discourse that emphasized labor discord, teacher-employer conflict, and a government that was strongly focused on measuring student achievement. Instead, they wanted to emphasize collaborative learning communities and make the experience of the individual learner the center of the discourse. The superintendent facilitated a consensus inside a districtwide planning group to conduct an AI entitled "What Do We Know About Learning?" A senior district level administrator was given responsibility for a $720,000 budget, and two teachers were appointed to be district AI consultants. All three attended a two-day course on AI and then hired an AI consultant to work with them. Beginning in January 2006, 21 schools in eight "sites" participated in a series of appreciative inquiries.

Project Scope

Eighteen secondary schools (grades 8–12), 88 elementary schools, and 7 adult learning centers were invited to apply to be part of the learning inquiry. Eight out of 20 applications were chosen. Some of these applications were from a single high school. A few were combined elementary and high school submissions. One was an adult learning center, and two combined all three types of institutions in common geographical areas. The district AI team managed the entire process and facilitated the summits.

Each site had one teacher who was given release time to be the site AI coordinator/change agent. Each site created an AI team that included administrators, teachers, students, and (in some cases) parents and school support staff. The two district AI consultants worked with each site. Funding was provided for teacher release time to attend team meetings, to conduct interviews, and to attend the summit.

AI Application

Soon after being chosen, AI site teams of six to ten members attended a two-day AI training course that resulted in high energy and enthusiasm for the project. Site teams began by interviewing others and asking for four or five stories; the interviewer would choose the "best" one to write up and give to the site coordinator. Each interviewee was asked if he or she would be willing to interview two other people and attend the summit. This viral interviewing strategy generated a large number of stories, created interest and enthusiasm in the AI process, and changed the discourse toward the hoped-for direction in most sites. Approximately three weeks before each AI Summit, the site team met for a series of *synergenesis* meetings, a technique for working with appreciative interview data.[23] The team created a Discovery Document that was circulated throughout the site.

At each of the two-day summits, which were held in April, there was an average of 80 people, mostly teachers and students with a few parents and others. The first day focused on developing a collective dream for the site. During the second day, teams worked on creating seven to ten Design Statements. To kick off Destiny, individuals made personal commitments to take action. Summits were widely seen as energizing and effective. Most participants completed surveys at the end of the summit; and the average response to the item "At this stage, I feel positive about the future because of my participation in the Appreciative Inquiry process" was 4.3 out of 5. The Dream mural and Design Statements were taken back to the sites to be shared with others, and various actions were taken to implement changes.

Project Milestones (Outcomes)

In most sites, the process engendered a heightened sense of community and empowerment. A variety of projects and processes emerging from the AI continued to influence the sites one year later. The district committed approximately $150,000 in its 2006–2007 budget to support these initiatives and almost $400,000 for new AI projects.

One year later it appeared that four sites experienced real transformational change in "how we do things around here." Those changes are expected to result in significant improvements in hard outcomes, which is being tracked, such as student enrollment and achievement. Two other sites showed positive incremental changes in that AI amplified or sped up changes that were already in process. Two of the sites showed little impact from AI.

At most sites, teachers and administrators commented on the important contribution that students' voices made to the summit. A common observation was that students opened doors that the adults might have left closed. In some sites, student empowerment increased dramatically. Another result that was important to the school district was an increase in "distributed leadership" at the various sites—greater informal leadership, particularly from more junior staff. The AI philosophy changed the discourse on organizing not only in the district but also in the government agency responsible for education. Many uses for AI were discussed and implemented in large and small ways.

---

23 Bushe, G. R. (2007). *Appreciative inquiry is not about the positive.* Unpublished paper available at http://www.gervasebushe.ca/AI_pos.pdf.

Summary of Learnings

What seems to have differentiated the transformational sites from the other sites was passionate and engaged leadership from high-status individuals combined with a shared concern or problem to which AI responded. The incremental change sites had good leadership but did not have any pressing issues related to AI. The no-change sites had problems with leadership and integration of the effort among the staff. The viral interviewing strategy accomplished the three objectives (to generate a large number of stories, to create interest and enthusiasm in the AI process, and to begin changing the discourse in the sites) where it was competently executed. The synergenesis process was a high-point learning experience for most everyone who participated in it. Utilizing an "improvisation" as opposed to "implementation" *Destiny* phase[24,25] and encouraging individual action was highly energizing for followers and leaders. A two-day summit was rushed, but it was just enough time to kick-start or amplify collective change processes at six of eight sites. Tracking specific changes showed that about half the changes could be attributed to things that happened during the *Discovery* phase and the other half to the *Design* phase. Analysis of observational data from spring 2006 showed that the degree of change was related to (1) the quality of insights generated during the *Discovery* phase and the quality of the Discovery Document that was created and (2) the degree of support for the Design Statements at the summit and the level of positive feeling at the end of the summit.

The AI process was surprisingly robust in that momentum was sustained even with a two-month summer gap in which nothing happened. While these are excellent outcomes, on reflection, some things could have been better. Some sites did not have the level of local sponsorship required and/or had the wrong people in the site coordinator role. More needed to be done at the selection phase to ensure that applications had solid local sponsorship and the right people on board. In particular, the credibility and status of the site coordinator seemed central to the success of the inquiry. While the synergenesis process proved powerful for those involved, only a few people at each site had the experience. Future AIs will look for ways to include many more in synergenesis sessions, either before or during the summit.

The original plan called for sponsors at the summit to decide which Design Statements would be adopted. This plan proved far too counter-cultural for this organization, where authorities were expected to be highly inclusive and participative in decision making. As a result, there was a great deal of variation at each site in what happened with Design Statements. In future AIs, plan-

---

24 Ibid.
25 Bushe, G .R., & Kassam, A. (2005). When is appreciative inquiry transformational? A meta-case analysis.

ning for validating and formally adopting Design Statements at each site will be encouraged early in the process. The summit will end with Design Proposals that go back to the school(s) for widespread discussion and comment. A half-day summit held two weeks after the two-day summit will consolidate those discussions into finalized Design Statements and launch the *Destiny* phase.

Contributors

Gervase R. Bushe PhD, Segal Graduate School of Business, Simon Fraser University, bushe@sfu.ca.

10

AI Worksheets

Worksheet 1:

Topic Choice Four Key Questions in Discovery

This worksheet lists the four key questions in the Discovery *phase. Take time to read the questions to the participants. Prior to reading the questions, ask participants to reflect and take a few minutes to jot down notes in response to the following questions. Then the partners will interview each other to explore the interview questions in-depth.*

What would you describe as being a peak experience or high point in your organization? This would be a time when you were most alive and engaged.

Without being modest, what is it that you most value about yourself, the nature of your work, and your organization?

What are the core factors that give life to your organization without which the organization would cease to exist?

What three wishes do you have to enhance the health and vitality of your organization?

Worksheet 2:

Topic Team Selection

This worksheet helps create the best topic team or core steering team for the AI initiative.

Suggested Team Members

Name	Title	Organizational Area	Best Reason for Invitation to Team

Worksheet 3:
Getting Started Discussion Checklist

This worksheet helps with the initial discussions to get a team started on an AI project.

Our organization will use AI because we want to _____
in order to _____.

Who will sponsor and lead this AI initiative?

What is the time frame for the effort?

Who are the organization's stakeholders?

How many people will be involved?

How will we select topics for the inquiry?

How many interviews will be conducted? Who will conduct them?

How will stories be collected, shared, and analyzed from the interviews?

What communication vehicles will be used to keep people "in the loop"?

Who (or what groups) will be involved in each stage of the project?

How will logistics be managed?

How will costs be shared?

How will AI be integrated and sustained in the organization's culture?

Worksheet 4:

Engaging AI Question Checklist

This worksheet helps ensure that the questions in the interview guide are framed in a positive tone and are engaging. In reviewing the question, ask yourself whether the question . . .

States an affirmative tone.

Builds on a half-full assumption.

Gives a broad definition to the topic.

Presents an invitation that:
- Is expansive.
- Uses positive-feeling words.
- Finds energizing stories.

Enhances the possibilities of storytelling and narratives.

Phrases itself in rapport talk, not report talk.

Values "what is." This will help spark the appreciative imagination by helping the person locate the experiences that are worth valuing.

Moves beyond common ground and elevates conversation to higher ground.

Conveys an unconditional positive regard

Evokes essential values, aspirations, and inspirations.

Worksheet 5:
Interview Packet Checklist

This worksheet helps create the interview guide because what we ask determines what we find. What we find determines how we talk. How we talk determines how we imagine together. How we imagine together determines what we achieve. The interview guide should incorporate the following components to work most effectively:

Introduction to explain the project and purpose

Instruction for preparing, conducting, and reporting the interviews

Stage-setting questions:
- How long have you been with the organization? Why did you join this organization? Where do you work? What do you enjoy most about your position?
- How would you describe a peak experience or high point in your organization? This would be a time when you were most alive and engaged.
- What do you value most about yourself, your work, and your organization?

Affirmative topic questions: formulate engaging questions with lead-ins (positive free fall) that assume that the subject matter in question already exists. Make sure these question look for the best of the past (continuity) and possibilities in the future (novelty).

Conclusion questions to wrap up the interview:
- What are the core life-giving factors that give life to this organization?
- Looking toward the future, what are we being called to become?
- What three wishes do you have for changing the organization (or the "miracle questions")?

Interview Summary Sheet to collect the best interview stories, quotes, and ideas:
- What was the best story that came out of the interview?
- What was the best quote that came out of the interview?

Demographic Summary Sheet (if appropriate)

Interview Consent Form

A sincere thank-you!

Worksheet 6:

Identifying Themes from Interviews

This worksheet helps the group identify all of the themes from their stories. After a review of these themes, the group selects those themes it believes are common among many of the stories and are important for moving the organization forward in its task.

A. Identifying Themes
  - Each person briefly shares the best story he or she heard from his or her interview partner. Group members take note of the themes they noticed in the stories.
  - After all stories are told, make a list of all of the themes in the stories. Look for high points, life-giving moments, and ideas that "grabbed" you.
  - List all of the themes on chart paper.

B. Select 3–5 Major Themes
  - From your group's list, come to agreement on the three to five most important themes.
  - Write the themes on the sheet provided.
  - Post or report out theme sheets.

C. Finding the Group Synergy among the Themes
  - When themes are reported and posted on a wall, each person can place a dot in the square to the right of three themes that describe what he or she believes are the most important themes. (It also can be a group discussion and vote). The key is to come to agreement on key themes and topics.

Worksheet 7:

Dreaming the Organization's Future

The goal is to create ideal future scenarios. The following activity can help create and visualize the discovery of the dream.

Self-manage the process to include a:
- Discussion leader: ensures that each person is heard and that the group stays on task.
- Recorder: writes on the flip chart(s) to take notes.
- Timekeeper: gives time checks to ensure that the assignment is completed in the allotted time frame.
- Reporter: reports out to the full group.

Visualize the dream you want from the themes or conversations identified in the Discovery phase. Ask yourself these questions:
- What is happening?
- How does this happen?
- What are the things that made this happen (e.g., leadership, structures, and systems)?
- What makes this dream (the vision) exciting?

Choose a creative way to present your dream (vision) to all participants. Your presentation can be a news report, a song, a poem, a skit, an interview, or a picture.

Capture the dream in a narrative statement.
- Use vivid language.
- Be positive and uplifting.

Worksheet 8:
Criteria for Creating Provocative Propositions

Provocative propositions begin to build positive images of the ideal organization. This worksheet helps ensure that provocative propositions meet the following criteria:

Is it provocative; that is, does it stretch, challenge, or interrupt?

Is it grounded; that is, do examples illustrate the ideal as real possibilities?

Is it desired; that is if it could be fully actualized, would the organization want it? Do you want it as a preferred future?

Is it stated in affirmative and bold terms?

Does it follow a social architecture approach?

Does it expand the zone of proximal development?

Does it use a third party (an outside appreciative eye)?

Is it complemented with benchmarking data?

Is it a high-involvement process?

Is it used to stimulate intergenerational organizational learning?

Is there balanced management of continuity, novelty, and transition?

Worksheet 9:

Design to Destiny Worksheet

This worksheet begins to translate provocative proposition into goals, strategies, commitments, and/or action items.

Self-manage the process to include a:
- Discussion leader: ensures that each person is heard and that the group stays on task.
- Recorder: writes on the flip chart(s) to take notes.
- Timekeeper: gives time checks to ensure that the assignment is completed in the allotted time frame.
- Reporter: reports out to the full group.

Select the provocative proposition to work with. Based on feedback from others, take 15–20 minutes to revise, edit, or improve the provocative proposition.

Write down targets, goals, strategies, and/or action items that can achieve the desired provocative proposition.

Brainstorm ideas about specific things that can occur now or in the near future to realize the dream.

Discuss and agree on what the key targets and goals are, what strategies and action items will be used to get there, and who will complete the tasks and by when.

Worksheet 10:

How to Build or Map the Positive Core

A field of work called graphical recording can help guide the mapping of the positive core of the organization. This worksheet provides a suggested process.

Organize as teams and ask participants to:
- Share the stories they collected in the interview process.

- Write down those key factors that create the organization's successes.

Use a visual creation to map the positive core, such as a:
- Graphic metaphor.
- Mosaic or collage.

Display and communicate to the stakeholders the visual of the positive core.

Worksheet 11:

AI: Valuation and Learning Worksheet

This worksheet can be used at the end of an AI initiative, workshop, or Destiny session to ask the participants the following questions:

What about the Appreciative Inquiry approach most enlivened you?

What excites you most about introducing or using Appreciative Inquiry in your work or personal life?

What Appreciative Inquiry competencies have you discovered that you already have?

What elevator story about Appreciative Inquiry would you like to share?

What can you envision to take Appreciative Inquiry to a higher level for yourself, for someone else, or for your organization?

What is one simple appreciative idea that you can act on tomorrow, or what is one simple appreciative action that you can do tomorrow?

WELCOME TO THE ORD SUMMIT

Igniting Leadership at All Levels

Working Together to Ensure the Earth's Vitality

Pervasive Leadership • Liberating Collaboration • Engendering Trust

"To advocate human conversation as the means to restore hope to the future is as simple as I can get. But I have seen there is no more powerful way to initiate significant change than to convene a conversation . . . It is always like this. Real change begins with the simple act of people talking about what they care about."
—Margaret Wheatley
   Author of *Leadership and the New Science*

"Contemporary society is not only profoundly shaped by organizations but also can be shaped for the better by them, through the leadership of great organizations. To an extent unimaginable a decade ago, the ideals of building a healthy, prosperous, and sustainable world future are taking on form and substance. Obstacles to cooperation and human enterprise that long seemed immovable have collapsed . . . Organizations are increasingly stepping forward to wrestle with complex issues that affect not only their shareholders, employees, and customers but also the quality of life in the world's communities and cities, the world's ecosystems, and countries around the globe. The best path to the good society, we believe, is the construction of great organizations that nurture and magnify the best in human beings."
—David Cooperrider and Suresh Srivastva
   Authors of *Organizational Wisdom and Executive Courage*

What Is an "AI" Organizational Summit?

The **WHOLE SYSTEM** participates—a cross section of as many interested parties as is practical. That means more diversity and less hierarchy than is usual in a working meeting and a chance for each person to be heard and to learn new ways of looking at the task at hand.

Future scenarios—for an organization, a community, or an issue—are put into **HISTORICAL** and **GLOBAL** perspective. That means thinking globally together before acting locally. This feature enhances shared understanding and greater commitment to act. It also increases the range of potential actions.

People **SELF-MANAGE** their work and use **DIALOGUE**—not problem solving—as the main tool. That means helping others do the tasks and taking responsibility for one's perceptions and actions.

COMMON GROUND and NARRATIVE RICH INTERACTION rather than conflict management or negotiation are the frame of reference. That means honoring differences rather than having to reconcile them and searching for meaning and direction in stories that honor and connect people to their "history as positive possibility."

APPRECIATIVE INQUIRY (AI)—To **appreciate** means to value—to understand those things worth valuing. To **inquire** means to study, to ask questions, to search. Therefore, AI is a collaborative search to identify and understand the organization's strengths, its potentials, the greatest opportunities, and people's hopes for the future.

INSPIRED ACTION ON BEHALF OF THE WHOLE—Because the whole system is involved, it is easier to make more rapid decisions and to make commitments to action in a public way—in an open way that everyone can support and help implement. The movement to action is guided by internal inspiration, shared leadership, and voluntary initiative. People work on what they share a passion about, what they most care about and believe will make the difference. Real change begins with the simple act of people acting on what they care about in the context of a shared vision that matters.

Appreciative Inquiry 4-D Cycle

Worksheet 1

Discovery: Articulating the Positive Core of ORD

Appreciative Inquiry—Opening Conversation in Pairs

> Note: Take brief notes and use your skills as an interviewer as you listen and go deeper into your partner's experiences, visions, and stories.

Question 1—High-Point Experience

As you look over your experience with ORD, there have been many ups and downs, peaks and valleys. We'd like you to reflect on one of the peaks, *one of the high points.* Can you remember a time that most stands out as a high point for you—a time when you felt most effective, alive, engaged, or really proud?

A. Please share the story. What happened? when? where? What were your feelings? What challenges did you encounter? How were they overcome? What insights do you have?

B. What was it *about you* and others around you that made the experience a high-point experience?

C. Based on this story and others like it, if we now had a conversation with people who know you best and asked them to share *the three best qualities they see in you, the best capabilities or qualities that you bring to ORD,* what would they say?

Question 2—Continuity and Change

A. Think back to when you were offered a position at ORD and you decided to say yes. What were the attributes that most attracted and excited you about your work, about the people, or even about the sense of purpose or mission of ORD as an organization? What made *the difference* for you when you decided to say yes?

B. Thinking today about the larger context of change and the purpose of ORD in the world, many **trends, events, and developments** indicate that ORD (like any high-purpose organization) will likewise change, develop, and perhaps be called to play a more significant role in the future. In your view, what are the most important events, trends, and developments in your profession or science, in the world, or in the needs and expectations of our constituencies? What do these trends suggest for ORD's future?

- What are the most important trends, events, or developments? Why?
- What do these trends, events, or developments imply for ORD's future—its larger purposes or future opportunities to grow, to change, to aim higher, and/or to lead in new ways?

Question 3—Pervasive Leadership:
Leadership is about changing and about bringing out the best in people. High-performing organizations empower and challenge people to initiate beyond what they believe is possible. In doing so, these organizations nurture the inherent leadership capacity within *each* employee—recognizing that leadership includes but also extends far beyond position or level.

You probably have seen or experienced a number of exemplars of leadership in your years at ORD—individual or group/team acts of leadership that you admire. Think for a moment about a story, one example, of the kind of leadership you value—something you have experienced, heard about, or seen at any level of ORD. What happened?

- What do you value most in this story of leadership?

- Based on this story, what is *leadership*? In your view, what does leadership involve? What are the key qualities?

Question 4—Collaboration, Trust, and Moments of Scientific or Organizational Achievement:
Increasingly, any kind of achievement requires crossing boundaries, often bringing improbable partners together for a free exchange of knowledge, skills, and abilities across disciplines, cultures, and organizational units.

A. Describe a time when you were inspired by working with a person or group in *a collaboration that utilized everyone's strengths*.
- What did you learn about ORD? about connecting across boundaries? about yourself?
- What were the outcomes?

B. Now let's build on that story. Imagine a time in the future when ORD has achieved a reputation in the world as a think tank of inspired collaborators with a shared vision of integrated solutions to ensure the earth's vitality.
- What behaviors would you expect?
- What kinds of organizational systems, norms, or practices would you see making the vision possible?

Question 5—Promising Innovations and Changes Happening at ORD—For Igniting Leadership at Every Level:
Building an empowered culture of leadership requires innovation and change; and projects, change initiatives, and bold pilots are already happening all over ORD. Some of the innovations or improvement efforts are small and not known; others are large. But small or large, the initiatives need to be singled out.

As you think about our topic, what initiatives, pilots, practices, or innovations stand out to you as being most noteworthy—things that have potential for helping us build pervasive leadership at every level?

- Please name the innovation or change, describe its strengths and potentials, and share where it is happening.

Question 6—Images of the Future ORD: 2005–2010

A. If you were to complete the following sentence with your highest aspiration and hope for ORD, what would you say?

"I will be most proud of ORD in the future when _____."

B. Actions we can take today to start creating the future
- What single small change could we make right now that would have the biggest impact in elevating ORD's capacity?
- What bolder change might we want to consider?

Self-Management and Group Leadership Roles
Each small group manages its own discussion, data, time, and reports. Here are useful roles for self-managing this work. **Leadership roles can be rotated.** Divide up the work as you choose.

DISCUSSION LEADER—Ensures that each person who wants to speak is heard within the time available. Keeps the group on track to finish on time.

TIMEKEEPER—Keeps the group aware of the time left. Monitors report-outs and signals the time remaining to the person talking.

RECORDER—Writes the group's output on flip charts using the speaker's words. Asks the person to restate long ideas briefly.

REPORTER—Delivers the report to the large group in the time allotted.

Worksheet 2

Discovering the Resources in Our Community

Purpose: To appreciate and welcome each other and to learn about special experiences, visions, capabilities, and resources people bring to this summit.

Self-Manage: Select a discussion leader, timekeeper, recorder, and reporter.

Steps:

1. Share highlights from what you learned about the person *you interviewed*. **Focus on questions 1 and 2.**

Go around the table. Introduce your interview partner—focus on highlights from his or her high-point story (question 1); best qualities people see in him or her (question 1); and key trends, events, and opportunities affecting the future of ORD (question 2). Everyone is introduced.

2. Assign a recorder to listen for patterns and common themes—for the high-point stories and trends/events/opportunities affecting the future of the ORD.

The recorder makes two lists—and the reporter is ready for a three-minute report-out. *Make notes on the next page.*

Common Themes and/or Unique Patterns

High-Point Analysis—Discovery of Patterns and Themes

When are people most passionate and effective at ORD?

1.

2.

3.

4.

5.

Events, Trends, and Developments à Discovery of Opportunities
From the perspective of serving the needs of our ORD stakeholders in the future and realizing our mission, what are the key trends, events, or developments affecting our future and how can we **translate them into opportunities or challenges to aim higher, to serve better, to lead?**

In your view, what are ORD's five highest opportunities for innovation, change, or leadership based on the trends, events, or developments?

1.

2.

3.

4.

5.

After recording common themes and any significant differences, please record answers to one more question: **What are our excitements or hopes for this ORD Summit—things that would make it significant and worthwhile?**

Worksheet 3

Discovering and Articulating the "Positive Core" of ORD

When *are* we at our best in terms of igniting leadership at all levels and working together to ensure the earth's vitality? Why?

Purpose: To share the most powerful, future-relevant, and inspiring stories of **igniting leadership at all levels** and to discover all of the factors in the stories contributing to an empowered culture of excellence.

Self-Manage: Select a discussion leader, timekeeper, recorder, and reporter.

Steps:

1. Share stories and discoveries from questions 3–5 of your interview.

2. As stories are shared, **identify the factors—ORD's strengths; special practices; and values, capacities, and root causes of success—things that make empowered leadership possible at every level.** Record the stories and analysis on the next page. Everyone should share. Make note of common themes and unique patterns. After your analysis, turn your attention to the next creative step.

3. Now create a metaphor to map or picture your insights into "the positive core" of ORD's strengths, special practices and values, capacities, and root causes of success—things that ignite good leadership at every level. For example the "positive core" might be pictured as a DNA double helix, a solar system, or a tree of life.

4. Be prepared for a 4–5 minute report. The reporter should be ready to:

- Share his or her metaphor and picture of his or her analysis of the positive core and causes of leadership at every level.

- Retell one of the actual stories of leadership that illustrates or helped inspire his or her thinking. The reporter should feel free to retell the story before or after sharing the metaphor.

Stories about Leadership
at Every Level

Root Causes of Success

Factors that make an empowered culture of excellence possible—things that are causing, creating, or supporting leadership at every level.

These factors can be at the following levels:
• Individual
• Work unit
• Organizational

Examples include current programs and initiatives that are effective and should be recognized.

Worksheet 4

External Stories about "Igniting Leadership at All Levels"

1. What did you find most important? What was it about those examples or ideas that particularly interested you?

2. When you think about institutional change *and* sustaining it, what were the things you heard that helped make progress and build momentum?

3. Name one implication or insight that might have relevance for our own work here—of building a future ORD that ignites leadership at every level?

Worksheet 5

Dreams and Visions of the Future

Ideal Future Scenario of "ORD Leadership at All Levels"
We Most Want

PRESENTATIONS ARE DUE AT _____ O'CLOCK

Purpose: To imagine and visualize ORD in the future—the ORD future you want to work toward based on these background questions:
- What is the world calling our organization to be?
- What does our positive core indicate we can be—taking ORD to a new level?
- What are the most enlivening and exciting possibilities that our organization can undertake to ignite leadership at all levels?
- I will be most proud of ORD in 2015 when what occurs?

Self-Manage: Select a discussion leader, recorder, timekeeper, and reporter.

1. Share stories and discoveries from question 6 of your interview/opening conversation.

2. Place yourself seven years into the future—it is 2015. From the perspective of the group or department of which you are part of the whole, visualize the ORD you really want—as if it exists now. What is happening that is new, better, and/or different as it relates to **Igniting Leadership at All Levels: ORD Working Together to Ensure the Earth's Vitality**?

3. Many changes have happened in the past seven years. Now envision the positive changes; pilot projects; and larger projects, innovations, and accomplishments since 2015, with possible reference to the following. (You choose; these are simply examples.)
- National images and reputation you want—what makes ORD become a magnet for good people?
- Nature of leader-follower relationships (What does this look like in the future you most want?)
- Quality of leadership education, research, and development
- Organizational practices and structures creating an empowered culture
- Decision making and planning processes
- Revolutionary training and learning
- HR practices (e.g., performance appraisals)

- Uses of technology, networks, and e-learning and sharing of information
- Collaboration, teamwork, and networking
- Commitment to the mission—preservation of the environment
- Change readiness and methods for increasing change capacity
- Communication practices
- Other highly desirable features that you choose

Spend enough time to imagine concretely the ORD leadership and culture your group wants to see. This is an exercise in imagination and dreaming—of the kind of ORD you want to work toward.

4. Choose a creative way to present your images of the future as if they are happening now.

Examples: * A TV Special   * A Magazine Cover Story * A Drama
*A Day in the Life   * A Panel Presentation * A Work of Art

5. Finally, after creating your presentation, on a flip chart, brainstorm the major **challenges** that you had to overcome on your way to your vision of ORD 2015 and the **opportunities** you worked with.

Ideal Future Scenario of "ORD Leadership at All Levels" We Most Want

Creative Presentations Notes:

Most Important, Provocative, Appealing Ideas for

Igniting Leadership at All Levels: ORD Working Together to Ensure the Earth's Vitality

Organizational Elements

What kind of organizational elements are necessary to bring these ideas to life (for example, systems, structures, culture, recruiting practices, mechanisms, strategies, education and training, and/or policies)?

Worksheet 6

Design Principles for Igniting Leadership at All Levels

Writing Provocative Propositions for Key Organizational Elements

PRESENTATIONS ARE DUE AT _____ O'CLOCK

Purpose: To lift our hopes and dreams of an ORD culture of excellence that ignites leadership at all levels. Here we consider elements such as practices, structures, policies, and technologies and other elements that would bring our dreams to life.

Self-Manage: Select a discussion leader, timekeeper, recorder, and reporter.

Steps:

1. At your table, review the examples of provocative propositions on the next sheet and the guidelines for great provocative propositions so that you all have a shared sense of what your product might look like at the end of this exercise (_____ minutes).

2. Discuss/brainstorm the "ingredients" you would like to see present in the ideal version of the "organizational element" assigned to your table (_____ minutes).

3. As a group, create and record on your flip chart a first draft provocative proposition of the organizational element assigned to your table—a short description of what the organizational element would look like when infused with the energy and essence of your dream (_____ minutes).

4. Finalize the draft of your design provocative proposition by printing a neat version on a single flip chart page. Type your proposition and save to a disk. Be prepared to report out (4 minutes).

Definitions and Guidelines

Appreciative Design through creating provocative propositions is a time for the creation of new forms, new containers, and new practices that embrace and are infused by the positive core unearthed in Discovery and imagined in our Dream.

"First we shape our structures and then our structures shape us."
—Winston Churchill

"Most people spend 50% of their time not just doing their job but fighting their own institutional bureaucracies."
—Dee Hock, Founder of Visa International

"All systems are perfectly designed to achieve the results they are currently getting."
—Marv Weisbord, Organizational Consultant

Great provocative propositions:

- Stretch and challenge.
- Are desired (people want to create them).
- Are exciting and use energizing language.
- Represent things people really believe in, such as constitutional *beliefs* as in "we hold these truths to be self evident."
- Describe what is wanted in a positive way (rather than saying what is not wanted).
- Are written in the present tense as if they are already happening.

Examples of Elements That Make Up the Organizational Architecture

Education and training	Reward and recognition practices
Leadership style and culture	Decision-making procedures
Staff/people/relationships	Beliefs about people
Work processes and job design	Beliefs about power and authority
Career structures and incentives	Recruiting practices
Organizational structures	Balance of personal/professional life
Stakeholder relationships	Information systems and technology
Communications	Empowering planning methods
Systems	

Definitions and Guidelines

Sample Provocative Propositions

Education and training are the foundation of the empowered culture of excellence in ORD. We foster leadership that encourages, challenges, and supports all members of the Agency to engage in ongoing learning, both personal and professional. ORD provides *lifelong training and education* opportunities that support a sense of purpose, direction, and continual growth. This, in turn, nurtures the strength and confidence people need to achieve their full personal and professional potential.

We recognize that all members want to contribute to a higher sense of purpose and service to a larger mission. *Jobs are designed* so that people have freedom and autonomy to take necessary action to achieve the mission of their department and to see the meaningfulness of their contributions. *All jobs are designed* to be meaningful, purposeful, and rewarding.

ORD recognizes that people from all levels of the organization have valuable knowledge and experience and immense potential. We have a culture that fosters *empowerment* at all levels of the Agency. Toward this end, decisions are made at the most local level possible and include all relevant and affected parties, ensuring the sharing of good information and creating the empowered involvement that breeds commitment.

Worksheet 7
Destiny Worksheet

Open Space Round One

Purpose: To create possible pilot projects, change initiatives, and actions that have the potential to move us toward the ORD future we want and as articulated in our design propositions.

Self-Manage: Select a discussion leader, timekeeper, recorder, and reporter.

1. Questions to discuss:
   - Vision of this initiative or learning pilot: What is needed for a learning experience to be successful?
   - Who needs to be involved in the implementation? champions?
   - What are possible locations? departments? divisions?
   - What are the learning potentials and possible impacts?
   - When should it be started?

2. Be prepared to summarize, write up, and submit the following:
   - Names of group members
   - Name of pilot project
   - A short purpose statement that relates to the propositions of the ideal future you want: "The purpose of this initiative or pilot is . . ."
   - A short description of the proposed pilot: what, when, where, how, etc.

Short-term action plans (over the next two months)

Actions	Help Needed From	Due Dates

Long-term actions (next year and beyond)

Actions	Help Needed From	Due Dates

Open Space Round Two

Purpose: To create possible pilot projects, change initiatives, and actions that have the potential to move us toward the ORD future we want and as articulated in our design propositions.

Self-Manage: Select a discussion leader, timekeeper, recorder, and reporter.

1. Questions to discuss:
   - Vision of this initiative or learning pilot: What is needed for a learning experience to be successful?
   - Who needs to be involved in the implementation? champions?
   - What are possible locations? departments? divisions?
   - What are the learning potentials and possible impacts?
   - When should it be started?

2. Be prepared to summarize, write up, and submit the following:
   - Names of group members
   - Name of pilot project
   - A short purpose statement that relates to the propositions of the ideal future you want: "The purpose of this initiative or pilot is . . ."
   - A short description of the proposed pilot: what, when, where, how, etc.

Short-term action plans (over the next two months)

Actions	Help Needed From	Due Dates

Long-term actions (next year and beyond)

Actions	Help Needed From	Due Dates

11

AI Classics:
Selected Articles*

Appreciative Inquiry in Organizational Life

David L. Cooperrider and Suresh Srivastva
Case Western Reserve University

Abstract

This chapter presents a conceptual refiguration of action-research based on a "socioarationalist" view of science. The position that is developed can be summarized as follows: For action-research to reach its potential as a vehicle for social innovation it needs to begin advancing theoretical knowledge of consequence; that good theory may be one of the best means human beings have for affecting change in a postindustrial world; that the discipline's steadfast commitment to a problem solving view of the world acts as a primary constraint on its imagination and contribution to knowledge; that *appreciative inquiry* represents a viable complement to conventional forms of action-research; and finally, that through our assumptions and choice of method we largely create the world we later discover.

> *We are sometime truly to see our life as positive, not negative, as made up of continuous willing, not of constraints and prohibition.*
>
> —*Mary Parker Follett*

> *We are steadily forgetting how to dream; in historical terms, the mathematicist and technicist dimensions of Platonism have conquered the poetical, mythical, and rhetorical context of analysis. We are forgetting how to be reasonable in nonmathematical dialects.*
>
> —*Stanley Rosen*

Introduction

This chapter presents a conceptual reconfiguration of action research. In it we shall argue for a multidimensional view of action-research which seeks to both generate theory and develop organizations. The chapter begins with the observation that action-research has become increasingly rationalized and encultured to the point where it risks becoming little more than a crude empiricism imprisoned in a deficiency mode of thought. In its conventional *unidimensional* form action research has largely failed as an instrument for advancing social knowledge of consequence and has not, therefore, achieved its potential as a vehicle for human development and social-organizational transformation. While the literature consistently signals the worth of action-research as a managerial tool for problem solving ("first-order" incremental change), it is conspicuously quiet concerning reports of discontinuous change of the "second order" where organizational paradigms, norms, ideologies, or values are transformed in fundamental ways (Watzlawick, et al., 1974).

Cooperrider, D. L., & Srivastva S. (1999). *Appreciative inquiry in organizational life. Appreciative management and leadership.* Euclid, OH: Lakeshore Communications, pp. 401–441.

In the course of this chapter we shall touch broadly upon a number of interrelated concerns—scientific, metaphysical, normative, and pragmatic. Linking these streams is an underlying conviction that action-research has the potential to be to the postindustrial era what "scientific management" was to the industrial. Just as scientific management provided the philosophical and methodological legitimacy required to support the bureaucratic organizational form (Clegg and Dunkerly, 1980; Braverman, 1974), action-research may yet provide the intellectual rationale and reflexive methodology required to support the emergence of a more egalitarian "postbureaucratic" form of organization. Unlike scientific management however, which provided the means for a technorational science of administration, action-research holds unique and essential promise in the sociorational realm of human affairs. It has the potential to become the paradigmatic basis of a truly significant—a humanly significant—generative science of administration.

In the first part of the essay it is suggested that the primary barrier limiting the potential of action-research has been its romance with "action" at the expense of "theory." This tendency has led many in the discipline to seriously underestimate the power of theory as a means for social-organizational reconstruction. Drawing largely on the work of Kenneth Gergen (1978, 1982), we re-examine the character of theoretical knowledge and its role in social transformation, and then appeal for a redefinition of the scientific aims of action-research that will dynamically reunite theory and practice. The aim of science is not the detached discovery and verification of social laws allowing for prediction and control. Highlighted here instead, is an alternative understanding that defines social and behavioral science in terms of its "generative capacity," that is, its "capacity to challenge the guiding assumptions of the culture, to raise fundamental questions regarding contemporary social life, to foster reconsideration of that which is 'taken for granted' and thereby furnish new alternatives for social actions" (Gergen, 1978, p. 1346).

Assuming that generative theory is a legitimate product of scientific work and is, in fact, capable of provoking debate, stimulating normative dialogue, and furnishing conceptual alternatives needed for social transformation, then why has action-research till now so largely downplayed creative theorizing in its work with organizations? Here we will move to the heart of the chapter and argue that the generative incapacity of contemporary action-research derives from the discipline's unquestioned commitment to a secularized problem-oriented view of the world and thus to the subsequent loss of our capacity as researchers and participants to marvel, and in marveling to embrace, the miracle and mystery of social organization. If we acknowledge Abraham Maslow's (1968) admonition that true science begins and ends in wonder, then we immediately shed light on why action-research has failed to produce innovative theory capable of inspiring the imagination, commitment, and passionate dialogue required for the consensual re-ordering of social conduct.

Appreciative inquiry is presented here as a mode of action-research that meets the criteria of science as spelled out in generative-theoretical terms. Going beyond questions of epistemology, appreciative inquiry has as its basis a metaphysical concern: it posits that social existence as such is a miracle that can never be fully comprehended (Quinney, 1982; Marcel, 1963). Proceeding from this level of understanding we begin to explore the uniqueness of the appreciative mode. More than a method or technique, the appreciative mode of inquiry is a way of living with, being with, and directly participating in the varieties of social organization we are compelled to study. Serious consideration and reflection on the ultimate mystery of being engenders a reverence for life that draws the researcher to inquire beyond superficial appearances to deeper levels of the life generating essentials and potentials of social existence. That is, the action researcher is drawn to affirm, and thereby illuminate, the factors and forces involved in organizing that serve to nourish the human spirit. Thus, this chapter seeks to enrich our conception of administrative behavior by introducing a "second dimension" of action-research that goes beyond merely a secularized problem-solving frame.

The proposal that appreciative inquiry represents a distinctive complement to traditional action-research will be unfolded in the following way: First, the role of theory as an enabling agent of social transformation will be considered; such consideration can help to eliminate the artificial dualism separating theory from practice. Second, we will challenge the problem-oriented view of organizing inherent in traditional definitions of action-research, and describe an affirmative form of inquiry uniquely suited for discovering generative theory. Finally, these insights will be brought together in a general model of the conceptual underpinnings of appreciative inquiry.

Toward Generative Theory in Action-Research

The current decade has witnessed a confluence of thinking concerning the paradigmatic refiguration of social thought. As Geertz (1980) notes, there is now even a "blurring of genres" as many social scientists have abandoned—without apology—the misdirected quest to mimic the "more mature" physical sciences. Turning away from a Newtonian laws-and-instances-type explanation rooted in logical empiricist philosophy, many social theorists have instead opted for an interpretive form of inquiry that connects organized action to its contextually embedded set of meanings, "looking less for the sorts of things that connect planets and pendulums and more for the sorts that connect chrysanthemums and swords" (Geertz, 1980, p. 165).

In the administrative sciences, in particular, this recent development has been translated into observable movement away from mechanistic research designs intended objectively to establish universal causal linkages between variables, such as organizational size and level of centralization, or between technology, environment, and organizational structure. Indeed, prominent researchers in the field have publicly given up the logical positivist idea of "certainly through science" and are now embarking on approaches to research that grant preeminence to the historically situated and ever-changing "interpretive schemes" used by members of a given group to give life and meaning to their actions and decisions (Bartunek, 1984). Indicative of the shift away from the logical positivist frame, researchers are converging around what has been termed the "sociorationalist" metatheory of science (Gergen, 1982). Recognizing the symbolic nature of the human universe, we now find a flurry of innovative work supporting the thesis that there is little about human development or organizational behavior that is "preprogrammed" or stimulus-bound in any direct physical or biological way. In this sense, the social universe is open to indefinite revision, change, and self-propelled development. And, this recognition is crucial because to the extent to which social existence is situated in a symbolic realm, beyond deterministic forces, then to that extent the logical positivist foundation of social science is negated and its concept of knowledge rendered illusionary.

Nowhere is this better evidenced than in the variety of works concerned with such topics as organizational paradigms (Brown, 1978; McHugh, 1970); beliefs and master scripts (Sproull, 1981; Beyer, 1981); idea management and the executive mind (Srivastva, 1983; 1985); theories of action and presumptions of logic (Argyris and Schon, 1980; Weick, 1983); consciousness and awareness (Harrison, 1982; Lukes, 1974); and, of course, an array of work associated with the concept of organizational or corporate culture (Ouchi and Johnson, 1978; Schein, 1983; Van Maanen, 1982; Deal and Kennedy, 1982; Sathe, 1983; Hofstede, 1980). As Ellwood prophetically suggested almost half a century ago, "This is the cultural view of human society that is [or will be] revolutionizing the social sciences" (Ellwood, 1938, p. 561).

This developing consensus on the importance of the symbolic realm—on the power of ideas—by such independent sources embracing such diverse objectives reflects the reality of organized life in the modern world. However reluctantly, even the most traditional social thinkers are now recognizing the distinctiveness of the postindustrial world for what truly is—an unfolding drama of human interaction whose potential seems limited or enhanced primarily by our symbolic capacities for constructing meaningful agreements that allow for the committed enactment of collective life.

Never before in history have ideas, information, and beliefs—or theory—been so central in the formulation of reality itself. Social existence, of course, has always depended on some kind of idea system for its meaningful sustenance. The difference now, however, is that what was once background has become foreground. Today, the very fact that society continues to exist at all is experienced not so much mechanistically (an extension of machines) or even naturalistically (a by-product of fateful nature) but more and more humanistically as a social construction of interacting minds—"a game between persons" (Bell, 1973). And under these conditions—as a part of the change from an agrarian society to a goods-producing society at first and then to an information society—ideas and meaning systems take on a whole new life and character. Ideas are thrust center stage as the prime unit of relational exchange governing the creation or obliteration of social existence.

This line of argument applies no less potently to current conceptions of social science. To the extent that the primary product of science is systematically refined idea systems—or theory—science too must be recognized as a powerful agent in the enhancement or destruction of human life. And while this presents an unresolvable dilemma for a logical empiricist conception of science, it spells real opportunity (and responsibility) for a social science that wishes to be of creative significance to society. Put most simply, the theoretical contributions of science may be among the most powerful resources human beings have for contributing to change and development in the groups and organizations in which they live. This is precisely the meaning of Kurt Lewin's early view of action-science when he proposed: "There is nothing so practical as good theory" (1951, p. 169).

Ironically, the discipline of action-research continues to insist on a sharp separation of theory and practice, and to underrate the role of theory in social reconstruction. The irony is that it does so precisely at a time when the cultural view of organizing is reaching toward paradigmatic status. The sad and perhaps tragic commentary on action-research is that it is becoming increasingly inconsequential just as its opportunity to contribute is on the rise (Argyris, 1983).

Observers such as Rappaport (1970) and Bartunek (1983) have lamented the fact that action-researchers have come to subordinate research aims to action interests. Levinson (1972) has gone even further by branding the discipline "atheoretical." And, Friedlander and Brown (1974) have noted that the definition of action-research in classic texts give virtually no mention to theory-building as an integral and necessary component of the research/diagnostic process, or the process of organizational change. Whenever theory is mentioned, it is almost always referred to as a springboard for research or diagnosis, not the other way around. Bartunek (1983, pp. 34) concludes that "even the most recent papers that describe action-research strategies tend to focus primarily on the process of action-research and only secondarily on the specific theoretical contributions of the outcomes of such research" (e.g., Frohman, Sashkin, and Kavanaugh, 1976; Shani and Pasmore, 1982; Susman and Evered, 1978; see Pasmore and Friedlander, 1982, for an exception). For those of us trained in the field this conclusion is not surprising. Indeed, few educational programs in organizational behavior even consider theory-building as a formal part of their curriculum, and even fewer place a real premium on the development of the theoretical mind and imagination of their students.

According to Argyris (1983), this lack of useful theorizing is attributable to two major factors. On the one hand practice-oriented scholars have tended to become so client-centered that they fail to question their clients' own definition of a problem and thereby to build testable propositions and theories that are embedded in everyday life. Academics, on the other hand, who are trained to be more scientific in their bent, also undercut the development of useful theory by their very insistence on the criteria of "normal" science and research—detachment, rigor, unilateral control, and operational precision. In a word, creative theorizing has literally been assaulted on all fronts by practitioners and academic scientists alike. It must also be noted that implicit in this critique by Argyris (1983), and others (e.g., Friedlander and Brown, 1974), is an underlying assumption that action-research has built into it certain natural conflicts that are likely to lead either to "action" (consulting) or "research" (diagnosis or the development of organizational theory), but not to both.

The situation is summed up by Friedlander and Brown (1974) in their comprehensive review of the field:

> We believe that research will either play a far more crucial role in the advancement of this field, or become an increasingly irrelevant appendage to it.... We have generally failed to produce a theory of change, which emerges from the change process itself. We need a way of enriching our understanding and action synergistically rather than at one or the other's expense—to become a science in which knowledge-getting and knowledge-giving are an integrated process, and one that is valuable to all parties involved (p. 319).

Friedlander and Brown concluded with a plea for a metatheoretical revision of science that will integrate theory and practice. But in another review over a decade later, Friedlander (1984) observed little progress coming from top scholars in the discipline. He then put words to a mounting frustration over what appears as a recurring problem:

> They pointed to the shortcomings of traditional research and called for emancipation from it, but they did not indicate a destination. There is as yet no new paradigm that integrates research and practice, or even optimizes useful knowledge for organizations.... I'm impatient. Let's get on with it. Let's not talk it, write it, analyze it, conceptualize it, or research it. Instead let's actively engage and experiment with new designs for producing knowledge that is, in fact, used by organizations (p. 647).

This recurrent problem is the price we pay for continuing to talk about theory and practice in dualistic terms. In a later section in this chapter another hypothesis will be advanced on why there is this lack of creative theorizing, specifically as it relates to action-research. But first we need to look more closely at the claim that social theory and social practice are, indeed, part of a synthetic whole. We need to elaborate on the idea that scientific theory is a means for both understanding and improving social practice. We need to examine exactly what it means to merge the idea and the act, the symbolic and the sociobehavioral, into a powerful and integral unity.

The Sociorationalist Alternative

As the end of the twentieth century nears, thinkers in organizational behavior are beginning to see, without hesitation, why an administrative science based on a physical science model is simply not adequate as a means for understanding or contributing in relevant ways to the workings of complex, organized human systems (see, for example, Susman and Evered, 1978; Beyer and Trice, 1982). Kurt Lewin had understood this almost half a century earlier but his progressive vision of an action science fell short of offering a clear metatheoretical alternative to conventional conceptions of science (Peters and Robinson, 1984). Indeed, the epistemological ambiguity inherent in Lewin's writing has been cited as perhaps the critical shortcoming of all his work. And yet, in hindsight, it can be argued that the ambiguity was intentional and perhaps part of Lewin's social sensitivity and genius. As Gergen (1982) suggests, the metatheoretical ambiguity in Lewin's work might well have been a protective measure, an attempt to shield his fresh vision of an action science from the fully dominant logical positivist temper of his time. In any event, whether planned or not, Lewin walked a tightrope between two fundamentally opposed views of science and never did make clear how theory could be used as both an interpretive and a creative element. This achievement, as we might guess, would have to wait for a change in the intellectual ethos of social science.

That change, as we earlier indicated, is now taking place. Increasingly the literature signals a disenchantment with theories of science that grants priority to the external world in the generation of human knowledge. Instead there is growing movement toward granting preeminence to the cognitive processes of mind and the symbolic processes of social construction. In *Toward Transformation in Social Knowledge* (1982), Kenneth Gergen synthesizes the essential whole of this movement and takes it one crucial step beyond disenchantment to a bold, yet workable conception of science that firmly unites theory with practice—and thereby elevates the status of theoretical-scientific work. From a historical perspective there is no question that this is a major achievement; it brings to completion the work abruptly halted by Lewin's untimely death. But more than that, what Gergen offers, albeit indirectly, is a desperately needed clue to how we can revitalize an action-research discipline that has never reached its potential. While a complete statement of the emerging sociorationalist metatheory is beyond the scope of this chapter, it is important at least to outline the general logic of the perspective, including its basic assumptions.

At the heart of sociorationalism is the assumption of impermanence—the fundamental instability of social order. No matter what the durability to date, virtually any pattern of social action is open to infinite revision. Accepting for a moment the argument of the social constructionists that social reality, at any given point, is a product of broad social agreement (shared meanings), and further granting a linkage between the conceptual schemes of a culture and its other patterns of action, we must seriously consider the idea that alterations in conceptual practices, in ways of symbolizing the world, hold tremendous potential for guiding changes in the social order. To understand the importance of these assumptions and their meaning for social science, let us quote Gergen (1982) at length:

> Is not the range of cognitive heuristics that may be employed in solving problems of adaptation limited only by the human imagination?
>
> One must finally consider the possibility that human biology not only presents to the scientist an organism whose actions may vary in an infinity of ways, but it may ensure as well that novel patterns are continuously emerging... variations in human activity may importantly be traced to the capacities of the organism for symbolic restruc-

turing. As it is commonly said, one's actions appear to be vitally linked to the man-
ner in which one understands or construes the world of experience. The stimulus world
does not elicit behavior in an automatic, reflex-like fashion. Rather, the symbolic trans-
lation of one's experiences virtually transforms their implications and thereby alters
the range of one's potential reactions. Interestingly, while formulations of this vari-
ety are widely shared within the scientific community, very little attention has been
paid to their ramifications for a theory of science. As is clear, without such regulari-
ties the prediction of behavior is largely obviated... to the extent that the individual
is capable of transforming the meaning of stimulus conditions in an indeterminate
number of ways, existing regularities must be considered historically contingent—
dependent on the prevailing meaning systems of conceptual structure of the times. In
effect, from this perspective the scientist's capacity to locate predictable patterns of
interaction depends importantly on the extent to which the population is both homo-
geneous and stable in its conceptual constructions (pp. 1617).

While this type of reasoning is consistent with the thinking of many social scientists, the ramifications are rarely taken to their logical conclusion: "Virtually unexam-
ined by the field is the potential of science to shape the meaning systems of the society
and thus the common activities of the culture" (Gergen, 1978, p. 1349). Virtually unex-
amined is the important role that science can—and does—play in the scientific construction of social reality.

One implication of this line of thought is that to the extent the social science conceives its role in the logical positivist sense, with its goals being prediction and control,
it not only serves the interests of the status quo (you can't have "good science" without stable replication and verification of hypotheses) but it also seriously underestimates the power and usefulness of its most important product, namely theory; it
underestimates the constructive role science can have in the development of the groups
and organizations that make up our cultural world. According to Gergen, realization
of this fact furnishes the opportunity to refashion a social science of vital significance
to society. To do this, we need a bold shift in attention whereby theoretical accounts are
no longer judged in terms of their predictive capacity, but instead are judged in terms
of their generative capacity—their ability to foster dialogue about that which is taken
for granted and their capacity for generating fresh alternatives for social action. Instead
of asking, "Does this theory correspond with the observable facts?" the emphasis for
evaluating good theory becomes, "To what extent does this theory present provocative
new possibilities for social action, and to what extent does it stimulate normative dialogue about how we can and should organize ourselves?" The complete logic for such
a proposal may be summarized in the following ten points:

1. The social order at any given point is viewed as the product of broad social agreement, whether tacit or explicit.
2. Patterns of social-organizational action are not fixed by nature in any direct biological or physical way; the vast share of social conduct is potentially stimulus-
   free, capable of infinite conceptual variation.
3. From an observational point of view, all social action is open to multiple interpretations, no one of which is superior in any objective sense. The interpretations (for
   example, "whites are superior to blacks") favored in one historical setting may be
   replaced in the next.
4 Historically embedded conventions govern what is taken to be true or valid, and
   to a large extent govern what we, as scientists and lay persons, are able to see. All

observation, therefore, is theory-laden and filtered through conventional belief systems and theoretical lenses.

5. To the extent that action is predicated on ideas, beliefs, meanings, intentions, or theory, people are free to seek transformations in conventional conduct by changing conventional codes (idea systems).

6. The most powerful vehicle communities have for transforming their conventions—their agreements on norms, values, policies, purposes, and ideologies—is through the act of dialogue made possible by language. Alterations in linguistic practices, therefore, hold profound implications for changes in social practice.

7. Social theory can be viewed as a highly refined language with a specialized grammar all its own. As a powerful linguistic tool created by trained linguistic experts (scientists), theory may enter the conceptual meaning system of culture and in doing so alter patterns of social action.

8. Whether intended or not, all theory is normative and has the potential to influence the social order—even if reactions to it are simply boredom, rebellion, laughter, or full acceptance.

9. Because of this, all social theory is morally relevant; it has the potential to affect the way people live their ordinary lives in relation to one another. This point is a critical one because there is no such thing as a detached/technical/scientific mode for judging the ultimate worth of value claims.

10. Valid knowledge or social theory is therefore a communal creation. Social knowledge is not "out there" in nature to be discovered through detached, value-free, observational methods (logical empiricism); nor can it be relegated to the subjective minds of isolated individuals (solipsism). Social knowledge resides in the interactive collectivity; it is created, maintained, and put to use by the human group. Dialogue, free from constraint or distortion, is necessary to determine the "nature of things" (sociorationalism).

In **Table 3.1** the metatheory of sociorationalism is both summarized and contrasted to the commonly held assumptions of the logical empiricist view of science. Especially important to note is the transformed role of the scientist when social inquiry is viewed from the perspective of sociorationalism. Instead of attempting to present oneself as an impartial bystander or dispassionate spectator of the inevitable, the social scientist conceives of himself or herself as an active agent, an invested participant whose work might well become a powerful source of change in the way people see and enact their worlds. Driven by a desire to "break the hammerlock" of what appears as given in human nature, the scientist attempts to build theories that can expand the realm of what is conventionally understood as possible. In this sense the core impact of sociorationalist metatheory is that it invites, encourages, and requires that students of social life rigorously exercise their theoretical imagination in the service of their vision of the good. Instead of denial it is an invitation to fully accept and exercise those qualities of mind and action that make us uniquely human.

Now we turn to a question raised earlier: How does theory achieve its capacity to affect social practice, and what are some of the specific characteristics of generative theory?

The Power of Theory in Understanding Organizational Life

The sociorationalist vision of science is of such far-reaching importance that no student, organizational scientist, manager, educator, or action-researcher can afford to ignore it.

Table 3.1: Comparison of Logical Empiricist and Socio-Rationalist Conceptions of Social Science

Dimension for Comparison	Logical Empiricism	Socio-Rationalism
01. Primary Function of Science	Enhance goals of understanding, prediction, and control by discerning general laws or principles governing the relationship among units of observable phenomena.	Enhance understanding in the sense of assigning meaning to something, thus creating its status through the use of concepts. Science is a means for expanding flexibility and choice in cultural evolution.
02. Theory of Knowledge and Mind	Exogenic—grants priority to the external world in the generation of human knowledge (i.e., the preeminence of objective fact). Mind is a mirror.	Endogenic—holds the processes of mind and symbolic interaction as preeminent source of human knowledge. Mind is both a mirror and a lamp.
03. Perspective on Time	Assumption of temporal irrelevance: searches for transhistorical principles.	Assumption of hstorically and contextually relevant meanings; existing regularities in social order are contingent on prevailing meaning systems.
04. Assuming Stability of Social Patterns	Social phenomena are sufficiently stable, enduring, reliable and replicable to allow for lawful principles.	Social order is fundamentally unstable. Social phenomena are guided by cognitive heuristics, limited only by the human imagination: the social order is a subject matter capable of infinite variation through the linkage of ideas and action.
05. Value Stance	Separation of fact and values. Possibility of objective knowledge through behavioral observation.	Social sciences are fundamentally nonobjective. Any behavioral event is open to virtually any interpretative explanation. All interpretation is filtered through prevailing values of a culture. "There is no description without prescription."
06. Features of "Good" Theory	Discovery of transhistorically valid principles; a theory's correspondence with face.	Degree to which theory furnishes alternatives for social innovation and thereby opens vistas for action; expansion of "the realm of the possible."
07. Criteria for Confirmation or Verification (Life of a Theory)	Logical consistency and empirical prediction; subject to falsification.	Persuasive appeal, impace, and overall generative capacity; subject to community agreement; truth is a product of a community of truth makers.
08. Role of Scientist	Impartial bystander and dispassionate spectator of the inevitable; content to accept that which seems given.	Active agent and coparticipant who is primarily a source of linguistic activity (theoretical language) which serves as input into common meaning systems. Interested in "breaking the hammerlock" of what appears as given in human nature.
09. Chief Product of Research	Cumulation of objective knowledge through the production of empiracally disconfirmable hypothesis.	Continued improvement in theory building capacity; improvement in the capacity to create generative-theoretical language.
10. Emphasis in the Education of Future Social Science Professionals	Rigorous experimental methods and statistical analysis; a premium is placed on method (training in theory construction is a rarity).	Hermenuetic interpretation and catalytic theorizing; a premium is placed on the theoretical imagination. Sociorationalism invites the student toward intellectual expression in the service of his or her vision of the good.

Good theory, as we have suggested, is one of the most powerful means we have for helping social systems evolve, adapt, and creatively alter their patterns over time. Building further on this metatheoretical perspective we can talk about five ways by which theory achieves its exceptional potency:

1. Establishing a conceptual and contextual frame;
2. Providing presumptions of logic;
3. Transmitting a system of values;
4. Creating a group-building language;
5. Extending visions of possibility or constraint.

Establishing a Perceptual and Contextual Frame

To the extent that theory is the conceptual imposition of order upon an otherwise "booming, bustling, confusion that is the realm of experience" (Dubin, 1978), the theorist's first order of business is to specify what is there to be seen, to provide an "ontological education" (Gergen, 1982). The very act of theoretical articulation, therefore, highlights not only the parameters of the topic or subject matter, but becomes an active agent as a cueing device, a device that subtly focuses attention on particular phenomena or meanings while obscuring others. In the manner of a telescope or lens, a new theory allows one to see the world in a way perhaps never before imagined.

For example, when American eugenicists used the lens of biological determinism to attribute diseases of poverty to the inferior genetic construction of poor people, they literally could see no systematic remedy other than sterilization of the poor. In contrast, when Joseph Goldberg theorized that pellagra was not genetically determined but culturally caused (as a result of vitamin deficiency and the eating habits of the poor), he could discover a way to cure it (Gould, 1981). Similarly, theories about the "survival of the fittest" might well help executives locate "predators," "hostile environments," and a world where self interest reigns, where it is a case of "eat or be eaten." Likewise, theories of leadership have been known quickly to facilitate the discovery of Theory X and Theory Y interaction. Whatever the theory, it provides a potential means for members of a culture to navigate in an otherwise neutral, meaningless, or chaotic sea of people, interactions and events. By providing an "ontological education" with respect to what is there, a theory furnishes an important cultural input that affects people's cognitive set. In this sense "the world is not so constituted until the lens is employed. With each new distinction the groundwork is laid for alterations in existing patterns of conduct" (Gergen, 1982, p. 23).

As the reader may already surmise, an important moral issue begins to emerge here. Part of the reason that theory is, in fact, powerful is that it shapes perceptions, cognition's, and preferences often at a preconscious level, much like subliminal communications or even hypnosis. Haley (1973) talks about how Milton Erickson has made this a central feature of this psychotherapeutic work. But Lukes (1974) cautions that such thought control may be "the supreme and most insidious exercise of power," especially when it prevents people from challenging their role in the existing order of things and when it operates contrary to their real interests.

Providing Presumptions of Logic

Theories are also powerful to the extent to which they help shape common expectations of causality, sequence, and relational importance of phenomena within a theoretical equation. Consider, for example, the simple logic underlying almost every formal performance-appraisal system. Stripped to essentials, the theoretical underpinnings run something like this: "If you want to evaluate performance (P), then you must evaluate the individual employee (E); in other words, 'P = E'." Armed with this theory, many managers have entered the performance-appraisal meeting shaking with the thought of having to pass godlike judgment on some employee. Similarly, the employee arrives at the meeting with an arsenal of defenses, designed to protect his or her hard-won self-esteem. Little genuine communication occurs during the meeting and virtually no problem-solving takes place. The paperwork is mechanically completed, then filed away in the personnel office until the next year. So powerful is this subtle P = E equation that any alternative goes virtually unnoticed, for example the Lewinian theory that behavior (performance) is a function of the person and the environment (in this case the organizational situation, the "OS" in which the employee works). Following this Lewinian line, the theory underlying performance appraisal would now have to be expanded to read P = E ´ OS. That is, P ? E. To adequately assess performance there must be an assessment of the individual in relation to the organizational setting in which he or she works and vice-versa. What would happen to the performance-appraisal process if this more complete theory were used as a basis for re-designing appraisal systems in organizations throughout the corporate world? Isn't it possible that such a theory could help shift the attribution process away from the person-blame to systems analysis? By attributing causality, theories have the potential to create the very phenomena they propose to explain. Karl Weick, in a recent article examining managerial thought in the context of action, contends that thought and action are part and parcel of one another; thinking is best viewed as a kind of activity, and activity as the ground of thought. For him, managerial theories gain their power by helping people overlook disorder and presume orderliness. Theory *energizes* action by providing a *presumption of logic* that enables people to act with certainty, attention, care, and control. Even where it is originally inadequate as a description of current reality, a forceful theory may provoke action that brings into the world a new reality that then confirms the original theory. Weick (1983) explains:

Once the action is linked with an explanation, it becomes more forceful, and the situation is thereby transformed into something that supports the presumed underlying pattern. Presumptions [theories] enable actions to be tied to specific explanations that consolidate those actions into deterministic events…

The underlying explanation need *not* be objectively "correct." In a crude sense any old explanation will do. This is so because explanation serves mostly to organize and focus the action. The focused action then modifies the situation in ways that confirm the explanation, whatever it is.

Thus, the adequacy of any explanation is determined by the intensity and structure it adds to potentially self-validating actions. More forcefulness leads to more validation and more perceived adequacy. Accuracy is subordinate to intensity. Since situations can support a variety of meanings, their actual content and meaning are dependent on the degree to which they are arranged in sensible, coherent configurations. More forcefulness imposes more coherence. Thus, those explanations that induce greater forcefulness become more valid, not because they are more accurate, but because they have a higher potential for self-validation…the underlying explanations they unfold (for example, "This is war") have great potential to intensify whatever action is underway (1983, pp. 230-232).

Thus, theories are generative to the extent that they are forceful (e.g., Marx), logically coherent (e.g., Piaget), and bold in their assertions and consistency (e.g., Freud, Weber). By providing a basis for focused action, a logic for attributing causality, and a sequence specification that grounds expectations for action and reaction, a theory goes a long way toward forming the common expectations for the future. "And with the alteration of expectation, the stage is set for modification of action" (Gergen, 1982, p. 24).

Transmitting a System of Values

Beyond abstract logic, it is often the affective core of social theory that provides its true force and appeal, allowing it to direct perception and guide behavior. From the tradition of logical positivism, good "objective" theory is to be value-free, yet upon closer inspection we find that social theory is infused with values and domain assumptions throughout. As Gouldner (1970) so aptly put it, "Every social theory facilitates the pursuit of some, but not all, courses of action and thus, encourages us to change or accept the world as it is, to say yea or nay to it. In a way, every theory is a discrete obituary or celebration of some social system."

Nowhere is this better exemplified—negatively—than in the role scientific theory played in the arguments for slavery, colonialism, and belief in the genetic superiority of certain races. The scientific theory in this case was, again, the theory of biological determinism, the belief that social and economic differences between human beings and groups—differences in rank, status, political privilege, education privilege—arise from inherited natural endowments, and that existing social arrangements accurately reflect biological limits. So powerful was this theory during the 1800s that it led a number of America's highest-ranking scientific researchers unconsciously to miscalculate "objective" data in what has been brilliantly described by naturalist Steven Jay Gould (1981, p. 54) as a "patchwork of fudging and finagling in the clear interest of controlling a priori convictions". Before dismissing this harsh judgment as simple rhetoric, we need to look closely at how it was determined. One example will suffice.

When Samual Morton, a scientist with two medical degrees, died in 1851, the *New York Tribune* paid tribute saying, "Probably no scientific man in America enjoyed a higher reputation among scholars throughout the world than Dr. Morton" (in Gould, 1981, p. 51). Morton gained this reputation as a scientist who set out to rank racial groups by "objectively" measuring the size of the cranial cavity of the human skull, which he regarded as a measure of brain size. He had a beautiful collection of skulls from races throughout the world, probably the largest such collection in existence. His hypothesis was a simple one: The mental and moral worth of human races can be arrived at objectively by measuring physical characteristics of the brain; by filling skull cavities with mustard seed or lead shot, accurate measurement of brain size is possible. Morton published three major works, which were reprinted repeatedly as providing objective, "hard" data on the mental worth of races. Gould comments:

Needless to say, they matched every good Yankee's prejudices—whites on top, Indians in the middle, and blacks on the bottom; and among whites, Teutons and Anglo-Saxons on top, Jews in the middle, and Hindus on the bottom…. Status and access to power in Morton's America faithfully reflected biological merit (p. 54).

Morton's work was undoubtedly influential. When he died, the South's leading medical journal proclaimed: "We of the South should consider him as our benefactor, for aiding most materially in giving the Negro his true position as an inferior race" (in Gould, 1981, p. 69). Indeed Morton did much more than only give "the Negro his true position," as the following remarks by Morton himself convey:

Negroes were numerous in Egypt, but their social position in ancient time, was the same as it is now, that of servants and slaves. The benevolent mind may regret the inaptitude of the Indian civilization… [but values must not yield to fact]. The structure of his mind appears to be different from that of the white man, or can the two harmonize in social relations except on the most limited scale. [Indians] are not only averse to restraints of education, but for the most part are incapable of a continued process of reasoning on abstract subjects (in Gould, 1981, p. 53).

The problem with these conclusions—as well as the numerical data, which supported them—was that they were based not on "fact" but purely and simply on cultural fiction, on Morton's belief in biological determinism. As Gould meticulously shows, all of Morton's data was wrong. Having reworked it completely, Gould concludes:

Morton's summaries are a patchwork of fudging and finagling in the clear interest of controlling a priori convictions. Yet—and this is the most intriguing aspect of the case—I find no evidence of conscious fraud; indeed, had Morton been a conscious fudger, he would not have published his data so openly.

Conscious fraud is probably rare in science…The prevalence of unconscious finagling, on the other hand, suggests the general conclusion about the social context of science…prior prejudice may be found anywhere, even in the basics of measuring bones and totaling sums (pp. 5556).

Morton represents a telling example of the power of theory. Theory is not only a shaper of expectations and perceptions. Under the guise of "dispassionate inquiry" it can also be a peddler of values, typecasting arbitrary value as scientific "fact." Along with Gould, we believe that we would be better off to abandon the myth of "value-free" science and that theoretical work "must be understood as a social phenomenon, a gutsy, human enterprise, not the work of robots programmed to collect pure information" (Gould, 1981, p. 21). Even if Morton's data were correct, his work still could not be counted as value-free. His data and theories were not only shaped by the setting in which he worked; they were also used to support broad social policy. This is akin to making nature the source of cultural values, which of course it never can be ("What is" does not equal "what should be").

Creating a Group-Building Language

The sociorationalist perspective is more than a pessimistic epitaph for a strictly logical positivist philosophy. It is an invitation to inquiry that raises the status of theory from mere appendage of scientific method to an actual shaper of society. Once we acknowledge that a primary product of science—theory—is a key resource for the creation of groups, the stage is set for theory-building activity intended for the use and development of human society, for the creation of human options.

Students of human behavior have been aware of the group as the foundation of society since the earliest periods of classical thought. Aristotle, for example, discussed the importance of bands and families. But it was not until the middle of the present century that scientific interest in the subject exploded in a flurry of general inquiry and systematic interdisciplinary research (for a sample review of this literature see Hare, 1976). Among the conclusions of this recent work is the crucial insight that:

The face-to-face group working on a problem is the meeting ground of individual personality and society. It is in the group that personality is modified and socialized and it is through the workings of groups that society is changed and adapted to its times (Thelen, 1954, p. vi).

Similarly, in the field of organization development, Srivastva, Obert, and Neilsen (1977) have shown that the historical development of the discipline has paralleled advances in group theory. And this, they contend, is no accident because:

Emphasis on the small group is responsive to the realities of social change in large complex organizations. It is through group life that individuals learn, practice, develop, and modify their roles in the larger organization. To enter programmatically at the group level is both to confront and potentially co-opt an important natural source of change and development in these systems (p. 83).

It is well established that groups are formed around common ideas that are expressed in and through some kind of shared language which makes communicative interaction possible. What is less clear, though, is the exact role that science plays in shaping group life through the medium of language. However, the fact that science frequently does have an impact is rarely questioned. Andre Gorz (1973) offers an explosive example of this point.

In the early 1960s a British professor of sociology by the name of Goldthorpe was brought in from a nearby university to make a study of the Vauxhall automobile workers in Luton, England. At the time, management at the factory was worried because workers in other organizations throughout the United Kingdom were showing great unrest over working conditions, pay, and management. Many strikes were being waged; most of them wildcat strikes called by the factory stewards, not by the unions themselves. Goldthorpe was called in to study the situation at Vauxhall, to find out for management if there was anything to worry about at their factory. At the time of the study there were at Vauxhall no strikes, no disruptions, and no challenges by workers. Management wanted to know why. What were the chances that acute conflict would break out in the "well-managed" and "advanced" big factory?

After two full years of research, the professor drew his conclusions. Management, he said, had little to worry about. According to the study, the workers were completely socialized into the system, they were satisfied with their wages and neither liked or disliked their work—in fact, they were indifferent to it, viewing it as boring but inevitable. Because their job was not intrinsically rewarding, most people did it just to be done with it—so they could go home and work on other more worthwhile projects and be with their family. Work was marginal and instrumental. It was a means to support other interests outside the factory, where "real life" began. Based then on his observations, Goldthorpe theorized that management had nothing to worry about: Workers were passively apathetic and well integrated into the system. They behaved according to middle-class patterns and showed no signs of strength as a group (no class-consciousness). Furthermore, most conflict with management belonged to the past.

The sociologist's report was still at the printer's when some employees got hold of a summary of his findings. They had the conclusions copied and distributed reports to hundreds of co-workers. Also at around this time, a report of Vauxhall's profits was being circulated, profits that were not shared with the employees. The next day something happened. It was reported by the London Times in detail:

Wild rioting has broken out at the Vauxhall car factories in Luton. Thousands of workers streamed out of the shops and gathered in the factory yard. They besieged the management offices, calling for managers to come out, singing the 'Red Flag,' and shouting. 'String them up!' Groups attempted to storm the offices and battled police which had been called to protect them (quoted in Gorz, 1973).

The rioting lasted for two days. All of this happened, then, in an advanced factory where systematic research showed workers to be apathetic, weak as a group, and resigned to accept the system. What does it all mean? Had the researchers simply misread the data?

To the contrary. Goldthorpe knew his data well. He articulated the conclusions accurately, concisely, and with force. In fact, what happened was that the report gave the workers a *language* with which to begin talking to one another about their plight. It brought them into interaction and, as they discussed things, they discovered that Goldthorpe was right. They felt alike, apathetic but frustrated; and they were apathetic because they felt as individuals working in isolated jobs, that no one could do anything to change things. But the report gave them a way to discuss the situation. As they talked, things changed. People were no longer alone in their feelings, and they did not want things to continue as they were. As an emergent group, they now had a means to convert apathy into action, noninvolvement into involvement, and individual powerlessness into collective strength. "In other words," analyzes Gorz, "the very investigation of Mr. Goldthorpe about the lack of class-consciousness helped tear down the barriers of silence and isolation that rendered the workers apathetic" (p. 334).

The Vauxhall case is an important one for a number of reasons. At a general level it demonstrates that knowledge in the social sciences differs in quality and kind from knowledge generated in the physical sciences. For instance, our knowledge of the periodic chart does not change the elements, and our knowledge of the moon's orbit does not change its path. But our knowledge of a social system is different. It can be used by the system to change itself, thus invalidating or disconfirming the findings immediately or at some later time. Thus the human group differs from objects in an important way: Human beings have the capacity for symbolic interaction and, through language, they have the ability to collaborate in the investigation of their own world. Because of our human capacity for symbolic interaction, the introduction of new knowledge concerning aspects of our world carries with it the strong likelihood of changing that world itself.

Gergen (1982) refers to this as the "enlightenment effect" of scientific work, meaning that once the formulations of scientific work are made public, human beings may act autonomously either to disconfirm or to validate the propositions. According to logical positivist philosophy, potential enlightenment effects must be reduced or—ideally—eliminated through experimental controls. In social psychology, for example, deception plays a crucial role in doing research; enlightenment effects are viewed as contaminants to good scientific work. Yet there is an alternative way to look at the reactive nature of social research: it is precisely because of the enlightenment effect that theory can and does play an important role in the positive construction of society. In this sense, the enlightenment effect—which is made possible through language—is an essential ingredient making scientific work worthwhile, meaningful, and applicable. It constitutes an invitation to each and every theorist to actively participate in the creation of his or her world by generating compelling theories of what is good, and just, and desirable in social existence.

Extending Visions of Possibility

The position taken by the sociorationalist philosophy of science is that the conduct of inquiry cannot be separated from the everyday negotiation of reality. Social-organizational research is, therefore, a continuing moral concern, a concern of social reconstruction and direction. The choice of what to study, how to study it, and what to report each implies some degree of responsibility. Science, therefore, instead of being considered an endpoint, is viewed as one means of helping humanity create itself. Science in this sense exists for one singular overarching purpose. As Albion Small (1905) proposed almost a century ago, a generative science must aim at "the most thorough, intense, persistent, and systematic effort to make human life all that it is capable of becoming" (pp. 3637).

Theories gain their generative capacity by extending visions that expand to the realm of the possible. As a general proposition it might be said that theories designed to empower organized social systems will tend to have a greater enlightenment effect than theories of human constraint. This proposition is grounded in a simple but important consideration which we should like to raise as it relates to the unity of theory and practice: Is it not possible that scientific theory gains its capacity to affect cultural practices in very much the same way that powerful leaders inspire people to new heights? Recent research on the functioning of the executive mind (Srivastva, 1983; 1985) raises a set of intriguing parallels between the possibilities of a generative science and the workings of the executive mind.

The essential parallel is seen in the primary role that ideas or ideals play in the mobilization of diverse groups in the common construction of a desired future. Three major themes from the research stand out in this regard:

1. **Vision:** The executive mind works largely from the present and extends itself out to the longer-term future. It is powerful to the extent that it is able to envision a desired future state which challenges perceptions of what is possible and what can be realized. The executive mind operates beyond the frontier of conventional practice without losing sight of either necessity or possibility.

2. **Passion:** The executive mind is simultaneously rational and intuitive, which allows it to tap into the sentiments, values, and dreams of the social collectivity. Executive vision becomes "common vision" to the extent that it ignites the imaginations, hopes, and passions of others-and it does so through the articulation of self-transcending ideals which lend meaning and significance to everyday life.

3. **Integrity:** The executive mind is the mental muscle that moves a system from the present state to a new and different future. As such, this muscle gains strength to the extent that it is founded upon an integrity able to withstand contrary pressures. There are three dimensions to executive integrity. The first, system integrity, refers to the fact that the executive mind perceives the world (the organization, group, or society) as a unified whole, not as a collection of individual parts. The second type of integrity is *moral integrity*. Common-vision leadership is largely an act of caring. It follows the "path of the heart," which is the source of moral and ethical standards. Finally, integrity of vision refers to consistency, coherence, and focus. Executive vision—to the extent to which it is compelling—is focused and unwavering, even in the midst of obstacles, critics, and conflicting alternatives.

Interestingly, these thematic dimensions of the executive mind have their counterparts in recent observations concerning the utilization of organizational research. According to Beyer and Trice (1982), the "affective bonding" that takes place during the research largely determines the attractiveness of its results and generates commitment to utilize their implications. For example, Henshel (1975) suggests that research containing predictions of an appealing future will be utilized and preferred over research that points to a negative or repelling future: "People will work for predicted states they approve of and against those they detest" (p. 103). Similarly, Weiss and Bucavalas (1980) report that results which challenge the status quo are most attractive to high-level executives because they are the persons expected to make new things happen, at least on the level of policy. And, with respect to passion and integrity, Mitroff (1980) urges social scientists to become caring advocates of their ideas, not only to diffuse their theories but also to challenge others to prove them wrong and thus pursue those ideas which have integrity in action.

This section has explored a number of ways in which social theory becomes a powerful resource for change and development in social practice. The argument is simple. Theory is agential in character and has unbounded potential to affect patterns of social action—whether desired or not. As we have seen, theories are not mere explanations of an external world lying "out there" waiting to be objectively recorded. Theories, like powerful ideas, are formative. By establishing perceptual cues and frames, by providing presumptions of logic, by transmitting subtle values, by creating new language, and by extending compelling visions of possibility or constraint—in all these ways social theory becomes a powerful means whereby norms, beliefs, and cultural practices may be altered.

Reawakening the Spirit of Action-Research

The key point is this: Instinctively, intuitively, and tacitly we all know that important ideas can, in a flash, profoundly alter the way we see ourselves, view reality, and conduct our lives. Experience shows that a simple economic forecast, political poll, or technical discovery (like the atomic bomb) can forever change the course of human history. Thus one cannot help but be disturbed and puzzled by the discipline of action-research in its wide-ranging indifference to theory. Not only does it continue to underrate the role of theory as a means for organizational development (Friedlander and Brown, 1974; Bartunek, 1983; Argyris, 1983) but it appears also to have become locked within an assumptive base that systematically distorts our view of organizational reality and inadvertently helps reinforce and perfect the status quo (Brimm, 1972).

Why is there this lack of generative theorizing in action-research? And, more importantly, what can be done to rekindle the spirit, excitement and passion required of a science that wishes to be of vital significance to organizations? Earlier we talked about a philosophy of science congenial to the task. Sociorationalism, it was argued, represents an epistemological point of view conducive to catalytic theorizing. Ironically though, it can be argued that most action researchers already do subscribe to this or a similar view of science (Susman and Evered, 1978). Assuming this to be the case, it becomes an even greater puzzle why contemporary action-research continues to disregard theory-building as an integral and necessary component of the craft. In this section we shall broaden our discussion by taking a look at some of the metaphysical assumptions embedded in our conventional definitions of action-research—assumptions that can be shown to govern our thought and work in ways inimical to present interests.

Paradigm 1: Organizing As A Problem to be Solved

The intellectual and spiritual origins of action-research can be traced to Kurt Lewin, a social psychologist of German origin who coined the term *action-research* in 1944. The thrust of Lewin's work centered on the need to bridge the gap between science and the realm of practical affairs. Science, he said, should be used to inform and educate social practice, and subsequent action would then inform science: "We should consider action, research, and training as a triangle that should be kept together" (Lewin, 1948, p. 211). The twofold promise of an action science, according to Lewin, was to simultaneously contribute to the development of scientific knowledge (propositions of an if/then variety) and use such knowledge for bettering the human condition.

The immense influence of Lewin is a complete puzzle if we look only to his writings. The fact of the matter is that Lewin published only 2 papers—a mere 22 pages—concerned directly with the idea of action-research (Peters and Robinson, 1984). Indeed, it has been argued that his enduring influence is attributable not to these writings but to the sheer force and presence of the man himself. According to biographer Alfred Marrow (1968), Lewin was a passionate and creative thinker, continuously knocking at the door of the unknown, studying "topics that had been believed to be psychologically unapproachable." Lewin's character was marked by a spirit of inquiry that burned incessantly and affected all who came in contact with him, especially his students. The intensity of his presence was fueled further by the belief that inquiry itself could be used to construct a more democratic and dignified future. At least this was his hope and dream, for Lewin had not forgotten his experience as a refugee from fascism in the late 1930s. Understanding this background, then, it is clear why he revolted so strongly against a detached ivory-tower view of science, a science that is immersed in trivial matters, tranquilized by its standardized methods, and limited in its field of inquiry. Thus, the picture we have of Lewin shows him to have been a committed social scientist pioneering uncharted territory for the purpose of creating new knowledge about groups and societies that might advance the democratic ideal (see, for example, Lewin, 1952). It was this spirit—a relentless curiosity coupled with a conviction of the need for knowledge-guided societal development—that marked Lewin's creative impact on both his students and the field.

Much of this spirit is now gone from action-research. What is left is a series of assumptions about the world which exhibits little, if any, resemblance to the process of inquiry as Lewin lived it. While many of the words are the same, they have been taken too literally and in their translation over the years have been bloated into a set of metaphysical principles—assumptions about the essence of social existence-that directly undermine the intellectual and speculative spirit. Put bluntly, under current norms, action-research has largely failed as an instrument for advancing social knowledge of consequence and now risks being (mis)understood as little more than a crude empiricism imprisoned in a deficiency mode of thought. A quick sketch of six sets of assumptions embedded in the conventional view of action-research will show exactly what we are talking about while also answering our question about the discipline's lack of contribution to generative theory:

Research equals problem-solving; to do good research is to solve "real problems." So ingrained is this assumption that it scarcely needs documentation. Virtually every definition found in leading texts and articles equates action research with problem solving—as if "real" problem solving is virtually the essence of the discipline. For example, as French and Bell (1978) define it, "Action-research is both *an approach to problem solving—a model or paradigm, and a problem-solving process—a series of activities and events.*" (p. 88)4 Or in terms of the Bradford, Gibb, and Benne (1964) definition, "It is an application of scientific methodology in the clarification and solution of practical problems" (p. 33). *Similarly, Frohman, Sashkin, and Kavanaugh (1976) state: "Action research describes a particular process model whereby behavioral science knowledge is applied to help a client (usually a group or social system) solve real problems and not incidentally learn the process involved in problem solving" (p. 203). Echoing this theme, that research equals problem solving, researchers at the University of Michigan's Institute in Social Research state,*

Three factors need to be taken into account in an organization development [action-research] effort: The behaviors that are problematic, the conditions that create those behaviors, and the interventions or activities that will correct the conditions creating the problems. What is it that people are doing or not doing, that is a problem? Why are they doing or not doing these particular things? Which of a large number of possible interventions or activities would be most likely to solve the problems by focusing on why problems exist? (Hausser, Pecorella and Wissler, 1977, p. 2).

Here it is unmistakably clear that the primary focus of the action-research approach to organizational analysis is the ongoing array of concrete problems an organization faces. Of course, there are a number of differences in the discipline as to the overall definition and meaning of the emerging action-research paradigm. But this basic assumption—that research equals problem solving—is not one of them. In a recent review intended to discover elements of metatheoretical agreement within the discipline, Peters and Robinson (1984) discovered that out of 15 different dimensions of action-research studied, only 2 had unanimous support among leaders in the field. What were these two elements of agreement? Exactly as the definitions above suggest: Social science should be "action oriented" and "problem focused."

Inquiry, in action-research terms, is a matter of following the standardized rules of problem solving; knowledge is the result of good method. "In essence," write Blake and Mouton (1976), "it is a method of empirical data gathering that is *comprised of a set of rather standardized steps:* diagnosis, information gathering, feedback, and action planning" (pp. 101102). By following this ritual list, they contend that virtually any organization can be studied in a manner that will lead to usable knowledge. As Chiles (1983) puts it, "The virtue of the model lies in the sequential process.... Any other sequence renders the model meaningless" (p. 318). The basic idea behind the model is that "in management, events proceed as planned unless some force, not provided against by the plan, acts upon events to produce an outcome not contemplated in the plan" (Kepner and Tregoe, 1973, p. 3). Thus, a problem is a deviation from some standard, and without precise diagnosis (step one) any attempt to resolve the problem will likely fail as a result of not penetrating the surface symptoms to discover the true causes. Hence, like a liturgical refrain which is seldom questioned or thought about, Cohen, Fink et al. (1984) tell the new student that *knowledge is the offspring of processing information through a distinct series of problem-solving stages:*

Action-research begins with an identified problem. Data are then gathered in a way that allows a diagnosis which can produce a tentative solution, which is then implemented with the assumption that it is likely to cause new or unforeseen problems that will, in turn, need to be evaluated, diagnosed, and so forth. *This action-research method assumes a constantly evolving interplay between solutions, results, and new solutions...This model is a general one applicable to solving any kind of problem in an ongoing organization* (pp. 359-360).

> *Action-research is utilitarian or technical; that is, it should be initiated and designed to meet a need in an area specified by the organization, usually by "top management." The search is controlled by the "felt need" or object of inquiry; everything that is not related to this object should be dismissed as irrevelant.*

As we are beginning to see, action-research conventionally understood does not really refer to research per se but rather to a highly focused and defined type of research called problem solving. Taken almost directly from the medical model, the disease orientation guides the process of inquiry in a highly programmed way. According to Levinson (1972), diagnostic action-research, "like a therapeutic or teaching relationship should be an alliance of both parties to discover and resolve these problems.... [The researcher] *should look for experiences which appear stressful to people. What kinds of occurrences disrupt or disorganize people*" (p. 37). Hence in a systematically limiting fashion, the general topic of research is largely prescribed—before inquiry even begins. As we would guess:

> Typical questions in [action-research] data gathering or "problem sensing" would include: *What problems* do you see in your group, including problems between people that are interfering with getting the job done the way you would like to see it done? And *what problems* do you see in the broader organization? Such open-ended questions provide latitude on the part of respon-

dents and encourage a *reporting of problems* as the individual sees them (French, 1969, pp. 183-185).

In problem solving it is assumed that something is broken, fragmented, not whole, and that it needs to be fixed. Thus the function of problem solving is to integrate, stabilize, and help raise to its full potential the workings of the status quo. By definition, a problem implies that one already has knowledge of what "should be"; thus one's research is guided by an instrumental purpose tied to what is already known. In this sense, problem solving tends to be inherently conservative; as a form of research it tends to produce and reproduce a universe of knowledge that remains sealed. As Staw (1984) points out in his review of the field, most organizational research is biased to serve managerial interests rather than exploring broader human and/or social purposes. But even more important, he argues, the field has not even served managerial interests well since research has taken a short-term problem focus rather than having formulated logic's of new forms of organization that do not exist. It is as if the discipline's *concept of social system development* means only clearing up distortions in current functioning (horizontal development) and does not include any conception of a stage-based movement toward an altogether new or transformed reality (vertical development or second-order change).

Action-research should not inquire into phenomena that transcend the competence of human reason. Questions that cannot be answered should not be asked and issues that cannot be acted upon should not be explored (i.e., action-research is not a branch of political philosophy, poetry, or theology). This proposition is a "smuggled-in" corollary to the preceding assumptions. It would appear that once one agrees with the ground rules of a pragmatic problem-solving science, the universe for inquiry is largely predetermined, defined, and delimited in scope. Specifically, what one agrees to a secularized view of a human universe that is predictable, controllable, and rational, one that is sequentially ordered into a series of causes and effects. As both a credit and a weakness, the problem-solving mode narrows our gaze in much the same manner that a blinder over one eye narrows the field of vision and distorts one's perception of depth. As a part of a long-term movement evidenced in social sciences, contemporary action-research embodies the trend toward metaphysical skepticism and denial (Quinney, 1982). That is, it operates out of a sacred void that cuts off virtually any inquiry into the vital forces of life. Indeed, the whole promise of modern science was that it would finally banish illusion, mystery, and uncertainty from the world. An inquiry process of immediate utility (problem solving), therefore, requires an anti-religious, secular spirit that will limit the realm of study to the sphere of the known. And because of the recognition that the formulation of a problem depends largely on one's views of what constitutes a solution, it is not surprising to find that *research on the utilization of research* shows a propensity for social scientists and organizations to agree on studying only those variables that can be manipulated (Beyer and Trice, 1982). As one might imagine, such a view has crippling implications for generative theorizing. For example, as typically practiced, action-research does little in the way of theorizing about or bringing beauty into organizational life. Does this mean that there is no beauty in organizing'? Does this mean that the realm of the esthetic has little or nothing to do with organizational dynamics'?

The tidy imagery of the problem-solving view is related to what Sigmund Koch (1981) has called, in his presidential address to the APA, the syndrome of "ameaningful thinking." One element of this syndrome is the perpetuation of the scientific myth which uses the rhetoric of prediction and control to reassure people that their lives are not that complex, their situations not all that uncertain—and that their problems are indeed manageable through causal analysis. In the process, however, science tends to trivialize, and even evade, a whole class of issues that "transcend the competence of human reason" yet are clearly meaningful in the course of human experience. One way in which the field of inquiry is restricted, according to Koch, has to do with one's choice of methodology:

There are times and circumstances in which able individuals, committed to inquiry, tend almost obsessively to frustrate the objectives of inquiry. It is as if uncertainty, moot-ness, ambiguity, cognitive infinitude were the most unbearable of the existential anguishes…. *Ameaningful* thought or inquiry regards knowledge as the result of "pro-cessing" rather than discovery. It presumes that knowledge is an almost automatic result of a gimmickry, an assembly line, a "methology"… So strongly does it see knowledge under such aspects that it sometimes seems to suppose the object of inquiry to be an ungainly and annoying irrelevance (1981, p. 259).

To be sure, this is not to argue that all action-research is "ameaningful" or auto-matically tied to a standardized problem-solving method. Likewise, much of the suc-cess achieved by action-research until now may be attributed to its restricted focus on that which is "solvable. " However, it is important to recognize that the problem-solv-ing method of organizational inquiry quite systematically paints a picture of organi-zational life in which a whole series of colors are considered untouchable. In this way the totality of being is obviously obscured, leading to a narrowed conception of human nature and cultural possibility.

Problems are "out there" to be studied and solved. The ideal product of action-research is a mirror-like reflection of the organization's problems and causes. As "objective third party " there is little role for passion and speculation. The action-researcher should be neither a pas-sionate advocate nor an inspired dreamer (utopian thinker). One of the laudable and indeed significant values associated with action-research has been its insistence upon a col-laborative form of inquiry. But unfortunately, from a generative-theory perspective, the term *collaboration* has become virtually synonymous with an idealized image of the researcher as a facilitator and mirror, rather than an active and fully engaged social par-ticipant. As facilitator of the problem-solving process, the action-researcher has three generally agreed-upon "primary intervention tasks": to help generate valid organiza-tional data; to enable others to make free and informed choices on the basis of the data, and to help the organization generate internal commitment to their choices. Elaborat-ing further, Argyris (1970) states:

One condition that seems so basic as to be defined as axiomatic is the gener-ation of valid information… *Valid information is that which describes the factors, plus their interrelationships that create the problem* (pp. 1617).

Furthermore, it is also assumed that for data to be useful there must be a claim to neutrality. The data should represent an accurate reflection of the observed facts. As French and Bell (1978) describe it, it is important for the action-researcher to stress the objective, fact-finding features: "A key value inculcated in organizational members is a belief in the validity, desirability, and usefulness of the data" (p. 79). Then through feedback that "refers to activities and processes that 'reflect' or 'mirror' an objective picture of the real world" (p. 111), the action-researcher facilitates the process of prior-itizing problems and helps others make choices for action. And because the overarch-ing objective is to help the organization develop its own internal resources, the action-researcher should not play an active role or take an advocate stance that might in the long run foster an unhealthy dependency. As French and Bell (1978) again explain, an active role "tends to negate a collaborative, developmental approach to improving organizational processes" (p. 203).

As must be evident, every one of these injunctions associated with the problem-solving view of action-research serves directly to diminish the likelihood of imaginative, passionate, creative theory. To the extent that generative theory represents an inspired theoretical articulation of a new and different future, it appears that action-research would have nothing to do with it. According to French and Bell (1978) "Even the presenting of options can be overdone. If the [action-researcher's] ideas become the focal point for prolonged discussion and debate, the consultant has clearly shifted away from the facilitator role" (p. 206).

At issue here is something even more important. The fundamental attitude embodied in the problem-solving view is separationist. It views the world as something external to our consciousness of it, something "out there." As such it tends to identify problems not here but "over there": Problems are not ours, but yours; not a condition common to all, but a condition belonging to this person, their group, or that nation (witness the acid-rain issue). Thus, the action-researcher is content to facilitate *their problem solving* because he or she is not part of that world. To this extent, the problem-solving view dissects reality and parcels it out into fragmented groups, families, tribes, or countries. In both form and substance it denies the wholeness of a dynamic and interconnected social universe. And once the unity of the world is broken, passionless, mindless, mirror-like inquiry comes to make logical sense precisely because the inquirer has no ownership or stake in a world that is not his or hers to begin with.

> *Organizational life is problematic. Organizing is best understood as a historically situated sequence of problems, causes, and solutions among people, events, and things. Thus, the ultimate aim and product of action-research is the production of institutions that have a high capacity to perceive, formulate, and solve an endless stream of problems.*

The way we conceive of the social world is of consequence to the kind of world we discover and even, through our reconstructions, helps to create it. Action-researchers, like scientists in other areas, approach their work from a framework based on taken-for-granted assumptions. To the extent that these assumptions are found useful, and are affirmed by colleagues, they remain unquestioned as a habitual springboard for one's work. In time the conventional view becomes so solidly embedded that it assumes the status of being "real," without alternative (Morgan, 1980; Mennhiem, 1936). As human beings we are constantly in symbolic interaction, attempting to develop conceptions that will allow us to make sense of and give meaning to experience through the use of language, ideas, signs, theories, and names. As many have recently shown, the use of metaphor is a basic mode under which symbolism works and exerts an influence on the development of language, science, and cognitive growth (Morgan, 1980; Ortony, 1979; Black, 1962; Keely, 1980). Metaphor works by asserting that A equals B or is very much like B. We use metaphors constantly to open our eyes and sensitize us to phenomenal realities that otherwise might go unnoticed. Pepper (1942) argues that all science proceeds from specifiable "world hypotheses" and behind every world hypothesis rests the boldest of "root metaphors."

Within what we are calling Paradigm I action-research, there lies a guiding metaphor which has a power impact on the theory-building activity of the discipline. When organizations are approached from the deficiency perspective of Paradigm I, all the properties and modes of organizing are scrutinized for their dysfunctional but potentially solvable problems. It is all too clear then that the root metaphor of the conventional view is that *organizing is a problem.* This image focuses the researcher's eye on a visible but narrow realm of reality that resides "out there" and is causally determined, deficient by some preexisting standard—on problems that are probably both understandable and solvable. Through analysis, diagnosis, treatment, and follow-up evaluation the sequential world of organizing can be kept on its steady and productive course. And because social existence is at its base a problem to be solved, real living equals problem solving, and living better is an adaptive learning process whereby we acquire new and more effective means for tackling tough problems. The good life, this image informs, depends on solving problems in such a way that problems of utility are identified and solutions of high quality are found and carried out with full commitment. As one leading theorist describes:

For many scholars who study organizations and management, the central characteristic of organizations is that they are problem-solving systems whose success is measured by how efficiently they solve problems associated with accomplishing their primary mission and how effectively they respond to emergent problems. Kilmann's approach (1979, pp. 214–215) is representative of this perspective: "One might even define the essence of management as problem defining and problem solving, whether the problems are well-structured, ill-structured, technical, human, or environmental... In this view, the core task of the executive is problem management. Although experience, personality, and specific technical expertise are important, the primary skill of the successful executive is the ability to manage the problem-solving process in such a way that important problems are identified and solutions of high quality are found and carried out with the full commitment of organizational members (Kolb, 1983, pp. 109–110).

From here it is just a short conceptual jump to the idealized aim of Paradigm 1 research:

Action-research tends to build into the client system an institutionalized pattern for continuously collecting data and examining the system's processes, as well as for the continuous review of *known* problem areas. *Problem solving becomes very much a way of organizational life* (Marguiles and Raia, 1972, p. 29).

I have tried in these few pages to highlight the almost obvious point that the deficiency/problem orientation is pervasive and holds a subtle but powerful grasp on the discipline's imagination and focus. It can be argued that the generative incapacity of contemporary action-research is securely linked with the discipline's guiding metaphor of social-organizational existence. As noted by many scholars, the theoretical output of the discipline is virtually nonexistent, and what theory there is, is largely problem-focused (theories of turnover, intergroup conflict, processes of dehumanization. See Staw, 1984 for an excellent review). Thus, our theories, like windsocks, continue to blow steadily onward in the direction of our conventional gaze. Seeing the world as a problem has become "very much a way of organizational life."

It is our feeling that the discipline has reached a level of fatigue arising from repetitious use of its standardized model. Fatigue, as Whitehead (1929) so aptly surmised, arises from an act of excluding the impulse toward novelty, which is the antithesis of the life of the mind and of speculative reason. To be sure, there can be great adventure in the process of inquiry. Yet not many action-researchers today return from their explorations refreshed and revitalized, like pioneers returning home, with news of lands unknown but most certainly there. Perhaps there is a different root metaphor from which to work.

Proposal for a Second Dimension

Our effort here is but one in a small yet growing attempt to generate new perspectives on the conduct of organizational research, perspectives that can yield the kind of knowledge necessary for both understanding and transforming complex social-organizational systems (Torbert, 1983; Van Maanen et al., 1982; Mitroff and Kilmann, 1978; Smirchich, 1983; Forester, 1983; Argyris, 1970; Friedlander, 1977). It is apparent that among the diverse views currently emerging there is frequently great tension. Often the differences become the battleground for fierce debate about theories of truth, the meaning of "facts," political agendas, and personal assertions of will. But, more fruitfully, what can be seen emerging is a heightened sensitivity to and interdisciplinary recognition of the fact that, based on "the structure of knowledge" (Kolb, 1984), there may be multiple ways of knowing, each of them valid in its own realm when judged according to its own set of essential assumptions and purposes. In this sense there are many different ways of studying the same phenomenon, and the insights generated by one approach are, at best, partial and incomplete. According to Jurgen Habermas (1971) different perspectives can be evaluated only in terms of their specified "human interests," which can broadly be differentiated into the realm of practical rationality and the realm of technical rationality. In more straightforward language Morgan (1983) states:

The selection of method implies some view of the situation being studied, for any decision on *how* to study a phenomenon carries with it certain assumptions or explicit answers to the question, "What is being studied?" Just as we select a tennis racquet rather than a golf club to play tennis because we have a prior conception as to what the game of tennis involves, so too, in relation to the process of social research, we select or favor particular kinds of methodology because we have implicit or explicit conceptions as to what we are trying to do with our research (p. 19).

Thus, in adopting one mode over another the researcher directly influences what he or she will finally discover and accomplish.

It is the contention of this chapter that advances in generative theorizing will come about for action-research when the discipline decides to expand its universe of exploration, seeks to discover new questions, and rekindles a fresh perception of the extra ordinary in everyday organizational life. In this final section we now describe the assumptions and philosophy of an applied administrative science that seeks to embody these suggestions in a form of organization study we call appreciative inquiry. In distinction to conventional action-research, the knowledge-interest of appreciative inquiry lies not so much in problem solving as in social innovation. Appreciative inquiry refers to a research perspective that is uniquely intended for discovering, understanding, and fostering innovations in social-organizational arrangements and processes. Its purpose is to contribute to the generative-theoretical aims of social science and to use such knowledge to promote egalitarian dialogue leading to social-system effectiveness and integrity. Whatever else it may be, social-system effectiveness is defined here quite specifically as a congruence between social-organizational values (the ever-changing non-native set of values, ideas, or interests that system members hold concerning the question, "How should we organize ourselves?") and everyday social- organizational practices (cf. Torbert, 1983). Thus, appreciative inquiry refers to both a search for knowledge and a theory of intentional collective action which are designed to help evolve the normative vision and will of a group, organization, or society as a whole. It is an inquiry process that affirms our symbolic capacities of imagination and mind as well as our social capacity for conscious choice and cultural evolution. As a holistic form of inquiry, it asks a series of questions not found in either a logical-positivist conception

Figure 3.1

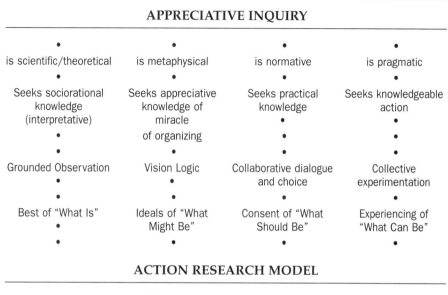

APPRECIATIVE INQUIRY

is scientific/theoretical	is metaphysical	is normative	is pragmatic
Seeks sociorational knowledge (interpretative)	Seeks appreciative knowledge of miracle of organizing	Seeks practical knowledge	Seeks knowledgeable action
Grounded Observation	Vision Logic	Collaborative dialogue and choice	Collective experimentation
Best of "What Is"	Ideals of "What Might Be"	Consent of "What Should Be"	Experiencing of "What Can Be"

ACTION RESEARCH MODEL

FOR A HUMANLY SIGNIFICANT
GENERATIVE SCIENCE OF ADMINISTRATION

of science or a strictly pragmatic, problem-solving mode of action-research. Yet as shown in **Figure 3.1**, its aims are both scientific (in a sociorationalist sense) and pragmatic (in a social-innovation sense) as well as metaphysical and normative (in the sense of attempting ethically to affirm all that social existence really is and should become). As a way of talking about the framework as it is actually practiced, we shall first examine four guiding principles that have directed our work in the area to date:

Principle 1: *Research into the social (innovation) potential of organizational, life should begin with appreciation.* This basic principle assumes that every social system "works" to some degree—that it is not in a complete state of entropy—and that a primary task of research is to discover, describe, and explain those social innovations, however small, which serve to give "life" to the system and activate members' competencies and energies as more fully functioning participants in the formation and transformation of organizational realities. That is, the appreciative approach takes its inspiration from the current state of "what is" and seeks a comprehensive understanding of the factors and forces of organizing (ideological, techno-structural, cultural) that serve to heighten the total potential of an organization in ideal-type human and social terms.

Principle 2: *Research into the social potential of organizational life should be applicable.* To be significant in a human sense, an applied science of administration should lead to the generation of theoretical knowledge that can be used, applied, and thereby validated in action. Thus, an applicable inquiry process is neither utopian in the sense of generating knowledge about "no place" (Sargent, 1982) nor should it be confined to academic circles and presented in ways that have little relevance to the everyday language and symbolism of those for whom the findings might be applicable.

Principle 3: *Research into the social potential of organizational life should be provocative.* Here it is considered axiomatic that an organization is, in fact, an open-ended indeterminate system capable of (1) becoming more than it is at any given moment, and (2) learning how to actively take part in guiding its own evolution. Hence, appreciative knowledge of what is (in terms of "peak" social innovations in organizing) is suggestive of what *might be* and such knowledge can be used to generate images of realistic developmental opportunities that can be experimented with on a wider scale. In this sense, appreciative inquiry can be both pragmatic and visionary. It becomes provocative to the extent that the abstracted findings of a study take on normative value for members of an organization, and this can happen only through their own critical deliberation and choice ("We feel that this particular finding is [or not] important for us to envision as an ideal to be striving for in practice on a wider scale"). It is in this way then, that appreciative inquiry allows us to put intuitive, visionary logic on a firm empirical footing and to use systematic research to help the organization's members shape the social world according to their own imaginative and moral purposes.

Principle 4: *Research into the social potential of organizational life should be collaborative.* This overarching principle points to the assumed existence of an inseparable relationship between the process of inquiry and its content. A collaborative relationship between the researcher and members of an organization is, therefore, deemed essential on the basis of both epistemological (Susman and Evered, 1978) and practical/ethical grounds (Habermas, 1971; Argyris, 1970). Simply put, a unilateral approach to the study of social innovation (bringing something new into the social world) is a direct negation of the phenomenon itself.

The spirit behind each of these four principles of appreciative inquiry is to be found in one of the most ancient archetypes or metaphorical symbols of hope and inspiration that humankind has ever known—the miracle and mystery of being. Throughout history, people have recognized the intimate relationship between being seized by the unfathomable and the process of appreciative knowing or thought (Marcel, 1963; Quinney, 1982; Jung, 1933; Maslow, 1968; Ghandi, 1958). According to Albert Schweitzer (1969), for example, it is recognition of the ultimate mystery that elevates our perception beyond the world of ordinary objects, igniting the life of the mind and a "reverence for life":

In all respects the universe remains mysterious to man... As soon as man does not take his existence for granted, but beholds it as something unfathomably mysterious, thought begins. This phenomenon has been repeated time and time again in the history of the human race. Ethical affirmation of life is the intellectual act by which man ceases simply to live at random... [Such] thought has a dual task to accomplish: to lead us out of a naive and into a profounder affirmation of life and the universe; and to help us progress from ethical impulses to a rational system of ethics (p. 33).

For those of us breastfed by an industrial giant that stripped the world of its wonder and awe, it feels, to put it bluntly, like an irrelevant, absurd, and even distracting interruption to pause, reflect deeply, and then humbly accept the depth of what we can never know—and to consider the ultimate reality of living for which there are no coordinates or certainties, only questions. Medicine cannot tell me, for example, what it means that my newborn son has life and motion and soul, anymore than the modern physicist can tell me what "nothingness" is, which, they say, makes up over 99 percent of the universe. In fact, if there is anything we have learned from a great physicist of our time is that the promise of certainty is a lie (Hiesenberg, 1958), and by living this lie as scientist doctrine, we short-circuit the gift of complementarity—the capacity for dialectically opposed modes of knowing, which adds richness, depth, and beauty to our lives (Bohr, 1958). Drugged by the products of our industrial machine we lose sight of and connection with the invisible mystery at the heart of creation, an ultimate power beyond rational understanding.

In the same way that birth of a living, breathing, loving, thinking human being is an inexplicable mystery, so too it can be said in no uncertain terms that *organizing is a miracle* of cooperative human interaction, of which there can never be final explanation. In fact, to the extent that organizations are indeed born and re-created through dialogue, they truly are unknowable as long as such creative dialogue remains. At this point in time there simply are no organizational theories that can account for the life-giving essence of cooperative existence, especially if one delves deeply enough. But, somehow we forget all this. We become lulled by our simplistic diagnostic boxes. The dilemma faced by our discipline in terms of its creative contribution to knowledge is summed up perfectly in the title of a well known article by one of the major advocates of action-research. The title by Marv Wiesbord (1976), has proven prophetic: "Organizational diagnosis: six places to look for trouble, with or without a theory." Content to transfer our conceptual curiosity over to "experts" who finally must know, our creative instincts lie pitifully dormant. Instead of explorers we become mechanics.

This, according to Koch (1981), is the source of "ameaningful" thinking. As Kierkegaard (1954) suggests, it is the essence of a certain dull-minded routine called "philistinism:

Devoid of imagination, as the Philistine always is, he lives in a certain trivial province of experience as to how things go, what is possible... Philistinism tranquilizes itself in the trivial (pp. 174–175).

As we know, a miracle is something that is beyond all possible verification, yet is experienced as real. As a symbol, the word *miracle* represents unification of the sacred and secular into a realm of totality that is at once terrifying and beautiful, inspiring and threatening. Quinney (1982) has suggested with respect to the rejuvenation of social theory, that such a unified viewpoint is altogether necessary, that it can have a powerful impact on the discipline precisely because in a world that is at once sacred and secular there is no place, knowledge, or phenomenon that is without mystery. The "miracle" then is pragmatic in its effect when sincerely apprehended by a mind that has chosen not to become "tranquilized in the trivial." In this sense, the metaphor "life is a miracle" is not so much an idea as it is—or can be—a central feature of experience enveloping (1) our perceptual consciousness; (2) our way of relation to others, the world, and our own research; and (3) our way of knowing. Each of these points can be highlighted by a diverse literature.

In terms of the first, scholars have suggested that the power of what we call the miracle lies in its capacity to advance one's perceptual capacity what Maslow (1968) has called a B-cognition or a growth-vs-deficiency orientation, or what Kolb (1984) has termed integrative consciousness. Kolb writes:

The transcendental quality of integrative consciousness is precisely that, a "climbing out of"... This state of consciousness is not reserved for the monastery, but it is a necessary ingredient for creativity in any field. Albert Einstein once said, "The most beautiful and profound emotion one can feel is a sense of the mystical... It is the dower of all true science" (p. 158).

Second, as Gabriel Marcel (1963) explained in his William James lectures at Harvard on *The Mystery of Being,* the central conviction of life as a mystery creates for us a distinctly different relationship to the world than the conviction of life as a problem to be solved:

A problem is something met which bars my passage. It is before me in its entirety. A mystery on the other hand is something I find *myself* caught up in, and whose essence is therefore not before me in its entirety. It is though in this province the distinction between "in me" and "before me" loses its meaning (p. 80).

Berman's (1981) recent analysis comes to a similar conclusion. The re-enchantment of the world gives rise to a "participatory consciousness" where there is a sense of personal stake, ownership, and partnership with the universe:

The view of nature which predominated the West down to the eve of the Scientific Revolution was that of an enchanted world. Rocks, trees, rivers, and clouds were all seen as wondrous, alive, and human beings felt at home in this environment. The cosmos, in short, was a place of *belonging*. A member of this cosmos was not an alienated observer of it but a direct participant in its drama. His personal destiny was bound up with its destiny, and this relationship gave meaning to his life.

Third, as so many artists and poets have shown, there is a relationship between what the Greeks called *thaumazein—an experience which lies on the borderline between wonderment and admiration—and a type of intuitive apprehension or knowing that we call appreciative. For Keats, the purpose of his work was:*

to accept things as I saw them, to enjoy the beauty I perceived for its own sake, without regard to ultimate truth or falsity, and to make a description of it the end and purpose of my appreciations.

Similarly for Shelley:

Poetry thus makes immortal all that is best and most beautiful in the world… it exalts the beauty of that which is most beautiful… it strips the veil of familiarity from the world, and lays bare the naked and sleeping beauty, which is in the spirit of its forms.

And in strikingly similar words, learning theorist David Kolb (1984) analyzes the structure of the knowing mind and reports:

Finally, appreciation is a process of affirmation. Unlike criticism, which is based on skepticism and doubt (compare Polanyi, 1968, pp. 269ff.), appreciation is based on belief, trust, and conviction. And from this affirmative embrace flows a deeper fullness and richness of experience. This act of affirmation forms the foundation from which vital comprehension can develop… Appreciative apprehension and critical comprehension are thus fundamentally different processes of knowing. Appreciation of immediate experience is an act of attention, valuing, and affirmation, whereas critical comprehension of symbols is based on objectivity (which involves a priori controls of attention, as in double-blind controlled experiments), dispassionate analysis, and skepticism (pp. 104–105).

We have cited these various thinkers in detail for several reasons: first, to underscore the fact that the powerful images of problem and miracle (in)form qualitatively distinct modes of inquiry which then shape our awareness, relations, and knowledge; and second, to highlight the conviction that the renewal of generative theory requires that we enter into the realm of the metaphysical. The chief characteristic of the modern mind has been the banishment of mystery from the world, and along with it an ethical affirmation of life that has served history as a leading source of values, hope, and normative bonding among people. In historical terms, we have steadily forgotten how to dream.

In contrast to a type of research that is lived without a sense of mystery, the appreciative mode awakens the desire to create and discover new social possibilities that can enrich our existence and give it meaning. In this sense, appreciative inquiry seeks an imaginative and fresh perception of organizations as "ordinary magic," as if seen for the first time—or perhaps the last time (Hayward, 1984). The appreciative mode, in exploration of ordinary magic, is an inquiry process that takes nothing for granted, searching to apprehend the basis of organizational life and working to articulate those possibilities giving witness to a better existence.

The metaphysical dimension of appreciative inquiry is important not so much as a way of finding answers but is important insofar as it heightens the living experience of awe and wonder which leads us to the wellspring of new questions—much like a wide-eyed explorer without final destination. Only by raising innovative questions will innovations in theory and practice be found. As far as action-research is concerned, this appears to have been the source of Lewin's original and catalytic genius. We too can re-awaken this spirit. Because the questions we ask largely determine what we find, we should place a premium on that which informs our curiosity and thought. The metaphysical question of what makes social existence possible will never go away. The generative-theoretical question of compelling new possibilities will never go away. The normative question of what kind of social-organizational order is best, most dignified, and just, will never go away, nor will the pragmatic question of how to move closer to the ideal.

In its pragmatic form appreciative inquiry represents a data-based theory building methodology for evolving and putting into practice the collective will of a group or organization. It has one and only one aim—to provide a generative theoretical springboard for normative dialogue that is conducive to self-directed experimentation in social innovation. It must be noted, however, that the conceptual world which appreciative inquiry creates remains—despite its empirical content—an illusion. This is important to recognize because it is precisely because of its visionary content, placed in juxtaposition to grounded examples of the extraordinary, that appreciative inquiry opens the status quo to possible transformations in collective action. It appreciates the best of "what is" to ignite intuition of the possible and then firmly unites the two logically, caringly, and passionately into a theoretical hypothesis of an envisioned future. By raising ever new questions of an appreciative, applicable, and provocative nature, the researcher collaborates in the scientific construction of his or her world.

Conclusion

What we have tried to do with this chapter is present conceptual refiguration of action-research; to present a proposal arguing for an enriched multidimensional view of action-research which seeks to be both theoretically generative and progressive in a broad human sense. In short, the argument is a simple one stating that there is a need to re-awaken the imaginative spirit of action-research and that to do this we need a fundamentally different perspective toward our organizational world, one that admits to its uncertainties, ambiguities, mysteries, and unexplicable, miraculous nature. But now we must admit, with a certain sense of limited capability and failure, that the viewpoint articulated here is simply not possible to define and is very difficult to speak of in technological, step-by-step terms. From the perspective of rational thought, the miraculous is impossible. From that of problem solving it is nonsense. And from that of empirical science, it is categorically denied (Reeves, 1984). Just as we cannot prove the proposition that organizing is a problem to be solved, so, too, we cannot prove in any rational, analytical, or empirical way that organizing is a miracle to be embraced. Each stance represents a commitment—a core conviction so to speak—which is given to each of us as a choice. We do, however, think that through discipline and training the appreciative eye can be developed to see the ordinary magic, beauty, and real possibility in organizational life; but we are not sure we can so easily transform our central convictions.

In sum, the position we have been developing here is that for action-research to reach its potential as a vehicle for social innovation, it needs to begin advancing theoretical knowledge of consequence—that good theory may be one of the most powerful means human beings have for producing change in a post-industrial world; that the discipline's steadfast commitment to a problem-solving view of the world is a primary restraint on its imagination, passion, and positive contribution; that appreciative inquiry represents a viable complement to conventional forms of action- research, one uniquely suited for social innovation instead of problem solving; and that through our assumptions and choice of method we largely create the world we later discover.

References

Argyris, C. (1973). Action science and intervention. *The Journal of Applied Behavioral Science,* 19, 115–140.

Argyris, C. (1970). *Intervention theory and methods.* Reading, MA: Addison-Wesley.

Argyris, C. and Schon, D. (1978). *Organizational learning: A theory of action perspective.* Reading. MA: Addison-Wesley.

Bartunek, J. (1983). How organization development can develop organizational theory. *Group and Organizational Studies.* 8, 303–318.

Bartunek, J. (1984). Changing interpretive schemes and organizational restructuring: The example of a religious order. *Administrative Science Quarterly,* 27, 355–372.

Bell, D. (1973). *The coming of the Post-Industrial society.* New York: Basic Books.

Beyer, J. (1981). Ideologies, values and decision making in organizations. In P. C. Nystrom and W. H. Starbuck (Eds.), *Handbook of organizational design, Vol. 2.* Oxford University Press.

Beyer, J. and Trice, H. (1982). Utilization process: Conceptual framework and synthesis of findings. *Administrative Science Quarterly,* 22, 591–622.

Blake. R. and Mouton. J. (1976). *Consultation.* Reading, MA: Addison Wesley.

Bohr, N. (1958). *Atomic theory and human knowledge.* New York: John Wiley.

Bradford, L. P., Gibb, J. R., and Benne, K. (1964). *T-group theory and laboratory method.* New York: John Wiley.

Braverman, H. (1974). *Labor and monopoly capital.* New York: Monthly Review Press.

Brimm, M. (1972). When is change not a change? *Journal of Applied Behavioral Science,* 1, 102–107.

Brown, R. H. (1978). *Leadership.* New York: Harper and Row.

Chiles, C. (1983). Comments on "design guidelines for social problem solving interventions." *Journal of Applied Behavioral Science* 19, 189–191.

Clegg, S. and Dunkerley. D. (1980). *Organization, class, and control.* Boston: Routledge and Kegan Paul.

Cohen, A. R., Fink, S. L., Gadon, H., and Willits, R. D. (1984). *Effective behavior in organizations.* Homewood, IL: Irwin.

Cooperrider, D. (I 986). *Appreciative Inquiry: Toward a methodology for understanding and enhancing organizational innovation.* Unpublished Ph.D. dissertation, Case Western Reserve University, Cleveland, OH.

Deal, T. E. and Kennedy, A. A. (1982). *Corporate cultures.* Reading, Mass.: Addison-Wesley.

Dubin, R. (1978). *Theory Building.* New York: The Free Press.

Ellwood, C. (1938). *A history of social philosophy.* New York: Prentice-Hall.

Forester, John (1983). Critical theory and organizational analysis. In G. Morgan (Ed.). *Beyond methods* Beverly Hills, CA: Sage Publications.

French, W. L. (1969). Organization development objectives, assumptions, and strategies. *Management Review,* 12(2), 23–34.

French, W. L. and Bell, C. H. (1978). *Organization development.* New Jersey: Prentice-Hall.

Friedlander, F. (1984). Producing useful knowledge for organizations. *Administrative Science Quarterly,* 29, 646-–648.

Friedlander, F. (1977). Alternative methods of inquiry. Presented at APA Convention. San Francisco, Ca.

Friedlander, F. and Brown, L. D. (1974). Organization development, *Annual Review of Psychology,* 25, 313–341.

Frohman, M., Sashkin, M., and Kavanaugh, M. (1976). Action-research as applied to organization development. *Organization and Administrative Sciences,* 1, 129–161.

Geertz, C. (1980). Blurred genres: The refiguration of social thought. *American Scholar,* 49, 165–179.

Gergen, K. (1982). *Toward transformation in social knowledge.* New York: Springer-Verlag.

Gergen, K. (1978). Toward generative theory. *Journal of Personality and Social Psychology,* 36, 1344–1360.

Ghandi, M. (1958). *All men are brothers.* New York: Columbia University Press.

Gorz, A. (1973). Workers' control is more than just that. In Hunnius, Garson. and Case (Eds.), *Workers control.* New York: Vintage Books.

Gould, S. J. (1981). *The mismeasure of man.* New York: Norton and Company.

Gouldner, A. (1970). *The coming crisis of Western sociology.* New York: Basic Books.

Habermas, J. (1971). *Knowledge and human interests.* Boston: Beacon Press.

Haley, J. *Uncommon therapy.* New York: W. W. Norton, 1973.

Hare, P. H. (1976). *Handbook of small group research.* New York: The Free Press.

Harrison, R. (1982). *Leadership and strategy for a new age: Lessons from "conscious evolution."* Menlo Park, CA: Values and Lifestyles Program.

Hausser, D., Pecorelia, P., and Wissler, A. (1977). *Survey-guided development 11.* LaJolla, Calif.: University Associates.

Hayward, J. (1984). *Perceiving ordinary magic.* Gouldner: New Science Library.

Hiesenberg, W. (I 958). *Physics and philosophy: The revolution in modern science.* London: Allen and Urwig.

Henshel, R. (1975). Effects of disciplinary prestige on predictive accuracy. *Futures,* 7, 92–106.

Hofstede, G. (1980). *Culture's consequences.* Beverly Hills, CA: Sage.

Jung, C. (1933). *Modern man in search of a soul.* New York: Harcourt, Brace and Company.

Keeley, M. (1980). Organizational analogy: Comparison of orgasmic and social contract models, *Administrative Science Quarterly,* 25, 337–362.

Kepner, C. and Trego, B. (1973). *Executive problem analysis and decision making.* Princeton, NJ.

Kierkegaard, S. (1954). *The sickness unto death.* New York: Anchor Books. Translated by Walter Lowrie.

Kilmann, R. (1979). Problem management: A behavioral science approach. In G. Zaltman (Ed.). *Management principles for non-profit agencies and organizations.* New York: American Management Association.

Koch, S. (1981). The nature and limits of psychological knowledge. *American Psychologist,* 36, 257–269.

Kolb, D. A. (1984). *Experiential learning.* Englewood Cliffs, NJ: Prentice-Hall.

Kolb, D. A. (1983). Problem management: Learning from experience. In S. Srivastva (Ed.), *The executive mind.* San Francisco: Jossey-Bass.

Levinson, H. (1972) The clinical psychologist as organizational diagnostician. *Professional Psychology,* 10, 485–502.

Levinson, H. (1972). *Organizational diagnosis.* Cambridge, MA: Harvard University Press.

Lewin, K. (1948). Action research and minority problems. In G. W. Lewin (Ed.), *Resolving social conflicts.* New York: Harper and Row.

Lewin, K. (1951). *Field theory in social science.* New York: Harper and Row.

Lukes, S. (1974). *Power: A radical view.* London: Macmillan.

Mannheim, K. (1936). *Ideology and utopia.* New York: Harcourt, Brace and World.

Marcel, G. (1963). *The existential background of human dignity.* Cambridge: Harvard University Press.

Margulies, N. and Raia, A. P. (1972). *Organization development: Values, process and technology.* New York: McGraw Hill.

Marrow, A. (1968). *The practical theorist.* New York: Basic Books.

Maslow, A. (1968). *Toward a psychology of being.* New York: Van Nostrand Reinhold Co.

McHugh, P. (1970). On the failure of positivism. In J. Douglas (Ed.), *Understanding everyday life.* Chicago: Aldine.

Mitroff, I. (1980). Reality as a scientific strategy: Revising our concepts of science. *Academy of Management Review,* 5, 513–515.

Mitroff, I. and Kilmann, R. (1978). *Methodological approaches to social sciences.* San Francisco: Jossey-Bass.

Morgan, G. (1983). *Beyond method.* Beverly Hills: Sage Publications.

Morgan, G. (1980). Paradigms, metaphors, and puzzle solving in organization theory. *Administrative Science Quarterly,* 24, 605–622.

Ortony, A. (Ed.) (1979). *Metaphor and thought.* Cambridge: Cambridge University Press.

Ouchi, W. G. and Johnson, J. B. (1978). Types of organizational control and their relationship to emotional well-being. *Administrative Science Quarterly,* 23, 293–317.

Pasmore, W., Cooperrider, D., Kaplan, M. and Morris, B. (1983). Introducing managers to performance development. In *The ecology of work,*. Proceedings of the Sixth NTL Ecology of Work Conference, Cleveland, Ohio.

Pasmore, W. and Friedlander, F. (1982). An action-research program for increasing employee involvement in problem solving. *Administrative Science Quarterly,* 27, 343–362.

Pepper, S. C. (1942). *World hypothesis.* Berkeley, CA: University of California Press.

Peters, M. and Robinson, V. (1984). The origins and status of action research. *Journal of Applied Behavioral Science,* 20, 113–124.

Quinney, R. (1982). *Social existence: Metaphysics, Marxism, and the social sciences.* Beverly Hills, CA: Sage Publications.

Rappaport, R. W. (1970). Three dilemmas of action-research. *Human Relations,* 23, 499–513.

Reeves, G. (1984). The idea of mystery in the philosophy of Gabriel Marcel. In J. Schlipp, and L. Hahn, (Eds.), *The philosophy of Gabriel Marcel.* LaSalle, IL: Open Court.

Sargent, L. T. (1982). Authority and utopia: Utopianisms in political thought. *Polity,* 4, 565–584.

Sathe, V. J. (1983). Implications of corporate culture. *Organizational Dynamics,* Autumn, 523.

Schein, E. (1983). The role of the founder in creating organizational culture. *Organizational Dynamics,* Summer, 12–28.

Schweitzer, A. (1969). *The teaching of reverence for life.* New York: Holt, Rinehart and Winston.

Small, A. (1905). *General sociology: An exposition of the main development in sociological theory from Spencer to Ratzenhofer.* Chicago: University of Chicago Press.

Smirchich, L. (1983). Studying organizations as cultures. In G. Morgan (Ed.), *Beyond method.* Beverly Hills, CA: Sage Publications.

Sproull, L. S. (1981). Beliefs in organizations. In P. C. Nystrom and W. H. Starbuck (Eds.), *Handbook of organizational design, Vol. 2.* New York: Oxford University Press.

Srivastva, S. (1985). *Executive power.* San Francisco: Jossey-Bass Publishers.

Srivastva, S. (1983). *The executive mind.* San Francisco: Jossey-Bass Publishers.

Srivastva, S. and Cooperrider, D. (1986). The emergence of the egalitarian organization. *Human Relations,* London: Tavistock.

Srivastva, S., Obert, S. and Neilsen, E. (1977). Organizational analysis through group process: A theoretical perspective for organization development. In C. Cooper (Ed.) *Organization development in the U.K. and U.S.A.* New York: The Macmillan Press.

Staw, B. (1984). Organizational behavior: A review and reformulation of the field's outcome variables. *Annual Review of Psychology,* 35, 626–666.

Susman, G. and Evered, R. (1978). An assessment of the scientific merits of action-research. *Administrative Science Quarterly,* 23, 582–603.

Thelen, H. (1954). *Dynamics of groups at work.* Chicago University of Chicago Press.

Torbert, W. (1983). Initiating collaborative inquiry. In G. Morgan (Ed.). *Beyond method.* Beverly Hills, CA: Sage Publications.

Van Maanen, J., Dabbs, J. M., and Faulkner, R. R. (I 982). *Varieties of qualitative research.* Beverly Hills, Calif.: Sage Publications.

Watzlawick, P., Weakland, J., and Fish, R. (1974). *Change: Principles of problem formation and problem resolution.* New York: Horton.

Weick, K. E. (1983). Managerial thought in the context of action. In S. Srivastva (Ed.), *The executive mind.* San Francisco: Jossey-Bass.

Wiesbord, M. (1976). Organization diagnosis: Six places to look for trouble with or without a theory. *Group and Organization Studies,* 1, 430–447.

Weiss, C. H. and Bucuvalas, M. (1980). The challenge of social research to decision making. In C. H. Weiss (Ed.), *Using social research in public policy making.* Lexington, MA: Lexington Books.

Whitehead, A. N. (1929). *The function of reason.* Boston: Beacon Press.

Whyte, W. F. (1982). Social inventions for solving human problems. *American Sociological Review,* 47, 113.

Referring document: http://www.stipes.com/aichap3.htm
Home page: http://www.stipes.com
Reprinted with permission from: *Appreciative Inquiry: An Emerging Direction for Organization Development,* David L. Cooperrider, Peter F. Sorensen, Jr., Therese F. Yaeger, and Diana Whitney, editors. Champaign IL: Stipes Publishing L.L.C., 2001. Copyright 2001 by Stipes Publishing L.L.C.
Posted: 9/20/01

Resources for Getting Appreciative Inquiry Started

An Example OD Proposal

David L. Cooperrider

"Appreciative Inquiry involves a paradigm shift, that will vitally transform, for example, how mergers or diversity intiatives are approached. The key, early on, is to prioritize several areas where there will be a high value-added contribution and, in those areas, take the appreciative approach to the hilt."

OVER THE PAST several years people have been asking more and more for practical tools that will help them transform their OD consulting practice away from the diagnostic problem-solving approaches toward more appreciative inquiry methods. One of the most common requests (when I do workshops on Appreciative Inquiry) is for examples of proposals – proposals that set the stage for OD contracting. This article presents a "composite picture" of several actual proposals that have led to major OD work. The "AMX" proposal represents the best of several projects that combine Appreciative Inquiry and Future Search. The corporate names used in this composite proposal are fictitious.

What I like most about the "whole system" change process spelled out here is that it completely lets go of problem solving. In my view, the problem solving paradigm, while once incredibly effective, is simply out of sync with the realities of today's virtual worlds. Problem solving is painfully slow (always asking people to look backwards historically to yesterday's causes); it rarely results in new vision (by definition we say something is a problem because we already implicitly assume some idea, so we are not searching to create new knowledge of better ideals, we are searching how to close gaps); and, in human terms, problem solving approaches are notorious for generating defensiveness (it is not my problem but yours).

Organizations are centers of human relatedness, first and foremost, and relationships thrive where there is an appreciative eye – when people see the best in one another, when they can share their dreams and ultimate concerns in affirming ways, and when they are connected in full voice to create not just new worlds but better worlds. Douglas McGregor was convinced of the power of positive assumptions about human beings. The AMX proposal is an example of an OD proposal that, in practical ways, mobilizes the appreciative process to the fullest extent I know how The proposal was written the week Congress passed legislation that would deregulate the telecommunications industry, changing the rules that guided the industry for over 60 years. AMX, one of the organizational giants, was literally in chaos with thousands being laid off. Facing the largest whole system transformation in their corporate history, the CEO asked, "How can we connect everyone to the adventure of creating the new century telecommunication organization?"

Cooperrider, D.L. (1996). Resources for getting appreciative inquiry started: An example OD proposal. *Organization Development Practitioner, 28,* 23–33.

THE AMX CONNECTS! PROPOSAL

Accelerating Organizational Learning For Winning the New Century

Background

During the past several years, AMX has positioned itself to take advantage of what may prove to be the greatest single business opportunity in history: the creation and management of the Information Superhighway Part of this positioning has been the clear articulation of the new strategic "ABC" vision and reaffirmation of the goal of being the most customer responsive business in the industry Along with the vision has come action. There are literally hundreds of successful new initiatives – reengineering, product innovations, new alliances, public relations campaigns, employee empowerment strategies, etc. – all combining to give birth to the new AMX. The entire system is in the thick of fundamental organizational transformation, and exists in a world where the economic, technological, and regulatory foundations of the business have radically changed. It simply is not the same business it used to be.

Important questions, therefore, are many: How can leaders accelerate positive transformation where the proof corporate change is revolutionary in result and evolutionary in execution? How can people reduce the time lag between exciting organizational innovations (initiatives, large and small, that illustrate what the new-century AMX organization can and should look like) and organizational storytelling, sharing, advocacy and mass learning from those innovations? How will employees sustain, over a period of years, corporate confidence and faith in AMX's abilities to make fundamental change even in the midst of inevitable setbacks? How can AMX complement its problemsolving culture with an appreciative mind set that selectively sees, studies, and learns from every positive new development? Can AMX develop and reclaim an oral tradition of storytelling that connects people across corporate generations and that propels the speed and spread of good news? How can AMX leaders decisively connect people throughout the system to the Future Search, and engage everyone in a "can do" way as social architects of the new century organization – a transformed organizational entity that lives its vision in all its structures, systems, strategies, management behaviors, job designs, partnerships; everything that the company does.[1]

Purpose

- The mission of AMX Connects! is to accelerate positive whole system transformation by actively connecting people to the "ABC" vision through the practice of Appreciative Inquiry.

Objectives

- To bring the "ABC" vision alive for 67,000 people at AMX by engaging a critical mass of people in an Appreciative Inquiry into the most positive and compelling

---

1. According to recent surveys by Yankelovich, 85% of Americans have lost confidence in the future. People report little confidence that current institutions and leaders will do the job. They see the gap between promised rhetoric about a better future and the continued breakdown, in the present, of many systems. Likewise the negative discourse and storytelling which dominates the media, politics, and the popular culture at large, is associated with increased levels of apathy among young and old, cynicism, fear, discrimination, and other damaging behavior. What is happening throughout society obviously has a spill-over effect in our corporations. Especially during times of major transition, ways are needed to rebuild essential connections, to renew hope, and to reinvigorate human creativity and leadership at all levels.

organizational innovations, practices, and traditions that (1) best illustrate the translation of the "ABC" vision into transformational action and (2) provide an anticipatory glimpse into the kind of organization AMX should and might become in the new century.

- To deliver tangible follow-up to the 1995 Leadership Workshop (which builds on the momentum of the Aspen, Colorado success where 140 regional and corporate executives were introduced to the theory of Appreciative Inquiry), and tie together executive education with real-time organization transformation. By co-leading the Appreciative Inquiry/Future Search process at the regional and corporate levels, the "action learning" design will contribute as much to leadership development as it does to organization development.

- To augment AMX's problem solving culture with an appreciative mind set that provides a paradigm shift in ways of looking at managerial analysis of all kinds – e.g., new options for approaching organization analysis, customer focus groups, strategic planning methods, reengineering studies, employee surveys, performance appraisal processes, public affairs methodologies, diversity initiatives, benchmarking approaches, merger integration methods, and many others.

- To build an affirmative atmosphere of hope and confidence necessary to sustain, over the next several years, the largest whole-system transformation in the company's history

- To discover and pioneer connections between Appreciative Inquiry/Future Search Conference methodologies (often involving hundreds of people interactively) and the voice, video, and data capabilities of AMX's advanced teleconferencing technologies. The potential for building connection and commitment to the future directions of the company are enormous: corporate visioning, advocacy, and good news telling will not be isolated to a few technical gurus, senior visionaries, or communication messengers, but will engage potentially thousands. When it comes to bringing vision alive, process is just as important as product. People want to be listened to and to be heard. The large group conference methodologies discussed below are truly impressive in their ability to cultivate the thrill of being a valued member in the creation of new and exciting futures.

Leadership

- AMX Connects! will be led by President Sheldon Abrahms; Susan Taft, Vice President Public Affairs; John Williams, Vice President of Organization Development, and the 140 individuals involved with the recent Leadership Conference. David L. Cooperrider and Associates from Case Western Re- Resources for Getting Appreciative Inquiry Started: An Example OD Proposal serve University's Weatherhead School of Management will provide outside guidance.

Timing

- The appreciative organizational inquiry and learning process will be formally inaugurated in 1996 with a workshop on Appreciative Inquiry Participants will be the leadership group of 140 through 1996 and 1997. Appreciative Inquiry will be introduced and Future Search Conferences completed in every region of Operations. Results from each of these will form the basis of a synthesizing corporate-wide Future Search in the spring of 1998 and will culminate with a future report – Images of The New Century AMX Organization – to be issued by the "think tank" group of 140.

THE ABC'S OF APPRECIATIVE INQUIRY

In a typical Appreciative Inquiry, the process will lead up to a major Future Search Conference, two or three days in length, where a whole organization or representatives of the whole (anywhere from 100 to 1,000 people) will come together to both construct images of the system's most desired future and to formulate creative strategies to bring that future about. Often, an organizational model like the 7-S framework will serve as a template for building "possibility propositions" in each of the key organizational design areas - for example, what will the ideal organizational structures or systems look like in the future (the conference organizers will specify how far into the future to think... usually 3-5 years out). The stages for bringing the whole thing off productively typically follow the ABC sequence:

A – Appreciative understanding of your organization (from the past to present);

B – Benchmarked understanding of other organizations (exemplary models to learn from); and

C – Creative construction of the future (sometimes called the Future Search Conference).

One possible design would be to launch, in each of the regions, a broad-based set of Appreciative Inquiry interviews leading to a regional Future Search conference. The design of the interviews would stress storytelling and study into the "ABC" vision in action – examples of being "the easiest company to do business with"; times when people feel truly "empowered", examples of new forms of "servant leadership"; illustrations of how AMX is "winning in the new world"; etc. All of these interviews would be done face-to-face by AMX managers and employees within the region. All the best quotes, stories, and illustrations would be compiled into a regional report and used to inspire a regionally based Future Search Conference into "AMX In the New Century: Images of Organizational Possibility". At the Future Search Conference, with 100 to 2,000 people, participants meet for two or three days to design the organization's most desired future and formulate creative strategies to bring that future about. The key product is a planning document made up of "possibility propositions" describing the collective hopes and dreams people feel inspired to bring about. In the search conference mode, people learn to think of the future as a condition that can be impacted and created intentionally out of values, visions, and what's technically and socially feasible. Such purposeful planning greatly increases the probability of making the desired future come alive. What is unique about the Future Search Conference method as described here is (1) its Appreciative Inquiry Foundation (often experienced as a liberating personal paradigm shift for people); and (2) the broad base of authentic participation that is demanded.

We live in a world of relentless economic and social change, based on 21st century technologies. Now we struggle to discover management methods equal to the complexity The power of Appreciative Inquiry and the whole system focus of Future Search combine, our experience shows, to both accelerate and sustain change. Transformation happens faster, at lower cost, and with more inspired collective follow-up than older, more piecemeal or fragmented approaches. Studies show that one well facilitated Future Search with "everybody" – a metaphor for a broad cross-section of stakeholders – will produce more whole systems learning, empowerment, and feelings of connection around business vision than hundreds of fragmenting small group meetings.

The Future Search Conferences, held in each of the regions, would then be capped off with a corporate-wide Future Search of the top 140, the leadership group and key stakeholders representing the whole. If held concurrently in each of the ten regions, the potential for linking up via teleconference for positive story-telling across regions might add a creative and powerful integrative dimension. Literally thousands could be involved in real-time inquiry and transformational planning around the "ABC" vision. Each Future Search would involve something like the following:

1. A conference coordinating committee at the regional level of 4-6 people would meet to plan dates, time, location, meals, group meeting tasks, and who should attend. The goal is to get ""the whole system"" in the room, or at least strong representation of all those that have a clear stake in the future of the organization. Often then, this includes people "outside" of the community members, partner rule is organization like customers, organizations, etc. The ground that whomever comes to the Future Search must be there for the whole meeting and has the opportunity for full voice in the deliberations.

2. Participants (from 100 to 1000 people) sit in groups of eight to ten, with flip chart paper or a chalkboard available. Depending on the focus and assigned tasks, groupings may vary during the conference. All output from small group discussion is recorded, all ideas are valid, and agreement is not required to get ideas recorded.

3. The conference has four or five segments, each lasting up to a half day Each segment requires that people (a) look at or build a data base; (b) interpret it together; (c) draw conclusions for action.

4. The first major activity focuses on macro-trends likely to affect the organization in the future. Each group is asked to make notes on significant events, changes, and trends they see merging by looking at each of the past three decades from three perspectives: significant changes and events that happened at the world, personal, and institutional/industry levels over each of the past three decades. Each table reports to the total group, and a facilitator notes trends. The total conference then interprets the most positive macro-trends – those trends that indicate opportunities for building a better organization, society, or industry Even the macro trends that appear negative or threatening often generate creative thinking on hidden opportunities or possibilities for creating the future people want.

5. The second major activity focuses on the appreciative analysis of the organization. Each group has a copy of the Appreciative Inquiry report that was compiled earlier, with quotes, stories, and comments from all the appreciative interviews. Three questions are then posed to each group: (a) What are the most outstanding moments/stories from this organization's past that make you most proud to be a member of this organization? (b) What are the things that give life to the organization when it is most alive, most effective, most in tune with it"s over-arching vision, etc. (make a list of up to ten factors)? and (c) Continuity: What should we try to preserve about our organization – values, traditions, best practices – even as we change into the future? Again, consensus is not needed as the results are displayed and discussed by the whole conference.

6. The third major activity focuses on the benchmark understanding of the best practices of other organizations. Each group is given the report from benchmarking studies and is asked to make a list of the most interesting or novel things being done in other organizations. The list should include things that are interesting, novel, or even controversial and provocative. The list is not an endorsement of any of the practices – it is simply a compilation of interesting or new ideas and practices. There is to be no discussion of whether or not to adopt the practices in the present organization. If benchmark studies have not been done as part of the

preconference Appreciative Inquiry process then group members should generate the list from things they have seen in other organizations have heard or read about. Reports are made to the whole conference and people are asked to comment on the most interesting or novel ideas.

7. The fourth major activity focuses on the future, especially it's creative construction. New groups are formed and are given a half day to develop a draft of a preferred, possible future. The focus is on translating the business vision into inspired organizational vision. The focus is on the organizational dimensions of the future. Using a model like the 7-S model or a homegrown model of organizational design elements, groups develop a set of "possibility propositions" of the ideal or preferred future organization (3-5 years into the future).

8. The fifth major activity focuses on the next action steps. Groups are then asked to reflect on what has surfaced and, depending on the nature of the groupings, to make three lists of suggested action steps: commitments they want to make as individuals to move the vision forward; action steps their region, and work unit, might take; and things the organization as a whole might do. Action proposals are shared in a total group session and a steering committee is formed to discuss proposals for the total organization, prioritize themes, and prepare a report to be presented at the capstone Future Search.

WHOLE SYSTEM INVOLVEMENT

In a comprehensive study of successful habits of visionary companies, Stanford University researchers Jerry Porras and James Collins put it simply:

It's become fashionable in recent decades for companies to spend countless hours and sums of money drafting elegant vision statements, values statements, purpose statements, aspiration statements, mission statements, purpose statements, objective statements, and so on. Such pronouncements are all fine and good – indeed, they can be quite useful – but they are not the essence of a visionary company Just because a company has a "vision statement" (or something like it) in no way guarantees that it will become a visionary company! If you walk away from this book thinking that the most essential step in building a visionary company is to write such a statement, then you will have missed the whole point. A statement might be a good first step, but it is only a first step.

—Taken from *Built to Last*, 1994

Translating core vision into everything the company does requires ways of connecting everyone – evoking ownership, commitment, under-standing, involvement, and confidence in the vision's promise. This proposal provides a do-able way to proceed: it is logistically possible and financially feasible to design a process where all of operations (67,000 people) are involved. Everyone, at a minimum, would be a participant in the Appreciative Inquiry as an interviewer, interviewee, or both. And up to 10,000 would participate in at least three other engaging activities of learning and doing: workshops on Appreciative Inquiry (one day long); conducting the interviews (doing 5-10 interviews); and one or more Future Search Conferences (three days in length). The working assumption, at the regional level, is that approximately 1,000 people would participate in a day long introduction to Appreciative Inquiry They would subsequently be charged with completing 5-10 interviews apiece, and then would serve as delegates to the regional Future Search Conference.

MEASURING FOR RESULTS

AMX Connects! will measure its results by asking how each step, and the whole process, achieves discrete, agreed upon objectives. This is a demanding approach that will force everyone involved to focus on how the method of Appreciative Inquiry actually affects the way people think, communicate, and act in relation to the process of whole system transformation. Some of the areas of expected impact include:

- Reduction in the time lag between organization innovations (innovations that are consistent with the "ABC" vision) and their spread throughout the corporation.
- The strengthening of a "can do" climate of hope and confidence in the corporation"s ability to manage the transition and realize its transformational goals.
- Significant increase in the corporation's positive internal dialogue about the future (e.g.,less cynical and deficit oriented discourse; less fear; less negativity; more vocabularies of positive possibility; more rapid spread of good news developments).
- Development of a more appreciative leadership mindset and culture which provides managers with new options for dealing with corporate and customer surveys, re-engineering, strategic planning analysis, team-building, merger integration, performance appraisal and others.
- Significant increase in the feeling of connection to the corporation's "ABC" vision at all levels and regions of AMX Operations.

SUSTAINABILITY

The telecommunications industry is going through a profound change that involves reassessment of economic foundations, technological infrastructures, organizational forms and processes, and managerial mindsets. The whole-system transformation being called for is both comprehensive in scope and fundamental in nature. There are a number of things, therefore, that must not be overlooked. First, we must not overlook the reality of people's resistance to such profound change – to even thinking about it – since it involves challenge to the inner assumptions which have become an inherent part of the culture and individual ways of constructing the "way things ought to be". Nor should we fail to note that the coming changes will bring about a great deal of fear and uncertainty; in fact, keeping down the fear is probably the greatest challenge of all, since only with low levels of fear can people see clearly and take the right actions. But perhaps most important is the need to address questions of sustainability What will make the appreciative inquiry/future search methodologies as outlined earlier more than just a one-time high? What will be done to sustain learnings at regional, corporate, and individual levels? Our own evaluations of Appreciative Inquiry and the evaluation studies of large group Future Search Conferences suggest the following five strategies for long term sustainability.[3]

---

3. See Wilmot, Tim (1995) "The Global Excellence in Management Program: A Two Year Evaluation of 25 Organizations Using Appreciative Inquiry" Case Western Reserve University For detailed analysis of large group methods and outcomes – from Ford Motor Company, First Nationwide Bank, SAS, Marriott, and Borning – see Jacobs, R. (1994) *Real Time Strategic Change: How to Involve an Entire Organization In Fast and Far Reaching Change,* San Francisco: BerrettKoeliler Publishers. For ten case studies of the Future Search methods see Weisbord, M. (1992) *Discovering Common Ground: How Future Search Methods Bring People Together To Achieve Breakthrough Innovation, Empowerment, Shared Vision, and Collaborative Action,* San Francisco: Berrett- Koehler

(1) **Skillbuilding: The Process of Organizational Transformation is a School for Leadership Development.** In many respects, there is really no such thing as organizational transformation, there is only individual transformation. Because of this, especially with the leadership group of 140, every major session will involve both organizational analysis and personal planning as well as skillbuilding modules around all the phases of appreciative inquiry and the methods of facilitating interactive, large group meetings. In GE's recent whole system "Workout Program", for example, it was found that the most important outcome of the initial large group Workouts was managerial skill development – the Workout conference methodologies have become a way of life for almost two-thirds of the work units. Of course, Chairman and CEO John F Welch played a major role in making the new participatory methods a priority He was notorious in his surprise appearances at local Workout sessions and was consistent in his message: 'building a revitalized "human engine" to animate GE"s formidable 'business engine.' "

(2) **Extending Appreciative Inquiry Into Change Efforts Where There Will Be High Value-Added.** Already there are plans being made by various AMX staff to use the appreciative methodologies to re-think and revitalize organization development practices like corporate surveys, customer focus groups, public affairs projects, etc. These efforts at extending Appreciative Inquiry should be made more systematic and priority driven. Our suggestions is that we should prioritize no more than five major extensions of Appreciative Inquiry – for example AI's contributions to merger integration methods, organizational surveys, process re-engineering, and diversity initiatives. Each of these efforts should be carefully documented and written up later in the form of a practitioner manual (e g, a merger integration manual, or a customer focus group manual). Appreciative Inquiry involves a paradigm shift that will vitally transform, for example, how mergers or diversity initiatives are approached. The key, early on, is to prioritize several areas where there will be a high value-added contribution and, in those areas, take the appreciative approach to the hilt.

(3) **Customized Regional Follow-up Consultation.** In preparation for the Future Search Conferences, and in response to needed follow-up at the regional level, there will be a consultant/facilitator team made up of internal AMX professionals (e.g., OD, HR, PA) and a specialist from Cooperrider and Associates. This consultant team will commit, up front, to ten days of consulting follow-up at the regional level to tailor-make a response to the initiatives generated at the Future Search Conferences. By definition, the customized response is unknown at this time, but our experience shows that the commitment to ten days of follow-up consultation is the single most important thing that can be done to ensure sustainability In a recent study of Appreciative Inquiry with 25 organizations, it has been found that ninety percent of the organizations are continuing with the appreciative methodologies, some two years after the start (see Wilmot, 1995). An essential attribute of the sustainability was that in each case, all ten days of promised follow-up consultations were in fact used. Likewise, the follow-up was completely at the initiative and request of the organizations themselves. Each organization had to "apply" in writing for the follow-up: what were the goals, what kind of support did they need facilitation, training, outside evaluation, retreat design, organization analysis, one-on-one personal counseling). The lesson is simple we must plan for sustainability from the beginning, and the commitment to the customized follow-up opportunity is critical.

(4) **Advanced "Internal Consultant " Learning Partnership.** Each year there will be two special sessions among all internal AMX change agents that are involved with Appreciative Inquiry and the Future Search Conferences. The learning partnership will deal with advanced theoretical and practice issues, and will use clinical/field-based modes of learning. The purpose will be to build internal skills and competencies, to build a support network among AMX units and regions, and to make good use of the program's evaluation studies for advanced professional development.

(5) **Appreciative Inquiry "On-line".** Already there have been discussions with specialists at AMX about how to accelerate the spread of innovations and good news storytelling by adding an Appreciative Inquiry protocol to the new AMX on-line suggestion program. An analogy here is useful: an ongoing Appreciative Inquiry will be to the "whole system transformation" what time-lapse photography is to the visible blossoming of an otherwise imperceptible flower. Putting Appreciative Inquiry on-line is a very exciting venture that has yet to be done anywhere. There is no question the time is ripe for this to happen; and it makes sense that it would be inaugurated at AMX, where leadership in the positive human impact of advanced technology lies at the forefront of the corporate mission. One way to introduce the on-line approach would be to conceive of the 67,000 interviews as mini-training sessions in Appreciative Inquiry After each interview, people would be given a short booklet with simple instructions on how to use the internal online "web page". Stories and new images would be made available on a continuous basis. An award could even be established for the stories that best anticipate and give a glimpse of the new AMX, living its vision today The implications of Appreciative Inquiry on-line are far reaching and exciting indeed. We are infants A when it comes to our understanding of the power of this kind of non-hierarchical information sharing and whole system dialogue. The results could be revolutionary.

In the course of developing the ideas described above, it has become clear that people at AMX have this hope that there's a little window of opportunity for really responding to a radically changed business environment. That window of opportunity, and the current season of hope being expressed, is going to last about as long as Sheldon Abrahms, in the early days of his new presidency, uses this occasion to boldly enroll everyone in the positive transformation. To make it all work we (as an internal/external team) will not only need to work collaboratively, responsively, and flexibly as a "learning organization," but we also will need to be united around a shared revolutionary intent.

CONCLUSION

The relational, large group, participatory methods outlined here fly in the face of old hierarchical, piecemeal problem-analytic approaches to change. Likewise the appreciative paradigm, for many, is culturally at odds with the popular negativism and professional vocabularies of deficit that permeate our corporations and society at large. Most important, however, there are people, many people throughout AMX, that feel the time has come to make the "positive revolution" happen. These are the individuals that are just waiting to step forward and lead. The constructive, creative, and indispensable voices of the new AMX already exist. But their critical mass has yet to be legitimized. AMX Connects is about mass mobilization, it is about the is in full voice. It is internal about systematic creation of an organization that is in full voice. It is about transformation of the corporation's dialogue. It is about creating, over the next several years of discovery and transition, a center stage for the positive revolutionaries.

Strategic Inquiry → Appreciative Intent: Inspiration to SOAR
A New Framework for Strategic Planning

Jacqueline Stavros, David Cooperrider, and D. Lynn Kelley

Overview: The Field of Strategic Planning

The corporate mantra over the last ten years has been change, change, and change. Many of the principles that corporations held as stable and immutable have been turned upside down. Books such as *Reengineering the Corporation*, *The Strategy Focused Organization*, *The Balanced Scorecard*, *Strategic Thinking: An Executive Approach*, *Strategy From the Top*, and *Leading Strategic Change* have become bestsellers in the corporate world. Corporations that were traditionally considered dominant within industries have shrunk or disappeared, and the march toward globalization has accelerated. For example, in 1976, the majority of the world's fifty largest companies were U.S.-based; by 1995, the number was just 17 (Pattison, 1996).

At the heart of the change, one often finds competition. When two similar entities compete for the same scarce resources, often one will win and the other will lose. Competition is not a new phenomenon. The very essence of Darwin's "survival of the fittest" is competition. The difference is that when similar species compete for the same scarce resources, the winning outcome is based not on a strategic but on the species that was naturally "most fit" to its environment. Look how far we have evolved! We now have the ability to plan for survival. Now it is not the company that unwittingly finds itself the "fittest" that survives—but the company that is best able to strategically think, plan, and manage its resources; lead its people; and sustain its future that becomes "fit" enough to survive and indeed thrive.

Given the acceleration of change in recent years, how are companies proactively responding? Obviously, some companies are ignoring the change and are being "left in the dust." However, the majority of companies that are responding to the change are limiting their responses to operational and tactical areas. Companies are answering the "call of the changing world" with such approaches as new processes, new procedures, downsizing, rightsizing, lean manufacturing, Six Sigma, virtual integration, core versus context exercises, value chain analysis, e-business models, and other new ways of running their business. These methods have shown the ability to produce dramatic results. However, the common theme that runs through all of these responses is their focus on new ways of performing the daily operations of the organization. There has been a great void in new methods used in the one area specifically designed to prepare for the changing future—an appreciative-based approach to strategic planning. We need to change the way we strategically think, plan, and implement strategy.

Think about this:
- Change requires action.
- Action requires a plan.

jstavros@comcast.net, dlc6@po.cwru.edu, lkelley@tfs.textron.com

- A plan requires a strategy.
- A strategy requires goals and enabling objectives.
- Goals and objectives require a mission.
- A mission is defined by a vision.
- A vision is set by one's values.

The Appreciative Inquiry (AI) approach to strategic planning starts by focusing on the strengths of an organization and its stakeholders' values and shared vision.

In spite of the tumultuousness of our competitive environment, with few exceptions, the core of the strategic planning approach used by U.S. corporations has been virtually unchanged over the last fifty years. For instance, almost all strategic planning processes contain the "old standby" of completing a SWOT (strengths, weaknesses, opportunities, threats) analysis or its counterpart TOWS (threats, opportunities, weaknesses, and strengths) analysis. The question this raises is if companies are using the traditional strategic planning approach (and are failing in spite of it), perhaps we need to change or challenge the approach. We want to offer an alternative to the SWOT analysis. Our alternative is to SOAR (strengths, opportunities, aspirations, results). But first let's take a brief look at the history of strategic planning.

The first writings on the topic predominantly relate to military strategy. The earliest surviving Western book on the subject, published in the fourth century BC, was written by Aineias the Tactician, an ancient Athenian. Within this book and others that followed the same vein (such as *The Art of War* by Sun Tzu), authors identified "job requirements" for strategists, guidelines for developing strategy, resource and manpower allocation, integration of different branches of the military, and characteristics held by good strategists. It was strategic thinking based on "divide and conquer."

Another serious writer in the Eastern tradition of strategic planning was the Samurai warrior, Miyamoto Mushahi, who wrote his book on strategic thinking in Japan over three hundred years ago. This book, full of ancient wisdom, was published in the United States in 1974 under the title *A Book of Five Rings* (Musashi, 1974). During the early 1980s, Japanese literature became required reading for American businesspeople. In particular, *A Book of Five Rings* was touted as being the key to understanding the Japanese mind in business. The author based his writings on the principles of Zen, stressing a victorious, warrior-like strategic attitude toward all aspects of life. The "tag line" on the book states, "The classic text of principles, craft, skill, and Samurai strategy that changed the American way of doing business." The cover drawing shows an archetypal Samurai warrior armed with the weapons of business: a phone and a computer printout. Although this novel approach was fundamentally different from the existing American-based writings on strategic planning, in spite of its self-promotion, it did little to "change the American way of doing business."

Around the same time as this tome was published in the United States, Americans were cutting their baby teeth on the formal notion of business strategic planning. Strategic planning was presented as a brand new discipline during the 1960s at Harvard Business School, when several pioneering professors taught and published articles on the holistic notion of business planning from the scope of the entire business rather than from individual disciplines such as marketing and finance. By the late 1970s, the key elements of strategic planning as we know it today began popping up in many of the publications on the topic. A typical strategic planning flowchart during that time looked like **Figure 1.**

Figure 1: Strategic Planning Process (1970s–1980s)

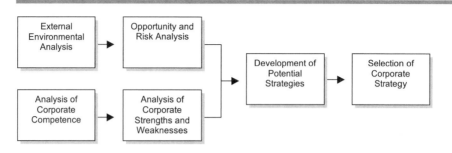

Look familiar? Although this flowchart is fifty years old, it is not radically different from the flowcharts published in today's strategic management textbooks. By the mid-1980s, Strategic Planning had become an official discipline, with courses offered at over 2,900 business schools, and some improvements to the strategic planning method were added. For instance, Peter Drucker's work in the 1970s urged companies to articulate the business they were in. This led to the development of a mission statement, a subsequent addition to the strategic planning model presented in **Figure 1**. Other additions to the model occurred when people realized that the best plan is useless unless it is acted upon.   Subsequent steps were added at the end of the original strategic planning process to help the organization deploy the plan and evaluate its success. Thus, steps such as establishing objectives, allocating resources, and monitoring the implementation of the plan appeared as additions to the original model.

Thus, a typical strategic planning flowchart in contemporary business textbooks looks like **Figure 2**.

Figure 2: Strategic Planning Process (1990s–Present)

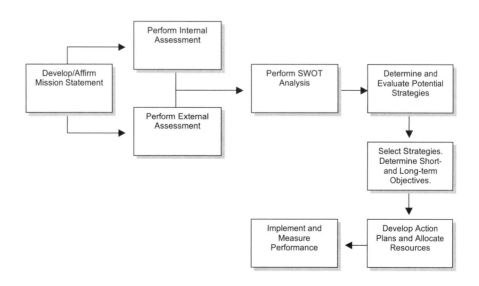

During the 1990s, several publications appeared decrying the existing strategic planning methodology. In 1994, Mintzberg published "The Rise and Fall of Strategic Planning" in the *Harvard Business Review*. The article denounced traditional strategic planning methods as producing rigid documents that are filed away and serve little or no purpose in the day-to-day activities of corporations. In *Beyond Strategic Planning*, Cowley and Domb (1997) noted additional problems with strategic planning:

- Unrealistic forecasts lead to overoptimistic strategic plans.
- Arbitrary goals have no support within the strategic plan.
- Companies fail to focus on a few high-leverage goals.
- Companies select the wrong goals.
- There is no "shared vision."
- The goals have no plans to support them.
- The planned activities are not frequently reviewed and evaluated.
- The review of progress toward strategic goals is punitive, which stifles risk taking.
- Planning is an event rather than a process.
- A department that is not responsible for implementation develops strategic plans.

Companies began looking for other methods of strategic planning that would address these problems. One of the proposed solutions was the Japanese method called Hoshin planning. During the 1960s, when the United States was first developing its form of strategic planning, Japan was independently inventing its own methods of strategic planning. American companies became aware of Hoshin planning in the early 1990s, following the translation into English publications on Hoshin planning. In the late 1980s, two books (Mizuno, 1988; Brassard, 1989) presented some of the tools used in Hoshin planning. However, since these tools were not overtly linked with strategic planning in the early publications, the strategic planning community did not immediately notice them. During the 1990s, additional books presented the Hoshin method as a form of strategic planning (Bechtell, 1995), and major U.S. companies such as Hewlett-Packard, Ford, and Xerox began using the method.

The Hoshin approach is based on the premise that organizations should choose just one or two "breakthrough strategy" areas each year. A major emphasis of the Hoshin method is the continuous improvement that occurs within the implementation cycle. Although many models for the Hoshin planning process have been published (including company-specific models, such as those of Xerox and Hewlett-Packard), a typical flowchart for Hoshin strategic planning looks as shown in **Figure 3**.

As you can see, Hoshin planning uses some of the same tools as the typical U.S.-based strategic planning methods. However, it should be noted that the specific inclusion of SWOT analysis is an American addition to the traditional Japanese approach—albeit one that is widely included in U.S. utilization of the method. Two of the advantages touted by Hoshin devotees are the associated tools that help gain employee involvement and buy-in during the development and the subsequent deployment of the plan and the built-in links between the strategic plan and the operations plans. In particular, a deployment matrix is used once the strategy is identified. The matrix is cascaded throughout the organization, creating a vehicle for each successive department to build its objectives in support of the preceding department's objectives—all of which are tied at the top to the strategic plan. The matrix shows the correlations and interrelationships necessary for strategy deployment. It also identifies corresponding measurements and subsequent impacts as the strategy is rolled out at all levels of the organization.

Figure 3: Hoshin Planning Process

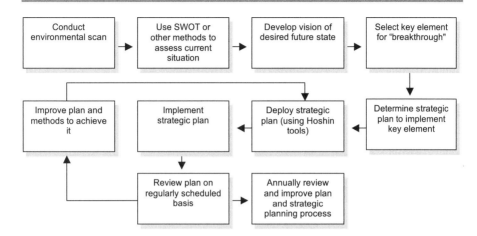

This brief review of strategic planning history over the last fifty years shows us that the process of planning has undergone some improvements—but very little deviation from its core structure that begins with a SWOT analysis. The biggest departure from the process that most U.S. companies use appears in the Japanese Hoshin process. Exposure to the Hoshin process has also led to other approaches, such as *A Systems Thinking Approach to Strategic Planning and Management* (Haines, 2000), wherein Haines says that we should "stamp out the outmoded way of planning, which no longer works in today's dynamic world" (p. i) (referring to traditional U.S. strategic planning).

We agree with Haines. Given the radical changes in the competitive environment, the old model is not up to the task of producing the types of strategy and strategic plans that will propel businesses forward in the rapidly evolving future.

Dozens of models have been available since the 1930s to help organizations do strategic planning. What is needed is not another strategic planning model, but a strategic thinking framework and approach to quickly and smoothly guide an organization through this complex process while engaging the whole system. We will present an emerging framework that involves an appreciative approach of creating an organization's future. This framework allows an organization's stakeholders to see where they are today and establish a vision of where they want to go. The strategic plan will be a cocreation involving various stakeholders at different levels in the organization. This new approach helps stakeholders to clearly identify, understand, and (most importantly) communicate individual and organizational values, direction (vision), purpose (mission), core and unique capabilities (internal analysis), strategic opportunities (external analysis), strategies and tactics, and structures and systems to create a positive organizational environment and to build upon an organization's positive core to sustain its unique value offering (UVO).

Appreciative Inquiry and Its Integration to Strategic Planning

Appreciative Inquiry (AI) is a vision-based approach of open dialogue that is designed to help organizations and their partners create a shared vision for the future and a mission to operate in the present (Srivastva & Cooperrider, 1990). Today's organizations can benefit from an appreciative approach of inquiry, which invites organizational members to learn and value the history of their organization and its culture. The AI approach allows them to:

- Build on their strengths (the positive core).
- Discover profitable opportunities.
- Visualize goals and strategic alternatives.
- Identify enabling objectives.
- Design strategies and tactics that are integrated with their most successful programs and supply chain partners.
- Implement a strategic plan that is a dynamic, continuous, and living document.

Such a plan will include the best organizational structure and systems to realize its vision. Numerous organizations that have used AI include:

- Private and public nonprofit organizations.
- For-profit organizations.
- Government and international agencies worldwide.

AI has allowed hundreds of organizations to discover and grow the best practices of **capacity building** for their organizations as well as for their value chain partners' organizations.

The AI approach to strategic planning involves identifying and building on existing strengths and profitable opportunities rather than dwelling on problems, deficiencies, weaknesses, and threats. Think about the traditional strategic planning process; at its very core is the good old standby SWOT analysis—strengths, weaknesses, opportunities, threats. If we split it 50/50, we would spend about half our time thinking about our positives (strengths/opportunities) and the other half thinking about our negatives (weaknesses/threats). But let's be honest. Even though the tool looks 50/50, human nature tends to dwell disproportionately on people's weaknesses and threats. Unfortunately, by concentrating on what people do wrong, we tend to amplify the negative. Welcome to the world of AI where, instead, we focus disproportionately on people's strengths and opportunities so that we can grow them until they crowd out the weaknesses and threats.

The AI approach also builds capacity by moving stakeholders of an association beyond organizational boundaries to form new relationships and thus expand the organization's potential. What do we mean by this? Many companies are bounded by the limitations of their organizations. Few executives think "outside the box" of their corporation when they are brainstorming their future strategies. AI opens up dialogues with the organization's partners and external stakeholders. These dialogues result in an expansion of the current capacity of the organization as partners look for ways to create shared directions that benefit both organizations. You can actually think of AI as an approach that expands organizational boundaries, the same way the familiar exercise below requires expansion beyond boundaries.

Instructions: Connect all nine dots using four straight lines without lifting your pencil from the page.

Answer: This can be accomplished only if you allow your pencil to move outside of the box.

Now imagine that box is your organization. When creating a strategic plan, most people are bound unconsciously within the rectangle, limiting their organizational capability. The AI approach actually creates opportunities and incentives to move outside the box so the organization's strategic plan may further expand organizational capacity to multiorganizational and global capacity.

One of the pitfalls of the traditional strategic planning process is that it is generally conducted by top management. The process fails to glean wisdom from all levels of the organization. In this failure, it also neglects to obtain stakeholder buy-in from the very people who must ultimately carry out the activities that support the strategic plan. Most of us have had the experience at some point in our careers of being presented with a strategic plan that we were expected to implement despite our lack of input into the plan. AI allows, and in fact encourages, all stakeholders to have a voice in the planning dialogue. This leads to full participation in an organization's future, resulting in stakeholder ownership of the strategic plan throughout the organization.

The collaborative process of open dialogue helps an organization and its partners understand what happens when their organizations are working at their best. This information is used to create an image of "the best of what can be" for the future. The power of AI is its potential to cocreate a visual image of the organization. Stakeholders participate in envisioning a shared set of values, a vision, a mission, goals and enabling objectives, strategic alternatives, integrated tactical programs to support the recommended strategies, an actionable implementation plan, and the best structure and systems for a sustainable future.

The advantages of the AI approach to strategic planning are that it:
• Focuses on the positive to crowd out the negative.
• Builds organizational capacity beyond existing boundaries.
• Invites stakeholders into the strategy process.
• Builds relationships with partners.

- Obtains input from all levels of the organization.
- Obtains buy-in from all levels of the organization.
- Allows the planning process to become more of a process that incorporates and connects values, vision, and mission statement to strategic goals, strategies, plans, and a positive and objective review of goals.
- Creates a shared set of organizational values and vision of the future organization.

AI allows for the strategic assessment process to take on a life of its own, starting with an inquiry to discover what has made the organization a success in the past and present. The process helps build a sustainable competitive advantage for the future by identifying the organization's Unique Value Offering (UVO). This phenomenon occurs through an ongoing dialogue with the identified stakeholders of the organization. Through this dialogue, appreciative ways of knowing and learning about an organization's history and core capabilities are enriched. Srivastva and Cooperrider (1990) explained it as follows:

> Organizations are, to a much larger extent than normally assumed, *affirmative systems*—they are guided in their actions by anticipatory "forestructures" of positive knowledge that, like a movie projects on a screen, project a horizon of confident expectation which energizes, intensifies, and provokes action in the present. The forestructures or guiding images of the future are not the property of individuals but cohere within patterns of relatedness in the form of dialogue. . . . In this view Appreciative Inquiry refers to a process of knowing that draws one to inquire beyond superficial appearances to the deeper life-enhancing essentials and potentials of organizational existence. (p.14)

AI is used as a coinquiry from multiple perspectives to understand organizational efforts to create a vision, serve its mission, obtain desired goals and objectives, and design the best strategies.

AI is best known for its 4-D Cycle:

> a cycle of activities that guide members of an organization, group, or community through four stages: *discovery*—finding out about moments of excellence, core values and best practices; *dream*—envisioning positive possibilities; *design*—creating the structure, processes and relationships that will support the dream; and *destiny*—developing an effective inspirational plan for implementation.

These four phases are closely linked to the phases of inquiry necessary in the strategic planning process, as shown at the end of this article.

AI plays a critical role in the strategic planning process. It provides a framework for the organization to complete a strategic assessment, and it emphasizes a collaborative process of open dialogue to help the organization's stakeholders understand what they see happening when the organization is working at its best. As the stakeholders identify and describe the "life-giving" forces of their organization, together they can imagine and impart innovation to the future of their organizations with energy, vitality, and commitment. The positive language and affirmation should fit with the value system of the organization. In addition, the process can be a helpful approach in any strategic planning effort because it requires a "strategic vision, collective action, multiple parties and an empowering context for innovation and development" (Liebler, 1997, p. 31).

The final part of this article introduces our relational approach to strategic assessment and planning to assist with cocreation of an organization's future. Our strategic planning framework serves only as a beginning to help organizations dialogue about how best to go about building and delivering their UVO. As demonstrated by case studies in the November 2003 issue of the *AI Practitioner*, when the strategic planning process is being implemented and sustained, the visible outcomes can be:

- Definition and communication of organizational values.
- Clarity of vision, mission, goals, and objectives.
- Openness to new ideas and opportunities from the outside.
- Self-confidence, self-reliance, and self-respect at the organizational level.
- Improved organizational capacities and individual and functional capabilities.
- The building of multiorganizational and global capacity.
- Stakeholder ownership and responsibility for the organization's existence and future.
- A participatory strategic planning process where everyone is free to voice concerns and opinions.
- Creation of new knowledge that is practical and useful.
- Consideration for important issues and needs of stakeholders.
- Acceptance of new relationships and responsibilities that will build strategic capacity at all levels.

Integrating AI and Strategic Planning is a living concept that has the freedom to grow and change through dialogue. It is much more than a plan. We believe that those organizations with the greatest capacity possess skills and the spirit, enthusiasm, energy, and synergy required for change. If leadership embraces the strategic planning process as an opportunity to work closely with its stakeholders for a profitable sustainable future, it will need the "spirit of cooperation" in which to pursue their organization's vision and mission. To this end, we offer our readers a road map to help organizations get focused and organized for growth.

Strategic Inquiry: Appreciative Intent: Inspiration to SOAR

To illustrate the application of SOAR within the strategic planning process, a corporation (Tendercare) is presented as it first pursued traditional strategic plan (and then how it applied the SOAR principles) to take its strategic plan to a higher level at three levels of strategy: corporate, business, and functional.

Typically, the first step in the traditional strategic planning process is to review the current strategic posture of an organization. It begins with a review of the existing *mission statement*. A mission statement is a statement of purpose or function for the organization. For example, the following is the mission statement of Tendercare, which is a company that operates in the long-term care industry:

The mission of Tendercare (Michigan) Inc. is to be a dynamic, quality-oriented, and significant provider of long-term care and diversified health care services.

To emphasize high standards of performance and integrity that will enhance the quality of life of our residents.

To provide our employees opportunities for growth through participation, achievement, recognition, and reward.

To maintain a strong economic base through sound practices in support of these goals.

The mission statement provides the reason the organization exists. It describes the products/services to be supplied, the markets served, and operating philosophy. Yet a mission statement should not be developed without a guiding *vision statement*. The vision statement answers the question, what do we ultimately want to become? For example:

To be the healthcare provider of choice in our market areas.

The vision statement represents senior management's *strategic intent*—"a broad (vision) statement that identifies the guiding business concept or driving force that will propel the company forward toward the achievement of that intent." (DeKluyver, 2002, p.9). Then prior year *goals, objectives, strategies, plans,* and *policies* are reviewed.

Goals are set as a refinement to open-ended statements about such wishes as "being profitable" or "achieving growth in the long-term care market." Then more specific measurables are defined, called *objectives*. For example, Tendercare's objective is to be number one in the long-term care market in Michigan by 2005. It is a quantifiable statement about a desired strategic goal. Next, the effectiveness of *strategies* is evaluated. A *strategy* is simply the "how-to" means or guiding actions to achieve the long-term objectives. Strategies are usually viewed at the following levels:

1. Corporate level: What type of business should we continue to be in? Where should we grow, remain status quo, or divest?
2. Business level: How do we compete?
3. Functional level: What should each functional area do to synchronize with the business and corporate level strategies?

After an audit of the current and past situation, a SWOT analysis begins. This analysis is also referred to as *environmental scanning*. During the environmental scan, data are collected to answer questions about the present and future of the organization and the markets/industry served. The strategic planning team fragments those forces that determine the present and future of the corporation into internal and external variables using the SWOT format to analyze strengths, weakness, opportunities, and threats.

Figure 4: SWOT Model

Internal Assessment	**S**trengths Where we can outperform others	**W**eaknesses Where others can outperform us
External Assessment	**O**pportunities How we might exploit the market	**T**hreats What/who might take our market

Based on the SWOT analysis, recommendations are made as to what strategic alternatives would best serve the organization. From these alternatives, policies are reviewed or created to link the formulation of strategy with implementation. Policies and guidelines provide clear guidance to employees for implementation, often in the form of programs, budgets, and procedures. Then *evaluation and control* mechanisms are put into place to measure activities and performance results.

This organization quickly discovered that the AI approach and SOAR framework to strategic planning offer several benefits over the traditional model. The first is that its strategic planning process is both results-oriented and coconstructive. Whereas the traditional process offers a distinct demarcation between the assessment, planning, implementation, and control stages, the AI framework actually allows participants to cocreate their desired future throughout the process by inquiry, imagination, innovation, and inspiration. This starts with a strategic inquiry that values the organizational members' insights. An inquiry is done to best understand organizational members' values and the peak moments/experiences of what has worked well in the past. The inquiry also includes questions about the core factor that gives life to the organization's continued existence and wishes for the future. Its internal focus is on organizational strengths. AI also is used with customers, suppliers, and partners to perform external analysis.

In many organizations, strategic planning takes place only at the highest levels of the organization and involves relatively few stakeholders. In contrast, this new framework encourages strategic planners and all possible stakeholders to embrace change based on a foundation of executive and organizational integrity. The issue of integrity is important because stakeholders must be aware of the underlying assumptions that drive corporate leaders as questions are developed for the strategic inquiry. The aspiration principle of AI suggests that systems grow toward the collective vision of the future. Through relational discourse, we build our desired image of the most preferred future.

The Appreciative Inquiry (AI) approach transforms the SWOT model into SOAR (strengths, opportunities, aspirations, results). It can liberate us to focus on what really matters: the future of our people and organization. The AI strategist or strategic planner poses the question of inquiry to shape the direction of the strategic planning process and inform the content based on its strengths and opportunities. This is what we call a strategic inquiry with an appreciative intent.

Figure 5: Strategic Inquiry → Appreciative Intent: Inspiration to SOAR

Strategic Inquiry	**S**trengths What are our greatest assets	**O**pportunities What are the best possible market opportunities
Appreciative Intent	**A**spirations What is our preferred future	**R**esults What are the measurable results

(Stavros, Cooperrider, and Kelley, 2003)

The SOAR approach to strategy starts with a **strategic inquiry**. During this inquiry, an organization's greatest Strengths and Opportunities are discovered and explored among the participants. The participants are invited to share their Aspirations and coconstruct their most preferred future. Then recognition and reward programs are designed to inspire employees to achieve measurable Results.

Like the original AI 4-D model, the AI approach to strategic planning starts with an **inquiry** using unconditional positive questions to discovery the organization's core values, vision, strengths, and potential opportunities. The inquiry is a time of reflection into the strengths of the past and how these have been constructed with an eye toward creating the change we may desire. Next, the participants enter the **imagination** phase, when time is spent dreaming and coconstructing the preferred future. At this transformation point, values are affirmed and a vision and mission statement are created or re-created. Long-term objectives and strategic alternatives and recommendations are presented in this phase. The third phase is a time of **innovation** to begin the strategic design of short-term objectives, tactical and functional plans, integrated programs, structures, and systems to best achieve the desired future. To ensure that measurable results are achieved, the AI approach and SOAR framework recognize that employees must be inspired through authentic recognition and reward systems. In short, the process of assessment, planning, implementation, and control is replaced with the concepts of "inquire," "imagine," "innovate," and "inspire."

Two Stories of Applying the SOAR Framework

Strategic planning is an opportunity to help organizations soar with their strengths and to elevate an entire system's learning capacity to innovate from initial thought to finish. It can be absolutely thrilling. While we do not often talk about strategic business planning this way, it is clear that strategic planning can be one of the most positive occurrences in an organization's life:

- A rarefied time that cultivates the most elevated thought and action.
- A ritual-like time for the public re-creation of high-quality connections across an entire system.
- A precious time for drawing upon the "positive core" of a system in ways that ignites upward spirals in purposeful vision and dynamic action.

When we reflected over the past several years of our organization development work across many types of corporations, we were surprised to find that every one of the high-point moments was linked with times of strategic planning.

- It is crucial to cultivate a context that inspires natural curiosity, that is, the thrill of something historians of business innovation have surprisingly called "esthetic appreciation" in contrast to the more limited attitude of calculation or practical utility.
- The second perspective is something that magnifies the first—and it does so more consistently and effortlessly than anything else we have ever experienced. It is the leap from talking *about* systems thinking to *doing* systems thinking. It is the enactment of the power of *wholeness, which* means, quite simply, bringing the whole system into the room together to do the inquiry and strategizing.

Esthetic appreciation and systems thinking are what the following two stories help illustrate. Each story is briefly described and then expanded upon in detail in the next section.

The first story involves the strength-based SOAR framework used at Roadway Express, one of the largest trucking companies in America. Terminals from Chicago Heights to Winston-Salem have used this methodology to perform strategic business planning at their decentralized locations. To date, Roadway has held over twenty strategic planning summits using the appreciative approach and now has twelve more summits planned for the upcoming year.

The second story is a story of a different kind. It is not one of great growth or amazing returns, but one of appreciative divestiture. For years Tendercare, a regional long-term care provider, had been operating an assisted living center in an eroding market. The company, hesitant to continue to invest more resources in a center that was failing, used the SOAR model. The company had come to the conclusion that the building did not fit into its aspirations and, as a result, needed to be closed.

Let's start with a brief overview of Roadway and explore its special techniques related to the mapping strengths, opportunities, aspirations, and results (or measures of success).

Roadway Express: An Amazing Story of Business Planning

A recent videotape captures it all: the energy, the positive connections between all levels, the enthusiasm of the SOAR model in action as Roadway Express, a Fortune 500 trucking company base in Akron, Ohio, holds a strategic planning summit. (You can see a web video of the summit at **http://ai.cwru.edu**.) Nearly 300 dockworkers and truck drivers gather with management and customers to discuss Roadway's strategy for becoming the leading "LTL carrier" in a fiercely competitive industry. The mix included dockworkers, sales reps, the CEO, drivers, administration, mechanics, customers, and more—literally "the whole system."

At a more recent strategic planning session at the organization's Winston-Salem facility, Joanne Gordon, a *Forbes* magazine business writer, surprised Roadway by asking if she could participate in the three-day event. The AI Summit would engage and involve every kind of stakeholder at the Winston-Salem, North Carolina, terminal. In the end, Joanne Gordon had never seen anything like it. We explained to her how Roadway was doing something nobody else in the industry was doing. Furthermore, Roadway had already successfully piloted this appreciative SOAR framework at 5 of its 300 terminals around the country.

Prior to the summit the *Forbes* journalist was convinced that the session was going to be some kind of large-group "cheerleading" or "therapy" session—not the real thing of joint business planning. She even talked about it that way. So she arrived at the summit asking tough, skeptical questions. Here are the opening lines in the feature story she later wrote: "Teamsters and managers writing business plans together? . . . It was a scene not often seen in the history of labor-management relations."

As the article unfolded, the reporter's skepticism began to soften. She even sounded shocked at the level of business capability and passion demonstrated, for example, by the dockworkers and drivers. It was clearly hard for this writer to let go of preconceptions such as how can a large group of hundreds come together to do the real business planning? Fortunately, she was involved firsthand. The Roadway team went through the powerful sequence:

- Day 1: They mind-mapped all of the distinctive strengths of Roadway in relationship to the marketplace.
- Day 2: They identified new business opportunities followed by a more selective
  articulation of aspirations—clear articulations of strategic intent for the future.
- Day 3: The aspirations were made more concrete and specific and were then
  translated into anticipated results including careful selection of business measures.

The skeptical *Forbes* journalist then wrote descriptively about what she saw:

> A team of short-haul drivers came up with 12 cost-cutting and
> revenue-generating ideas. One of the most ambitious: Have each of the 32 driv-
> ers in Winston-Salem deliver just one more customer order each hour. Using
> management data, the drivers calculated the 288 additional daily shipments,
> at average revenue of $212 each and with a 6% margin, would generate just
> about $1 million a year of operating profit.

Still cautious, however, Gordon offered her view that the visions in the business
plan were too much of a stretch and that results would be "unlikely." But the gloomy
prediction was soon shattered. At its analyst meeting several months later on January
22, 2003, Roadway Corporation reported that revenues for the 16 weeks constituting
the company's fourth quarter were $1,074,110,000, up 25.7% over revenues of
$854,640,000 for the same period the previous year. For the fourth quarter of 2002, the
company reported income from continuing operations of $25,923,000, or $1.37 per share
(diluted), compared to income from continuing operations of $13,477,000, or $0.72 per
share (diluted), for the fourth quarter of 2001. Operating ratios improved significantly; and according to later analysis, the employee-driven "W&I" improvements translated into an additional $17 million in additional revenue for the year and $7 million
annual profit. This exciting breakthrough was a result of the combined efforts across
all 300 terminals of the 27,000 employee system. But here is the telling fact: of the five
terminals leading the company in the gains, *all* were sites that had worked as organizational effectiveness sites using AI in one way or another, and three of the top five
sites leading the company in gains had, in fact, held large-scale summits using the SOAR
sequence for business planning.

So what would Roadway's approach be in 2004? Twelve more locations had already
been selected as sites for introducing this kind of strength-based, opportunity-focused
strategic planning. For Roadway, the more business-focused, the better. Here the goal
is not only better strategies but also human development. Roadway wants leadership
at every level and realizes that strategy is not simply a one-moment special event. Roadway wants to embed a strategic thought process that can be used every day to seize
new opportunities and to make strategizing an ongoing occurrence. After the Akron
terminal summit, for example, a team of switchers and mechanics created a vision that
has the potential to save the company millions every year. At Winston-Salem, the drivers have voluntarily become some of the organization's best salespeople. Within months
of their summit, the drivers secured over $1 million of new business. One driver used
his "off-time" to take a potential customer trout fishing. The result was a major new
account. Strategic thinking is becoming part of the culture. Jim Staley, Roadway's CEO,
spoke in another magazine article about strategy as a way to build leadership at every
level: "The AI approach unleashes tremendous power, tremendous enthusiasm, and

gets people engaged in the right way in what we're trying to accomplish."

Formulating sound strategy requires both analysis and synthesis; it is as much a rational act as a creative and emergent one. But this case emphasizes the latter. The strength-based framework we call SOAR creates an energy that lasts. It fuels creative emergence. It supports a view of strategy where every success and strength is noticed—not just in the planning session itself, but all of the time. And this is how it works: big things emerge from little things with one condition as key—they are noticed and appreciated.

Cultivating a Positive Core at Tendercare

Strategic planning is not always about finding new ways to grow a company. The other two alternatives can be to remain status quo or to divest of assets. Tendercare is a regional long-term care provider that operates a chain of skilled nursing homes, assisted living residences, and various other long-term care services in Michigan. Tendercare's vision is to be the provider of choice in each of the markets in which it operates; and while most of its centers live up to this vision, a few do not. In 2002, the company embarked on a carefully thought-out strategic plan that included a thorough review of its properties and their contribution to the company's vision and mission. For years, the company had taken a defensive posture in their markets, working hard to maintain a solid footing in the communities in which it operated. This meant that even when a center did not meet its vision of being the provider of choice, rather than seek alternatives, the company maintained the center. While senior management recognized that a couple of buildings regularly lost money, no action was taken for fear of losing market share, stirring up regulatory issues, attracting negative press, angering families and residents, and damaging the company's reputation.

In early 2002, the company brought in a team of consultants to one center that had been losing money for more than three years. This assisted living center had a unionized staff and currently operated at 75 percent of capacity. The initial goal of using AI was to bring the staff, management, residents, and family members together as a unified team to create a positive working culture and then to get them to work together toward a final attempt to improve the center's census and reputation.

Using the SOAR-based framework, the core care team worked with the center and its stakeholders over a six-week period. During this time, a strategic inquiry with a purposeful appreciative intent was carried out using the new five "I" model (inquiry, imagine, innovation, and inspiration built on a foundation of integrity). Integrity was maintained in that employees were told the facility may be closed or sold. With a focus on the center's strengths, opportunities, aspirations, and results (SOAR), it became clear that the best option for the company might be to discontinue operation of the center. While measurable results included an 8 percent increase in census and a successful de-unionization vote, the center was not able to compete effectively within its market. As a result, 18 months later, the company made the decision, for the first time in its history, to take the bold step of closing one of its centers due to a significant change in the uncontrollable environment.

Closing an assisted living center that residents have considered as their home for many years is not a simple task in the best of circumstances. Because the staff, residents, families, and management had the opportunity to work together openly and honestly in sharing information, ideas, stories, and plans, the transition went very smoothly. From the date the closure was announced until the last resident moved out, the timeframe was less than 30 days. Several noteworthy points include the fact that during the entire transition, every staff member showed up for work, no one left his or her position prematurely, the company worked to find employment opportunities for every interested employee, and every resident was placed without incident.

Because of this successful divestiture, the company is planning to use the strategic inquiry with appreciative intent approach and the SOAR model to review several additional centers that do not meet its vision and mission. In the words of Tendercare's vice president of market development, "We have seen a dramatic shift from a defensive posture of fear to a new level of excitement about our ability to truly make the company into what we want it to be while considering each and every stakeholder. By taking a positive and proactive approach we are able to invest in our good centers instead of spending enormous amounts of time, energy and resources in the couple of centers that seem to drain energy and resources." The corporate Tendercare marketing and business development team is also planning to use the SOAR framework in 2004 to take one of its strongest regions to the next level of growth.

Summary

We started this article by stating that the corporate mantra over the past couple of decades has been change, change, and change. While change is inevitable, no one has ever advocated change for the sake of change. So don't. Instead, change with purpose. Decide what you are going to be—the best, the most customer service-oriented, the friendliest, the most profitable, whatever it might be—and then don't begrudge your weaknesses. Instead, celebrate what you do well. The unconditional strategic inquiry into strengths and opportunities is the quest. The SOAR framework is an exciting breakthrough and a new way of thinking about strategic planning. Just as AI has brought a bold new approach to the field of organizational development and change, SOAR offers a break from the tradition deficit-based planning process. It is, quite literally, the inspiration to SOAR.

References

Bechtel, M. (1995). The Management Compass, AMA Management Briefing, New York.

Brassard, M. (1989). *The Memory Jogger Plus+*. Meuthuen, MA: Goal/QPC.

Cowley, M., & Domb, E. (1997). *Beyond Strategic Vision*. Boston: Butterworth-Heinemann.

Cooperrider D., Whitney D., & Stavros, J. (2003). *Appreciative Inquiry Handbook: The First in a Series of AI Workbooks for Leaders of Change*. Cleveland, OH: Lakeshore Communications.

DeKluyver, C. (2000). *Strategic Thinking: An Executive Perspective*. Upper Saddle River, NJ: Prentice Hall.

Haines, S. G., (2000). *The Systems Thinking Approach to Strategic Planning and Management*. New York: St. Lucie Press.

Kotter, J. (2002). *Heart of Change*. Boston: Harvard Business School Press.

Mintzberg, H. (January/February 1994). "The Fall and Rise of Strategic Planning, *Harvard Business Review*, 107–114.

Mizuno, S. (1988). *Management for Quality Improvement: The Seven New QC Tools*, Cambridge, MA: Productivity Press.

Musashi, M. (1974). *A Book of Five Rings*. Woodstock, NY: The Overlook Press.

Pattison, J. E. (1996). *Breaking Boundaries*. Princeton, NJ: Pattersons/Pacesetter Books.

Srivastva, S., & Cooperrider, D. (1990). *Appreciative Management and Leadership: The Power of Positive Thought and Action in Organizations*. Cleveland, OH: Lakeshore Communications.

Sun Tzu. (1971). *The Art of War*. Oxford, UK: Oxford University Press.

Strategic Impact: Inspiration to SOAR!

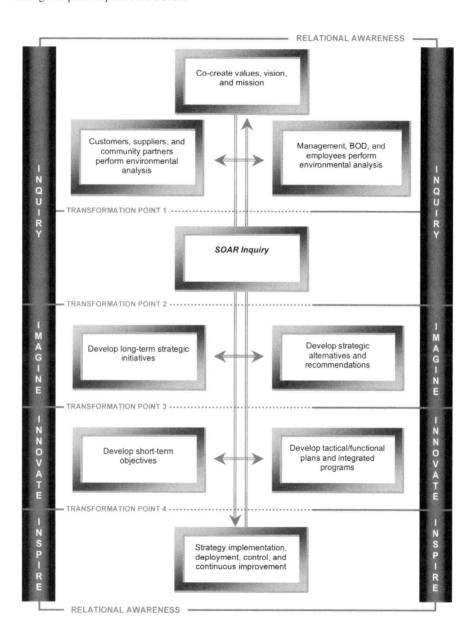

Stavros, Cooperrider & Kelley, 2005
(Updated from original SOAR diagram 2003)

Appreciative Inquiry Bibliography
(includes references cited within the handbook)

Adamson, J., Samuels, N., & Willoughby, G. (2002, March). Changing the way we change at Heathside School. *Managing Schools Today*.

AI Practitioner Collection CD 1998–2004. (2005, December 10). *AI Practitioner Journal*.

Anderson, H., Cooperrider D., Gergen, K., Gergen, M., McNamee, S., & Whitney, D. (2001). *The appreciative organization*. Chagrin Falls, OH: Taos Institute Publications.

Aram, J. D. (1990). Appreciative interchange: The force that makes cooperation possible. In S. Srivastva & D. L. Cooperrider (Eds.), *Appreciative management and leadership: The Power of Positive Thought and Action in Organization* (Rev. ed.). (pp. 175–204). Euclid, OH: Lakeshore Communications.

Ashcraft, M. (1998). *Fundamentals of cognition*. Reading, MA: Addison-Wesley-Longman.

Ashford, G., & Parry, J. (2001). *Integrating Aboriginal values into land use and resource management*. Winnipeg, Manitoba, Canada: International Institute for Sustainable Development/Skownan First Nation.

Ashford, G., & Patkar, S. (2001). *The positive path: Using appreciative inquiry in rural Indian communities*. Winnipeg, Manitoba, Canada: Kromar Printing Ltd.

Assistance, V. T. (1996). *Appreciative inquiry: An approach to organizational analysis and learning*. Rosslyn, VA: Volunteers in Technical Assistance.

Babcock, P. (2005, September). A calling for change. *Society for Human Resource Management, 50*.

Balousek, M. (2004, September 29). Downtown summit has ideas on freeing up owners. *Wisconsin State Journal*, Retrieved from http://www.madison.com/wsj.

Banaga, G. (1998). A spiritual path to organizational renewal. In S. Hammond & C. Royal (Eds.), *Lessons from the field: Applying appreciative inquiry* (pp. 260–271). Plano, TX: Practical Press, Inc.

Barrett, F. (1995). Creating appreciative learning cultures. *Organizational Dynamics, 24*(2), 36–49.

Barrett, F. (1999). Knowledge creating as dialogical accomplishment: A constructionist perspective. In A. Montuori & R. Purser (Eds.), *Social creativity: Volume 1* (pp. 133–151). Cresskill, NJ: Hampton Press.

Barrett, F. (2000). Cultivating an aesthetic of unfolding: Jazz improvisation as a self-organizing system. In S. Linstead & H. Hopfl (Eds.), *The aesthetics of organization* (pp. 228–245). London: Sage Publications.

Barrett, F. (2000). Learning to appreciate the sublime: Don't knock the rock. In R. Pellegrini & T. R. Sarbin (Eds.), *Between fathers and sons: Pivotal narratives in men's lives*. London: Sage Press.

Barrett, F., & Fry, R. (2005). *Appreciative inquiry: A positive approach to building cooperative capacity*. Chagrin Falls, OH: Taos Institute Publications.

Barrett, F., & Peterson, R. (2000). Appreciative learning cultures: Developing competencies for global organizing. *Organization Development Journal, 18*(2), 10–21.

Barrett, F., Thomas, G. F., & Hocevar, S. P. (1995). The central role of discourse in large-scale change: A social construction perspective. *Journal of Applied Behavioral Science, 31*(3), 352–372.

Barrett, F. J. (1998). Creativity and improvisation in jazz and organizations: Implications for organizational learning. *Organization Science, 9*(5), 605–622.

Barrett, F. J., & Cooperrider, D. L. (1990). Generative metaphor intervention: A new approach for working with systems divided by conflict and caught in defensive perception. *Journal of Applied Behavioral Science, 26*(2), 219–239.

Barrett, F. J., & Cooperrider, D. L. (2001). Generative metaphor intervention: A new approach for working with systems divided by conflict and caught in defensive perception. *Appreciative Inquiry: An Emerging Direction for Organization Development.*

Barros, I., & Cooperrider, D. L. (2000). A story of Nutrimental in Brazil: How wholeness, appreciation, and inquiry bring out the best in human organization. *Organization Development Journal, 18,* 22–28.

Barros, I., & Cooperrider, D. L. (2001, August 14). Appreciative inquiry fostering wholeness in organizations: A story of Nutrimental in Brazil. *Nutrimental Industria e Comercio de Alimentos S.A.*

Bergquist, W. H., Bergquist, W., Merritt, K., & Phillips, S. (1999). *Executive coaching: An appreciative approach.* Sacramento, CA: Pacific Soundings Press.

Bilimoria, D. et al. (1995). A call to organizational scholarship: The organization dimensions of global change: No limits to cooperation. *Journal of Management Inquiry, 4*(1), 71–90.

Bilimoria, D., Wilmot, T. B., et al. (1996). Multi-organizational collaboration for global change: New opportunities for organizational change and development. In R. W. Woodman & W. A. Pasmore (Eds.), *Research in organizational change and development, vol. 9* (pp. 201–236). Greenwich, CT: JAI Press.

Blair, M. (1998). Lessons from using appreciative inquiry in a planning exercise. In S. Hammond & C. Royal (Eds.), *Lessons from the field: Applying appreciative inquiry* (pp. 186–214). Plano, TX: Practical Press, Inc.

Bloom, J. L., & Martin, N. A. (2002, August 29). Incorporating appreciative inquiry into academic advising. *The Mentor.*

Booy, D., & Sena, S. (2000). Capacity building using the appreciative inquiry approach: The experience of world vision Tanzania. *Global Social Innovations, 3*(1), 4–11.

Bosch, L. (1998). Exit interviews with an "appreciative eye." In S. Hammond & C. Royal (Eds.), *Lessons from the field: Applying appreciative inquiry* (pp. 230–243). Plano, TX: Practical Press, Inc.

Bosch, L. (2005). Good leadership: An appreciative discovery of expectations. *OD Practitioner, 37,* 25–30.

Bowling, C., Ludema, J., & Wyss, E. (1997). *Vision twin cities appreciative inquiry report.* Cleveland, OH: Case Western Reserve University.

Branson, M. (2004). *Memories, hopes, and conversations: Appreciative inquiry and congregational change.* Herndon, VA: Alban Institute.

Brittain, J. (1998). Do we really mean it? How we change behavior after the provocative propositions are written. In S. Hammond & C. Royal (Eds.), *Lessons from the field: Applying appreciative inquiry* (pp. 216–229). Plano, TX: Practical Press, Inc.

Browne, B. (1998). Imagine Chicago: A study in intergenerational appreciative inquiry. In S. Hammond & C. Royal (Eds.), *Lessons from the field: Applying appreciative inquiry* (pp. 76–89). Plano, TX: Practical Press, Inc.

Buckingham, S. T. (1999). *Leadership skills in public health nursing: An appreciative inquiry.* Victoria, British Columbia: Royal Roads University.

Bukenya, G. et al. (1997). *Manual of district health management for Uganda.* McKinleyville, CA: Fithian Press.

Bunker, B. B. (1990). Appreciating diversity and modifying organizational cultures: Men and women at work. In S. Srivastva & D. L. Cooperrider (Eds.), *Appreciative management and leadership: The power of positive thought and action in organizations* (Rev. ed.). (pp. 126–149). Euclid, OH: Lakeshore Communications.

Bunker, B. B., & Alban, B. T. (1997). Large group interventions: Engaging the whole system for rapid change. San Francisco: Jossey-Bass.

Bushe, G. R. (1995). Advances in appreciative inquiry as an organization development intervention. *Organization Development Journal, 13*(3), 14–22.

Bushe, G. R. (1997). *Attending to others: Interviewing appreciatively.* Vancouver, BC: Discovery and Design Inc.

Bushe, G. R. (1998). Appreciative inquiry with teams. *Organization Development Journal, 16*(3), 41–50.

Bushe, G. R. (2000). Clear leadership: How outstanding leaders make themselves understood, cut through the mush, and help everyone get real at work, Mountain View, CA: Davies-Black.

Bushe, G. R. (2001). Meaning making in teams: Appreciative inquiry with pre-identity and post-identity groups. In F. Barrett, R. Fry, & D. Whitney (Eds.), *Appreciative inquiry: Applications in the field.*

Bushe, G. R., & Coetzer, G. (1995). Appreciative inquiry as a team-development intervention: A controlled experiment. *Journal of Applied Behavioral Science, 31*(1), 13–30.

Bushe, G. R., & Pitman, T. (1991). Appreciative process: A method for transformational change. *OD Practitioner, 23*(3), 1–4.

Carter, L., Mische, A., & Schwarz, D. R. (1993). *Aspects of hope: The proceedings of a seminar on hope.* New York: ICIS Center for a Science of Hope.

Chaffee, P. (1997). Ring of breath around the world: A report of the United Religions Initiative global conference. *Journal of the United Religions Initiative, 4.*

Chaffee, P. (1997). *Unafraid of the light: Appreciative inquiry and faith communities* (unpublished paper). San Francisco: Interfaith Center at the Presidio.

Chaffee, P. (2005). Claiming the light: Appreciative inquiry and congregational transformation. Herndon, VA: Alban Institute.

Chapagain, C. P. (2005). Appreciative inquiry for building human capacities: An innovative approach for the new millennium. Katmandu, Nepal: Plan-International.

Cobb, N. B. (2002). *Project management workbook.* New York: McGraw-Hill.

Coffey, A., & Atkinson, P. (1996). *Making sense of qualitative data.* Newbury Park, CA: Sage Publications.

Cojocaru, S. (2005). The appreciative perspective in multicultural relations. *Journal for the study of religions and ideologies, 10,* 36–48.

Collins, J., & Porras, J. (1994). *Built to last: Successful habits of visionary companies*. New York: Harper Business.

Cooperrider, D. (2000). An appreciative inquiry conversation guide: Creating a small forum in which leaders of the world religions can gather in mutual respect and dialogue. *Global Social Innovations, 1*(3), 23–26.

Cooperrider, D. (2002). Here's a way to negotiate the Mideast Crisis. *MWorld* (Summer edition).

Cooperrider, D., & Avital, M. (2004). *Advances in appreciative inquiry: Constructive discourse and human organization*. Oxford, UK: Elsevier Publishing.

Cooperrider, D. et al. (2003). *The appreciative inquiry trilogy*. Chagrin Falls, OH: Taos Institute Publications.

Cooperrider, D., Sorenson, P., Yaeger, T., & Whitney, D. (2001). *Appreciative inquiry: An emerging direction for organizational development*. Champaign, IL: Stipes Publishing.

Cooperrider, D., Sorensen, P., Yaeger, T., & Whitney, D. (2003). *Appreciative inquiry: Foundations in positive organization development*. Champaign, IL: Stipes Publishing.

Cooperrider, D., & Srivastva, S. (1999). Appreciative inquiry in organizational life. In S. Srivastva & D. L. Cooperrider, *Appreciative management and leadership* (Rev. ed.). (pp. 401–442). Euclid, OH: Lakeshore Communications.

Cooperrider, D., & Srivastva, S. (1999). The emergence of the egalitarian organization. In S. Srivastva & D. L. Cooperrider. *Appreciative management and leadership: The Power of Positive Thought and Action in Organization* (Rev. ed.). (pp. 443–484). Euclid, OH: Lakeshore Communications.

Cooperrider, D. L. (1995). Introduction to appreciative inquiry. In W. French & C. Bell (Eds.), *Organization development*. Englewood Cliffs, NJ: Prentice Hall.

Cooperrider, D. L. (1996). Resources for getting appreciative inquiry started: An example OD proposal. *OD Practitioner, 28*(1 & 2), 23–33.

Cooperrider, D. L. (1996). Special issue: OD and the global agenda. *Organization development journal, 14*(4).

Cooperrider, D. L. (1996). The "child" as agent of inquiry. *OD Practitioner, 28*(1 & 2), 5–11.

Cooperrider, D. L., Barrett, F., & Srivastva, S. (1995). Social construction and appreciative inquiry: A journey in organizational theory. In D. Hosking, P. Dachler, & K. Gergen (Eds.), Management and organization: Relational alternatives to Individualism (pp. 157–200). Aldershot, England: Avebury Press.

Cooperrider, D. L., & Bilimoria, D. (1993). The challenge of global change for strategic management: Opportunities for charting a new course. *Advances in strategic management, 9*, 99–141.

Cooperrider, D. L., & Dutton, J. (1999). *The organizational dimensions of global change: No limits to cooperation*. Thousand Oaks, CA: Sage Publications.

Cooperrider, D. L., & Khalsa, G. S. (1997). The organization dimensions of global environmental change. *Organization and Environment, 10*(4), 331–341.

Cooperrider, D. L., & Pasmore, W. A. (1991). Global social change: A new agenda for social science? *Human Relations, 44*(10), 1037–1055.

Cooperrider, D. L., Sorensen, P. F., Whitney, D., & Yaeger, T. F. (2000). *Appreciative inquiry: Rethinking human organization toward a positive theory of change*. Champaign, IL: Stipes Publishing.

Cooperrider, D. L., & Srivastva, S. (1987). *Appreciative inquiry in organizational life*. In W. Pasmore & R. Woodman (Eds.), *Research in organization change and development* (pp. 129–169). Greenwich, CT: JAI Press.

Cooperrider, D. L., & Srivastva, S. (1998). An invitation to organizational wisdom and executive courage. In S. Srivastva & D. L. Cooperrider (Eds.), *Organizational wisdom and executive courage* (pp. 1–24). San Francisco: New Lexington Press.

Cooperrider, D. L., & Thachenkery, T. (1995). Building the global civic culture: Making our lives count. In P. Sorenson, T. C. Head, N. J. Mathys, J. Preston, & D. Cooperrider (Eds.), *Global and international organization development* (pp. 282–306). Champaign, IL: Stipes Publishing.

Cooperrider, D. L., & Whitney, D. (1999). *Collaborating for change: Appreciative inquiry*. San Francisco: Berrett-Koehler.

Cooperrider, D. L., & Whitney, D. (1999). When stories have wings: How "relational responsibility" opens new options for action. In S. McNamee & K. Gergen (Eds.), *Relational responsibility: Resources for sustainable dialogue* (pp. 57–64). Thousand Oaks, CA: Sage Publications.

Cooperrider, D. L., & Whitney, D. (2005). *Appreciative inquiry: A positive revolution in change*. San Francisco: Berrett-Koehler.

Cottor, R., Asher, A., Levin, J., & Weiser, C. (2004). *Experiential learning exercises in social construction: A field book for creating change*. Chagrin Falls, OH: Taos Institute Publications.

Covey, S. (1990). *The 7 Habits of Highly Effective People*. New York: Simon & Schuster.

Cowling, W. R. (2004, Jul/Aug/Sept). Pattern, participation, praxis, and power in unitary appreciative inquiry. *Advances in Nursing Science, 27*(3), 202–214.

Cummings, T. G. (1990). The role of executive appreciation in creating transorganizational alliances. In S. Srivastva & D. L. Cooperrider (Eds.), *Appreciative management and leadership: The power of positive thought and action in organizations* (Rev. ed.). (pp. 205–227). Euclid, OH: Lakeshore Communications.

Cummings, L. L., & Anton, R. J. (1990). The logical and appreciative dimensions of accountability. In S. Srivastva & D. L. Cooperrider (Eds.), *Appreciative management and leadership: The power of positive thought and action in organizations* (Rev. ed.). (pp. 257–286). Euclid, OH: Lakeshore Communications.

Curran, M. (1991, December). Appreciative inquiry: A third wave approach to OD. *Vision/Action*, 12–14.

DeKluyver, C. (2000). *Strategic thinking: An executive perspective*. New York: Prentice Hall.

Easley, C., Yaeger, T., & Sorensen, P. (2002, July 24). Appreciative inquiry: Evoking new ways of understanding, valuing and loving and changing the youth we have lost to gangs. *Proceedings of the Organization Discourse: From Micro-Utterances to Macro-Inferences Conference*. The Management Centre, Kings College, University of London, England.

Elkington, J. (1998). *Cannibals with forks*. Gabriola Island, BC: New Society Publishing.

Elliott, C. (1999). *Locating the energy for change: An introduction to appreciative inquiry.* Winnipeg, Manitoba, Canada: International Institute for Sustainable Development.

Finegold, M. A., Holland, B. M., & Lingham, T. (2002). Appreciative inquiry and public dialogue: An approach to community change. *Public Organization Review, 2,* 235–252.

Fitzgerald, S., Murrell, K., & Miller, M. (Spring 2003). Appreciative inquiry: Accentuating the positive. *Business Strategy Review, 14*(1), 5–7.

Fredrickson, B. L. (2001). The role of positive emotions in positive psychology: The broaden-and-build theory of positive emotions. *American Psychologist, 56.*

Fredrickson, B. L. (2003, July). The value of positive emotions. *American Scientist, 91.*

Frost, P. J., & Egri, C. P. (1990). Appreciating executive action. In S. Srivastva & D. L. Cooperrider (Eds.), *Appreciative management and leadership: The power of positive thought and action in organizations* (Rev. ed.). (pp. 289–322). Euclid, OH: Lakeshore Communications.

Fry, R., Whitney D., Seiling, J., & Barrett, F. (2001). *Appreciative inquiry and organizational transformation: Reports from the field.* Westport, CT: Quorum Books.

Fuller, C., Griffin, T., & Ludema, J. (2000). Appreciative future search: Involving the whole system in positive organization change. *Organization Development Journal, 18*(2), 29–41.

Gergen, K. J. (1990). Affect and organization in postmodern society. In S. Srivastva and D. L. Cooperrider (Eds.), *Appreciative management and leadership: The power of positive thought and action in organizations* (Rev. ed.). (pp. 153–174). Euclid, OH: Lakeshore Communications.

Gergen, K. J. (1991). *The saturated self.* New York: Basic Books Publishing.

Gergen, K. J. (1994). *Realities and relationships: Soundings in social construction.* Cambridge, MA: Harvard University Press.

Gergen, K. J. (1999). *An invitation to social construction.* Thousand Oaks, CA: Sage Publishing.

Gergen, K. J., & Gergen, M. (2004). *Social construction: Entering the dialogue.* Chagrin Falls, OH: Taos Institute Publications.

Gergen, K. J., McNamee, S., & Barrett, F. J. (2001). Toward transformative dialogue. *International Journal of Public Administration, 24*(7), 679–709.

Gibbs, C. (2002). The United Religions Initiative at work: Interfaith dialogue through appreciative inquiry, sowing seeds of transformation, interfaith dialogue and peacebuilding. Washington, DC: United States Institute of Peace.

Gibbs, C., & Ackerly, S. (1997). United Religions Initiative global summit summary report. Paper presented at the United Religions Initiative Global Summit, San Francisco.

Goldberg, R. A. (2001, March 21). Implementing a professional development system through appreciative inquiry. *Leadership and Organization Development Journal, 22,* 56–61.

Golembiewski, B. (2000). Three perspectives on appreciative inquiry. *OD Practitioner, 32*(1), 54–58.

Golembiewski, R. T. (1998). Appreciating appreciative inquiry: Diagnosis and perspectives on how to do better. In R. W. Woodman and W. A. Pasmore (Eds.), *Research in organizational change and development* (pp. 1–45). Greenwich, CT: JAI Press.

Golembiewski, R. T. (1999). Fine-tuning appreciative inquiry: Two ways of circumscribing the concept's value-added. *Organization Development Journal, 17*(3), 21–28.

Gordon, J. (2003, January 20). Meet the freight fairy. *Forbes,* 171.

Gotches, G., & Ludema, J. (1995). Appreciative inquiry and the future of OD. *Organization Development Journal, 13*(3), 5–13.

GTE. (1997). GTE asks employees to start a grassroots movement to make GTE unbeatable in the marketplace. *GTE Together.*

Hagevik, S. (2000). Appreciative inquiry and your career. *Journal of Environmental Health, 63*(1), 39, 44.

Hammonds, K. (2001, July). Leaders for the long haul, *Fast* Company, 56–58.

Hammond, S. (1996). *The thin book of appreciative inquiry.* Plano, TX: Thin Book Publishing.

Hammond, S. (1998). What is appreciative inquiry? *The Inner Edge, 1*(2), 36–27.

Hammond, S. (2006). *Chinese translation of the thin book of appreciative inquiry.* Plano, TX: Thin Book Publishing.

Harman, W. W. (1990). Shifting context for executive behavior: Signs of change and revaluation. In S. Srivastva and D. L. Cooperrider (Eds.), *Appreciative management and leadership: The power of positive thought and action in organizations* (Rev. ed.). San Francisco: Jossey-Bass.

Hart, S. (2005). *Capitalism at the crossroads.* Upper Saddle River, NJ: Pearson Education.

Head, R. (1999). *School of management.* Cleveland, OH: Case Western Reserve University.

Head, R. L. (1999). Appreciative inquiry as a team-development intervention for newly formed heterogeneous groups. *OD Practitioner, 32*(1), 59–66.

Head, R. L., & Young, M. M. (1998). Initiating culture change in higher education through appreciative inquiry. *Organization Development Journal, 16*(2), 65–72.

Head, T. (2006, Summer). Appreciative inquiry in the graduate classroom: Making group dynamics a practical topic to address. *Organization Development Journal, 24*(2), 83–88.

Head, T. C. (2000). Appreciative inquiry: Debunking the mythology behind resistance to change. *OD Practitioner, 32*(1), 27–32.

Head, T. C., Sorensen, P. F., Jr., Preston, J. C., & Yaeger, T. (2000). Is appreciative inquiry OD's philosopher's stone? In D. L. Cooperrider, P. F. Sorensen, Jr., D. Whitney, & T. F. Yaeger (Eds.), *Appreciative inquiry: An emerging direction for organizational development* (pp. 363–378). Champaign, IL: Stipes Publishing.

Henry, R. (2004). Leadership at every level: Appreciative inquiry in education. *New Horizons for Learning,* Retrieved from http://www.newhorizons.org.

Henry, R. (2005, February). Discovering and growing what gives life: Appreciative inquiry in community colleges. *Instructional Leadership Abstracts, 3.*

Herasymowych, M. (1997, May). Tapping into the power of learning part 4A: Appreciating potential and possibilities. *InfoMine, 4.*

Herrick, C., & Stoneham, D. (2005). Unleashing a positive revolution in medicine: The power of appreciative inquiry. *Utah Medical Association Bulletin, 52.*

Hock, D. (1999). *Birth of the chaordic age.* San Francisco: Berrett-Koehler.

Hubbard, B. M. (1998). Conscious evolution: Awakening the power of our social potential. Novato, CA: New World Library.

Isen, A. M., Estrada, C. A., & Young, M. J. (1998). Positive affect facilitates integration of information and decreases anchoring in reasoning among physicians. *Organizational Behavior and Human Decision Processes, 72,* 117–135.

Jacobsgaard, M. (2000). Appreciative inquiry in action. *Global Social Innovations, 1,* 59–60.

Johnson, G., & Leavitt, W. (2001, March 22). Building on success: Transforming organizations through appreciative inquiry. *Public Personnel Management, 30,* 129.

Johnson, G., & Leavitt, W. (2005). Building on success: Transforming organizations through appreciative inquiry. *Public Personal Management, 30.*

Johnson, P. C., & Cooperrider, D. L. (1991). Finding a path with heart: Global social change organizations and their challenge for the field of organizational development. In R. W. Woodman & W. A. Pasmore (Eds.), *Research in organizational change and development* (pp. 223–284). Greenwich, CT: JAI Press.

Johnson, P. C., & Cooperrider, D. L. (1991). Global integrity: Beyond instrumental rationality in transnational organizing. *Journal of Transnational Associations.*

Johnson, S., & Ludema, J. (1997). Partnering to build and measure organizational capacity: Lessons from NGOs around the world. Grand Rapids, MI: CRC Publications.

Johnston, C. (2002, May 1). The best possible world. *CWRU Magazine, 14.*

Jonas, H., Fry, R., & Srivastva, S. (1989). The office of the CEO: Understanding the executive experience, *Academy of Management Executive, 3*(4).

Jones, D. A. (1998). A field experiment in appreciative inquiry. *Organization Development Journal, 16*(4), 69–78.

Kaczmarski, K. M., & Cooperrider, D. L. (1997). Constructionist leadership in the global relational age. *Organization and Environment, 10*(3), 235–258.

Kaczmarski, K. M., & Cooperrider, D. L. (1998). Constructionist leadership in the global relational age: The case of the mountain forum. In D. L. Cooperrider & J. E. Dutton (Eds.), *The organizational dimensions of global change: No limits to cooperation* (pp. 57–87). Thousand Oaks, CA: Sage Publications.

Kamini, R. S., & Soon, S. (2002, August 9). Appreciative inquiry and the media (SWOT ed.). *New Straits Times,* Malaysia.

Kanungo, R. N., & Conger, J. A. (1990). The quest for altruism in organizations. In S. Srivastva & D. L. Cooperrider (Eds.), *Appreciative management and leadership: The power of positive thought and action in organizations* (Rev. ed.). (pp. 228–256). Euclid: OH: Lakeshore Communications.

Kaye, B., & Jacobson, B. (1999). True tales and tall tales: The power of organizational storytelling. *Training & Development, 53*(3), 44–50.

Kelm, J. B. (2005). *Appreciative living*. Wake Forest, NC: Venet Publishers.

Khalsa, G. S. (2000). A case story of the United Religions Initiative first global summit. Paper presented at the Appreciative Summit Conference, Cleveland, OH.

Khalsa, G. S. (2000). The pilgrimage toward global dialogue: A practical visionary approach. *Breakthrough News*, 8–10.

Khalsa, G. S., & Kaczmarski, K. M. (1996). The United Religions Initiative summit conference summary. Paper presented at the United Religions Initiative Summit Conference, San Francisco.

Khalsa, G. S., & Kaczmarski, K. M. (1997). Chartering and appreciative future search. *Global Social Innovations, 1*(2), 45–52.

Khalsa, G. S., & Steingard, D. S. (1999). The relational healing dimension of organizational development: Transformative stories and dialogue in life-cycle transitions. In W. A. Pasmore & R. W. Woodman (Eds.), *Research in organizational change and development* (pp. 269–318). Stamford, CT: JAI Press.

Kind, M. (2004, January 16). Yellow roadway will keep area workers, expand with terminals in other towns. *Kansas City Business Journal*.

Kinni, T. (2003, September 22). The art of appreciative inquiry. Harvard Business School—Working Knowledge for Business Leaders, Retrieved from http://hbswk.hbs.edu/archive/3684.html.

Knight, P. (2002). Small-scale research: Pragmatic inquiry in social science and the caring professional. London: Sage Publications.

Krattenmaker, T. (2001, October). Change through appreciative inquiry. *Harvard Management Communication Newsletter, 4*.

Krouse, P. (2006, October 25). Global compact recruits locally. *The Plain Dealer*, Cleveland, OH.

Krouse, P. (2006, October 23). Using business to make the world better. *The Plain Dealer*, Cleveland, OH.

Lawn, M., & Morris, D. (2005, February). A positive approach to shaping the future. *Perdido: Leadership with a Conscience, 11*, 19–24.

LeJeune, M. (1999, February). Companies turning to appreciative inquiry to ask staff what's right. *Boulder County Business Report*.

Liebler, C. J. (1997). Getting comfortable with appreciative inquiry: Questions and answers. *Global Social Innovations, 1*(2), 30–40.

Liebling, A., Elliott, C., & Arnold, H. (2001, May). Transforming the prison: Romantic optimism or appreciative realism? *Criminal Justice, 1*, 161–180.

Liebling, A., Price, D., & Elliott, C. (1999). Appreciative inquiry and relationships in prison. *Punishment & Society, 1*(1), 71–98.

Liedman, J. (2002, January). HR pros may favor appreciative inquiry. *Human Resource Executive*.

Livingston, J. (1999). The human and organizational dimensions of global change: An appreciative inquiry interview with Robert Golembiewski. *Organization Development Journal, 17*(1), 109–115.

Lord, J. G. (1995). The philanthropic quest: A generative approach for professionals engaged in the development process. Cleveland, Ohio: Philanthropic Quest International.

Lord, J. G. (1998). The practice of the quest: Evolving a new paradigm for philanthropy and social innovation—A casebook for advancement professionals grounded in the quest. Cleveland, OH: Philanthropic Quest International.

Ludema, J., Wilmot, T., & Srivastva, S. (1997). Organizational hope: Reaffirming the constructive task of social and organizational inquiry. *Human Relations, 50*(8), 1015–1052.

Ludema, J. D. (2000). Leadership symposium 2000: Global staffing and retention. Appreciative Inquiry report on global staffing and retention presented at McDonald's Worldwide Convention, Orlando.

Ludema, J. D., Cooperrider, D. L., & Barrett, F. (2001). Appreciative inquiry: The power of the unconditional positive question. In P. Reason & H. Bradbury (Eds.), *Handbook of action research: Participative inquiry and practice* (pp. 189–199). London: Sage Publications.

Ludema, J.D., Whitney, D., Mohr, B., & Griffin, T. (2003). The appreciative inquiry summit: A practitioner's guide for leading positive large-group change. San Francisco: Berrett-Koehler.

Luechauer, D. L. (1999). Applying appreciative inquiry instead of problem-solving techniques to facilitate change. *Management Development Forum, 2*(1).

Mahé, S., & Gibbs, C. (2003). Birth of a global community: Appreciative inquiry as midwife to the United Religions Initiative. Euclid, OH: Lakeshore Communications.

Mann, A. et al. (2006, January). Adapting appreciative inquiry. *Consulting Today,* Retrieved from http://www.consultingtoday.com/topicindex/index.html.

Mann, A. J. (1997). An appreciative inquiry model for building partnerships. *Global Social Innovations, 1*(2), 41–44.

Mann, A. J. (2000). Variations on a theme: The flexibility of the 4-D model. *Global Social Innovations, 1*(3), 12–15.

Mantel, M. J., & Ludema, J. D. (2000). From local conversations to global change: Experiencing the worldwide web effect of appreciative inquiry. *Organization Development Journal, 18*(2), 42–53.

Markova, D., & Holland, B. (2006). Appreciative inquiry: A strategy for change in systemic leadership that builds on organizational strengths, not deficits. *School Administrator, 62.*

Marshak, R. J. (2005, March). Is there a new OD? *Seasonings: A Journal by Senior OD Practitioners.*

Martinetz, C. F. (2002, September). Appreciative inquiry as an organizational development tool. *Performance Improvement.*

McGehee, T. (200a). WHOOSH: Business in the fast lane: Unleashing the power of a creation company. Cambridge, MA: Perseus Publishing.

Mead, Margaret and her work on intergenerational learning, the Mead Centennial 2001, The Institute for Intercultural Studies, http://www.interculturalstudies.org/Mead/2001centennial.html.

Mellish, L. (2001). Appreciative inquiry at work. *AI Newsletter, 12*, 8.

Miller, C. J., Aguilar, C. R., Maslowski, L., & McDaniel, D. (2003). *The nonprofit's guide to the power of appreciative inquiry.* Denver: Community Development Institute.

Miller, M. G., Fitzgerald, S. P., Murrell, K. L., Preston, J., & Ambekar, R. (2005, March). Appreciative inquiry in building a transcultural strategic alliance. *Journal of Applied Behavioral Science, 42*(1), 91–110.

Mirvis, P. H. (1988). Organization development: Part I—An evolutionary perspective. In W. A. Pasmore & R. W. Woodman (Eds.), *Research in organizational change and development* (pp. 1–57). Greenwich, CT: JAI Press.

Mirvis, P. H. (1990). Merging of executive heart and mind in crisis management. In S. Srivastva & D. L. Cooperrider (Eds.), *Appreciative management and leadership: The power of positive thought and action in organizations* (pp. 55–90). San Francisco: Jossey-Bass.

Mirvis, P. H. (1997). "Soul work" in organizations. *Organization Science, 8*(2), 193–206.

Mohr, B. (2001). *A guide to appreciative inquiry.* Waltham, MA: Pegasus Communications.

Mohr, B., & Watkins, J. (2002). *The essentials of appreciative inquiry: A roadmap for creating positive futures.* Waltham, MA: Pegasus Communications.

Mohr, B. J. (2001). Appreciative inquiry: Igniting transformative action. *The Systems Thinker, 12*(1), 1–5.

Mohr, B. J., Smith, E. J, & Watkins, J. M. (2000). Appreciative inquiry and learning assessment. *OD Practitioner, 32*(1), 33–53.

Muscat, M. (1998). Imagine Chicago: Dreams and visions for a 'second city' of the future. *The Inner Edge, 1*(2), 23–24.

Muscat, M. (1998). The federal quality consulting group: Using the vision story process to rebuild an organization. *The Inner Edge, 1*(2), 18–19.

Newman, H. L., & Fitzgerald, S. P. (2001). Appreciative inquiry with an executive team: Moving along the action research continuum. *Organization Development Journal, 19*, 37–44.

Nicholas, S. (2005). Appreciative inquiry in hypnotherapy. *Hypnotherapy News.*

Nordbye, M., & Yaeger, T. (2003, November). Team development, the appreciative inquiry way. *Training Today.*

Odell, M. (2000). From conflict to cooperation: Approaches to building rural partnerships. *Global Social Innovations, 1*(3), 16–22.

Olson, E. E., & Eoyang, G. H. (2001). *Facilitating organization change: Lessons from complexity science.* San Francisco: Jossey-Bass/Pfeiffer.

Orem, S., Binkert, J., & Clancy, A. (2007). *Appreciative coaching: A positive process for change.* San Francisco: Jossey-Bass.

Paddock, S. S. (2003). *Appreciative inquiry in the Catholic Church.* Plano, TX: Thin Book Publishing.

Pages, M. (1990). The illusion and disillusion of appreciative management. In S. Srivastva & D. L. Cooperrider (Eds.), *Appreciative management and leadership: The power of positive thought and action in organizations* (Rev. ed.). (pp. 353–380). Euclid, OH: Lakeshore Communications.

Paine, L. S., & Rogers, G. C. (2001, July 27). Avon products. *Harvard Business Review*.

Pascale, R. T., & Sternin, J. (2005). Your company's secret change agents. *Harvard Business Review*.

Pepitone, J. S. (1995). Future training: A roadmap for restructuring the training Function. Dallas: AddVantage Learning Press.

Peterson, R. (1993). Design aid ™: A multimedia tool for appreciative organization design. *Organizational Development and Transformation*. California Institute of Integral Studies, 87.

Polak, F. (1973). *The image of the future*. San Francisco: Jossey-Bass.

Preskill, H., & Catsambas, T. T. (2006). *Reframing evaluation through appreciative inquiry*. Thousand Oaks, CA: Sage Publications.

Preskill, H., & Coghlan, A. (2004). *Using appreciative inquiry in evaluation: New directions for evaluation: No. 100*. San Francisco: Jossey-Bass.

Pullen, C. (2001, October). Appreciative inquiry in financial planning and life. *Journal of Financial Planning, 14*, 52–54.

Quinn, R. E. (2000). Change the world: How ordinary people can achieve extraordinary results. San Francisco: Jossey-Bass.

Radford, A. (1998–2007). Appreciative Inquiry Newsletter.

Raimy, E. (1998). Precious moments. *Human Resource Executive, 12*(11), 1, 26–29.

Rainey, M. A. (1996). An appreciative inquiry into the factors of culture continuity during leadership transition. *Organization Development Practitioner, 28*(1 & 2), 34–41.

Reed, J. (2006). *Appreciative inquiry: Research for change*. Thousand Oaks, CA: Sage Publications.

Reed, J., Pearson, P., Douglas, B., Swinburne, S., & Wilding, H. (2002, January). Going home from hospital—An appreciative inquiry study. *Health & Social Care in the Community, 10*, 36–45.

Reed, J., & Turner, J. (2005). Appreciating change in cancer services—An evaluation of service development strategies. *Journal of Health Organization Management, 19*(3), 163–176.

Ricketts, M. (2002). The glass is half full—Appreciative inquiry, experiential learning and organizational change. *Association of Experiential Education's AEE Horizon Newsletter* (Summer ed.).

Ricketts, M., & Willis, J. (2001). *Experience AI: A practitioner's guide to integrating appreciative inquiry and experiential learning*. Chagrin Falls, OH: Taos Institute Publications.

Rosenthal, R. (1969). *Pygmalion in the classroom*. New York: Holt, Rinehart and Winston.

Royal, C. (1994). The NTL diversity study: The use of appreciative inquiry to discover best experiences around diversity in a professional OD organization. Alexandra, VA: NTL Institute for Applied Behavioral Science.

Royal, C., & Hammond, S. (Eds.). (2001). *Lessons from the field: Applying appreciative inquiry*. Plano, TX: Thin Book Publishing.

Ryan, F. J., Soven, M., Smither, J., Sullivan, W. M., & VanBuskirk, W. R. (1999). Appreciative inquiry: Using personal narratives for initiating school reform. *The Clearing House, 72*(3), 164–167.

Salter, C. (2000, November). We're trying to change world history. *Fast* Company, 230.

Schiller, M. (1998). A dialogue about leadership & appreciative inquiry. *Organization Development Journal, 16*(4), 79–84.

Schiller, M., Riley, D., & Holland, B. M. (Eds.). (2001). *Appreciative leaders: In the eye of the beholder.* Chagrin Falls, OH: Taos Institute Publications.

Seligman, M. (1992). Helplessness: On development, depression and death. New York: W.H. Freeman.

Snyder, C. R., & McCullough, M. E. (2000). A positive psychology field of dreams: If you build it they will come. *Journal of Social and Clinical Psychology, 19.*

Sorensen, P. F., Gironda, L. A., Head, T. C., & Larsen, H. H. (1996). Global organization development: Lessons from Scandinavia. *Organization Development Journal, 14*(4), 46–52.

Sorensen, P. F., & Yaeger, T. F. (1997). Exploring organizational possibilities: Appreciative inquiry. *Training Today*, 7–8.

Sorensen, P. F., & Yaeger, T. F. (1998). A universal approach to change: Appreciative inquiry. *Training Today*, 7–8.

Sorensen, P. F., Yaeger, T. F., & Nicoll, D. (2000). Appreciative inquiry 2000: Fad or important new focus for OD? *OD Practitioner, 32*(1), 3–5.

Srivastva, S., & Barrett, F. J. (1986). *Executive power.* San Francisco: Jossey-Bass.

Srivastva, S., & Barrett, F. J. (1988). Foundations for executive integrity: Dialogue, diversity, development. In S. Srivastva (Ed.), *Executive integrity: The search for high human values in organizational life* (pp. 290–319). San Francisco: Jossey-Bass.

Srivastva, S., Bilimoria, D., Cooperrider, D. L., & Fry, R. E. (1995). Management and organization learning for positive global change. *Management Learning, 26*(1), 37–54.

Srivastva, S., & Cooperrider, D. L. (1986). The emergence of the egalitarian organization. *Human Relations, 39*(8), 683–724.

Srivastva, S., & Cooperrider, D. L. (Eds.). (1998). *Organizational wisdom and executive courage.* San Francisco: New Lexington Press.

Srivastva, S., & Cooperrider, D. L. (Eds.). (1999). *Appreciative management and leadership: The power of positive thought and action in organization* (Rev. ed.). Euclid, OH: Lakeshore Communications.

Stavros, J. M. (2000, Winter). Northern and southern perspectives of capacity building using an appreciative inquiry approach. *Journal of Global Social Innovations.*

Stavros, J. M., Cooperrider, D., & Kelley, L. (2003). Appreciative intent: Inspiration to SOAR. *AI Practitioner.*

Stavros, J. M., & Meda, A. K. (2003). An assisted living center: Cultivating the positive core through appreciative inquiry. Paper presented at the Southwest Academy of Management Annual Meeting, Houston, TX, and the Organization Development Institute Annual Conference, Williamsburg, VA.

Stavros, J. M., & Torres, C. B. (2005). *Dynamic relationships: Unleashing the power of appreciative inquiry in daily living.* Chagrin Falls, OH: Taos Institute Publications.

Stavros, J. M., Seiling, J., & Castelli, P. (2007). Appreciative form of capacity building for organizational accomplishment: Lessons from a network of nonprofit organizations. *Journal of North American Management Society.*

Stavros, J. M., & Sprangel, J. (in press). Applying appreciative inquiry to deliver strategic change: OTC. In *Creative conversations for organisational change*. United Kingdom: Kogan Page.

Stetson, N., & Miller, C. (2003, April 1). Appreciative inquiry: A new way of leading change without resistance. *Community College Times, 15*.

Stetson, N., & Miller, C. (2003, May). Lead change in educational organizations with appreciative inquiry. *Consulting Today*.

Stetson, N. E., & Miller, C. R. (2004). *Appreciative inquiry in the community college: Early stories of success*. Phoenix: League for Innovation in the Community College.

Strauss, A., & Corbin, J. (1990). *Basics of qualitative research: Grounded theory procedures and techniques*. Newbury Park, CA: Sage Publications.

Sullivan, M. (2004, June). The promise of appreciative inquiry in library organizations. *Library Trends*.

Sutherland, J., & Stavros, J. (2003, November). The heart of appreciative strategy. *AI Practitioner*.

Tang, Y., & Joiner, C. (2006). *Synergic inquiry: A collaboration action methodology*. Thousand Oaks, CA: Sage Publications.

Tenkasi, R. (2000). The dynamics of cultural knowledge and learning in creating viable theories of global change and action. *Organization Development Journal, 18*(2), 74–90.

Thatchenkery, T. J. (1996). Affirmation as facilitation: A postmodernist paradigm in change management. *OD Practitioner, 28*(1), 12–22.

Thatchenkery, T. (2005). *Appreciative sharing of knowledge*. Chagrin Falls, OH: Taos Institute Publications.

Thatchenkery, T. (2007). *Appreciative inquiry and knowledge management: A social constructionist perspective*. Cheltenham, United Kingdom: Edward Elgar Publishing.

Thatchenkery, T., & Metzker, C. (2006). *Appreciative intelligence: Seeing the mighty oak in the acorn*. San Francisco: Berrett-Koehler.

Trosten-Bloom, A., & Whitney, D. (1999). Appreciative inquiry: The path to positive change. In Key, M. K. (Ed.), *Managing change in healthcare: Innovative solutions for people-based organization*. New York: McGraw-Hill Healthcare Financial Management Association.

Trosten-Bloom, A., & Whitney, D. (2001). Creative AI approaches for whole-system culture change: Hunter Douglas Window Fashions Division. Golden, CO: Corporation for Positive Change.

Trosten-Bloom, A., & Whitney, D. (2001). *Positive change @ work: The appreciative inquiry approach to whole system change at Hunter*. [Videotape and accompanying workbook]. (Available from Corporation for Positive Change, PO Box 3257, Taos, NM, 87571)

UC Berkeley Extension guides higher education to positive change. (2002, April 18). Business Wire, Retrieved from http://home.businesswire.com.

Van Marter, J. (2006, September 27). Executives Look for "A New Way." Article archived at http://www.pcusa.org/pcnews/2006/06491.htm.

Van Vuuren, L. J., & Crous, F. (2005, April). Utilizing appreciative inquiry (AI) in creating a shared meaning of ethics in organizations. *Journal of Business Ethics, 57*(4), 399–412.

Watkins, J. M., & Cooperrider, D. L. (1996). Organizational inquiry model for global social change organizations. *Organization Development Journal, 14*(4), 97–112.

Watkins, J. M., & Cooperrider, D. L. (2000). Appreciative inquiry: A transformative paradigm. *OD Practitioner, 32*(1), 6–12.

Watkins, J. M., & Mohr, B. J. (2001). *Appreciative inquiry: Change at the speed of imagination*. San Francisco: Jossey-Bass/Pfeiffer.

Webb, L., & Rockey, S. (2005). Organizational change inside and out. *Journal for Nonprofit Management*, 17–27.

Webb, L. D. (1999). Appreciative inquiry as a way to jump start change. *At Work, 8*(2), 16–18.

Weisbord, M. (1994). *Discovering common ground*. San Francisco: Berrett-Koehler.

Weisbord, M., & Janoff, S. (2000). *Future search: An action guide to finding common ground in organizations and communities*, (2nd ed.). San Francisco: Berrett-Koehler.

West, D., & Thomas, L. (2001). *Looking for the 'bigger picture': An application of the appreciative inquiry method in Renfrewshire Council for Voluntary Services*. Weinheim, Germany: Beltz Publishing.

Whalley, C. (1998). Using appreciative inquiry to overcome post-OFSTED syndrome. *Management in Education, 12*(3), 6–7.

White, T. H. (1996). Working in interesting times. *Vital Speeches of the Day, 62*(15), 472–474.

Whitney, D. (1996). Postmodern principles and practices for large scale organization change and global cooperation. *Organization Development Journal, 14*(4), 53–68.

Whitney, D. (1998). Let's change the subject and change our organization: An appreciative inquiry approach to organization change. *Career Development International, 3*(7), 314–319.

Whitney, D. (2001). Postmodern challenges to organization development. *HRD Strategies for 2000 AD.*

Whitney, D. (2004). Appreciative inquiry and the elevation of organizational consciousness. In D.L. Cooperrider & M. Avital (Eds.), *Constructive discourse and human organization: Advances in appreciative inquiry* (Vol. 1). Oxford, UK: Elsevier Science.

Whitney, D. (2007). Designing organizations as if life matters: Principles of appreciative organizing. In M. Avital, R. J. Boland, & D. L. Cooperrider (Eds.), *Designing information and organizations with a positive lens: Advances in appreciative inquiry* (Vol. 2). Oxford, UK: Elsevier Science.

Whitney, D., & Cooperrider, D. L. (1998). The appreciative inquiry summit: Overview and applications. *Employment Relations Today, 25*(2), 17–28.

Whitney, D., & Cooperrider, D. L. (2000). The appreciative inquiry summit: An emerging methodology for whole system positive change. *OD Practitioner, 32*(1), 13–26.

Whitney, D., Cooperrider, D. L., Garrison, M., & Moore, J. (2001). Appreciative inquiry and culture change at GET: Launching a positive revolution. In *Appreciative inquiry and organization transformation*. Westport, CT: Quorum Books.

Whitney, D., Cooperrider, D. L., Kaplin, B., & Trosten-Bloom, A. (2001). *Encyclopedia of positive questions, volume one: Using appreciative inquiry to bring out the best in your organization.* Euclid, OH: Lakeshore Communications.

Whitney, D., & Schau, C. (1998). Appreciative inquiry: An innovative process for organization change. *Employment Relations Today, 25*(1), 11–21.

Whitney D., & Trosten-Bloom, A. (2003). *The power of appreciative inquiry: A practical guide to positive change.* San Francisco: Berrett-Koehler.

Whitney, D., Trosten-Bloom, A., Cherney, J., & Fry, R. (2004). Appreciative team building: Positive questions to bring out the best in your team. *iUniverse.*

Williams, R. F. (1996). Survey guided appreciative inquiry: A case study. *OD Practitioner, 28*(1&2), 43–51.

Wilmot, T. B., & Ludema, J. D. (1995). Odyssey into organizational hope. In D. Marcic (Ed.), *Organizational behavior: Experiences and cases* (3rd ed.). (pp. 109–112). Eagan, MN: West Publishing.

Wilson, T. (1995). Imagine shaping a better Chicago. *Chicago Tribune,* p. 2.

Woodman, R. W., & Pasmore, W. A. (Eds.). (1987). *Research in organizational change and development: An annual series featuring advances in theory, methodology and research.* Greenwich, CT: JAI Press.

Yaeger, T. (1999). Responses from Russia: An appreciative inquiry interview with Konstantin Korotov, RODP. *Organization Development Journal, 17*(3), 85–87.

Yaeger, T. F., & Sorensen, P. F. (2005, July). A seasoned perspective on appreciative inquiry. *Seasonings: A Journal by Senior OD Practitioners.*

Yballe, L., & O'Connor, D. (2000). Appreciative pedagogy: Constructing positive models for learning. *Journal of Management Education, 24*(4), 474–483.

Zakariasen, K. L., Zakariasen, K. A., & Lodding, D. (2002, February). The practice of your future: Creating a vision. *JADA, 133,* 213–218.

Zantua, M. (2005, Oct 17). Appreciative inquiry as a tool for self-sufficiency and peace. Center for Learning Connections, Retrieved from http://learningconnections.org.

Zemke, R. (1999, June 1). Don't fix that company. *Training Magazine, 36,* 26.

Zemke, R. (2000). David Cooperrider: Man on a mission. *Training, 37*(11), 52–53.

Zhexembayeva, N. (2006, August). Becoming sustainable: Tools and resources for successful organizational transformation. GreenBiz.com, Retrieved from http://www.greenbiz.com/news/columns_third.cfm?NewsID=33335.

Zhexembayeva, N. (2006, November). Management knowledge leading positive change: Are we ready to tip? GreenBiz.com, Retrieved from http://www.greenbiz.com/news/columns_third.cfm?NewsID=34204.

Zolno, S. (2002). Appreciative inquiry: New thinking at work. In E. Biech, *The 2002 Annual: Developing human resources.* San Francisco: Jossey-Bass/Pfeiffer.

ZurBonsen, M., & Maleh, C. (2001). *Appreciative inquiry (AI): Der Weg zu Spitzenleistungen.* Weinheim, Basel, Germany: Beltz Publishing.

AI Dissertations and Theses

(Unless noted, dissertations can be found on the AI Commons.)

Aitken, J. (1996). *Growing the empowerment organization*. San Francisco: California Institute of Integral Studies.

Allen, M. D. (in progress). *What makes an effective public service agency?* San Francisco: California Institute of Integral Studies.

Arcoleo, D. P. (2001). *Underneath appreciative inquiry*. Santa Barbara, CA: The Fielding Institute.

Bieschke, J. M. (in progress). *Transgenerational transference of organizational values*. Culver City, CA: Pepperdine University.

Bowling, C. J. (2000). *Human cooperation: Appreciative processes for creating images of governance*. Cleveland, OH: Case Western Reserve University.

Buckingham, S. T. (1998). *Leadership skills in public health nursing: An appreciative inquiry*. Victoria, British Columbia, Canada: Royal Roads University.

Chandler, D. T. (1998). *Appreciative inquiry as a means of engaging commitment, loyalty, and involvement among members of an organization*. Malibu, CA: Pepperdine University.

Chapagain, C. P. (2004). *Human resource capacity building through appreciative inquiry approach in achieving developmental goals*. Gulfport, MS: College of Business and Economics, Human Resource Management, Madison University.

Cockell, J. (2005). *Making magic: Facilitating collaborative processes*. Vancouver, British Columbia, Canada: University of British Columbia.

Cooperrider, D. L. (1986). *Appreciative inquiry: Toward a methodology for understanding and enhancing organizational innovation*. Cleveland, OH: Case Western Reserve University.

Drabczyk, A. L. (2005). *Citizen and emergency responder shared values*. Terre Haute, IN: Indiana State University.

Drogin, S. L. (1997). *An appreciative inquiry into spirituality and work*. Seattle, WA: Seattle University.

Furman, D. (in progress). *The qwest for excellence in formal education in the United States: The Mexican experience*. Rexburg, ID: University of Idaho.

Hargis, L. C. (2006). *Appreciative inquiry in higher education as an effective communication tool: A case study*. ProQuest/UMI.

Head, R. L. (1999). *Appreciative inquiry as a team development intervention for newly formed heterogeneous groups*. Lisle, IL: Benedictine University.

Hlatshwayo, G. (2001). *Innovative strategies for building collaborative capacity in large-scale global organizing: A case narrative of birthing the United Religions Initiative*. Cleveland, OH: Case Western Reserve University.

Hopper, V. L. (1991). *An appreciative study of highest human values in a major healthcare organization*. Cleveland, OH: Case Western Reserve University.

Johnson, P. C. (1998). *Straight to the heart: Cleveland leaders shaping the next millennium*. Cleveland, OH: Case Western Reserve University.

Johnson, P. C. (1992). *Organizing for global social change: Toward a global integrity ethic*. Cleveland, OH: Case Western Reserve University.

Jones, D. A. (1999). *Appreciative inquiry: A field experiment focusing on turnover in the fast food industry.* Lisle, IL: Benedictine University.

Ludema, J. A. (1997). *Narrative inquiry: Collective storytelling as a source of hope, knowledge, and action in organizational life.* Cleveland, OH: Case Western Reserve University.

Maber, T. B. (2006). *Creating a great workplace: Exploring shared values and employee engagement through appreciative inquiry.* Victoria, British Columbia, Canada: Royal Roads University.

Magee, J. A. (2002). *A condition of the heart.* Victoria, British Columbia, Canada: Royal Roads University.

McGough, L. (2006). *A comparison of appreciative inquiry and nominal group techniques in the evaluation of a college counseling center.* Buffalo, NY: University at Buffalo, State University of New York.

Mellish, L. E. (2000). *Appreciative inquiry at work.* Brisbane, Australia: Mellish & Associates.

Moehle, M. R. (in progress). *Student perceptions of band.* Cleveland, OH: Case Western Reserve University.

Ohs, A. (in progress). *Appreciative inquiry supporting literacy coach empowerment.* Prescott, AZ: Prescott College.

Peelle, III, H. E. (2005). *Appreciative inquiry and creative problem solving in cross-functional teams.* Phoenix, AZ: University of Phoenix.

Petersen, B. A. (2001). *Developing effective staff teams.* Vermillion, SD: University of South Dakota.

Peterson, R. A. (1993). *Designaid ™: A multimedia tool for appreciative organization design.* San Francisco, CA: California Institute of Integral Studies.

Portzline, B. J. (2006). *An appreciative inquiry approach to evaluation practice.* Albuquerque, NM: University of New Mexico.

Pratt, C. S. (1996). *Constructing unitary reality: An appreciative inquiry.* Cleveland, OH: Case Western Reserve University.

Pullicino, E. J. (2002). *Information technology as a marketing tool.* Ibragg, Malta: C. Testa & Co.

Quintanilla, G. L. (1999). *An appreciative inquiry evaluation of a science enrichment program for children and youth: Preliminary findings.* San Diego, CA: San Diego State University.

Rabinowitz, S. L. (2005). *Organizational stress management: A case for positive psychology-based psychoeducational interventions.* Silver Spring, MD: Pepperdine University: MSOD Program.

Rafferty, T. M. (1999). *Whose children are these? An appreciative inquiry.* Cincinnati, OH: The Union Institute.

Richer, M. (in progress). *Effect of appreciative inquiry on personnel retention in healthcare.* Montreal, Quebec, Canada: McGill University School of Nursing.

Robinson-Easley, C. A. (1998). *The role of appreciative inquiry in the fight to save our youth.* Lisle, IL: Benedictine University.

Royal, C. A. (1997). *The fractal initiative: Appreciative inquiry and rethinking social identities*. Santa Barbara, CA: Fielding Institute.

Seifert, T. (2001). *Creating exceptional customer service in a register of deeds office*. Vermillion, SD: University of South Dakota.

Smith, S. R. (2003). *Creating a growth oriented environment using appreciate inquiry in a nondenominational church*. Cleveland, OH: Cleveland State University.

Sperry, S. L. (1999). *A descriptive study of the impact of appreciative processes on self and organization-based self-esteem*. Malibu, CA: Pepperdine University.

Stavros, J. M. (1998). *Capacity building: An appreciative approach: A relational process of building your organization's future*. Cleveland, OH: Case Western Reserve University.

Tamang, B. B. (2004). *Appreciative inquiry approach*. Kathmandu, Nepal: Central Department of Sociology/Anthropology, Tribhuvan University.

Thatchenkery, T. J. (1994). *Hermeneutic processes in organizations: A study in relationships between observers and those observed*. Cleveland, OH: Case Western Reserve University.

Tripp, P., & Zipsie, M. (2002). *The introduction of appreciative inquiry to the U.S. Navy using appreciative inquiry interviews and the large group intervention with applications to U.S. Marine Corps logistics strategic management*. Monterey, CA: Naval Postgraduate School.

van der Haar, D. (2002). *A positive change*. Tilburg, Netherlands: University of Tilburg.

Wasserman, I. C. (2004). *Discursive processes that foster dialogic moments*. Santa Barbara, CA: The Fielding Graduate Institute.

Wilmot, T. M. (1995). *The global excellence in management program: A two year evaluation of 25 organizations using appreciative inquiry*. Cleveland, OH: Case Western Reserve University.

Wishart, C. G. (1998). *Toward a language of human abundance: The holistic human logic of sustainable development*. Cleveland, OH: Case Western Reserve University.

Withers, D. A. (2006). *Appreciative inquiry: Designing for engagement in technology-mediated learning*. Vancouver, British Columbia, Canada: Simon Fraser University.

Wood, K. D. (in progress). *Appreciative inquiry participant's understanding and meaning making of transformative experiences and transformative learning*. Santa Barbara, CA: Fielding Graduate University.

Web Sites

Appreciative Inquiry Commons: http://appreciativeinquiry.cwru.edu

AI Practitioner: http://www.aipractitioner.com

Case Western Reserve University Weatherhead School of Management, Center for Business as an Agent of World Benefit: http://worldbenefit.cwru.edu

IISD (International Institute of Sustainable Development) MYRADA Appreciative Inquiry Project: http://iisd.ca/ai/myrada.htm

Images and Voices of Hope: http://www.ivofhope.org

Imagine Chicago: http://www.imaginechicago.org

Nepal Appreciative Inquiry National Network (NAINN): http://nainn.blogspot.com

SIKT, Scandinavian Institute for Creative Thinking: http://www.sikt.se

The Taos Institue: http://www.taosinstitute.net

United Religions Initiative: http://www.uri.org

Glossary

A

Affirmative competence—The organization draws on the human capacity to appreciate positive possibilities by selectively focusing on current and past strengths, successes, and potentials.

Affirmative topic choice—A topic identified in the *Discovery* phase that guides the formation of the interview guide. It is a positive descriptive phase representing the organization's focus for change.

AI Summit—A large-scale meeting process that focuses on discovering and developing an organization's positive change core and designing it into the organization's strategic business processes, systems, and culture.

Anticipatory learning—A type of learning that creates positive images of the future.

Anticipatory Principle—A fundamental principle that says one's positive images of the future lead one's positive actions. This is the increasingly energizing basis and presumption of Appreciative Inquiry.

Appreciate—A verb that means "to value something." It's the act of recognizing the best in the people or the world around us; to affirm the past and present strengths, successes and potentials; to perceive those things that give life (health, vitality, and excellence) to living systems. It also means to increase in value (e.g., the economy has appreciated in value). Synonyms: valuing, prizing, esteeming, and honoring.

Appreciative Inquiry—The cooperative search for the best in people, their organizations, and the world around them. It involves systematic discovery of what gives a system "life" when the system is most effective and capable in economic, ecological, and human terms.

Appreciative Inquiry Summit—A three- to four-day Appreciative Inquiry intervention that seeks to gather the whole system in one room to collectively go through all phases of the 4-D Cycle. This process can include hundreds to thousands of participants.

Appreciative interview—An interview that uncovers what gives life to an organization, a department, or a community when at its best.

Appreciative learning culture—An organizational culture that fosters and develops the following competencies to create an appreciative learning system: affirmative, expansive, generative, and collaborative competencies.

Appreciative paradigm—A unique perspective of the organizational world that views organizations as mysteries to be embraced.

C

Capacity building—A relational process that builds an organization's future to pursue its vision, mission, and goals and sustain its existence. This process pushes boundaries to develop and strengthen an organization and its people.

Change agent—A person adept in the art of reading, understanding, and analyzing organizations as living, human constructions.

Chaordic organization—An organizational structure (such as Appreciative Inquiry Consulting, LLC) that allows its owners to be autonomous while at the same time connecting all of them around a compelling shared identity and meaningful purpose.

Coconstruct (cocreate)—A term used to describe a collaborative construction of an organization's future state. It is developed out of social construction theory, which states that human systems create their social reality by the words they speak.

Cognitivism—In contrast to behaviorism, this school of thought claims that psychology should be concerned with a person's internal representations of the world and with the internal or functional organization of the mind.

Collaborative competence—The organization creates forums in which members engage in ongoing dialogue and exchange unique perspectives.

Constructionist Principle—A fundamental principle and belief in Appreciative Inquiry that says human knowledge and organizational destiny are interwoven. To be effective, organizations must be understood as human constructs.

Continuity—A part of the Appreciative Inquiry process that seeks to maintain the best of an organization's history, image, and culture during the time of the organization's transformation into the future state envisioned by its stakeholders.

Continuity search—A search that seeks out and then preserves what the organization does best.

Core competencies—The value capabilities that assist an organization in creating strength bases relative to key competition.

D

Deficit-based approach to problem solving—An approach that begins with seeking out the problem, the weak link in the system. Then diagnosis and alternative solutions are recommended. Appreciative Inquiry challenges this traditional paradigm with an "affirmative" approach to embrace an organization's challenges in a positive light.

Design—The third phase of the 4-D model in which participants create the provocative proposition by determining the ideal, "how can it be?" The organization's future is coconstructed. This is where the stakeholders work together to transfer the dreams.

Design elements—Those elements that are considered in the social architecture of the organization's future.

Destiny—The fourth phase of the 4-D model in which participants continue to coconstruct their preferred future by defining "what will be?" Stakeholders begin the planning and implementation process to bring to life the dreams that have been designed. Stakeholders create action plans and assign responsibility commitments.

Dialogue—An exchange of ideas or opinions: *achieving constructive dialogue with all elements*. It is about understanding and learning that builds trust and enables people to create new possibilities.

Discover, Dream, Design, Destiny—4-D Cycle—The model that displays the Appreciative Inquiry approach in four phases that is designed to meet the unique challenges of an organization and its industry.

Discovery—The first phase of the 4-D model in which participants inquire into the life-giving forces of the organization to begin to understand and build their positive core. Participants uncover and value the best of "what is?" This information is generated through the engaging appreciative interviews.

Distinctive competencies—Strengths that give an organization a superior advantage in the marketplace.

Dream—The second phase of the 4-D model in which participants dialogue and create a dream for the organization. A collective vision is defined as "What might be?"

E

Expansive competence—The organization challenges habits and conventional practices, provoking stakeholders to experiment in the margins, make expansive promises that challenges them to stretch in new directions, and evoke a set of higher values and ideals that inspire them to passionate engagement.

F

Fateful—The words one chooses and the questions one asks determine the events and answers one finds.

Future Search—A methodology created by Marv Weisbord and Sandra Janoff that allows the whole system (stakeholders) to cocreate the organization's future.

G

Generative competence—The organization constructs integrative systems that allow stakeholders to see the results of their actions, to recognize that they are making a meaningful contribution, and to experience a sense of progress.

Generative learning—The type of organizational learning that emphasizes continuous experimentation, systematic thinking, and a willingness to think outside the limits of an issue.

Generative metaphor intervention—A form of intervention used to help a group build (1) liberated aspirations and the development of hope, (2) interpersonal relationships, (3) strategic consensus around a positive vision for the future, (4) a renewed collective will to act, and (5) egalitarian language to reflect a new sense of unity and mutuality in the joint creation of the group's future. (Definition is from the article "Generative Metaphor Intervention: A New Approach for Working with Systems Divided by Conflict and Caught in Defensive Perception" by Frank J. Barrett.)

H

Habitus mentalis—Habitual styles of thought.

Heliotropic—A term that implies that people have an observable and largely "automatic" tendency to move in the direction of affirming images of the future.

I

Imagination—The phase of the AI approach to strategic planning when time is spent dreaming and coconstructing the preferred future.

Improvisational capacity—The capacity to allow for change to happen with endless variation. Appreciative Inquiry is not just one way of change; there are infinite ways for the *Destiny* phase to occur.

Indra's Net—A web of relationships that sparkle, nourish, and amplify. It is an ancient image of oneness and diversity.

Inner dialogue—A term used to describe the conversation that goes on within the mind of a person and within the collective mind of the organization. An organization's inner dialogue can typically be ascertained by listening to the informal communication channels within the organization.

Innovation—The phase of the AI approach to strategic planning that begins the strategic design of short-term objectives, tactical and functional plans, integrated programs, structures, and systems to best achieve the desired future.

Inquiry—A verb that describes the act of exploration and discovery. It also refers to the act of asking questions and of being open to seeing new potentials and possibilities. Synonyms: discovery, search, study, and systematic exploration.

Interview guide—The primary data collection tool used during the *Discovery* phase of Appreciative Inquiry. Interview questions are determined based on the affirmative topic choice. These questions are open-ended and designed to elicit rich storytelling from the interviewee. Also known as the interview protocol.

L

Learned helpfulness—Learning that understands what went well and applies what might be done to strengthen the next time.

Life-giving forces—Those elements or experiences within an organization's past and/or present that represent the organization's strengths when it is operating at its very best. A life-giving force can be a single moment in time, such as a particular customer transaction; or it can be large in scope. It can be any aspect that contributes to the organization's highest points and most valued experiences or characteristics.

Logical empiricism—Logical positivism (later referred to as logical empiricism) holds that philosophy should aspire to the same sort of rigor as science. Philosophy should provide strict criteria for judging sentences true, false, and meaningless.

M

Metacognitive—The awareness of one's own cognitive systems and knowledge and insight into its workings. It is the awareness that prompts a person to write reminders to himself or herself to avoid forgetting something.

Metaphor—An element or a figure of speech in which an expression is used to refer to something that denotes a suggested similarity. In Appreciative Inquiry, metaphors are used because they have the power to facilitate "meaning making" and to generate a better understanding within the minds of the receiver and listener.

N

Novelty—Taking the new parts of the positive core identified in the Discovery and Dream phases and integrating them with the past strengths of the system to design what it takes to move the system forward.

O

Open space technology—A process created by Harrison Owen that allows the stakeholder to discuss what he or she can and will do to contribute to the realization of the organizational dream as articulated in the provocative propositions. This technique can be used during the *Design* phase and Appreciative Inquiry Summit.

Organization architecture—The model for designing an organization's future. This is where the design elements are selected to create the ideal organization.

P

Paradigm—The generally accepted perspective of a particular discipline, theory, or mind-set at a given time.

Placebo effect—A process created in the twentieth century in which projected images, as reflected in positive belief, ignite a healing process that can be as powerful as conventional therapy.

Poetic Principle—A fundamental principle and belief in the Appreciative Inquiry approach that says human organizations are like open books. The story of the system is constantly being coauthored, and it is open to infinite presentations.

Positive core—That which makes up the best of an organization and its people.

Positive image—positive action—An Appreciative Inquiry theory that posits the more positive and hopeful the image of the future, the more positive the present day action.

Positive Principle—A fundamental principle and belief in the Appreciative Inquiry approach that says that momentum for change requires large amounts of positive affect and social bonding, attitudes such as hope, inspiration, and the sheer joy of creating with one another.

Pragmatic—A school of philosophy that is characterized by consequences, utility, and practicality as vital components of truth.

Principle of Simultaneity—A fundamental principle and belief within Appreciative Inquiry thought that recognizes that inquiry and change are not separate moments, but are simultaneous.

Problem-solving paradigm—A fundamental perspective that views organizations as problems to be solved.

Provocative propositions—Statements that bridge the best of "what is" with an organization's vision of "what might be." It becomes a written articulation of the organization's desired future state that is written in the present tense to guide the planning and operations in the future. Also known as possibility proposition and possibility statements.

Pygmalion effect—An area of research that provides empirical understanding of the relational pathways of the positive image-positive action dynamic.

S

Sense-making—A term from action research that represents the analytical process within Appreciative Inquiry where the organization defines and learns about the change.

Social architecture—It addresses the design elements critical to an organization to support the positive core. The first step in the *Design* phase is to identify this architecture.

Social constructionism—The idea that a social system creates or determines its own reality.

Strategic inquiry—Part of the SOAR approach to strategy in which an organization's greatest **S**trengths and **O**pportunities are discovered and explored among the participants. The participants are invited to share their **A**spirations and coconstruct their most preferred future. Then recognition and reward programs are designed to inspire employees to achieve measurable **R**esults.

Sustainable development—Forms of progress that meet the needs of the present without compromising the ability of future generations to meet their needs.

Sustainable enterprise—A firm or an organization that maintains and re-creates itself over time while simultaneously attending to the triple bottom line of social, environmental, and economic benefits being distributed to the entire world..

Systematic management—A style of management that uses a fixed and organized plan.

T

Theme identification—Part of the *Dream* phase of the Appreciative Inquiry process where participants identify important threads from the interview data and summary sheets that pinpoint life-giving forces within the organization.

Transformative—Having the power or tendency to transform. To change a system in nature, disposition, heart, character, or the like; to convert. Appreciative Inquiry is a transformative process for any organization.

Triple bottom line—Focuses on economic prosperity, environmental quality, and (the element business has tended to overlook) social justice and people. Also, financial well-being is one of three important criteria for success; the other two are environmental sustainability and social well-being.

U

Utopian—Utopia, in its most common and general meaning, refers to a hypothetical perfect society. The word has also been used to describe actual communities founded in attempts to create such a society. The adjective *utopian* is often used to refer to good (physically, socially, economically, or politically) but impossible proposals.

W

Whole system—In an AI organizational summit, a cross section of as many interested parties as is practical.

Whole System Change—A term used to refer to the ultimate goal of Appreciative Inquiry to transform an entire organization at one time. Methodologies used include AI Summits, Future Search, and Open Space Technologies.

Whole systems process—A framework for integrating multiple organizational change initiatives into a well-designed, highly effective coherent whole.

Wonder—Rapt attention or astonishment at something awesomely mysterious or new to one's experience.

Index

THE
TAOS
INSTITUTE PUBLICATIONS
▲▲▲▲▲▲▲▲▲▲▲▲▲▲▲▲▲▲▲▲▲▲▲▲

The Taos Institute is a nonprofit organization dedicated to the development of social constructionist theory and practices for purposes of world benefit. Constructionist theory and practice locates the source of meaning, value, and action in communicative relations among people. Chief importance is placed on relational process and its outcomes for the welfare of all. Taos Institute Publications (TIP) offers contributions to cutting-edge theory and practice in social construction. These books are designed for scholars, practitioners, students, and the openly curious. The **Focus Book Series** provides brief introductions and overviews that illuminate theories, concepts, and useful practices. The **Books for Professionals Series** provides in-depth works focusing on recent developments in theory and practice. Books in both series are particularly relevant to social scientists and to practitioners concerned with individual, family, organizational, community, and societal change. Some of the earliest and leading books on Appreciative Inquiry and one of the core principles of AI—social construction—are found within the series of TIP books. We invite you to join in the conversation through these books.

Kenneth J. Gergen
President, Board of Directors
The Taos Institute

For information about the Taos Institute, visit http://www.taosinstitute.net.

Taos Institute Publications

Focus Book Series

Appreciative Inquiry: A Positive Approach to Building Cooperative Capacity (2005), by Frank Barrett and Ronald Fry

Dynamic Relationships: Unleashing the Power of Appreciative Inquiry in Daily Living (2005), by Jacqueline Stavros and Cheri B. Torres

Appreciative Sharing of Knowledge: Leveraging Knowledge Management for Strategic Change (2004), by Tojo Thatchekery

Social Construction: Entering the Dialogue (2004), by Kenneth J. Gergen and Mary Gergen

The Appreciative Organization (2001), by Harlene Anderson, David Cooperrider, Ken Gergen, Mary Gergen, Sheila McNamee, and Diana Whitney

Appreciative Leaders: In the Eye of the Beholder (2001), edited by Marge Schiller, Bea Mah Holland, and Deanna Riley

Experience AI: A Practitioner's Guide to Integrating Appreciative Inquiry and Experiential Learning (2001) by Miriam Ricketts and Jim Willis

Books for Professionals Series

Horizons in Buddhist Psychology: Practice, Research & Theory (2006), edited by Maurits Kwee, Kenneth J. Gergen, and Fusako Koshikawa

Therapeutic Realities: Collaboration, Oppression and Relational Flow (2006), by Kenneth J. Gergen

SocioDynamic Counselling: A Practical Guide to Meaning Making (2004), by R. Vance Peavy

Experiential Exercises in Social Construction: A Fieldbook for Creating Change (2004), by Robert Cottor, Alan Asher, Judith Levin, and Cindy Weiser

Dialogues About a New Psychology (2004), by Jan Smedslund

For online ordering of books from Taos Institute Publications, visit

http://www.taospub.net or http://www.taosinstitutepublications.net.

For further information, call 1-888-999-TAOS or 1-440-338-6733 or write books@taosinstitute.net or taosinstitutepublishing@alltel.net.

Mission

The Center for Positive Organizational Scholarship is a community of scholars devoted to energizing and transforming organizations through research on the theory and practice of positive organizing and leadership.

Key Activities	Domains of Excellence	

Key Activities

- Create and test new theories of positive organizational behavior and research instruments to measure positive organizational phenomena
- Develop and market POS educational cases and tools
- Disseminate POS ideas and intellectual products to scholars, students, corporations, nonprofits, and communities.
- Develop co-learning partnerships with select companies and nonprofit organizations.

Domains of Excellence

- Compassion
- Organizational Virtuousness
- Positive Emotions
- Positive Identity
  - Reflected Best Self
- Positive Leadership
  - Empowerment
  - Fundamental State of Leadership

- Positive Social Capital
  - Energy Networks
  - Generalized Reciprocity
  - High-Quality Connections
- Resilience
- Thriving
- Values

Faculty

The Core Faculty of the Center are Wayne Baker (director), Kim Cameron, Jane Dutton, Bob Quinn, Gretchen Spreitzer, and Lynn Wooten, who are joined by Faculty Associates (POS scholars at the University of Michigan) and Faculty Affiliates (POS scholars at institutions and organizations around the world). The faculty of the Center are members of a large, global network of scholars working to push the frontiers of POS.

Positive Organizational Scholarship

Positive Organizational Scholarship (POS) is an exciting new movement in organizational studies that draws on path-breaking work in the organizational and social sciences. "Positive" indicates the discipline's affirmative bias; "organizational" focuses on processes and conditions in organizational contexts; and "scholarship" reflects the rigor, theory, and scientific procedures that ground the POS approach.

The premise of POS research is that by understanding the drivers of positive behavior in the workplace, organizations and individuals can flourish. POS does not adopt one particular theory or research method but draws from the full spectrum of theories and methods to understand, explain, predict, and create high performance.

Center for Positive Organizational Scholarship • 701 Tappan Avenue • Stephen M. Ross School of Business

› University of Michigan • Ann Arbor, MI 48109

(734) 647-8154 • positiveorg@umich.edu • http://www.bus.umich.edu/Positive/ • Projects Coordinator: Janet Max

STEPHEN M. ROSS SCHOOL OF BUSINESS
AT THE UNIVERSITY OF MICHIGAN

Statement of Appreciative Inquiry Consulting

Appreciative Inquiry Consulting, LLC (AIC) is a global network of consultants, academic researchers, business leaders, and individuals committed to creating a positive revolution in change by using Appreciative Inquiry (AI) to engage the "positive core" of all people and all living systems and to expand that rich potential, creating organizations that are themselves agents of world benefit.

AIC is committed to the conceptual and practical advancement of Appreciative Inquiry, including its constructionist, scientific, and spiritual foundations. As a community, we realize that AI is in a state of evolution; and as long as the inquiry part of AI is alive, it will continue to contribute to break new ground. We as a community are constantly seeking creative links and synergies with related and diverse approaches that share in the search for new frontiers of positive change. At the heart of AIC is the sharing of knowledge and practices, the collaboration on projects and research of mutual interest, and peer-to-peer sharing and conferences. The AIC community benefits from a common identity in creating marketing materials, products, and services.

The AIC web site showcases our members' work and provides an evolving resource pool of designs, templates, working papers, protocols, and other artifacts of members' collective work and learning in AIC. Our office and web site can assist those looking for AI practitioners and coordinate a referral system to link practitioners throughout the network for global consulting and collaboration.

Membership in AIC is open to all who share its purpose and principles. The web site (www.aiconsulting.org) lists the purpose and principles and includes a description of the process for joining the positive revolution in change for which AIC stands.

Appreciative Inquiry Consulting, LLC
ManagingPartner@aiconsulting.org
www.aiconsulting.org

About the Authors

Dr. David L. Cooperrider is professor and chair of the SIGMA Program for Human Cooperation and Global Action at the Weatherhead School of Management at Case Western Reserve University. He has served as researcher and consultant to a wide variety of organizations, including Allstate, Capgemini, Ernst & Young, GTE-Verizon, Roadway Express, Nutrimental, World Vision, Cleveland Clinic, Imagine Chicago, American Red Cross, and United Religions Initiative. These projects are inspired by the Appreciative Inquiry (AI) methodology, of which he is co-originator. He has been recipient of Best Paper of the Year Awards at the Academy of Management. GTE was awarded the 1998 Best Organization Change Program by ASTD.

David has designed a series of dialogues using AI with 25 of the world's top religious leaders, started in 1998 by His Holiness the Dalai Lama, who said, "If only the world's religious leaders could just know each other . . . the world will be a better place." Using AI, the group has held meetings in Jerusalem and at the Carter Center in Atlanta. David was recognized in 2000 as among "the top ten visionaries" in the field by Training magazine and has been named in *Five Hundred People of Influence*. He is past president of the National Academy of Management's Division of Organization Development and a cofounder of the Taos Institute. He has lectured and taught at Stanford University, MIT, the University of Chicago, Katholieke University in Belgium, Pepperdine University, and others. David has published 7 books and authored more than 40 articles and book chapters.

His wife Nancy is an artist, and his daughter and two sons are in college. The AI Commons web site he helped create is http://appreciativeinquiry. case.edu. David's e-mail address is david.cooperrider@case.edu.

Dr. Diana Whitney, president of Corporation for Positive Change is cofounder and director emeritus of the Taos Institute. She is an internationally recognized consultant and keynote speaker and a pioneering thought leader on the subjects of Appreciative Inquiry, positive change, and spirituality at work. She is a fellow of the World Business Academy.

She is an award-winning writer and author of six books and dozens of articles and chapters, including *Appreciative Inquiry* with David Cooperrider and *The Power of Appreciative Inquiry* with Amanda Trosten-Bloom. In addition, Diana has edited five collections on Appreciative Inquiry, including *Appreciative Inquiry and Organizational Transformation* and *Positive Approaches to Peace Building*.

Diana teaches and consults in the Americas, Europe, and Asia. She has lectured and taught at Antioch University, Case Western Reserve University, Ashridge Management Institute in London, and Eisher Institute in India and for Human Value in Japan. She is a Distinguished Consulting Faculty at Saybrook Graduate School and Research Center.

The focus of Diana's consulting is the application of Appreciative Inquiry to strategic planning, mergers, large-scale transformation, service excellence and leadership, and management development. With 30 years of consulting, her clients include business, government, and social profit organizations: Merck, British Airways, Hunter Douglas, GTE-Verizon, GE Capital, Johnson & Johnson, and Sandia National Labs.

Diana serves as adviser to the United Religions Initiative, a global interfaith organization dedicated to peace and cooperation among people of different religions, faiths, and spiritual traditions.

Diana lives in Chapel Hill, North Carolina, and can be reached at diana@positivechange.org.

Dr. Jacqueline (Jackie) M. Stavros possesses 20 years of strategic planning, international, and organizational development and change experience. Jackie is an associate professor for the College of Management, Lawrence Technological University, where she teaches and integrates Appreciative Inquiry and other approaches to strength-based change in her MBA and DBA course work.

She uses Appreciative Inquiry (AI) to work with clients to build dynamic relationships and to facilitate strategic planning and leadership development sessions. Clients have included ACCI Business System; BAE Systems; Fasteners, Inc.; General Motors of Mexico; Jefferson Wells; NASA; Tendercare; United Way; Girl Scouts USA; Orbseal Technologies; and several Tier 1 and Tier 2 automotive suppliers and organizations in education.

Jackie has worked and traveled to more than a dozen countries in Asia, Europe, and North America. She has presented on AI and SOAR framework at Hewlett-Packard, the American Dietetic Association, PricewaterhouseCoopers, National City Bank, and the Detroit Chamber of Commerce. She has coauthored another book in AI, *Dynamic Relationships: Unleashing the Power of Appreciative Inquiry in Daily Living*, and dozens of book chapters and articles. She recently coauthored a book chapter for Berrett-Koehler's new *Change Handbook* titled "SOAR™: A New Approach to Strategic Planning" and coedited a series of articles for the international journal The Ai Practitioner on "SOARing to High and Engaging Performance: An Appreciative Approach to Strategy (http://www.aipractitioner.com).

She earned a doctorate in Management at Case Western Reserve University on *Capacity Building Using an Appreciative Approach: A Relational Process of Building Your Organization's Future*. Her MBA is from Michigan State University, and she has a BA from Wayne State University. Jackie is an associate for the Taos Institute and an editor for Taos Institute Publishing. She is a board member of the Positive Change Corps, a virtual global organization that focuses on strength-based approaches to teaching and learning in primary education (Pk–12th grade). She is a member of the Academy of Management, the Organization Development Network, and the Organization Development Institute.

Jackie lives with her family in Brighton, Michigan, and can be reached at jstavros@comcast.net.

About Berrett-Koehler Publishers

Berrett-Koehler is an independent publisher dedicated to an ambitious mission: Creating a World that Works for All.

We believe that to truly create a better world, action is needed at all levels – individual, organizational, and societal. At the individual level, our publications help people align their lives with their values and with their aspirations for a better world. At the organizational level, our publications promote progressive leadership and management practices, socially responsible approaches to business, and humane and effective organizations. At the societal level, our publications advance social and economic justice, shared prosperity, sustainability, and new solutions to national and global issues.

A major theme of our publications is "Opening Up New Space." They challenge conventional thinking, introduce new ideas, and foster positive change. Their common quest is changing the underlying beliefs, mindsets, institutions, and structures that keep generating the same cycles of problems, no matter who our leaders are or what improvement programs we adopt.

We strive to practice what we preach -- to operate our publishing company in line with the ideas in our books. At the core of our approach is stewardship, which we define as a deep sense of responsibility to administer the company for the benefit of all of our "stakeholder" groups: authors, customers, employees, investors, service providers, and the communities and environment around us.

We are grateful to the thousands of readers, authors, and other friends of the company who consider themselves to be part of the "BK Community." We hope that you, too, will join us in our mission.

Be Connected

Visit Our Website

Go to www.bkconnection.com to read exclusive previews and excerpts of new books, find detailed information on all Berrett-Koehler titles and authors, browse subject-area libraries of books, and get special discounts.

Subscribe to Our Free E-Newsletter

Be the first to hear about new publications, special discount offers, exclusive articles, news about bestsellers, and more! Get on the list for our free e-newsletter by going to www.bkconnection.com.

Get Quantity Discounts

Berrett-Koehler books are available at quantity discounts for orders of ten or more copies. Please call us toll-free at (800) 929-2929 or email us at bkp.orders@aidcvt.com.

Host a Reading Group

For tips on how to form and carry on a book reading group in your workplace or community, see our website at www.bkconnection.com.

Join the BK Community

Thousands of readers of our books have become part of the "BK Community" by participating in events featuring our authors, reviewing draft manuscripts of forthcoming books, spreading the word about their favorite books, and supporting our publishing program in other ways. If you would like to join the BK Community, please contact us at bkcommunity@bkpub.com.

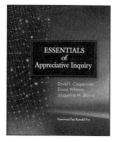

ISBN: 978-1-933403-205
$34.95 (pb)

ESSENTIALS of Appreciative Inquiry

David L. Cooperrider, Diana Whitney, and Jacqueline M. Stavros

Consisting of the first seven chapters of the *Appreciative Inquiry Handbook*, 2nd. Edition, this shortened version is aimed at academicians, students and workshop leaders. The book covers the theoretical background and core elements of the AI process. In addition, it offers six "mini-lectures" which succinctly introduce adherents to the process of AI.

CONTENTS

Place your order by simply...

Calling toll free: **(877) 225-8820** from 8:30 a.m.–4:30 p.m., EST

Or by faxing at **(330) 225-9932**

Or email to **carl@crowncustompublishing.com**

Or visit us online at **www.crowncustompublishing.com**

Crown Custom Publishing, Inc.
Brunswick, OH

Encyclopedia of Positive Questions, Vol. 1

Using AI to Bring Out the Best in Your Organization

Diana Whitney, David L. Cooperrider,
Amanda Trosten-Bloom, and Brian S. Kaplan

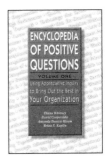

This timely book is composed of generic interview questions central to the "Discovery" phase of the Appreciative Inquiry process. This workbook on the power of positive questions has implications for every aspect of business—measurement systems, custom focus groups, quality management, team building, performance appraisal, surveys—indeed everywhere we ask questions or gather data related to positive change efforts.

ISBN: 1933403-055
212 pp
$18.95

Birth of a Global Community: Appreciative Inquiry in Action

The Story of the United Religions Initiative
Charles Gibbs and Sally Mahé

The birth of the United Religions Initiative (URI) is the story of how hundreds, then thousands of people across cultures, oceans, and faith traditions began to share a common call to make the world they live in more like the world they yearned for in their dreams. The book also tells the story of how an emergent processs of organizational change—the Appreciative Inquiry (AI) process—came along at just the right time to provide the engine for the new organization and its development.

ISBN: 1893435-423
384 pp
$24.95

Appreciative Management and Leadership Revised Edition

The Power of Positive Thought and Action in Organizations
Suresh Srivasta and David L. Cooperrider

"Based on the theory and practice of Appreciative Inquiry, Appreciative Management and Leadership offers a revolutionary alternative—a positive approach to organizing intended to unleash the entrepre- neurial spirit of all organizational members and mobilize system-wide action in pursuit of a common purpose. This book is a "must read" for all thought leaders—chief executives, managers, change agents, scholars, and practitioners—who want to create and sustain vital organizations in a world of rapid change."

ISBN: 1893435-059
548 pp
$49.50

James D. Ludema
Professor of Organization Development
Benedictine University, Chicago, IL

Crown Custom Publishing, Inc.
Brunswick, OH